EUROPEAN PEASANTS AND THEIR MARKETS

European Peasants and Their Markets

Essays in Agrarian Economic History

Edited by
WILLIAM N. PARKER AND ERIC L. JONES

Princeton University Press, Princeton, New Jersey

Library of Congress Cataloging in Publication Data will
be found on the last printed page of this book

This book has been composed in linotype Baskerville
Printed in the United States of America
by Princeton University Press, Princeton, New Jersey

Acknowledgments

The authors of the essays in this volume are all teachers of economics or of history and stand within roughly ten years of the receipt of their Ph.D.'s from North American institutions. They have many acknowledgments to make, and many left unsaid, to colleagues, wives, dissertation advisers, students, and to European scholars who have helped them. The two editors, being scholars of a somewhat earlier vintage, feel obligations largely to the foundations and institutions that have supported the work and the collection of it into this form. A grant from the National Science Foundation helped to turn the individual papers into a joint effort, and the Council on Western European studies at Yale University added its support for a seminar and conference in April 1972, which drew things together. Our obligation to two anonymous readers at the Princeton University Press and especially to Sanford Thatcher, the Social Science editor, is obvious not only in the fact that the book has appeared, but in the technical quality of its production. Eric and Sylvia Jones prepared the index and earned the relieved thanks of each of the authors, of the Press itself, and of the senior editor.

Contents

Part One

EUROPEAN PEASANTS AND THEIR MARKETS

Introduction

WILLIAM N. PARKER

"The Old World was tough in wickedness anyhow; the Old World's
heart of stone might blunt the sharpest blade of the bravest
knight-errant."

J. M. Keynes,
The Economic Consequences of the Peace

So Keynes reflected, with a sardonic chuckle, tinged with *Schaden-
freude,* at the fate of an eminent Princeton professor at the peace
conference of Versailles. And perhaps every American idealist,
setting foot on Europe's dark and bloody ground, risks a similar
end. If so, then the present volume by eight young American
scholars is indeed a venture brave and bold. No ground is darker
or bloodier than Europe's agrarian past, and none is guarded
with a more jealous ferocity by her historians. Nothing in American experience, except perhaps the experience of slavery, would
prepare either a farmer or a scholar for the effort to wrest a
living from so tangled a terrain.

Ferocity is often generated in proportion to love; everywhere
in Europe, agrarian history has sprung first of all from a scholar's
love for his native landscape and local habitation. Historians of
wider sympathies or capacities have extended their view to a
province or a county, lifting the work out of the narrower con-
fines of genealogical and antiquarian research. Books such as
Joan Thirsk's *English Peasant Farming* and E. Le Roy Ladurie's
Les Paysans de Languedoc have a range and depth that give them
a relevance beyond even the provinces they treat. The national
histories of Friedrich Lütge and Wilhelm Abel on Germany have
made a version of the national agrarian experience available to
the national historian. In England only the old and imperfect
work of Lord Ernle claims to cover the whole country and
history, pending the distant completion of the multivolumed
Agrarian History of England and Wales initiated under the

editorship of the late H. P. R. Finberg. For France, the beautiful syntheses by March Bloch and Georges Duby stop with the sixteenth century, just as modern nationhood begins to be achieved. Despite its claim to a longer time period, much the same may be said for the remarkable, if occasionally eccentric, recent work of B. H. Slicher van Bath: *The Agrarian History of Western Europe, A.D. 500–1850*—a book whose great value is the bringing of some coherence, based on economic movements, to the history of just those periods where the documentation is most scarce. The *Cambridge Economic History*, too, gives best coverage to agrarian matters in the medieval period, where there is not much else to talk about, and where the cunning editorial and creative hand of Professor Postan made itself felt. Of treatments of European agriculture as a whole for periods since 1800, only the valuable and original chapter of Folke Dovring in the *Cambridge Economic History*, volume VI, and the same author's *Land and Labor in Europe in the Twentieth Century* are readily available to English-reading students. Surely the need exists for a general history devoted to the great economic and social issues that have lain within the experience of lords, peasants, and commercial farmers in western Europe.

Some necessary simplifications

The volume here presented claims to be but a small step in the direction of a European agrarian history. Its contribution comes in good part from its point of view—the perspective of men educated in North America, loving those portions of Europe they know as intensely as any native—perhaps on occasion even more intensely than those who know better—but perceiving and judging the historical record from a certain cultural distance. Whether such a distance is an appreciative or a distorting one, and whether the novelty or scope it allows compensates for its foreignness, must be left to others (including Europeans) to judge. Only the first four essays, and Professor Jones' Afterword, lay claim to an explicitly pan-European perspective. The last four essays are case studies, contributing primarily to the histories of the areas from which their data are drawn, and only indirectly to a general European history. Franklin Mendels and Jan de Vries study peasant demand and rural industry in Belgium and Holland respectively (essays 5 and 6), but surely the

Fragestellung, as German scholarship would call it, is different from that of Hedda Gabler's husband when he studied the domestic industries of the Middle Ages. In both essays there is a hidden purpose of exploring what this experience can explain about the relation of peasant industry to industrialization taken as an economic process, if not in the world at large, at least in the wide areas of peasant industry in Europe as a whole. Robert Dickler's and George Grantham's essays (essays 7 and 8), treating eastern Prussia and France, are essays in the adjustment of an agrarian region, with a certain organizational form, to the threats and opportunities of the nineteenth-century world market. These essays, like all good case studies, are contributions to the specific histories of the areas they treat; but beyond (or beneath) that, they offer cases of a phenomenon observed with many similarities and many differences in the regional histories of other portions of Europe and the world. In this they are similar to the work of a modern European scholar writing about, say, Latin America, Africa, or Southeast Asia. Do they not add something to what even such a European might produce when writing about the history of his native soil?

This larger, or at least more impersonal, view is apparent even more clearly in the first four essays, by Richard Hoffmann, Donald McCloskey, and Jon Cohen and Martin Weitzman on the organizational phenomena of European agriculture: the common (or "open") fields and their enclosure. Here, though many of the references are to England (particularly in McCloskey and Cohen-Weitzman), the intention is clearly to write essays of general applicability to the whole common-field system which, as Hoffmann's map shows, ran like a great flooded river across the European plain. Hoffmann's essay is written in the style of an historian's description of a great movement: the adoption of the common-field form in the early Middle Ages; McCloskey and Cohen-Weitzman treat that form's persistence and its transmutation into enclosed and compact fields almost as an essay in economic theory. Yet all the essays address a general question. Taken together, they seek to pick out of the multitudinous examples and events the outlines of a general theory for the existence, persistence, and disappearance of common-field agriculture, wherever it occurred, and to suggest, by implication at least, why it did not occur elsewhere and at other times.

These essays exemplify, then, two methods of science: the case study, and the search for generalizations. These may both be applied to social studies only with great care and at high risk. The case study method, widely used in medical science, is useful early in the study of every complex phenomenon. It requires that the investigator distinguish one "case" from another, frame each in a self-contained and internally consistent model, and examine the interrelation of the elements—themselves selected and defined—in some specific context. No less than the more general or sweeping approach, it requires definition, abstraction, and theoretical structure. The more sweeping or abstract method used in the first four essays is an effort to develop the general relationships that a large number of cases will illustrate, the "laws"—if one adopts that term so hated by most historians—that explain the behavior of the cases. But in all the essays the treatment is based on an abstraction from historical reality, a simplification without which general history cannot be written. Whether, indeed, general history can be written at all is admittedly subject to dispute; but if the attempt is to be made, it must be based on such simplification. Common to the case studies and to the more explicitly analytical essays, then, are the categories of economic theory as they are broadly and rather loosely conceived in studies of economic organization and development, such categories as capital, labor, population, market, property, demand, firm, household, tenancy, contract.

Economic theory! Words to conjure with these days in North American socio-scientific circles. What is meant here are simply the categories of a market economy, categories a Marxist would perceive as those of capitalism. Behind them all is another simplifying concept around which controversies rage in modern social science: the concept of "rational behavior." This assumption is easy to understand when the history under study is that of a capitalistic enterprise; it is, indeed, central to Max Weber's ideal type of capitalistic economic enterprise. The successful analysis of rational behavior requires objective standards of achievement and the quantification of the main alternative elements. Human activity must be taken as a process, implying ends and means, costs and revenues, and choices made in response to calculation of the expected net result. So far as possible, the uncertainty must be removed even from risky ventures by an estimate of the probabilities of success, and by devices to spread risk—to turn the wrath of God into an insurable contingency.

Our authors have devoted themselves to showing how, within a market economy, the demands of peasants, lords, laborers, and rural industrial workers from the late seventeenth century onward work to produce the observed patterns of consumption and production—the sheets, pillow cases, and other bourgeois comforts of Dutch rural households; the intense industrial activity of a Flemish rural proletariat; the drive to efficiency on Prussian estates; the ambivalent reactions to landholding and market production of the French *mainouvrier*. In these case studies we come to understand history in terms of a reasonable reaction of the actors within a certain economic environment, given the built-in demands, suspicions, and ambitions that peasants may be assumed to have had. But there is of course a deeper question of rationality, into which it is not possible to enter. Why did Dutch farmers want certain standards of comfort instead of some others of life's goods? Why did Prussian landowners, like the English, want efficient management, instead of spending their energies or ambitions along other lines? Why did French peasants so love the land and cling to the security it offered? We can observe that those who possessed these traits responded to the situations they were in "rationally." But why they had these traits is a question not of economic but of psychohistory.

Even more intriguing, because less definable, is the concept of rationality in human behavior elsewhere than in the marketplace. Where the influence of the market begins and ends in history is a matter of speculation. Mendels traces peasant work and production patterns to the pressures of population growth, but in a study published elsewhere he also indicates that he has found that population change itself, in particular the marriage rate, fluctuated with the price of linen. Hoffmann shows a probable relation between the spread of the common-field system and the periods and places of population pressure. McCloskey argues that both the persistence and final decline of the system can be traced to rational behavior on the part of lords or village communities concerned with spreading risk. Cohen and Weitzman similarly show the inevitability of population contraction on enclosed land as a result of a rational process. In all these cases the market appears to have been partly at work, allowing

for the estimation of benefits and costs, but much of the activity
appears to have been more directly motivated by the need to
accommodate growing populations, risky weather and soil conditions, or the increase of a lord's surplus, even in the absence of
markets.

In all these cases one is pushed back to the most fundamental
question with which economic history has to deal: underlying all
human social behavior may one postulate a generalized and
universal "human nature"—universal not in the sense of giving
identical responses to identical stimuli, but in the sense of
possessing a common susceptibility to the molding forces of the
environment? Treatment of this question is obviously beyond
our scope here; it is the fundamental question in all general history or anthropology. It is a tribute to the penetration of the
essays in this volume that reflection on them as a group leads one
through specific institutional arrangements and specific economic
behavior to speculate on this fundamental problem.

Reflections of socio-economic history

Even within the limitations of theoretical simplification, and
guided by an economic philosophy well known for its poverty,
our group of essays reflects many of the phases and features of
that great moving stream of human events that has flooded across
the European landscape over the past thousand years. A full
agrarian history cannot be reconstructed from these studies,
much less a full economic or social history, but these studies do
suggest portions of an outline for such a history.

The first phase, for instance, might be called a Malthusian
cycle in modern European social history, extending from the
thirteenth to the mid-seventeenth century. If Slicher van Bath's
estimates of population movements in this period are accepted
(they are admittedly not very firmly based), then population
growth against the limits of agricultural resources and techniques
emerges as its dominant feature. The dynamics of the formation
of common-field agriculture, as presented by Hoffmann, then fall
into place as an innovative response to new population pressures,
a response that sets the agrarian pattern (and affects the population growth) for centuries to come. The strength of this institutional arrangement is reinforced by the division into strips and

the provisions of common rights, analyzed by McCloskey. But another, political, ingredient of that strength was the dominance of feudal overlords with power to enforce enclosure, in order to achieve the economic results discussed by Cohen and Weitzman, who are fully supported by some standard theorems of economic theory.

In these latter essays we can see the first pressures from a growth of trading opportunities and changes in the balance of political power, which mark the inception of what may ultimately be called the mercantile or, slightly later, Smithian, phase of the European economy's growth. Trading opportunities were opened up, initially by the political unification of national areas; then through the extension of overseas empires; always by the development of the military power and splendor of a royal court, a royal monetary system, royal grants of monopoly and all the other characteristics of mercantilism; and ultimately by the partial ascendancy within those states of the commercial classes themselves. All this is reflected in agrarian history: the movements of enclosure, and the growth of peasant industries and peasant prosperity—or, in some contexts, peasant misery, discussed or sampled in essays three through six.

Finally, in the nineteenth century, Europe moves into a phase I would call Schumpeterian, after the great Austrian-American economist who defined capitalism as "technological change financed by credit," and deduced from that definition many of the main characteristics of the modern world economy, its incessant technical revolution, the continuous penetration of its producers into one another's markets, its cyclical instability. In essays seven and eight on East Prussia and France, we see two forms of agrarian adjustment to the changes of such a world. It obviously makes a great difference to the history of a region with what agrarian constitution it enters the maelstrom of the modern world economy, what distribution of power and property prevails there, what habits of enterprise, thrift, and risk-taking its producers have inherited, what image of the good life they hold. The larger European socio-economic history is thus adumbrated in the agrarian history, and flickering glimpses of the latter are themselves revealed in the studies of this volume.

But there is of course much more European social and economic history that has slipped through our net. The progression of agricultural technology, for example, underlies many of the issues of change from one period to another. Organizational change, the growth of "surplus" rural populations, competitiveness on world markets—all these subsume a process of technical change which has, in fact, a history of its own. It is in the interface between economic change and the growth of knowledge about nature and about ways to find out about nature that the understanding of Europe's evolving agricultural technology is to be found. Some of the problems of this complex bit of socio-intellectual history are alluded to in the interesting Afterword by Eric Jones.

Or again, to consider population growth as a "given" in agrarian history, to which field systems, demand patterns, and techniques or rural work patterns must adjust, is obviously an example of what economists call "partial equilibrium analysis." A mass of demographic studies coming out of the French and English family reconstitution projects and from the regional statistics exploited by Professor Easterlin's project at the University of Pennsylvania indicate the sensitivity of rural birth rates and marriage rates to economic opportunity. Markets, crop types, tenancy systems, and inheritance customs and laws all have their effect in controlling or releasing the Malthusian devil (and the Old Adam). Indeed it seems most likely that Europe's surge of population in the eighteenth and early nineteenth centuries, if traceable to a rising birth rate in the presence of a long-run constancy in death rates, had as its active cause the growth of opportunities for rural industry. What the American census calls a "rural nonfarm" population, freed from the constraints of land holding and peasant custom, but still near enough to the relatively lower rural death rates to survive, began to grow in the areas where enough food and jobs could be provided.

Piecing together the technological and demographic elements for the earlier period might provide a test for one of the most momentous issues in modern economic history: the interrelation of population pressure and agrarian technology. It is the thesis of Ester Boserup's famous little book *The Conditions of Agricultural Progress*[1] that is here at issue. Population pressure has, no doubt, often caused a change in agrarian techniques from a system with high yields per man-hour and low yields per acre

---

[1] Ester Boserup, *The Conditions of Agricultural Progress*, London, 1965.

and per man-year, to a more labor-intensive system that supports a larger population by using both the land and the agricultural labor force more intensively over the year. The mechanism by which a society accomplishes such a shift is not clear, but in Boserup's model the process is presumably precipitated by declines in standards of nutrition under the earlier system. In such a model, *population pressure is, as its name implies, a prod*, inducing improvement through an intolerable accumulation of human misery. But the application of such a model to early modern Europe neglects two important points in the history: the presence of markets and the growth of trade, and the technical changes in the agricultural "revolution" itself. The presence of trade and markets meant that very appreciable gains in productivity could be achieved through the familiar practices of agricultural specialization and through the diffusion of improvements that accompany such trade. Much of this occurred even under village agriculture, and capitalistic-minded landlords and peasants in a flexible land-holding system who realized such gains were motivated by greed and ambition rather than by the threat of widespread starvation.

Now, the "new husbandry" that was diffused in the grain and livestock agriculture of northern Europe was peculiarly suited to respond to the stimulus, not of peasant demand for grain, but of urban demand for meat and wool. It is true, as the Boserup model avers, that a shift occurred from a triennial fallow rotation to continuous cropping, and that this increased effective land supplies above the old open field levels by as much as fifty percent. But the new crop grown on the field formerly held fallow was not a grain crop directly for human consumption, but a feed crop—hay, clover, or roots. The gains in grain yields came as these feeds had the chance to work their way through the animals' digestive systems and produce fertilizer as a product along with the increased supplies of wool, meat, and dairy products. By this peculiarity in the agricultural production function, the demand for high-grade food, cloth, and leather then produced the larger amounts of lower-cost foods by which a growing mass of rural population could be kept alive.

History is not a straightforward story of population pressure and productivity increase; it is an exercise, indeed, in one of the favorite themes of certain perverse eighteenth-century philosophers, in particular Mandeville (the William Buckley of his day). For it shows how private vice—ostentatious urban consumption of meat—could produce vast public benefit.[2]

The interrelation with political history

In turning over the rocky soil of agrarian history, one comes ultimately to the bedrock of politics. The peasant in Europe is never thought of—by historians, at least—as simply, or even mainly, a producer; nor the lord or landowner as a manager or innovator. Agricultural reorganization in the European countries has been closely, though obscurely, connected with that change in political status which nineteenth-century historians identified as the growth of human freedom, the shift from status to contract, the growth of "bourgeois" liberty and democracy, and the move from seigneurial and communal forms of property to private, individual landed property under capitalism. Agrarian history, then, does not yield to simple explanations in terms of economic or historical geography. It refuses to fit exactly a technological or environmental determinism. But neither is it wholly a history of politics and power relationships free of natural, technical, and economic influences. Rather it is a blend of the two—the natural and the social, the technical and the political—and in analyzing it, the right balance is difficult to achieve. The importance and complexity of the relationship may justify a short excursus, particularly since the essays in our volume leave the political side of things largely to the reader's imagination or recollection.

Perhaps the oldest and sturdiest scholarly theme in European agrarian history is the establishment of private property in land, the replacement of a personal and political relationship between lord and peasant with a market relationship between landowner and tenant or laborer. Relationships within the seigneurial framework were complex and many-faceted, and took a long time to break down. At some points dues were commuted to rents as early as the thirteenth century; in other places and in other forms, dues in labor or in kind at rates set by custom rather than

---

[2] This point is made also by Eric Jones in the introduction to his edited volume, *Agriculture and Economic Growth in England, 1650–1815*, London, 1967, p. 8. See also his "Agriculture and Economic Growth in England, 1660–1750: Agricultural Change," *Journal of Economic History* 25 (March 1965), 6–7. It is not clear whether demand led supply or vice versa, but both grew faster than the population in England between 1650 and 1730.

by contract remained or reappeared as late as the mid-eighteenth century. The development was scrutinized by legal and constitutional historians and by socialist historians in the mid and late nineteenth century, as they traced the growth of political and personal freedom under capitalism. The market, with its money relationships, was not looked on, as Marx had it, as an enslaving and alienating force, but as the liberator from patriarchal and local despotism, the tyranny of lord and village. That this development in law and social status was based on economic change was obvious, but the historians' interest was not in the economic effects of freedom but in the fact of freedom itself.

The economic effects were not negligible. Two of our essays (McCloskey and Cohen-Weitzman on enclosures) deal not simply with the physical fact of enclosure, but with the effect of the shift from communal to private control over the various decisions involved in the use of land. Of equal importance is the effect of private control over land, agricultural capital, and labor on these factors' mobility. The possibility of the conversion of land from one use to another and one crop to another, its use in innovation and experiment, and its movement into the hands of owners interested in extracting a maximum of revenue from it by intelligent use were increased as the rules for its control shifted from the feudal to the modern law of property, and the decisions on its use were shifted from village tradition to individual initiative. From this point of view, many obstacles lay in the way of the complete conversion of land into an economic commodity. Inheritance laws and customs, the lingering remains of feudal titles and feudal dues, the growth of a vast array of types of title to rights in the land, and most especially the persistence of the social prestige that landholding had given when it was the source of political and even judicial power—all served to make land markets imperfect and to limit wholly rational exploitation. At best, one might say that land remained a consumer's, as well as a producer's good, and so was susceptible to unproductive use.

Changes in the laws and customs surrounding land use also had the effect of increasing the mobility of capital. Not only could agricultural land be pledged on mortgage so that it served, like a national debt, to provide a stable base for the proliferation of other credit instruments, but its purchase and sale permitted the transfer of liquid capital in and out of agriculture. The

effects ran both ways: landowners were responsible for investment both on their estates and in ancillary industries, such as
milling, transport, and mining; and they might use estate revenues or mortgage proceeds to finance nonagricultural activities,
not only gambling and high living in town, but also voyages,
foreign investment, and a government's wars. At the same time,
bourgeois wealth could buy into agriculture; partly as a source
of conspicuous consumption, or rather conspicuous investment,
but partly in the hope of profit from operating or reselling the
property and improving its cultivation and its rent-earning
capacity.

The benefits of turning land into a commodity and extending
a capital market to permit the conversion of assets into trans-
ferable, liquid form were not wholly without cost. Land in
private and experimental use might be wasted more readily than
when under the control of traditional techniques, and "free"
capital markets, on which borrowing is easy, may actually discourage saving. Traditional societies and their folkways generally
take the past and future more fully into account than did the
ebullient commercial capitalism of the seventeenth and eighteenth centuries or the science-based enterprise of the ninteenth
and twentieth century. The freeing of a peasantry similarly
meant in many cases simply their dispossession from customary
tenures and rights within the village and manorial systems.

Three different states of the agricultural labor force, then,
emerged as feudal society declined. In England in the sixteenth
and seventeenth centuries, the commutation of feudal dues that
had occurred much earlier developed into complex patterns of
cash tenancy; while some of the rural labor force, dispossessed
or simply supernumerary because of population growth, became
wage laborers, remaining largely in their own localities, but
available for considerable wandering among agricultural districts and for movement into industrial occupations. This was
probably the condition most favorable to formation of an industrial labor force both in the countryside and in the cities.
More or less the same pattern, especially the elimination and
proletarianization of poorer tenants, was repeated in Prussia
after the agricultural "reforms" between 1815 and 1850.

To the east and south of Prussia, well outside western Europe,
a different transformation of village agricultural organization

occurred, partly in reaction to market growth and commercial opportunity in the west. Between 1500 and 1700, an actual enserfment of the peasants by lords, supported in Russia by the central authority, took place.[3] Through political action by lords and territorial rulers, commercial production and the sale of surplus grain were extended, while open fields and most of the communal production organization were retained. When one compares Russian, Polish, and Hungarian estates with those of England and eastern Prussia in the first half of the nineteenth century, there can be no doubt that the "reforms"—gradual in England, sudden in Prussia—freeing the labor force from the soil, helped also to stimulate agricultural improvement. The mobility of labor, and perhaps the greater mobility of capital, together with closer contact with industrial areas and commercial markets, helped to produce this effect.

The third typical formation of the rural labor force in Europe was the independent, or semi-independent, peasantry of southern and western Germany, the Scandinavian and Low Countries, and of France even before the Revolution. The status of peasants in all these areas between 1500 and 1800 is varied and ambivalent, but the fragmentation of political authority in Germany and the growth of royal authority dependent on sources other than the landed nobility in France added to the peasants' political and legal independence. The question an economist asks is, "what did peasants do with their independence?" Did the opportunity of owning land and deriving for themselves and their families the whole of its revenue motivate them to work more carefully, to improve and watch their economic advantage? Ordinarily we have taken the course of enclosure and the abandonment of communal village custom and practice as indicative of the answer to this question. In many regions (figure 1–1), to be sure, properties had always been consolidated. But where this was not so, consolidation came rather slowly during the nineteenth century. A certain backwardness clung to peasant agriculture, as to the agriculture of serf estates. In both cases, labor supplies were more plentiful than where labor had been dipossessed and, in the presence of alternative employment, made mobile. The peasant, even more than the eastern landowner,

---

[3] Jerome Blum, *Lord and Peasant in Russia from the Ninth to the Nineteenth Century*, Princeton, 1961, chapter 13.

always also had the possibility of withdrawing into a greater degree of self-sufficiency and abandoning commercial production. The "irrationally" high value put on the security of land owner-ship slowed land transfers and efficient resource allocation as much among a peasantry as among a collection of landed aristo-crats. In addition, the peasant did not have the resources to bear the risks of innovation, but depended for improvements largely on the very slow and cautious borrowing of advanced techniques and novelties from the estates of larger producers.

At this point mention must be made of the dramatic "theses" of one recent writer, Barrington Moore, which assign a central role in European political development—and in particular the development of the forms of organization of state and industry—to the political status and spirit of the peasantry.[4] Moore's thesis is that where modern industry was introduced after a revolution that overthrew the preindustrial classes—church, di-vine right monarchs, landowners, or (in the case of the United States) slaveowners—a free rural population in conjunction with the bourgeoisie was able to establish, maintain, and broaden political democracy. Where such a cleansing did not occur, it was an easy matter for new industrial wealth to combine with old landed wealth to produce the concentrated forms of an authoritarian, and eventually a fascistic, state and industry. Moore extends this thesis, with further variations to Russia and Asia, and though one might not think it possible, he explains the English case in these terms. But he stops short of answering the antecedent question: why did a peasant revolution in con-junction with a bourgeois one occur in the "Western democ-racies," and why did it fail to occur, or to succeed, in central Europe and the East?

The answer to this question lies, in my opinion, in the com-mercial and agrarian conditions of all these regions as they stood in the early modern period, that is, in the sixteenth and seventeenth centuries. Possibly for reasons of military tech-nology, it would appear that the feudal scale of political power could no longer maintain itself against the centralizing power of larger-scale armies and rulers.[5] But for the latter to consoli-

[4] Barrington Moore, Jr., *Social Origins of Dictatorship and Democracy: Lord and Peasant in the Making of the Modern World,* Boston, 1966, pp. xiv–xvii.

[5] Douglass C. North and Robert P. Thomas, *The Rise of the Western*

date their territories, they needed access to revenues outside the feudal system, with which to hire armies, maintain a navy and a royal household, bribe nobles, and sustain a bureaucracy to gather taxes. Some such revenue could come from crown estates, some from levies on the nobility, and some from direct taxation of peasants. But the latter was possible only once power was established; in the period of its establishment, when there were no routes of direct connection between king and peasantry short-circuiting ancient local allegiances and loyalties, it was not possible. The prime source of revenue free of the feudal structure was then the mercantile and industrial classes. The state could perform services for these groups, give protection, establish currency, regulate and defend foreign trade, grant patents of monopoly, sustain colonial enterprises, and establish factories of its own. Mercantilism was the body of policy that produced this alliance, and its success presupposed a body of mercantile enterprise. So where the opportunities for trade existed on a scale wide enough to permit the finance of royal and bourgeois power—that is, in the coastal economies of the north and west, either royal authority was strengthened, or else it was under-mined or overthrown, as in England and the Netherlands, in favor of a mercantile oligarchy.

These facts of economic history help to explain the differences between the political development in Europe west of the Elbe, and Europe to the east.[6] To explain the differential develop-ment of Britain, France, Germany, and the Netherlands is a much more delicate job; I am not sure it can be done in a way that takes into account all the variables involved. Even if it could be done, it would be inappropriate to try it as an introduction to a group of essays devoted to economic rather than political issues. A fundamental issue, at least before the eighteenth century, ap-pears to be the relative proportions of royal, bourgeois, noble, and peasant power. In eastern Europe, these proportions were

---

World, Cambridge, 1973, pp. 81–82, 94–96. North and Thomas, however, emphasize the role of institutional adaptation, in particular the development of property rights, in determining the outcome in various regions.

[6] For the period before 1700, the foregoing and following discussions in this section are derived, with some differences of emphasis, from the treat-ment in Marc Bloch's *Caractères Originaux de l'Histoire Rurale Française,* translated by Janet Sondheimer under the title *French Rural History,* Berkeley and Los Angeles, 1966, especially chapter IV.

weighted heavily in favor of the nobility, so that royal power, with its policy of peasant protection, remained weak. In England and the Netherlands a preponderance of power lay with the merchant classes, so that they could overcome royal power. In France the proportions were ideal for the advancement of royal power and with it, at least in the fifteenth and sixteenth centuries, some advance in the position of the peasantry. Some allowance must also be made for the role of wool production in England, which, expanding in the critical times of the sixteenth century, permitted a nobility with growing mercantile interests to consolidate and extend its holdings—even in a time of growing royal political power—at the expense of the peasantry. On the continental plain, arable husbandry kept the peasantry on the land, either enserfed or with tenants' rights and status.

Somewhere, then, in the exact conditions—exact with respect to timing and to physical environment—of the early modern period, the political constitutions of western European nations were forged. It was a process that went on under different economic conditions in Germany and Italy in the nineteenth century, where it can be observed at closer hand, and in "emerging" nations today, where it is too close for accurate observation. When examined scientifically, exactly, and comparatively on a Europe-wide basis, it will surely be found that the incidents of the agrarian history—the labor requirements of different crops, the timing and shape of demand growth, the internal organization of estates, the penetration of land and capital markets into the countryside—have a place alongside the growth of armies and the changes in weapons, the growth of mercantile wealth, the shifting religious allegiances and marital alliances of princes, and the ambitions of reformers, kings, and popes.

Whatever their origins, the different agrarian constitutions of the European states produced in the nineteenth century somewhat different reactions to the world-wide mercantile and industrial expansion. Nowhere—perhaps not even in eastern Europe—was the direct influence of the landed classes on state policy dominant. The strength of urban industrial expansion determined policy in the states that enjoyed such expansion, and fear of that strength distorted policy in the kingdoms and empires, including the Russian, which remained predominantly agricultural in their economies. In the more open, less peasant-ridden economies—British, Dutch, Danish—the agricultural adjustment was all that could have been desired even by von Thünen himself. Here the spatial adjustment of crops to the intense concentration of industrial populations at the ports and coal basins, and the competition of grains from broad plains of the "periphery" of northern Europe was notable. In France and Germany, a compromise between the industrial and agrarian interests produced a set of mutually protective tariffs. And on the estates east of the Elbe and into Russia, changes in techniques and structures began to occur, whose end, after the colossal disturbances of war and collectivization, is not yet in sight.

A concluding cautionary word

Scholars venturing into a thinly settled area usually find very soon that there are good reasons for its neglect. The reasons in the case of large-scale agrarian history lie, not only in the focus and techniques of previous scholarship, but in the nature of the subject itself. Nature in all her variety seems to defy the historian's efforts to generalize. What can one say *in general* about northwestern Europe—its mountains, coasts, plains, and forests, its variety of soils, terrains and climates? The agriculture and stock rearing of highland Europe are to be sharply distinguished from practices on the plains and rolling terrains, and the latter from those in river valleys and lowlands. Farming on light soils has always presented problems and solutions very different from that on clay soils; the adaptations to the Mediterranean climate are very different from those to the climate of the Rhine Valley, the central European plain, or the humid areas of northwestern France or the British Isles. And the variety of organizations and techniques by which Europeans have coped with varied nature is even greater and more complex. Unlike the townships of the American Middle West, no two common-field villages were of exactly the same dimensions, nor were the holdings of peasants divided along the lines of a uniform rectangular survey. Implements, made locally, were far from being of standard manufacture, and crops and livestock types present all that genetic variation which is the source of successful adaptation to varied natural conditions.

Added to these natural and technical sources of variety is the fact that Europe has always been a region of uneven economic development. Markets grew first around the seacoast, along rivers, and at a few administrative centers and junctions of overland trade routes. The agriculture around such points was early affected both by the "pull" of market demand, raising the value of produce and so of land and peasants' time, and by the easier spread of knowledge of technical improvements by which that demand could be supplied. Demands for grain, continuing to draw on inland areas, affected practices and organization far into the interior of the continent, and hill and mountain areas as well as wet lowlands were permitted specialization in livestock and pasturage. One may doubt whether the degree of self-sufficiency, even on an isolated manor, ever approached that on backwoods farms in North America or other new areas in the nineteenth century. And the relationship to markets in Europe before 1800 was a far stabler one, less subject to the sudden shifts that characterized the frontier. Adjustments, which constitute the synthesizing principle of the economic side of agrarian history, occurred only very slowly, over centuries, at rates almost invisible to the political historian, and more suitable to the lens of the geographer or the geologist.

Even where the slow rhythm of the economic movements in agrarian history can be observed, the changes—as we have seen—appear hopelessly entangled with questions of political and social organization. When a synthesis of all these elements can be achieved over a small region by someone immersed in the history and landscape of a subculture, and animated by his own sense of connection with a farming population, its interests, and its folklore, it is a great triumph of sensitive scholarship. Despite the claims made and the hopes exposed in this volume, is a similar synthesis on a continental level really possible without the sacrifice of rigor, realism, and fidelity to detail? And even if it could be achieved, is there any point to achieving it?

From an economist, such questions should receive an affirmative answer. Northwestern Europe, with its extension in northeastern United States, represents the world's central experience of industrialization under capitalistic institutions. An agricultural base, however varied in natural character or social organization, was involved in this development, and was in turn affected by it. Economic history, moving toward a synthetic treatment of the process of industrialization in western Europe, must include a full and coherent picture of the accompanying process of agricultural change. Agricultural and industrial developments ought to be studied together to show where each impeded or accelerated the other. It is no detraction from the unity of such a treatment to emphasize the possibilities of comparative history that lie within it. Industrialization, like Tennyson's God, "reveals Himself in many ways," and comes to different European regions at different times and in different forms. In agriculture, changes in productivity, growth of population, and migration of labor occur under different ownership patterns; family structures and inheritance systems evolve at different times and in different sequences in the various national and regional histories. And although the sources of diversity should not be underestimated, it would seem myopic from the economist's point of view to focus solely on them and to laugh to scorn the sorts of formulations alluded to here. Western European agriculture at the end of the Middle Ages was pursued under a few standard organizational forms. It was all temperate zone agriculture, employing similar techniques, equipment, practices, and genetic materials. And over the following five hundred years it has faced a similar succession of economic events, opportunities, and impulses. The political responses and the timing of the economic responses have been indeed quite different from one part of Europe to another. But these only give variety and movement to a narrative that is rather firmly held within a single natural, technological, and economic frame.

The historian, no doubt, has trouble seeing matters in this way. If he is a conscientious scholar, he has a fear of heights and of broad expanses of time and space. His concern with sensitive political and social movements and with the mental states of the actors in them would seem to call for local or national emphases even more loudly than do the economist's facts of technology and geography. Yet if European unity becomes a political as well as an economic reality, as seems possible and sometimes even likely, surely its history is not to be found solely in the local or national historiography which is the inheritance to us from an Hegelian historicism of nineteenth-century Germany. The national state, which inspired the highest flights of nineteenth-century history-writing, is no longer in anyone's mind the highest expression of Western consciousness and civilization. The political development that has accompanied industrialization in Western Europe has led to a formation of national states that evolved out of the dominance by a landed aristocracy, through the hegemony of a bureaucratic monarchy, to the pluralistic, semioligarchic structures of the present day. In this evolution the landed classes have had an important part, and one not dissimilar in different states. It is the similarity of this development, and of the social class formations that have underlain it in different parts of Europe, that forms the basis for a united Europe—at least as far as the Elbe. The agrarian history of the whole continent helps to show why there is a dividing line at the Elbe, and what the areas to the west of it have in common. To the west feudal lords became settled aristocracies, and feudal property in land became ownership in fee simple, whether on large or small scale. In Western continental Europe a free peasantry came to form an economic and political force down to the present.

Modern economics and modern European politics then both call for an examination of European agrarian history as a single body of phenomena, which has helped in several dimensions to create the European economy and society to whose prospective development so many hopes and fears are attached today. If this volume serves to startle or disturb even one sound European scholar who, like the peasants he writes about, "leans on his hoe and gazes on the ground," it will have served a purpose as useful as that of most works of the human mind and imagination. For when men's thoughts are turned in a certain direction in reflection on their past, who can tell what reinforcement is given to those activities by which they build their future? That is perhaps a sentiment on which both Keynes and Woodrow Wilson might have agreed.

1

Medieval Origins of the Common Fields*

RICHARD C. HOFFMANN

During the medieval and early modern periods, the greater portion of the north European plain was farmed under arrangements now known as the common or open fields. Recent research
has greatly enlarged our understanding of the origins, expansion,
and functions of the cluster of institutions that made up this
agricultural system. This essay endeavors to synthesize recent investigations, considering the common fields as a means of agricultural management, and suggesting that they began as a response to the pressures of a growing population against a base
of relatively fixed resources and technology. The early history of
European agriculture is seen, therefore, as a slow and contingent
movement from arrangements that left managerial control largely
in the hands of the individual cultivator to a system regulated
by constraints imposed by the village community.

Common field agriculture: characteristics and location

The stereotyped features of the common-field system are almost
so commonplace that "every schoolboy knows them," but it may
be useful to summarize them before describing their distribution
in the later Middle Ages, and calling attention to certain aspects
of peasant life that must be considered in any discussion of

* I wish to thank E. Le Roy Ladurie, J. Ambrose Raftis, Thomas V. Cohen,
and Hermann Rebel for valuable suggestions and criticism.
    The following abbreviations appear in the notes to this essay: *AgHR,
Agricultural History Review; Annales, Annales: économies, sociétés, civilisa-
tions; ZAA, Zeitschrift für Agrargeschichte und Agrarsoziologie.*

Europe's agrarian evolution. More than just a way of raising crops, common fields were part of a way of life that combined social, legal, and purely agricultural institutions in a cultural unity. Our immediate purpose, however, here requires emphasis on the three uniquely diagnostic features of the complete or "mature" common-field system: [1]

(1) the "open fields" in their physical layout;
(2) the practice of common pasture on the stubble and fallow;
(3) the regulation of cropping, grazing, and other facets of farm management by an assembly of cultivators.

In the European context the coincidence of these defines a common-field system.[2]

The term "open fields" refers to the arable land of each village lying in several large portions without further subdivision by permanent fences, hedges, or the like. The holding of each cultivator lay in numerous unfenced parcels, normally strips, scattered about the fields. Several parallel strips of various holders composed a bundle called a "furlong" (*Gewann*), and several furlongs made up the "field" (*Zelge, sole*). Although a spatial arrangement of scattered unfenced strip parcels might seem sufficient to imply all the other features of a common-field system, it is possible to find examples where this was not the case.[3] More seriously, equating "openness" with "commonness" leads to the fallacious assumption that identity of origin and function may be inferred from mere formal similarity.[4] Thus operational characteristics

[1] In discussing a "mature" system I follow the suggestion of Joan Thirsk, "The Common Fields," *Past and Present* 29 (1964), 3–25, despite the objections of J. Z. Titow, "Medieval England and the Open Field System," *Past and Present* 32 (1965), 88–89.

[2] Thirsk, "Common Fields," pp. 5–6, adds common pasture on the waste as a necessary definitive element in a common field system, but Titow, "Open Field System," pp. 86–88, rightly points out that the arrangement could function even in the absence of waste. As becomes apparent below, however, common waste pasture is here seen as a variable central to the evolution of common field agriculture.

[3] One such case is the open field Fenland villages of Lincolnshire and Cambridgeshire mentioned in Joan Thirsk, "Field Systems of the East Midlands," in Alan R. H. Baker and Robin A. Butlin, eds., *Studies of Field Systems in the British Isles* (Cambridge, 1973), pp. 252–53.

[4] Alan R. H. Baker and Robin A. Butlin join Thirsk in advancing this

must be added to the purely morphological arrangement of the fields.

The second feature, common pasture, implied that an individual's sole right to the product of his land extended only over arable crops; otherwise (that is, after harvest and during the recurring fallow years) the forage that remained belonged to the stock of all the villagers.

Finally, individual cultivators retained the power to make only such decisions about cropping and other agricultural practices as remained after the fundamental elements of rotations, plowing dates, harvest dates, stock quotas, and the like had been determined, usually on a customary basis, by all the cultivators in common.[5] Where these three characteristics coexisted, a mature common-field system prevailed; where one or more was weak or absent, agricultural societies bore greater or lesser differences in character, which, in the European case, tended to favor greater individual control.

In Figure 1.1 much of the literature, including many local and regional studies, has been sifted and combined to show the importance of the common fields in northwestern Europe at the close of the medieval phase of secular economic growth in about 1300.[6] This form of agriculture dominated large areas of the north European plain which had particular characteristics of both physical and human geography. The common-field region avoids extremes both of climate (the Mediterranean climatic zone, wet Atlantic climates, subarctic regions) and relief (mountains and extensive marshlands). In terms of human geography, common-field agriculture was closely associated with a nucleated settlement pattern. In fact, it is almost inconceivable in any area where the rural population was dispersed in isolated farmsteads

position against Titow. See their "Conclusion: Problems and Perspectives," in Baker and Butlin, *Field Systems*, pp. 622–24.

[5] The variety and detail of community regulation of agriculture is well illustrated in Warren O. Ault, *Open Field Husbandry and the Village Community: A Study of Agrarian By-Laws in Medieval England* (Transactions of the American Philosophical Society, new series, vol. 55, part 7; Philadelphia, 1965).

[6] The map was compiled from the local and regional studies cited throughout these notes and, in addition, those similar works that appear in Appendix 1.2. Suggestions for revision that are based on evidence for different conditions in a given area or region around 1300 will be welcomed.

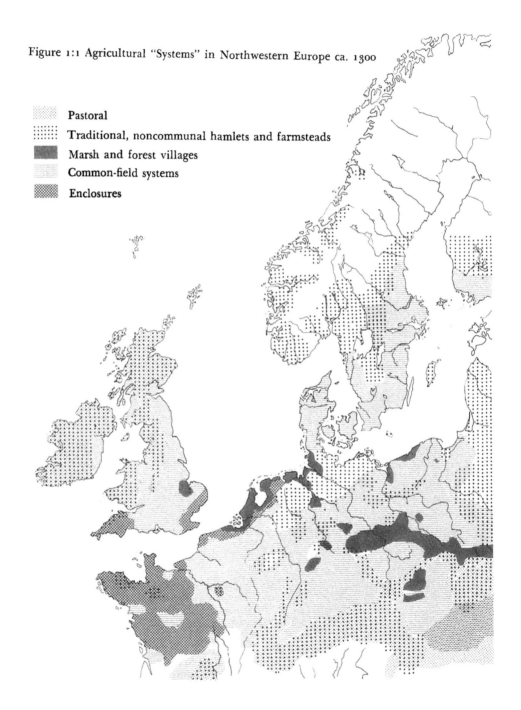

Figure 1:1 Agricultural "Systems" in Northwestern Europe ca. 1300

Pastoral

Traditional, noncommunal hamlets and farmsteads

Marsh and forest villages

Common-field systems

Enclosures

or in hamlets of less than, say, ten households. All its elements depended upon peasants living together in villages where mutual contact, neighborly cooperation, and some sort of community organization (whether spontaneous or imposed by a lord) shaped social and economic life. On the other hand, the proximity of towns with strong commercial markets for farm produce to feed workers who specialized in nonagricultural occupations also militated against common-field institutions in the immediately surrounding countryside. Finally, these agricultural arrangements tended to appear first and most densely in the regions of Europe with the strongest manorial systems, and to spread geographically along the same lines as that form of government and social control.

Common fields originated in the heartland of seigneurialism: northern France, Flanders, and southwestern Germany. By the late thirteenth century they dominated the plains of central and southern England, northern France, Germany, and east-central Europe, as well as outlying areas, such as southern Sweden or those portions of Ireland and Wales that had been more or less assimilated to the Anglo-Norman variety of medieval civilization. But in the uplands of Germany, the marshes of the North Sea coast, the high moors of the northern and western British Isles, the narrow valleys of Norway, northern Sweden, and the Alps, and in the immediate environs of the growing mercantile and industrial cities, more peasants were free from more elements of landlord influence, and the common-field system, with its additional communal constraints, was weaker or entirely absent.

The Common Fields and Peasant Economics

When we try to understand common-field agriculture in the context of an operating peasant society, research on surviving modern peasantries can help us connect and arrange the exiguous medieval evidence. The first parameter of a peasant's existence is that he lives in a starkly hierarchical society.[7] He is dominated by a nonpeasant elite group. Thus any peasant agri-

---

[7] For a useful synthesis of contemporary thinking about the analytical difficulties of peasant study (with a full bibliography) see Henri Mendras, "Un schéma d'analyse de la paysannerie occidentale," *Peasant Studies Newsletter* 1 (1972), 79–93 and 126–44. The following discussion draws in particular upon pp. 126–30.

culturist faces two primary economic demands: to provide for the
continued subsistence of his own household, and to meet the exac-
tions imposed upon him and his fellows from outside. Peasants
normally seek to satisfy these needs in the context of broadly
similar household economic units, which serve as the locus of
decisions on both consumption and production. In Europe,
specifically, in each of an indeterminate sequence of years each
household in a common field village had to produce enough to
cover payments to the lord and the church, seed for the coming
year, and the consumption needs of its members. Each household could mobilize nearly identical skimpy resources and techniques. Such subsistence agriculture meant that total production
did not much exceed total necessary expenditures, and that
peasant households lived close to famine, eating well only after
good years and starving after bad ones. In these constrained
circumstances, a peasant operates with a somewhat different set
of priorities than does a capitalist farmer. Central to the individual's decision-making is a desire to maximize the product of
his family's labor, to squeeze all he can from his land even after
diminishing returns set in.[8] As a group, therefore, the peasant
community seeks to retain its members on the land, and endeavors to provide for the greatest possible number its technology can sustain.[9] Finally, the pressure of marginal subsistence, coupled with a relatively static technology and little
variation in resources among the households, discouraged excessive risk-taking. Many features of the common-field system—
dispersion of plots, common pasture, crop rotation, communal
control—served to mitigate the uncertainties of farming and to
ensure a minimal production level to all families.

The peasant's relation to the market also differs from that of
a capitalist farmer. We might characterize his position as market
involvement without market orientation. Although few peasants

[8] A. V. Chayanov, *The Theory of Peasant Economy,* edited by Daniel
Thorner, Basile Kerblay, and R. E. F. Smith (Homewood, Ill., 1966), pp.
70–90.

[9] "The old economic order asked: How can I give, on this piece of land,
work and sustenance to the greatest possible number of men? Capitalism
asks: From this given piece of land how can I produce as many crops as
possible for the market with as few men as possible?" Max Weber, "Capitalism and Rural Society in Germany," in H. H. Gerth and C. Wright Mills,
editors and translators, *From Max Weber: Essays in Sociology* (New York.
1958), p. 367.

dwell in economies entirely innocent of money, prices, and exchange, and though few remain utterly separate from the market sector, they tend not to structure their economic activity around the market.[10] The goal is rather maximum self-sufficiency of each household, and entry into the market only to obtain the minimal cash required for money dues or for purchase of the few consumption items (salt and, perhaps, iron) that could not be raised or fabricated at home. The peasant's desire for household self-sufficiency severely reduces the potential liquidity of his product; within the household, cabbages cannot be substituted for a basket or excess cattle for a shortage of seed grain. When self-sufficiency is coupled with the need to maximize the family labor product in a subsistence economy, we find peasants seeking not the greatest possible volume or cash value of their product, but rather a qualitative mix of various required products.[11] Hence common-field institutions functioned not to yield the largest feasible grain harvest, but to maintain an equilibrium between maximum regular cereal production and the minimum livestock required by existing technology and resources. Before the fourteenth century most peasants lived, if not by bread alone, most often by bread and porridge. Still, they needed livestock to provide not only protein to their diets, but also power for field work and dung to maintain the fertility of the soil. Without knowledge of fodder crops or enough arable land to plant them in place of cereal grains, the peasant turned to the woods and wastes to feed his beasts. But if waste pasturage failed to support the stock he needed (and it always meant dissipation of precious manure),

[10] Mendras, "Un schéma d'analyse," especially pp. 126–27 and 130. Monetary values arise externally to the peasant economy. Since, however, money at times becomes an invaluable necessity for the peasant, we have the phenomenon of rural usury.

The important analytical distinction between market involvement and market orientation might be further elucidated by the parallel case of a modern suburbanite's vegetable garden. Although the modern gardener may well seek to maximize his self-sufficient return on vegetable production, he does not thereby lose his primary economic orientation to the market. Nor does a peasant who seeks to maximize his return from a marketing venture thus lose his fundamentally nonmarket characteristics. Two further parallels between the gardener and the peasant also come to mind. Neither considers labor costs so long as those remain within the household unit. And, like the peasant, the suburban gardener seeks, in his self-sufficient production, a qualitative mix of product (not as many tomatoes as possible, but some lettuce, some beans, some corn, some beets, and some tomatoes).

[11] Chaynov, *Theory of Peasant Economy*, pp. 121–24.

he was caught in a vicious spiral: too little stock to provide the power and fertilizer necessary to work enough good land to produce the fodder crops needed to keep up stocking levels. To a degree, then, common pasture on the stubble of the grain fields and on the weeds of the fallow offered feed for the animals and made them deposit manure on the fields. It provided poor feed and little manure, but it brought each peasant closer to the stocking levels he required.

The combination in peasant agriculture of low productivity with organization into many relatively similar household production and consumption units, each trying to achieve self-sufficient subsistence at minimum risk, encourages uniformity in agricultural practices. Given their comparable resources and technical capabilities, most men in a village want to do about the same thing with a similar portion of their land at about the same time of year.[12] The common condition of social subordination to a nonpeasant elite with infinitely greater access to resources strongly reinforces this conformist tendency.[13] As a result, modern peasants seem to manifest extreme "scarcity consciousness"[14] and to behave as if their perceptual orientation stressed the narrow limits which circumscribe all possible "good fortune" accessible to them.[15] Assumptions of scarcity, uniformity, and social subor-

[12] George C. Homans, *English Villagers of the Thirteenth Century* (Cambridge, Mass., 1941), pp. 8off., emphasizes this point for the common fields.
[13] Chandra Jayawardena, "Ideology and Conflict in Lower Class Communities," *Comparative Studies in Society and History* 10 (1968), 434–41.
[14] See the thought-provoking discussion by Manfred Stanley, "Nature, Culture and Scarcity. Foreword to a Theoretical Synthesis," *American Sociological Review* 33 (1968), 855–70.
[15] This statement seems to articulate fairly an area of agreement within the involved anthropological controversy over George M. Foster's formulation of "the image of limited good." See George M. Foster, "Peasant Society and the Image of Limited Good," *American Anthropologist* 67 (1965), reprinted in J. M. Potter, M. N. Diaz, and G. M. Foster, eds., *Peasant Society. A Reader* (Boston, 1967), pp. 300–23; David Kaplan and Benson Saler, "Foster's Image of Limited Good—An Example of Anthropological Explanation," *American Anthropologist* 68 (1966), 202–205; John W. Bennett, "Further Remarks on Foster's Image of Limited Good," *American Anthropologist* 68 (1966), 206–10; George M. Foster. "Foster's Reply to Kaplan, Saler, and Bennett," *American Anthropologist* 68 (1966), 210–14; Steven Piker, "The Image of Limited Good—Comments on an Exercise in Description and Interpretation," *American Anthropologist* 68 (1966), 1202–11; John G. Kennedy, "Peasant Society and the Image of Limited Good—A Critique," *ibid.*, *American Anthropologist* 68 (1966), 1212–25; John J. Honigmann, "Interpersonal Relations in Atomistic Communities," *Human Organization* 27 (1968), 224–25. Note that Foster sought a model for modern peasants (and,

dination combine, in the absence of known available alternatives, to encourage strong social pressures toward normative and static behavior patterns.[16]

The operation of common-field agriculture reflects this self-reinforcing set of attitudes. With land arranged in intermingled parcels, any individual who departed from routine could encounter difficulties of access or lack turning space for his plow. Conversely, if he decided to pasture his cattle on a plot surrounded by the ripening grain of his neighbors, disputes would be inevitable. Thus even a moderate antipathy toward social conflict could informally approximate the effects of conscious community regulation of economic activity. And if the community as a whole felt threatened by departures from the norm, it sought to eliminate them, especially if the deviation endangered that slim margin between subsistence and starvation. Individual initiative and innovation in the management of arable land could well threaten the narrowly limited possibilities for survival of each household. The advantages seized by an individual might come at the expense of every other family. In a world of static technology and limited opportunity, this could not be tolerated. Thus the entire peasant value system discourages change, and seeks to avoid its effects. What we might call a subsistence-sufficiency orientation provides the framework for peasant decision making.[17]

Change does come to peasant economies, however. In the modern world they are infected, so to speak, with opportunities and pressures originating in the exchange economy outside, but large-scale, long-term change in premodern peasant economies

---

as he admits, perhaps for other segments of premodern societies), but that, as formulated, it has little power to explain changes over time.

[16] Jayawardena, "Ideology and Conflict," pp. 434–41. On norm enforcement through social pressure or village courts see the discussion of "law and custom" in Max Gluckman, *Politics, Law and Ritual in Tribal Society* (New York, 1968), pp. 231–35.

[17] The term "subsistence sufficiency" is derived from Edward Miller's description of economic attitudes among pre-thirteenth-century English monastic landlords, and itself echoes the vocabulary of twelfth-century charters for the farm of a manor. Thus the nonmarket orientation is in no way to be construed as always confined to the peasantry. See Edward Miller, "England in the Twelfth and Thirteenth Centuries· An Economic Contrast?" *Economic History Review* 2d series 24 (1971), 1–14, especially pp. 7–8. Miller sees the development of policies to maximize production on thirteenth-century ecclesiastical manors as linked to attitudinal changes away from subsistence sufficiency.

has been much less easily understood. For this reason the work of Ester Boserup provides valuable assistance to our analysis.[18] Boserup argues that traditional agricultural economies change when the pressures of a growing population against a fixed resource and technological base force them to do so. As increased subsistence needs exhaust resources amenable to extensive exploitation, the people must intensify, apply greater labor to the same land, increase frequency of cropping, and thereby achieve the newly required production levels. In particular, she postulates a historical sequence of land utilization, wherein early long fallow techniques are successively replaced by short fallow, annual cropping, and multiple cropping, each as an economy is compelled by demographic pressures. Boserup's argument assumes the availability of more intensive techniques and the willingness of a society to use them.[19] She thus neglects the possibility of a society choosing or being forced to evolve other means of adaptation to situations of population pressure. And there is the further problem that intensification can itself create new disruptions of the social order. Some further work, however, suggests that agricultural intensification is but one possible reaction to population pressure and that increased and formalized social controls can be yet another (not necessarily exclusive) alternative.[20] Clearly the stresses engendered by population growth in a peasant economy offer an important point of departure for an investigation into the origins and development of common fields.

It is within the intellectual context of the technical constraints on medieval peasant society, its subsistence-sufficiency orientation, and the explanatory paradigm suggested by the Boserup

[18] Ester Boserup, *The Conditions of Agricultural Growth: The Economics of Agrarian Change under Population Pressure* (Chicago, 1965), pp. 11–18. Boserup's association of growing agricultural production with a growing population is also echoed by Colin Clark and Margaret Haswell, *The Economics of Subsistence Agriculture,* 2d ed. (New York, 1966), p. 69, where it is called "the characteristic mark of a peasant community."

[19] For carefully reasoned and multidisciplinary criticism of Boserup see the symposium on her work by Julius Rubin, Edward Nell, and Jan de Vries, *Peasant Studies Newsletter* 1 (1972), 35–53.

[20] Brian Spooner and Robert Netting, "Humanized Economics," *ibid.,* pp. 54–58, and the various contributions to Brian Spooner, ed., *Population Growth: Anthropological Implications* (Cambridge, Mass., 1972), especially that by Robert Netting, "Sacred Power and Centralization: Aspects of Political Adaptation in Africa," pp. 219–44.

thesis, that we here explore the development of common field agriculture in medieval Europe. Succeeding sections of this essay describe the considerably more individualistic and less intensive agricultural system that antedated the common fields; delineate the origins, maturation, and diffusion of common-field institutions; and finally suggest an explanatory model for those developments that takes account of both the historical evidence and modern understandings of the dynamics of a peasant society. We shall advance the hypothesis that common-field agriculture, with its subordination of individual initiative to communal control, arose as the response of formerly individualistic European peasants who were faced with growing social conflict when an increasing population with a relatively fixed agrarian technology threatened its limited resources. Their choice of a communal response is explained by their general subsistence-sufficiency orientation, and by long experience with both informal cooperation in agriculture and communal institutions of peace and order.

Agriculture before the common fields: traditional individualistic subsistence

Common-field agriculture first came under close scrutiny by writers and reformers in the eighteenth century and by legal historians in the nineteenth century. At that time European peasant communities had worked within it "since time immemorial." It is little wonder that its critics and students could not imagine, much less investigate or describe, its origins and early development. These were transposed to an unknowable prehistoric past in the forests of primitive Germany [21] or tribal Gaul,[22] and linked indissolubly with the character of specific national or ethnic groups. For England the common-field system in its entirety was

[21] A classic statement is, of course, August Meitzen, *Siedlungen und Agrarwesen der Westgermanen und Ostgermanen, der Kelten, Römer, Finnen und Slaven,* 3 vols. with atlas (Berlin, 1896).

[22] André Déléage, *La vie économique et sociale de la Bourgogne dans le haut Moyen Age,* Thèse pour le doctorat ès lettres présentée à la Faculté dans lettres de l'Université de Paris, 2 vols. in one with atlas (Mâcon, 1941), pp. 694–98, would derive the dichotomy in agrarian institutions that prevails between northeast and southwest Burgundy from the ancient distinctions between prehistoric dolmen and tumulus peoples, and between Indo-European Celts and Mediterranean peoples.

connected to the Anglo-Saxon settlement [23] or to pre-Roman Belgic invaders.[24] Such interpretations assumed implicitly that any group of institutional arrangements that functioned in such complex interdependence and displayed such apparent stability must have been created almost simultaneously in all its parts, and have existed almost without a history or a development.

In recent decades European historical scholarship has significantly revised the traditional interpretation. No longer is it assumed that the settlement patterns and agricultural institutions portrayed in so much detail by postmedieval maps, commentators, and court records had remained fixed from the "Dark Ages" of the great migrations until the "enlightened" age of agricultural reform. German historical geographers have been among the leaders in the new view.[25] French scholars are pursuing a similar, though independent line,[26] and even in England the revisionist thesis seems to be making converts, despite fierce opposition.[27] Certainly more regional and local research, in par-

[23] This is the stance of the classics, H. L. Gray, *English Field Systems* (Cambridge, Mass., 1915), and C. S. and C. S. Orwin, *The Open Fields*, 2d ed. (Oxford, 1954), pp. 23–29 and 60–61, as well as that of Titow, "Open Field System," pp. 95–102.

[24] Frederic Seebohm, *The English Village Community Examined in its Relations to the Manorial and Tribal Systems and to the Common or Open Field System of Husbandry. An Essay in Economic History*, 4th ed. (London, 1905), pp. 412–441.

[25] See, for example, Hans Mortensen, "Die mittelalterliche deutsche Kulturlandschaft und ihr Verhältnis zur Gegenwart," *Vierteljahrsschrift für Sozial- und Wirtschaftsgeschichte* 45 (1958), 17–36. German scholarship on this and related issues has recently been summarized for the English reader by Alan Mayhew, *Rural Settlement and Farming in Germany* (London, 1973), pp. 13–90, and especially pp. 22–28.

[26] Among the earliest statements are Étienne Juillard, *Structures agraires et paysages ruraux. Un quart de siècle de recherches françaises* (Annales de l'Est Mémoire No. 17; Nancy, 1957), 54, and Xavier de Planhol, "Essai sur la genèse du paysage rurale en champs ouverts," in *Géographie et histoire agraires, Actes du colloque international organisé par la faculté des Lettres de l'Université de Nancy* (Annales de l'Est Mémoire No. 21; Nancy, 1959), pp. 414–24.

[27] A post-Anglo-Saxon origin for English common fields was proposed in 1964 by Thirsk, "Common Fields," and immediately assaulted by Titow, "Open Field System." Joan Thirsk replied in "The Origin of the Common Fields," *Past and Present* 33 (1966), 142–47. Jerome Blum adopted the new interpretation on a European scale in "The European Village as Community: Origins and Functions," *Agricultural History* 45 (1971), 158–63, while in a recent collaborative British work, Baker and Butlin, *Field Systems*, most contributors of regional chapters seem to agree with the strongly revisionist conclusion of the editors, pp. 653–56.

ticular efforts designed to test explicit descriptive interpretations and causal hypotheses, must precede a definitive synthesis; still, we can now outline the development of the common-field system and its spread across Europe in a way that corresponds with the archeological and historical evidence as we know it.

To begin with the age of migrations and early medieval period (fourth to eighth centuries), as "Europe" began to emerge from the ruins of classical civilization, both the spade and the scanty texts reveal a traditional agriculture devoid of the essential and associated elements of the common-field system. Rather than assembling into the large villages typical of the common-field system, the early Germanic invaders settled in isolated farm-steads, or in hamlets inhabited by a local leader and his handful of followers or bondsmen. For example, this pattern prevailed in Thuringia before the Frankish conquest, the central Rhine-land, and even the southwest German Alemannic region, where common-field institutions made an extremely early appearance.[28] Likewise, in areas of Bavaria that were later exclusively village-based—the Gäuboden, for example—the hamlet form originally prevailed.[29] Outside Germany less attention has been paid to this problem, but Juillard has suggested similar conditions in those areas of northern France where a densely nucleated Gallo-Roman population failed to survive the invasions,[30] while Pocock's recent study of the morphogenesis of the fields of an Oxfordshire village clearly shows its origins in four separate sites more than a mile from one another.[31] Pre-Norman Yorkshire featured hamlet set-tlements.[32] Above these basically familial holdings, territorial

[28] Friedrich Lütge, *Die Agrarverfassung des frühen Mittelalters im mittel-deutschen Raum vornehmlich in der Karolingerzeit*, 2d ed. (Quellen und Forschungen zur Agrargeschichte; Stuttgart, 1966), p. 336; Franz Steinbach, *Ursprung und Wesen der Landgemeinde nach rheinischen Quellen* (Arbeits-gemeinschaft fur Forschung des Landes Nordrhein-Westfalen, Geisteswis-senschaften, Heft 87; Köln, 1960), 5–15; Willi A. Boelcke, "Die frühmittel-alterlichen Wurzeln der südwestdeutschen Gewannflur," *ZAA* 12 (1964), 134–37.

[29] Pankraz Fried, "Zur Geschichte der bayerischen Landgemeinde," in *Die Anfänge der Landgemeinde und ihr Wesen*, vol. 1 (Vorträge und Forschungen, vol. 7; Konstanz, 1964), 88.

[30] Juillard, *Structures agraires*, p. 54.

[31] Ernest A. Pocock, "The First Fields in an Oxfordshire Parish," *AgHR* 16 (1968), 88–89.

[32] June A. Sheppard, "Field Systems of Yorkshire," in Baker and Butlin, *Field Systems*, pp. 176–87.

communities throughout Europe served to keep the peace and to ensure equitable access to unseparated common wastes.[33]

If the peasantry of the earliest Middle Ages lived more separated from one another than did their common-field descendants, their parcels of arable land were likewise more clearly distinguished. The archeological evidence, in particular, demonstrates that the classic form of open fields with numerous small strip parcels did not prevail at this time. Before the ninth century the land worked by each peasant in Basse-Auvergne lay in a few large blocks.[34] In northwest Germany the hamlet's arable land was divided into a single set of long strips,[35] while in southern Germany an involved scholarly controversy seems to have ended with agreement that both long strips and large blocks occurred as the earliest forms of holdings in the oldest settlements.[36] Homans' unsubstantiated assertion "that the institutions of open-field England resembled those of at least part of Lower Saxony" and that therefore "people familiar with the institutions on the continent brought them to England during the invasions of the Dark Ages as part of their cultural equipment" [37] fails to take cognizance of some recent archeological and other evidence. Niemeier, for example, finds that in the entire northwest German area a hamlet arrangement, with the relatively little arable land divided into a few easily accessible long strips, prevailed before and during the migrations. Niemeier even proposes that the core of the arable land in England's last surviving common-field village, Laxton, suggests by the pattern of holdings that it too began

[33] As Joan Thirsk points out in "East Midlands," p. 246, shared use of the waste was a feature of all European peasant communities from prehistoric times. On territorial communities see Blum, "Village as Community," p. 159.

[34] Gabriel Fournier, "Les transformations du parcellaire en Basse-Auvergne au cours du haut Moyen-Age," in *Géographie et histoire agraires*, pp. 203–208.

[35] For a synthesis see Mayhew, *Rural Settlement*, pp. 22–28, or Anneliese Krenzlin, "Blockflur, Langstreifenflur und Gewannflur als Ausdruck agrarischer Wirtschaftsformen in Deutschland," in *Géographie et histoire agraires*, pp. 353–69; for a somewhat different interpretation, see Martin Born, "Langstreifen in Nordhessen?" *ZAA* 15 (1967), 105–33.

[36] Boelcke, "Wurzeln der Gewannflur," p. 131; K. H. Schröder, "Die Gewannflur in Süddeutschland," in *Die Anfänge der Landgemeinde und ihr Wesen*, vol. 1, 20–24; Dietrich Fliedner, "Zur Problematik der römischen und frühalemannischen Flurformen im Bereich der südwestdeutschen Gewannsiedlungen," *ZAA* 18 (1970), 16–35.

[37] George C. Homans, "The Explanation of English Regional Differences," *Past and Present* 42 (1969), 30.

as such a long-strip hamlet.[38] Most recently, Baker and Butlin have decisively rejected the possibility that the open fields arrived with the baggage of the Anglo-Saxons.[39]

A more simplified field structure suggests a higher degree of agricultural individualism during the earliest medieval centuries than under "open-field" arrangements, where difficulties of access to each strip could force some mutual restraint. Most recent scholars, at least, interpret the extremely sparse evidence this way. For example, the oldest settlements in southwest Germany are those with names ending in -*ingen* and -*heim;* they predate the sixth century. Boelcke finds that at least half of these began as isolated farms.[40] Likewise, the place name and field name *Bohl,* a common usage in areas of Württemburg settled during the Merovingian period, is derived from a term for an area of individual use.[41] Steinbach further asserts that both Tacitus' description of early Germanic agriculture and the pertinent passages of Salic and other Merovingian law codes are devoid of evidence for communal regulation of arable land, confining their references solely to neighborly rights enforceable in the courts.[42]

[38] Georg Niemeier, "Agrarlandschaftliche Reliktgebiete und die Morphogenese von Kulturlandschaften im atlantischen Europa," *Geografiska Annaler* 43 (1961), 229–33. More specific investigation of a region in the lower Jutland peninsula suggests that, until the ninth century, the Saxon inhabitants farmed walled square fields: Herbert Jahnkuhn, "Die Entstehung der mittelalterlichen Agrarlandschaft in Angeln," *ibid.,* pp. 151–64. The Anglo-Saxon origin of the long strips is supported by David M. Wilson, "Anglo-Saxon Rural Economy. A Survey of the Archaeological Evidence and a Suggestion," *AgHR* 10 (1962), 70–71.

[39] Baker and Butlin, *Field Systems,* pp. 624–25.

[40] Boelcke, "Wurzeln der Gewannflur," p. 150.

[41] Hans Jänichen, "Der Bohl im Schwäbisch-Alemannischen," *Zeitschrift für württemburgischen Landesgeschichte* 22 (1963), 29–53.

[42] Steinbach, *Ursprung der Langemeinde,* pp. 10–13, refers specifically to Tacitus, *Germania,* section 26: "Agri pro numero cultorum ab universis in vicis occupantur, quos mox inter se secundum dignationem partiuntur; facilitatem patiendi camporum spatia praestant. Arva per annos mutant, et superest ager." The Alfred J. Church and William J. Brodribb translation, edited by Moses Hadas, *The Complete Works of Tacitus* (New York, 1942), p. 721, gives a meaning as used by Steinbach: "Land proportioned to the number of inhabitants is occupied by the whole community in turn, and afterwards divided among them according to rank. A wide expanse of plains makes the partition easy. They till fresh fields every year, and they have still more land than enough." Interpretation is, however, by no means unanimous; Homans, "English Regional Differences," p. 33, seems to prefer an older view that Tacitus here describes communal management and use.

Faucher's study of the origins of the three-course rotation in France also suggests that a stage of dominant individualism preceded the communal controls of the later common-field system.[43] Such interpretations gain support from the treatment of arable agriculture in the early Germanic law codes. One of the earliest, the late fifth-century Burgundian *Lex Gundobada,* not only implies that arable land was separate and individual, but also, by its very concern with stock damages to arable crops,[44] indicates the absence of significant village law concerning a matter of immense importance in later common-field bylaws. Similar conclusions may be drawn from the emphasis on individual possession of fields in the sixth through ninth-century Salic and the seventh and eighth-century Alemannic codes.[45]

Early medieval peasants lived in small settlements scattered sparsely through the forests and wastes. Although they worked their arable land in a relatively individualistic manner, the limited technology and virtual absence of a market sector meant that their practices were largely controlled by tradition and custom. And they were, of course, subsistence farmers with little need for or access to products that could be brought in from outside. But during this early phase, arable agriculture may have played a secondary role to a sort of sedentary pastoralism. In virtually all of the early legal compilations, those few sections that directly concern economic activities strongly emphasize stock, while barely mentioning arable agriculture.[46] The islands

[43] Daniel Faucher, "L'Assolement triennal en France," *Etudes rurales* 1 (1961), 15–16.

[44] *Lex Gundobada* XXIII; edited by Friderico Bluhme in *Leges Burgundionum,* in Monumenta Germaniae Historica, *Leges in folio* III, edited by G. H. Pertz (Hannover, 1863), 543. This particular article was revised twice before the end of the seventh century (*ibid.,* pp. 569–70 and 574–75). For an English translation see Katherine F. Drew, *The Burgundian Code* (Philadelphia, 1972), p. 39.

[45] See Karl A. Eckhardt, ed., *Pactus legis Salicae,* 2 vols. in 4 (Germanenrechte, neue Folge, Historisches Institut des Werralandes, Westgermanisches Recht, vols. 1–2; Göttingen, 1954–1957), II:1, 231–232 (article XXXIV:3–4), and his *Leges Alamannorum,* 2 vols. (Germanenrechte, neue Folge, Historisches Institut des Werralandes, Westgermanisches Recht, vol. V:1–2; Göttingen, 1958, and Witzenhausen, 1962), I, 144 (Pactus legis Alamannorum, XLII:1–2).

[46] The evidence is admittedly impressionistic, but the impression gained by reading through the codes is a strong one. A pair of late and brief examples may serve to illustrate the point. The Saxon law code, written down under Frankish auspices around 785, has four articles (34, 56, 57, 58) dealing with theft of or damage to stock, but the only mention of any arable land or crops occurs in certain late manuscripts, where the money values of

of light soils best suited to the simple techniques of early medieval agriculture [47] lay in a green sea of woods and wastes. Here
was ample fodder for small, rangy cattle and half-wild swine.
The Alemannic codes refer to woodland shelters for pigs and
cattle and then, in prescribing the damages due for illegally
killing the animals of another, thoroughly mix articles referring
to "domestic" stock (swine, geese, doves) and those for game
(bison, deer, bear), clearly implying that all were to be found in
the same place.[48] Likewise, the early ninth-century Thuringian
code, by specifying the compensation due from anyone who
caught or killed another's cattle or draft stock in game traps
that he had set in the woods,[49] demonstrates both the extensive
use of woodland pasture and its separation from private ownership and use. The forests and waste belonged to no individual;
their wide expanses provided enough for all.[50]

The traditional individualistic subsistence agriculture detectable in long-settled areas in the heartland of western Europe
at the beginning of the Middle Ages closely resembles that known
from relatively "backward" noncommon-field areas at its fringes,
which appear only in later documents. For example, students of
Scandinavia, especially Sweden, before and during the early

---

a measure of wheat, barley, or oats are fixed by article 66. See Claudius von
Schwerin, ed., *Leges Saxonum und Lex Thuringorum* (Fontes iuris Ger-
manici antiqui in usum scholarum ex Monumentis Germaniae Historicis
separatim editi; Leipzig and Hannover, 1918), pp. 26, 31–32, and 34. Likewise
the laws of two Thuringian clans dwelling along the Unstrut and between
the Saale and the Elster, which were written down in 802/803, discuss stock in
eight articles, without ever mentioning arable land at all. See *ibid.*, pp. 62
and 65–66. The pastoral emphasis of early medieval Germanic peoples is
also accepted by the most active postwar student and editor of their laws,
Karl A. Eckhardt; see his revision of Hans Planitz, *Deutsche Rechtsgeschichte*,
2d ed. rev. (Graz and Köln, 1961), pp. 26–28 and 70–72.

[47] Bernard Wailes, "Plow and Population in Temperate Europe," in
Spooner, *Population Growth*, pp. 173–74, points out that evidence on the
distribution of early Anglo-Saxon settlements confirms that they initially
avoided heavy clay soils, both in the Midlands as a whole and within smaller
regional landscapes.

[48] In the Eckhardt edition, I, 120 and 124–31, for the seventh century
Pactus, and II, 66, for the eighth century *Lex*.

[49] Von Schwerin, *Leges*, p. 66: "in silva . . . ubique pecus vel iumentum
alterius captum vel mortuum fuerit." Similar measures appear in the
Saxon code, *ibid.*, pp. 31–32.

[50] Krenzlin, "Blockflur," pp. 364–65; Albrecht Timm, *Die Waldnutzung
in Nordwestdeutschland im Spiegel der Weistümer. Einleitende Untersuchungen über die Umgestaltung des Stadt-Land-Verhältnisses im Spätmittel-
alter* (Köln, 1960), pp. 52–53 and 86–88.

Viking period, find no evidence for village settlements or open fields. Instead, the peasants dwelt in hamlets of a few farms, raised crops on individual fields at the center of their lands, and pastured cattle on the common surrounding wastes.[51] Before the late twelfth and early thirteenth centuries the agricultural institutions and practices of Slavic east-central Europe displayed a similar pattern,[52] while the well-known infield-outfield system of much of medieval and modern Ireland, Scotland, and the Atlantic fringes of Norway and Brittany shares numerous common traits.[53] There are even some traces from as late as the twelfth century in sparsely inhabited sections of France and the thirteenth century in Poland of groups practicing genuine forest fallow agriculture,[54] the most extensive stage in Boserup's scheme.

[51] Hilbert Andersson, *Parzellierung und Gemengelage: Studien über die ältere Kulturlandschaft in Schonen* (Meddelande fran Geografiska Institutet vid Stockholms Högskola, nr. 122; Lund, 1959); Sigurd Erixon, "Swedish Villages without Systematic Regulation," *Geografiska Annaler* 43 (1961), 69–73; Sven-Olof Lindquist, "Some Investigations of Field-Wall Areas in Östergotland and Uppland," *Geografiska Annaler* 43 (1961), 213–14; John Granlund, "Dorf- und Flurformen Schwedens," *Die Anfange der Landgemeinde und ihr Wesen,* vol. 2 (Vorträge und Forschungen, vol. 8; Konstanz, 1964), 308; Michael Müller-Wille, "Vor- und frühmittelalterliche Flurwüstungen in Skandinavien," *ZAA* 13 (1965), 147–74, especially pp. 172–74.

[52] Maria Dobrowolska, "The Morphogenesis of the Agrarian Landscape of Southern Poland," *Geografiska Annaler* 43 (1961), 27–33; Marie Kiełczewska-Zaleska, "Various Trends of Transformation of Polish Rural Settlements," *Ibid.,* pp. 321–22; Paul Johansen, "Einige Funktionen und Formen mittelalterlicher Landgemeinden in Estland und Finnland," *Die Anfänge der Landgemeinde und ihr Wesen* II, 282–83 and 287; Kazimierz Slaski, "Agrarstruktur und Agrarproduktion in Pommern vor Beginn der deutschrechtlichen Kolonisation," *ZAA* 16 (1968), 181–89; B. Baranowski *et al., Histoire de l'économie rurale en Pologne jusqu'à 1864* (Institut d'Histoire de la Culture Matérielle près l'Académie Polonaise des Sciences; Wrocław, 1966), 25–31; Karol Maleczyński, ed., *Historia Śląska Tom I, Do Roku 1763, Część I do połowy XIV w.* (Polska Akademia Nauk, Instytut Historii; Wrocław, 1960), pp. 162–70.

[53] See the useful synthesis by Harold Uhlig, "Old Hamlets with Infield and Outfield Systems in Western and Central Europe," *Geografiska Annaler* 43 (1961), 285–312, and, more recently, G. Whittington, "Field Systems of Scotland," in Baker and Butlin, *Field Systems,* pp. 550–79, and Ronald H. Buchanan, "Field Systems of Ireland," in Baker and Butlin, *Field Systems,* pp. 608–16. Whittington even suggests that a formally recognizable infield developed in Scotland only during the twelfth and thirteenth centuries, when population growth compelled abandonment of a former shifting oats monoculture.

[54] Teodor Tyc, *Die Anfänge der dörflichen Siedlung zu deutschem Recht in Grosspolen (1200–1333),* translated by Maria Tyc (Breslau, 1930), pp. 42–43, proposes forest fallow agriculture as the distinctive characteristic of special peasant status groups in early thirteenth-century Polish texts, the

What emerges, therefore, is a somewhat standardized European *pattern of extensive sedentary pastoralism and mixed farming on* nuclei of suitable land, whether permanent or shifting, farmed for subsistence by a thinly distributed population that knew certain elements of neighborly cooperation, but had none of the complex field arrangements, common rights over the arable land, and communal regulations of the later common-field system. This pattern, called here traditional individualistic subsistence agriculture,[55] antedated the common-field system throughout northern and western Europe. As we shall see in the next two sections, this system disappeared first and most completely in the densely populated heartlands of the common-field system, but survived, sometimes well beyond the Middle Ages, in areas that lay at the periphery of medieval civilization or otherwise lacked the climatic, geographic, or demographic prerequisites for the more intensive cereal production that lay at the foundation of the shift towards the common fields.

The appearance of the common fields

Evolution from an individualistic towards a communal system of agricultural management has two different aspects. In the first place, there is the problem of origins—the time, sequence, and region in which the various elements of the common-field arrangement first appeared alone and in association—and, secondly, there occurs the process of diffusion and acculturation whereby other regions assimilated these institutions and came to share a common agricultural system. Current research informs us best about the acculturation process in those peripheral areas that

---

łazęcy, the *popraznici*, and the *strozones.* He also cites a twelfth-century French text that describes people who cleared woodland by fire to take two consecutive years' crops from it before moving on.

[55] The term "individualistic," here applied to early medieval agriculture, describes a form of agricultural management that is well away from the communal end of a spectrum running from the purely collective to the purely individual, but it does not imply individualism in the abstract nineteenth-century sense. As mentioned in the text, this was a household economy; the individuals who mattered were patriarchal heads, whose capacity for radically innovative decisions was bound by narrow subsistence needs, seigneurial lordship, and technological poverty. In her attempt to synthesize the early historical development of the common fields Anneliese Krenzlin, "Blockflur," pp. 364–65, describes this earliest phase as "Waldviehweidewirtschaft mit geringem Ackerbau in ungeregelter Wechselwirtschaft" on "Blockflur mit Einzelhöffen und Hofgruppensiedlungen."

adopted common fields rather late, and also suggests a convincing interpretation of the initial centers of innovation, but considerable ignorance remains concerning the intervening phase of penetration into those old-settled regions where the system was a secondary phenomenon. Our discussion here centers on recent views of common-field origins in old-settled sections of northern France and southwestern Germany, and then briefly surveys the subsequent expansion across northwestern Europe.

In certain favored localities the pattern of settlement and cultivation in the age of migrations began to change by the early seventh century. In Frankish Gaul north of the Loire, some old centers of dense Gallo-Roman population, which seem to have retained a degree of nucleation despite the invasions, now experienced renewed population increase and concentration; such seems to have occurred in the vicinity of Ghent.[56] Elsewhere, Alemannic regions on both sides of the Rhine are the best studied, but also probably the most pronounced case on the continent. Here definite signs of population growth, increased nucleation, and subdivision of the old unitary block fields into strips held by multiple individual heirs all begin to appear. The regional demographic upswing manifested itself in the successful establishment by Merovingian and early Carolingian rulers of many new villages in former royal forests.[57] Recent German investigators label the period one of "villagization" (*Verdorfung*) because peasants left several hamlets to assemble in a single site, which thereby became a large village. The hamlets' arable land did not, however, go out of cultivation, but merged to create the large arable acreage of the new core village. Kornwestheim in Swabia, for example, had thus absorbed eight other hamlets by the early thirteenth century.[58] One impetus for such increased nucleation may have come from local lords, who saw in a more concentrated populace improved opportunities for social control and exploitation of peasant labor.

[56] In general, see Juillard, *Structures agraires*, p. 54, or Robert-Henri Bautier, *The Economic Development of Medieval Europe* (London, 1971), p. 29. On the Ghent and Aalst districts, see Adrian E. Verhulst, "En Basse et Moyenne Belgique pendant le haut moyen age: differents types de structure domainale et agraire," *Annales* 11 (1956), 61–70, and his "Probleme der mittelalterlichen Agrarlandschaft in Flandern," *ZAA* 11 (1963), 34–35.

[57] Hans-Jürgen Nitz, "Siedlungsgeographische Beiträge zum Problem der frankischen Staatskolonisation im süddeutschen Raum," *ZAA* 11 (1963), 34–35.

[58] Boelcke, "Wurzeln der Gewannflur," pp. 150–57.

Population growth and nucleation was, of course, accompanied by the need to fill the consumption demands of more people. The response was to use the additional labor now available by intensifying agricultural production through transferring resources from pastoralism to cereals. As will be shown, "cerealization" (*Vergetreidung*) and "destocking" (*Depekoration*) were everywhere an initial step in the transition from earlier arrangements to the common fields. By early Carolingian times this particular shift apparently had been carried out in many of the older-settled and more densely populated regions of the Frankish heartland.[59]

So the seventh and eighth centuries seem to have been a time of growing population, growing nucleation of settlement, and transition from the older, stock-oriented, extensive type of agriculture to a more intensive one that approached a cereal monoculture, at least in those areas once most favored by the first settlers. Those same localities simultaneously offer the earliest traces, not only of small strip parcels, but also of multistrip bundles (that is, furlongs) that were jointly managed as rotational units. The first documentary evidence for the sets of separately held strip parcels that make up a classic open field comes from the early eighth century,[60] but the institution may well be a bit older, since it clearly predates the use of whole fields as rotational units.[61] In both cases, however, the earliest evidence comes from the Alemannic region along the upper Rhine. Here a two-course rotation originally prevailed; the still more intensive three-course rotation seems to have been an

[59] *Ibid.;* Wilhelm Abel, "Landwirtschaft und ländliche Gesellschaft in Deutschland," *Agricoltura e mondo rurale in occidente nell' alto medioevo 22–28 aprile 1965* (Settimane di Studio del Centro Italiano di Studi sull' Alto Medioevo, vol. 13; Spoleto, 1966), pp. 172–73 and the discussion, pp. 262–63.

[60] Schröder, "Gewannflur," pp. 15–28; Abel, "Landwirtschaft," pp. 172–73. Boelcke, "Wurzeln der Gewannflur," p. 153, finds the strip parcels of the *Pactus legis Salicae* (early sixth century) to be of the long strip rather than the common field variety.

[61] Hans Jänichen, "Über den mittelalterlichen und neuzeitlichen Ackerbau im westlichen Schwaben. Beiträge zur Geschichte der Gewannflur," *Jahrbuch zür Statistik und Landeskunde von Baden-Württemberg* 7 (1962), 40–71; Gertrud Schröder-Lembke, "Nebenformen der alten Dreifelderwirtschaft in Deutschland," *Agricoltura e mondo rurale,* pp. 287–88, and her "Zum Zelgenproblem," *ZAA* 17 (1969), 44–51, in which she finds the earliest appearance of the south German dialect term for a field used as a rotational unit in documents from the area around Lake Constance in the late eighth century.

innovation of the more strictly Frankish northern French-Flemish
area that spread with especial rapidity into other places of early
and intense Frankish influence.[62] The consensus of recent research seems to be that the open fields with strip parcels, and
the notion of managing each field as a rotational unit, which
implies a certain degree of joint control of cropping, first appeared in the upper Rhenish region, but only after the local
Alemannic inhabitants had come under Frankish hegemony.
It is probable that the three-course rotation, the specific set of
techniques most commonly associated with the common fields,
was a Frankish development, but early combined with the field
arrangements devised by Alemannic peasants.

Both the rotational practices and the small open-field strips
with, perhaps, some regulation of cropping, spread to old-settled
areas to the north and east during the remainder of the early
Middle Ages. By the late ninth or early tenth century old hamlets had begun to subdivide their former block and large strip
fields into small strip parcels, and to follow the evolution toward
a common-field system in Franconia, Hesse, Dijonnais, Artois,
and the Paris basin, to mention only some continental areas so
far subjected to detailed study.[63] Fournier's careful study of
Basse-Auvergne establishes that in the ninth and tenth centuries
population growth in the already more densely settled sections
was accompanied by subdivision of early large block fields into
small parcels of an open-field structure; in marginal and thinly
inhabited mountainous places, however, the old forms survived
much longer.[64] In England, where late seventh-century legal
evidence suggests the presence of unfenced individual shares in

[62] Niemeier, "Reliktgebiete," p. 233; Schröder-Lembke, "Nebenformen der
Dreifelderwirtschaft," pp. 287–88. Theodor Mayer, "Vom Werden und
Wesen der Landgemeinde, Ein Nachwort," *Die Anfänge der Landgemeinde
und ihr Wesen*, vol. 2, 474–77, emphasizes the role of the Carolingian state
in this process more than other authors seem willing to accept.

[63] Anneliese Krenzlin and Ludwig Reusch, *Die Entstehung der Gewann-
flur nach Untersuchungen in nördlichen Unterfranken* (Frankfurter geographische Hefte, 35. Jahrgang, 1. Hefte; Frankfurt, 1961); Born, "Langstreifen," pp. 127–29; Déléage, *Bourgogne*, pp. 261–75; George W. Coopland, *The
Abbey of Saint-Bertin and its Neighbourhood 900–1350* (Oxford Studies in
Social and Legal History, vol. 4, no. 8; Oxford, 1914), pp. 22–44; Charles
Higounet, "L'Assolement triennal dans la plaine de France au XIIIᵉ siècle,"
Comptes rendus de l'Académie des inscriptions et belles-lettres, Année 1956,
p. 509.

[64] Fournier, "Basse-Auvergne," pp. 205–207.

fields, there is no question that the Domesday Book portrays an old-settled landscape, and describes agricultural holdings in terms indicative of loose, probably neighborly rather than communal, open-field forms.[65]

Maturation and diffusion of common field agriculture

We have found that a loose but recognizable form of the common-field system took shape in old-settled areas of southwestern Germany, northern France, and England when localized population growth was associated with transition from an extensive combination of pastoral and arable husbandry to one in which cereals played the dominant subsistence role. Then, from the later tenth century to the late thirteenth or early fourteenth, nearly all of Europe experienced major demographic and economic growth with, however, significant local and regional variations in timing and duration. This period likewise brought increasing maturation, even solidification, of the institutional cluster of the common-field system in older areas, and expansion into large new ones.[66] But, of course, the general process of diffusion varied widely in its impact on specific regions. Among the influences affecting any given area's adoption of common fields, we should probably include its place in the large-scale sequence of settlement expansion, its suitability for short-fallow grain cultivation, the rate at which growth-induced resource shortages forced intensification, and the previous cultural experience and expectations of indigenous and immigrant populations. Reference to a few cases should clarify both the general trend and the kinds of regional peculiarities that seem to have occurred.

Although by the year 1000 many old-settled areas were already moving towards the common fields, new settlements established in the tenth and eleventh centuries at the edge of inhabited and uninhabited landscapes still began as hamlets and isolated farms reminiscent of the age of migrations. In those districts of central and eastern Yorkshire where it took more than a century to

[65] Thirsk, "Common Fields," pp. 6–7 and "Origin," pp. 145–47; Wilson, "Anglo-Saxon Rural Economy," pp. 70–71, note 4, points out that the reading of this passage in the Laws of Ine, which would see it as confirming common field strips, is a mistranslation of the original.

[66] The general association between settlement expansion and formation of common fields in high medieval Germany is outlined in Mayhew, *Rural Settlement*, pp. 39–58.

replace population losses during the 1069 rebellion, new assarts began as independent farmsteads, and only gradually were amalgamated with the adjoining common fields.[67] A similar pattern of individual assarts at the periphery of older common fields and in areas where topography had postponed colonization appears in East Anglia and the region of the Chiltern Hills.[68] In southwestern Germany, where despite the dense early medieval settlement large upland tracts remained to be pioneered, many of the villages dating to this period show in their morphology an origin as private clearances. The Black Forest, for example, was mostly opened up by individual farmers who, with their households, established isolated farms.[69] In almost all of these instances, the initially individualistic agriculture of the eleventh century gave way to common fields as local supplies of new land ran out during the course of the twelfth century. The developmental pattern, though temporally compressed, follows that established earlier in the oldest settlements: an orientation toward individualism and subsistence under conditions of abundant resources during early phases of the medieval growth cycle gave way to communalism under the pressure of local conditions of scarcity.

The behavior pattern derived from expectations of abundant resources changed as the twelfth century passed, and as medieval peasant culture entered a phase of major expansion into distant regions. After about 1150 western European peasants migrated to far-away new lands across the Elbe and later deep into Poland in the east, and across the Irish Sea in the west. In both instances they now carried with them from central Germany and from England the entire set of common-field institutions, transplanting them in their entirety to the new environment. The unusually large German villages of Brandenburg and certain parts of the Odra basin in Silesia date to the late twelfth and thirteenth centuries. From the start they possessed communal institutions to regulate short fallow cereal cultivation on planned open fields

[67] T. A. M. Bishop, "Assarting and the Growth of the Open Fields," *Economic History Review* 6 (1935), as reprinted in E. M. Carus-Wilson, ed., *Essays in Economic History* (London, 1954), pp. 35–36.

[68] M. R. Postgate, "Field Systems of East Anglia," in Baker and Butlin, *Field Systems*, pp. 293–96; David Roden, "Field Systems of the Chiltern Hills and Their Environs," *ibid.*, pp. 360–63.

[69] Schröder, "Gewannflur," pp. 18–28; Mayhew, *Rural Settlement*, pp. 59–60.

with regular strips, furlongs, and fields which had often been laid
out according to a regionally standard pattern.[70] English peasants
brought to Ireland after the 1170s by Anglo-Norman adventurers
likewise created common-field villages around Dublin.[71] Closer
to home, but still a migration in the sense of crossing a frontier
into relatively uninhabited land separate from the old arable
areas, the first twelfth-century settlers in the forest of Arden in
Warwickshire established open-field villages from the beginning.[72]
The contrast between individualistic pioneering in the period
before 1150 and the extensive common fields established *ex nihilo*
soon thereafter suggests a concurrent transformation in the expectations and cultural experience of peasant emigrants from
the old regions of western Europe.

About the same time that emigrants from western Europe
began to carry the common-field system with them as part of
their cultural baggage, indigenous populations even in areas not
subject to significant immigration began to adopt similar agricultural practices. With the wholesale acculturation to the common fields of peasantries around the periphery of transalpine
Europe, we have the final phase in the diffusion of this institutional cluster. For example, first Bohemia in the later twelfth
century, then Poland in the thirteenth century (and, in some far
eastern regions, still later), assimilated the western pattern under
the rubric of "German law." [73] From as early as the eleventh

[70] Anneliese Krenzlin, *Dorf, Feld und Wirtschaft im Gebiet der grossen
Täler und Platten östlich der Elbe; eine siedlungs-geographische Unter-
suchung* (Forschungen zur deutschen Landeskunde, vol. 70; Remagen,
1952), pp. 25–50; Herbert Helbig, "Die Anfänge der Landgemeinde in
Schlesien," *Die Anfänge der Landgemeinde und ihr Wesen*, vol. 2, 112–13;
Mayhew, *Rural Settlement*, pp. 50–58 and 77–84.

[71] James H. Johnson, "The Development of the Rural Settlement Pat-
tern of Ireland," *Geografiska Annaler* 43 (1961), 167–69; Ronald H. Buchanan,
"Field Systems of Ireland," in Baker and Butlin, *Field Systems*, pp. 608–16.
Unlike the case of east-central Europe discussed below, the indigenous
Irish population did not itself adopt the common field system.

[72] B. K. Roberts, "A Study of Medieval Colonization in the Forest of
Arden, Warwickshire," *AgHR* 16 (1968), 103–104. During the thirteenth
century, however, new clearings in Arden were developed as isolated farms
entirely exempt from common field constraints. This, however, was part
of a general reaction against communal control noticeable throughout Europe
wherever increasing market opportunities offered profit to aggressive individuals. See Roberts' further discussion in "Field Systems of the West
Midlands," in Baker and Butlin, *Field Systems*, 229–31.

[73] Dobrowolska, "Southern Poland," p. 34; Kiełczewska-Zaleska, "Polish
Rural Settlements," pp. 321–22; Slaski, "Pommern," pp. 188–89; Wilhelm

century Danes converted their hamlets to common-field arrangements in a local adaptation called *Bol,* while some two centuries
later Swedes naturalized this in turn as *solskifte,* an elaborate
scheme for determining the distribution of strips in the common
fields according to the sequence of houses in the village.[74] Here,
at the frontiers of the medieval west, population growth and
economic development got under way somewhat later than in the
medieval heartland; the regular and pervasive contacts that
would encourage cultural borrowing were likewise delayed. But
again in these areas of late adoption we find the common fields
established during times of demographic increase, and the transfer of resources from stock-raising to cereal cultivation. By the
end of the thirteenth century a relatively mature form of the
common-field system had spread over the great north European
plain and pressed against the mountains, marshes, and forests
that surrounded it, still sheltering peasantries who followed
more extensive and archaic forms of husbandry.

This discussion of the origins and spread of the open fields
and communal regulation of tillage should not leave the impression that the system was installed as a whole in any given region
or village at some specific instant when local inhabitants felt
themselves forced to acquire greater cereal production, stubble-
grazing resources, or the like.[75] Scattered arable parcels of the
small strip type can, of course, be detected quite early in some
localities, and regulated cropping in others. Adjustment of vil-

---

Weizsäcker, "Die Entstehung der Landgemeinde in Böhmen," *Die Anfänge
der Landgemeinde und ihr Wesen,* vol. 2, 379–86.

[74] Andersson, *Parzellierung und Gemengelage;* Granlund, "Dorf- und
Flurformen Schwedens," pp. 319–22; Sölve Göransson, "Regular Open-Field
Pattern in England and Scandinavian Solskifte," *Geografiska Annaler* 43
(1961), 80–104, suggests that *solskifte,* which is also known from Denmark,
may have originated in England; David Hannerberg, "Solskifte and older
methods of partitioning arable land in Central Sweden during the Middle
Ages," *Géographie et histoire agraires,* pp. 245–59.

[75] The exceptions are, of course, certain areas of planned settlement such
as Brandenburg, and places such as Lithuania, where a formalized variant
of the common field system was imposed from above on crown estates in
1557 and rapidly spread to those of other landlords. On the latter see R. A.
French, "The Three-Field System of Sixteenth Century Lithuania," *AgHR*
18 (1970), 106–125. More recently Karl von Loewe has argued for the
priority of the nobility in the "modernization" of Lithuanian agriculture;
Karl von Loewe, "Commerce and Agriculture in Lithuania, 1400–1600,"
Economic History Review 2d series 26 (1973), 23–35, which is, however, rightly
more concerned with advances in agricultural technology and direct exploitation of the demesne than with peasant social institutions *per se.*

lage landholdings, sometimes to the point of complete redistribution, is not unknown.[76] But the overall process was gradual, piecemeal, and continuing, not a medieval "Agricultural Revolution" in the temporal sense. In general, open-field strips seem to antedate common grazing on the stubble, and full regulation of cropping developed only slowly from informal *ad hoc* agreements among cultivators of adjoining plots. In Lorraine, one of the purest open-field provinces in Europe, evidence for strict community control over grazing on the stubble dates only from the thirteenth century.[77] Jänichen found a similar sequence of field-wide cropping units following well after the open-field strips in his study of western Swabia.[78] Some villages of the Palatinate adopted strict cropping regulations of a two-course rotation in the thirteenth century, but others waited until the fourteenth century, or even the fifteenth.[79] In the thirteenth century, likewise, peasants in at least one village in Beauce retained complete freedom in cropping their own parcels in the open fields,[80] and the Ostfalian rural customary law of the *Sachsenspiegel* gives the impression of rather free individuality, certainly without cropping regulation or communal management.[81] Carefully designed local studies alone offer a possibility of fully explaining such subtle nuances.

Emphasis must be placed, however, on the late twelfth and thirteenth centuries as a time of unusually pronounced increase in the extent and severity of communal restrictions on individual management of arable resources. In certain areas of Rhine-Hesse, where a closely regulated two-course rotation provided subsistence to peasants who also engaged in intensive viticulture, most villages installed it during the thirteenth century, as did twelve of the twenty-two similar places in nearby parts of the Palatinate.[82]

---

[76] Sheppard, "Yorkshire," pp. 176–87; Baker and Butlin, "Conclusion" of *Field Systems*, pp. 649–53.

[77] Planhol, "Genèse du champs ouverts," pp. 418–22.

[78] Janichen, "Mittelalterlichen Ackerbau im Schwaben," pp. 68–71.

[79] Gertrud Schröder-Lembke, "Wesen und Verbreitung der Zweifelderwirtschaft im Rheingebiet," *ZAA* 7 (1959), pp. 20–24, does not, however, suggest possible reasons for the differences.

[80] Georges Duby, *Rural Economy and Country Life in the Medieval West*, translated by Cynthia Postan (Columbia, S. C., 1968), pp. 93–94.

[81] Gerhard Buchda, "Die Dorfgemeinde im Sachsenspiegel," *Die Anfänge der Landgemeinde und ihr Wesen*, vol. 2, 15.

[82] Schröder-Lembke, "Zweifelderwirtschaft," pp. 20–24; the other ten Palatinate villages went to strict regulation somewhat later.

In the villages around Osnabrück communal organization and
mutual limitations developed rapidly from the late twelfth
century.[83] West of the Rhine, the earliest Alsatian evidence for
the communally controlled use of whole fields as cropping units
dates from 1249[84] and for common stubble pasturage in Normandy from 1214.[85] Higounet, in his survey of the three-course
rotation in thirteenth century France, and Fournier, in his local
study of Basse-Auvergne, agree that the expansion of all elements
of the common-field system reached a climax around 1250.[86]
Across the Channel, where arable expansion had severely reduced
waste pasture resources in most lowland districts by at least
1200,[87] Thirsk finds the earliest detectable village-wide cropping
in England in 1156/57, and communally controlled stubble pasturage only around 1240.[88] She further points out the absence of
any village institutions to regulate agricultural practices before
manorial courts began to display an interest in such matters in
the late twelfth and early thirteenth centuries.[89] During this
same thirteenth century, the demographic curve approached its
medieval peak, with more people in some districts by 1300 than
would again live there until modern times.[90]

To the simple population pressure should be added, especially
from the later twelfth century in the older regions of the west, a

[83] Gunther Wrede, "Die Entstehung der Landgemeinde im Osnabrucker
Land," *Die Anfänge der Landgemeinde und ihr Wesen*, vol. 1, 294.

[84] Schröder-Lembke, "Nebenformen der Dreifelderwirtschaft," p. 295.

[85] Léopold V. Delisle, *Etudes sur la condition de la classe agricole et
l'état de l'agriculture en Normandie, au moyen age* [Burt Franklin Research
and Source Work Series, no. 105; New York, 1967 (originally published 1851)],
pp. 160–65.

[86] Higounet, "L'Assolement triennal," pp. 507–12; Fournier, "Basse-
Auvergne," p. 203.

[87] Baker and Butlin, "Conclusion" to *Field Systems*, p. 631.

[88] Thirsk, "Common Fields," pp. 17–20. Ault, *Open Field Husbandry*, pp.
5–7, accepts these in the context of a full study of village agricultural regulations.

[89] Thirsk, "Origin," p. 147; the manorial courts previously dealt with
simple matters of agricultural management only as these involved the
demesne. In her later "Field Systems of the East Midlands," p. 232, Thirsk
notes that the earliest record of a village meeting outside the manorial
context dates from the fourteenth century.

[90] Duby, *Rural Economy*, pp. 123–26; Josiah C. Russell, "Population in
Europe 500–1500," in Carlo Cipolla, ed., *The Fontana Economic History of
Europe*, vol. 1, *The Middle Ages* (London, 1972), 39–40; B. H. Slicher van
Bath, *The Agrarian History of Western Europe A. D. 500–1850*, translated by
Olive Ordish (New York, 1963), pp. 77–81 and 132–37.

new contender for increasingly limited resources: the market. Recognizing the enriching possibilities in production for sale to the newly resurgent urban centers, some countrymen, lords and peasants, sought to create their own independent agricultural enterprises. Their abandonment of the old subsistence-sufficiency orientation brought them into conflict with the larger groups who retained it. Lawsuits between such innovators and peasant communities threatened with the loss of joint resources helped induce and evolve still harsher communal controls.[91]

Around 1300 the expansion of the medieval European economy and population reached a certain climax. The difficulties of the next generations need no demonstration here. During the population decline of the later middle ages, expansion and hardening of communal control over peasant agricultural practices also slowed down in many areas, to begin anew only with the return of buoyancy in the sixteenth century.[92] We detect, therefore, a direct association between the advance of common fields and population growth, both on the widest chronological scale and on the narrower level of specific regions and periods.

To recapitulate the historical evidence, during the age of migrations all the north European regions so far subjected to careful investigation reveal a rural economy geared to extensive use of abundant resources by a sparse and scattered peasant population. In these conditions an individual who experimented with the crops growing on his lands posed no problem of access, no unusual dangers to his neighbors. When he cleared more woodland to make it arable for a growing family, he did not thereby discernibly reduce the waste pasture available to his fellows. But

[91] Duby, *Rural Economy*, pp. 157–64, gives considerable exemplary detail. A further example of the antipathy between extensive market access and the common fields is found in Roberts, "West Midlands," pp. 229–31; enclosures made in the forest of Arden under the 1235 Statute of Merton were concentrated in the areas closer to Coventry; further south the common fields were untouched. Remember, as well, the change in economic mentality represented in the move to regular market production as described by Miller, "Twelfth and Thirteenth Centuries," pp. 12–14.

[92] Agreement on this chronology is virtually unanimous. See the general statements of, for example, Abel, "Landwirtschaft," pp. 262–63; Abel, "Verdorfung und Gutsbildung in Deutschland zu Beginn der Neuzeit," *Geografiska Annaler* 43 (1961), 1–7; Thirsk, "Common Fields," p. 7; and even, it seems to this reader, Titow, "Open Field System," pp. 88–89. For two specific local studies see Krenzlin and Reusch, *Gewannflur in Unterfranken*, and Wilhelm Matzat, *Flurgeographische Studien im Bauland und Hinteren Odenwald* (Rhein-Mainsche Forschungen, Heft 53; Frankfurt, 1963).

such activities had to be viewed in a different light when, perhaps as early as the seventh century in a few old-settled areas,
more generally from the tenth century, and in some places only
in the thirteenth century, population growth, the expansion of
agriculture, and a shift to more nucleated settlement patterns
began to curtail the local abundance of free resources.

The emerging competition for increasingly limited resources
might have been resolved by sheer power; certainly seigneurial
lords never ceased to appropriate their share of the peasants'
"surplus." It might have been met, as it was in the modern
period, by a massive shift to a market economy; market-oriented
individualism did appear, but its few rural adherents aroused
fierce opposition among the peasantry. For centuries there was
no greater technological intensification than that provided by the
heavy plow, improved harness, and three-course rotation (all *early*
medieval innovations) for the great mass of peasant agriculture.[93]
Historical evidence indicates instead a gradual spread from the
oldest-settled areas of institutions designed for communal control
of resources. By the late twelfth century the mentality of communal control had penetrated so deeply into European peasant
culture that it went along into new lands, where it may not have
been initially needed. With the thirteenth century acceptance of
common-field agriculture by many peripheral peasantries, and
the growing rigidity of the system in its well-populated regions of
origin, it prevailed over most of the best lands of transalpine
Europe. The task that remains is to suggest a causal explanation
that links the impact of population growth on the traditional
individualism of the early Middle Ages to the communal response that sacrificed individual control over production for the
sake of preserving minimal subsistence levels for a maximum
peasant population.

Population growth, peasant priorities, and communal control

Our explanatory scenario or model (presented in schematic form
in Appendix 1.1) focuses on the emergence of the three diag-

---

[93] Despite severe disagreement on the diffusion and significance of these
innovations in medieval England, both Lynn T. White, Jr., *Medieval
Technology and Social Change* (London, 1962), pp. 39–78, and J. Z. Titow,
English Rural Society 1200–1350 (London, 1969), pp. 37–42, would seem to
agree on this point. See also Wailes, "Plow and Population," pp. 154–79.

nostic elements of the common-field system: "open fields," stubble and fallow pasture, and communal control. Although the causal chains that are seen to result in the first two features resemble those proposed by some other authors, Baker and Butlin or Blum,[94] for example, they are here presented in a more explicit (and hence testable) form. The communal response to problems inherent in pasturing stock on open fields is then considered not as the necessary reaction of any agriculturists so faced, but as contingent upon the experience, priorities, and options of medieval European peasants.[95] As any causal model must, we start from the antecedent system: traditional individualistic subsistence agriculture. Before the coming of the common fields we found a general European pattern of extensive pastoralism and mixed farming carried out by a sparse population that, with limited technical equipment, exploited large block or strip fields and extensive "free" waste pastures to achieve self-sufficient household subsistence under a regime of seigneurial lordship. Communal institutions lacked control over agricultural management.

Traditional subsistence agriculture changed in accord with Boserup's paradigm that population growth induces agricultural intensification. Early medieval peasants adopted and came to emphasize several new technical items, heavier plows, improved harness, and the three-course rotation, which permitted more intensive cultivation. Further intensification, however, was not possible in the small areas previously farmed, and population growth required creation of new arable land. Arable expansion

[94] Baker and Butlin, "Conclusion" to *Field Systems*, pp. 635–56 (more or less confined to Britain), and Blum, "Village as Community," p. 161 (a brief and generally descriptive discussion).

[95] Both of the works cited in the previous note seem to argue directly from the problems posed by stock pastured on open fields to a necessarily communal response. But, short of assuming an undemonstrated general proposition that internal conflict always (or under specified additional conditions) produces a group response, or fallaciously confusing motive with sufficient cause, this explanation is inadequate. The alternative response, individualism and private property, of certain market-oriented agriculturalists in the Middle Ages and of the entire modern agricultural reform movement, affirms its insufficiency, especially since the common fields appear to contravene the very principle of maximizing behavior that economists seem to hold so dear. An adequate and testable explanation therefore requires explicit consideration of those elements of the medieval peasant condition which led to rejection of market-oriented individualism in favor of communal control.

converted waste from an extensive use (livestock production) to a more intensive use (cereal production). The inescapable consequence was reduction of available waste pasture, at first insignificantly by comparison with the vast remainder, but eventually with important effects. The continual diminution of waste pasture as a result of the expansion of arable land is central to our model, but its consideration must follow an examination of the way "open fields" arose in the context of population growth and assarting.

Whence came the mixture of unfenced parcels that characterized the common fields? The early medieval evidence suggests two probable prior situations: in the first, a single peasant household managed and worked a unitary block of arable land in the midst of the waste; in the second, several such households were grouped loosely into a hamlet, and each likewise exploited one or more good-sized blocks or strips in the immediate vicinity of the settlement. In the absence of stubble or fallow pasture, that is, given the sufficient waste pasture resources then available, the only fencing required in either case was peripheral, intended to keep beasts, wild or domestic, out of the crops.[96] The second variant demands some way to delineate individual parcels, but this need be no more than the double furrow or grass baulk known from the later open fields. The very population growth that impelled assarting, however, took place in the family; family growth created population growth. Thus it was the growing family that first expanded its arable land to meet its larger cereal demands and to absorb its additional labor supply, and, eventually, as new families hived off, either subdivided the old holding[97]

[96] This limited concern is clear in the oldest and largest Germanic law codes: the Burgundian *Lex Gundobada,* all of the Salian compilations, and the Alemannic laws. See *Lex Gundobada,* edited by Bluhme, 543, 569–70, and 574–75; *Pactus legis Salicae,* edited by Eckhardt, I:2, 255–356 (Article LXI of the post-830 "systematic text"; the earlier versions are substantively identical); *Leges Alamannorum,* edited by Eckhardt, I, 136 and II, 66 (Articles XXX and XCVI of the seventh-century *Pactus legis Alamannorum* and of the eighth-century *Lex Alamannorum,* respectively).

[97] In this context the findings of Yver and Faith that impartible inheritance customs replaced a general practice of subdivision among heirs in the predominantly common-field areas of France and England only during and after the twelfth and thirteenth centuries is of the greatest importance. For the first time the most plausible mechanism for the fragmentation of holdings has been demonstrated as normal peasant behavior in the period of open field formation. See Jean Yver, *Egalité entre héritiers et exclusion des enfantes dotés. Essai de géographie coutumière,* (Société d'histoire du

or created new ones beside it. The result tended toward either the cluster form of hamlet fields mentioned above, or a bundle of strips, as in the open fields. Likewise, any assart undertaken cooperately by a group of neighbors or kinsmen could start as a joint holding, but ultimate division again tended to yield the strip pattern. The speed with which a process of subdivision can convert large block holdings into small and intermingled strips has been demonstrated by the work of Sventozar Ilešič on nineteenth-century Slovenia.[98] It is in the context of subdivision from old large fields to smaller parcels that the various forces favoring strips over blocks must be seen as operating.[99] The transformation of the morphology of the European arable land from relatively large to small and scattered parcels is, therefore, quite understandable under conditions of population growth.

The absence of internal fencing may be a moot point. The traditional agriculture apparently lacked it and, in the continued absence of livestock using the fields, it remained unneeded. Poor technical equipment raised the cost of structures more sturdy than the simplest boundary markers, while the tendency of parcels to depart from the square much increased the total quantity of internal fencing required. With similar routines and informal neighborly collaboration among the holders of adjoining unfenced parcels, serious confrontations could be avoided without the need for elaborate and systematic communal regulation.

droit; Paris, 1966), especially pp. 11–23 and 290–303; Rosamond J. Faith, "Peasant Families and Inheritance Customs in Medieval England," *AgHR* 14 (1966), 81–84.

[98] Sventozar Ilešič, "Die jungeren Gewannfluren in Nordwest-Jugoslawien," *Geografiska Annaler* 43 (1961), 130–37.

[99] See, for example, the discussion of the heavy plow technique, drainage, and ease of division in White, *Medieval Technology and Social Change*, pp. 41–57. In addition, strip parcels offered ease of access from a path bordering one end of the old field, and also simplified equity of quality in the division. That the desire to avoid risk (seen in this essay as part of the subsistence-sufficiency orientation) may have contributed still more to the enduring scatter and intermingling of parcels has been suggested by Donald N. McCloskey, "The Enclosure of Open Fields: Preface to a Study of Its Impact on the Efficiency of English Agriculture in the Eighteenth Century," *Journal of Economic History* 32 (1972), 19, and in his contributions to the present volume. Baker and Butlin, "Conclusion" to *Field Studies*, pp. 635–41, similarly emphasize the role of assarting and subsequent subdivision as central to the emergence of intermingled parcels, rejecting any necessary role of or significant evidence for co-aration in this regard, and proposing that piecemeal leasing of former demesne and formal reapportionment and redistribution are, respectively, minor and late contributors to the process.

Private arrangements for management by furlongs, which are well known from both England and the continent, allowed considerable room for conflict-free experimentation and innovation, so long as the number of interested individuals remained relatively small.

The historical evidence suggests that significant exploitation of stubble and fallow pasture postdated the open fields. Here again, increasing population and accompanying intensification provides a causal explanation, this time through its eventually constricting effects on the supply of waste pasture. The simple transformation curve shown in Figure 1.2 helps to depict the process involved. As was shown above, early medieval peasants grew relatively little grain but exploited good-sized herds on the extensive wastes. Even under these initial conditions of high stock levels by comparison to the human population, it is unlikely that they fully used the capacity of the land for stock. Stock-per-area ratios were probably very low, and waste pasturage must be considered a free good during the early Middle Ages (point I on Figure 1.2). Hence the first stages of arable expansion had little effect on pasture resources and herd sizes; technical inadequacies, especially seasonal fodder shortages caused by the very ignorance of fodder crops that would continue to harass the common field peasant, placed more immediate limits on herd sizes. Up to a point (M), then, additional land and labor could be devoted to more intensive cereal production without sacrificing stock. When, however, the limits of the surplus land were reached, waste pasturage and cultivation became competing uses for the same land. As an economic good, land would be allocated between the two uses on the basis of their relative desirability, with a production mix along curve XN in the figure. For the capitalist farmer, the point of production will be determined by market forces, which set the relative costs of production against the prices obtainable. Individual medieval entrepreneurs often enclosed the waste to retain it for commercial livestock production.[100] But before the fourteenth century the main historical trend was continued cerealization at the expense of pasture and stock, a movement completely in accord with Boserup's theory, and a direct manifestation of the peasant desire to maximize the product of family labor. The latter could well demand arable

[100] Duby, *Rural Economy*, pp. 141–43.

Figure 1.2: The Productivity Advantage of Stubble and Fallow Pasture

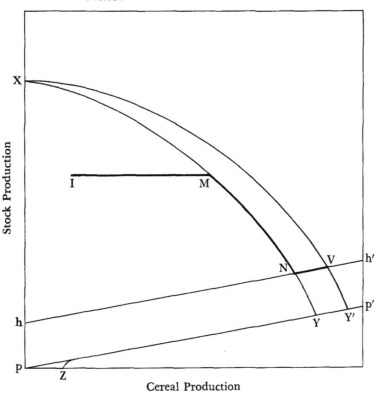

Where:

XYZ = transformation curve between stock and cereal production on a fixed amount of land convertible between
arable and waste pasture, requiring stock as a production input for cereals but without significant cultivation
of fodder crops.

pp' = minimum stocking level to provide animal power for
cereal production alone.

hh' = minimum stocking level to provide both animal power
for cereal production and animal products for minimum
human consumption.

I = initial stock-cereal relation of early middle ages with
large surplus of waste pasturage.

M = maximum cereal production achieved by arable expansion without diminishing initial stocking level through
reduction of utilized waste pasturage.

N = maximum cereal production achieved by arable expansion at expense of utilized waste pasturage but without
thereby reducing stocking level below requirements for
human consumption and cereal production.

XY' = new, larger transformation curve achieved by pasturing
stubble and fallow

expansion beyond the point where capitalist economic thinking
justifies retention of pasture. In this case its applicability gains
strong support from both the shortages of pasture and the
severely suboptimal stocking levels known for peasant holdings
of the high Middle Ages.[101] Thus the actual trend in the Middle
Ages is from M in the figure to N, the point of minimal stock
necessary for subsistence and production requirements, with some
peasant households even sliding below the minimum (toward Y).

Yet another characteristic difference between capitalist and
peasant economics explains why the peasantry persisted in raising
any stock at all: their subsistence-sufficiency orientation demanded a mix of necessary products. In the present context,
remember that livestock provided not only meat, hides, and
fiber, but also the sole nonhuman energy source crucial to cereal
production itself. Therefore, as shown by the floors hh' and pp',
and the rapid retreat of the transformation curve from Y to Z,
diminution of pasture resources can be tolerated only to the
point where they can still support a minimal subsistence level of
stock.[102] Two implications follow. In the first place, at this
marginal stage waste pasture itself becomes a vital but severely
limited good, the object of competition among lords, market
producers, and peasants, as well as among peasants themselves.
Within the peasant group, communal institutions of a territorial
or local sort, often informal, had long overseen access to the
waste. Barring the intervention of the powerful, such control
was easily extended. Secondly, under these conditions of a crying
need for additional forage, stubble and fallow pasture provided
a small but important increment to available fodder. Point V in
the figure indicates the productivity increase permitted to the
marginal situation by using these additional resources. The net
effect is to allow a further increase in arable land without a
corresponding reduction of stock levels below the minimum, or
an increase in stock inventories without loss of cereal production.
Added incentive came from concentration of manuring on the
arable land itself, and, perhaps, augmentation of seasonal short-

---

[101] Michael M. Postan, "Village Livestock in the Thirteenth Century,"
Economic History Review, 2d series 15 (1962), 219–49, especially p. 235.

[102] It is, of course, possible to produce along curve NY, but only by
sacrificing certain of the nutritional benefits of meat consumption and the
other items stock-raising offers to self-sufficiency. Reducing stock levels
below those at Y, however, means that cereal production itself will suffer.

falls. Admittedly, the stock per capita that could be sustained through stubble and fallow pasture fell well short of that once obtained from the waste, and, calculating in both instances on the basis of all land exploited (as arable or pasture) by the village, the stock-per-acre figure had probably dropped, too.[103] For a peasant household operating on the subsistence margin, however, the least increment could well have been invaluable. Adoption of stubble and fallow pasture on the arable land can be seen, therefore, as a small but perhaps vital increase in the productivity of limited land resources. Pasture on arable land is, of course, an advanced stage in Boserup's successive levels of intensification. Though not multicropped in the narrowest sense, the same land now served two uses, and contributed two products, grain and animals, in the same year. The problem of pasture shortage, itself due to intensification under population pressure, was solved by still further intensification.

The advent of grazing on open-field arable land created the problem to which communal regulation of agricultural management was a response: two potentially conflicting uses were combined on the same land or on adjacent parcels without effective separation. How do you keep the cows out of the corn? Medieval peasants lacked an easy technical solution. Separate herding or tethering of each household's beasts did not work. The labor expended was, from the standpoint of the stock owner, unproductive. He had little direct incentive to be continuously vigilant that his animals did not get fat on someone else's wheat. Eighteenth-century evidence from open-field villages in Cumberland and Westmoreland shows that the rash of litigation that followed attempts at tethered grazing inspired both schemes for close communal regulation and demands for enclosure.[104] Similar technical inadequacies made adequate permanent fencing of each parcel costly to construct, an impediment to access, and wasteful

[103] This point deserves further investigation. Until the fourteenth and fifteenth centuries, even the most advanced European agriculturists normally harvested cereals with the sickle, and left half of the stalk as stubble. If this were left to the stock, a substantial fodder supply remained. If this were cut by the individual, only a short stubble was left. See Charles Parain, "The Evolution of Agricultural Technique," *The Agrarian Life of the Middle Ages*, 2d ed. rev., edited by Michael M. Postan (Cambridge Economic History of Europe, vol. I; Cambridge, 1966), pp. 155–57.

[104] G. Elliott, "Field Systems of Northwest England," in Baker and Butlin, *Field Systems*, p. 60.

of valuable land. Temporary fencing would be needed at the very time harvesting got under way. So conflicting land use would easily precipitate endemic social conflict among neighbors. Population growth itself, simply by pushing more and more people into contact with one another, and the rise of that competing market-oriented demand for resources which was described earlier, could only exacerbate the tensions. But the immediate, central impetus for strict and systematic communal control was a shortage of pasture, which forced use of the stubble and fallow. The demonstration of this lies in the sharp contrast between the free cultivation of sparsely settled regions that had ample wastes (the Fenland, the Kentish Weald, uplands in southwestern Yorkshire), and the tight regulations of more densely settled regions that had very little pasture (the Midlands, eastern Yorkshire).[105] The conflict demanded a solution, and medieval peasants found it in communal control. Pasture was made common. The village required but one herdsman and no new fencing. But then general community agreement had to control harvest dates, plowing the fallow, sowing, and the like, and sharply to curtail each individual farmer's ability to make his own independent plans and operational management decisions.

Conflict over land use demanded a solution, but imposed no specific solution. The general choice of the communal alternative in the Middle Ages contrasts with a few medieval and most modern European responses. We must, therefore, suggest certain contingencies that disposed the peasantry to respond as they did. One obvious candidate is the open fields themselves, that crazy quilt of small parcels held by various villagers, which would have to be changed before the limited available techniques could permit a thorough-going system of private property. But an existing institution is an impediment, not an absolute barrier to change. The fields were not necessarily fixed, for we know instances of reconstruction and redistribution during the high Middle Ages, some of which resulted in separate farms, others in highly systematic and "classical" open fields.[106] The deeper

---

[105] A number of examples are to be found in Baker and Butlin, *Field Systems:* Thirsk, "East Midlands," pp. 246–55; Alan R. H. Baker, "Field Systems of Southeast England," 393–419; Sheppard, "Yorkshire," 175–76; and Baker and Butlin, "Conclusion," p. 631.

[106] Duby, *Rural Economy*, pp. 161–62, gives a general sketch of thirteenth-century enclosure by market farmers, while Sheppard, "Yorkshire," pp. 176–

question, therefore, is why one institutional change, communal control, rather than another, redistribution, served to resolve the problem of conflict in land use. The open fields contributed, but are insufficient to explain communal control.

We return, therefore, to those characteristic experiences and priorities that produce the mentality of peasants, to that subsistence-sufficiency orientation of a dependent group in a hierarchical society. Certain such attributes have already explained the unusual propensity of medieval peasants to expand their arable land well beyond the point of pasture shortage, and at the same time to persist in stock raising as well. A further review of that orientation and its applicability in the high Middle Ages makes the communal response far more understandable. Subsistence-sufficiency involves a mutually reinforcing connection whereby uniformly limited technical abilities and severe social subordination join with rough comparative equality within the peasant group to promote strongly conformist and static behavior patterns. Living at a marginal subsistence level, the peasant knows scarcity as a basic fact of his life, especially by comparison with the apparent abundance enjoyed by his non-peasant rulers. With no visible opportunities for advancement at the expense of others than his neighbors, disaster is so much more likely than gain that all risks are feared. The goal, therefore, is survival; maximization can scarcely be imagined. Thus, as we stated earlier, the subsistence-sufficiency orientation discourages change and seeks to avoid its effects.

The socially subordinate position of high medieval peasants surely needs no explication. Seigneurial lordship prevailed in all of the common-field regions of Europe. At the same time, as the resources accessible to peasants became noticeably limited under the pressures of population growth, the opportunities open to nobles and townsmen expanded enormously. Whole new industries and trades appeared. Wealthy European consumers in the high Middle Ages drew for luxuries on the production of most of the known world. Simultaneously, social differences hardened into increasingly formalized and sharp legal definitions of class.

---

87 argues for post-eleventh-century reorganization to explain the elaborate open field systems of the northeast. In their "Conclusion" to *Field Systems,* pp. 649-53, Baker and Butlin support Sheppard's interpretation with strong and direct early modern evidence. Field systems are fixed only if men fix them.

Noble, townsman, and peasant became three distinct status
groups and upward social mobility that much more difficult.[107]
Thrown back on his own scant resources, the peasant could perceive his limitations while further recognizing the rough equality
he shared with others of his station. Especially by comparison
with the nobles who raked in their rents, the mercantile townsmen, or those entrepreneurs who brought the market mentality
to the countryside, the peasants were subsistence farmers seeking
self-sufficiency on family-operated holdings with similar unso-
phisticated techniques. All endured similar risks of crop failure
and starvation. Common goals of basic security promoted group
solidarity, a strong sense of social norms, and, relative to their
superiors, a sense of rough equality within peasant society. The
result was a strong bias in favor of joint action to preserve what
little they had.

But the common-field system was, in its application and operation, not simply egalitarian. Communal control of limited resources rested not in the hands of all inhabitants nor, with
exceptions, even in those of all heads of households. The assembly of cultivators was everywhere dominated, if not monopolized,
by the better-off peasants.[108] Those who had the most to lose
from unregulated admission of stock to the open fields, those who
stood to suffer greatly from arbitrary changes in the cropping
cycle, in short, those who stood the best chance of achieving that
self-sufficient household subsistence that we see as the core of the
peasant value system, took charge to prevent damage to their
traditional relative position. Communal control minimized
change and its effects. It served to maintain the equilibrium of
the peasant economy and to reduce the dangers that its disruption threatened. In this context, the imposition of social control
over agricultural management in the form of the common fields
can be seen as the manifestation of values common to subject
groups in a hierarchical society. Leadership in the realization
of those values came from the traditionally successful members
of the group, and served to avert dangers that might threaten
their continued success within the bounds of the traditional

---

[107] Marc Bloch, *Feudal Society*, translated by L. A. Manyon, 2 vols. (Chicago,
1964), II, 320–22.

[108] Jerome Blum, "The Internal Structure and Polity of the European
Village Community from the Fifteenth to the Nineteenth Century,"
Journal of Modern History 43 (1971), 549–52.

orientation. Those peasants who perceived opportunities outside this accepted system came, by their very excess of individualism, into conflict with the imposed norms and the values that upheld them. Such people were forced to submit, or sought to withdraw from the community. Their success was confined to areas of peculiar advantage (easy market access) within the larger medieval economy.

But the forces promoting the communal response were not confined to risk aversion, group solidarity, and other such elements of the subsistence-sufficiency orientation. Medieval European peasants faced with the danger of social conflict in their vital agricultural sphere were not without experience of communal institutions. From as far back as the migrations, territorial assemblies had helped regulate law and order, accepting additions to their membership, and overseeing the use of common wastes.[109] We have already seen how strengthened communal regulation served to defend common access to unimproved land against the efforts of those who would have appropriated it. Informal cooperation between holders of adjacent strips in open fields offered yet another background element favorable to extension of social control over economic activity. The common fields originated, therefore, as a conservative and equilibrium-maintaining response by a group whose outlook and experience easily and not irrationally guided them in that direction.

Nor, in a final brief aside, should we think that the peasantry stood utterly alone in the high medieval West with its mental orientation toward sufficiency and its stability-seeking corporatism. Only around 1200 do English ecclesiastical landlords seem to have abandoned management policies aimed at subsistence in favor of others that sought to maximize their incomes.[110] The stiffening of antiusury legislation by post-1150 canonists is clearly linked to assumptions of an ideally stable society whose proper order was being upset by the pursuit of wealth and individualism.[111] During that "Age of Lawyers" when legal compila-

---

[109] The active sphere of the early territorial community is succinctly summarized in the mid-ninth-century compilation of Salian Frankish law called the "Italian fragment": "Non potest homo migrare, nisi convicinia et herba et aqua et via [ei concessa sunt]" (Eckhardt, *Pactus legis Salicae*, I:2, 370).

[110] Miller, "Twelfth and Thirteenth Centuries," pp. 12–14.

[111] Werner Stark, "The Contained Economy: An Interpretation of Medieval Economic Thought," in *Pre-Capitalist Economic Thought: Three Modern Interpretations* (New York, 1972), pp. 17–21.

tions, law codes, and careful definition of rights and privileges
concerned members of budding bureaucracies in both church and
state, intellectuals such as John of Salisbury and Saint Thomas
Aquinas emphasized the organic analogy and other corporate
aspects of social organization. And their contemporaries restored
to European thought an idea lost since late antiquity, the village
as a corporate entity, a *corpus mysticum*.[112] With communalism
and anti-individualism so much a part of the larger mental environment as well as of their own, the medieval European peasantry could easily sacrifice ease of innovation for the greater
assurance of minimal subsistence and self-sufficiency offered by
the common fields.

We see the emergence of the mature common-field system in
medieval Europe, therefore, as the end result of population
growth impinging on traditional subsistence agriculture. Growing numbers of peasants forced agricultural intensification, and
resulted in pressures against ultimately limited resources. The
social conflict that ensued elicited from the peasants, whose
economic priorities closely reflected their marginal position
and limited opportunities, an equilibrium-maintaining response,
communal control of agricultural management. The response
worked. It worked so well that after the mid-fourteenth century,
when fearsome losses to the European population had removed
many of the pressures against the supply of agricultural land,
communal control could be turned to the preservation of yet
other balances favored by the leading villagers. After 1350,
English village bylaws served surviving old families in their
on-going struggle with newcomers who arrived to take over
abandoned lands,[113] and those well endowed with land in their
search for cheaper hired labor. Thus the common-field system
survived to grow still more rigid in later periods of population
growth until, with technological change and the greatly increased
penetration of a market orientation into the countryside, it
posed a major obstacle to further intensification and the eventual

[112] Otto von Gierke, *Das deutsche Genossenschaftsrecht*, 4 vols. (Berlin,
1868–1913), vol. 3 (1881), 544–45, and the English edition in his *Political
Theories of the Middle Age* [*sic*], translated by Frederic W. Maitland
(Boston, 1958), pp. 20–21; Fritz Kern, *Humana civilitas (Staat, Kirche und
Kultur). Eine Dante-Untersuchung* (Mittelalterliche Studien, edited by
Fritz Kern, vol. I, No. 1; Leipzig, 1913), p. 11.

[113] Personal suggestion of Professor J. Ambrose Raftis, Pontifical Institute
of Medieval Studies, Toronto.

market-based rationalization of European agriculture in modern times.

The common fields have a history. They did not spring fully formed from the head of a Germanic deity and survive immutable until their wholesale destruction. The outline of the system they replaced is becoming fairly clear, and so are the conditions under which they emerged and spread across Europe. The process of common-field formation and diffusion is, however, less transparent. This essay suggests a view of that process that joins the effects of population growth to the economic outlook of peasants, a view that seems to accord with the evidence as we now know it. Further understanding of this institution so central to the medieval experience and to the agrarian history of Europe will come from continued and focused investigation, much of it at the most local level, into the historical interaction among populations, markets, institutions, and mentalities in the medieval countryside.

Appendix 1.1: Causal Model for the Medieval Origins of the Common Fields

Solid lines indicate positive and dashed lines negative relationships.

Appendix 1.2 Additional Sources for Map: Agricultural "Systems" in Northwestern Europe ca. 1300.

British Isles

Francis R. H. Du Boulay, *The Lordship of Canterbury: An Essay on Medieval Society* (London, 1966), pp. 130–42.

M. Elliot, "The System of Cultivation and Evidence of Enclosure in the Cumberland Open Fields in the Sixteenth Century," pp. 118–36 in *Géographie et histoire agraires. Actes du colloque internationale organisé par la Faculté des Lettres de l'Université de Nancy:* Annales de l'Est, Memoires, no. 21 (Nancy, 1959). Henceforth this collection will be cited as *Géographie et histoire agraires* [Nancy colloquium].

F. Emery, "The Farming Regions of Wales," pp. 113–41 in *The Agrarian History of England and Wales, 1500–1640,* edited by Joan Thirsk (Cambridge, 1967), esp. pp. 115 and 128.

H. P. R. Finberg, "Recent Progress in English Agrarian History," *Geografiska Annaler* 43 (1961), 77–78.

———, Review of Darby and Finn, *The Domesday Geography of South-West England,* in *AgHR* 17 (1969), 78.

Paul Flatrès, *Géographie rurale de quatre contrées celtiques: Irlande, Galles, Cornwall et Man* (Rennes, 1957), pp. 349–477.

———, "Les structures rurales de la frange atlantique de l'Europe," pp. 193–202 in *Géographie et histoire agraires* [Nancy colloquium].

John Hatcher, "Non-Manorialism in Medieval Cornwall," *AgHR* 18 (1970), 1–3.

T. J. Pierce, "Pastoral and Agricultural Settlements in Early Wales," *Geografiska Annaler* 43 (1961), 182–89.

Michael M. Postan, "Medieval Agrarian Society in Its Prime: England," pp. 549–632 in *The Agrarian Life of the Middle Ages;* The Cambridge Economic History of Europe, Vol. 1, 2d ed. (Cambridge, 1966), esp. pp. 571–74.

David Roden, "Demesne Farming in the Chiltern Hills," *AgHR* 17 (1969), 22–23.

Dorothy Sylvester, *The Rural Landscape of the Welsh Borderland: A Study in Historical Geography* (London, 1969), 220–54.

Joan Thirsk, "The Farming Regions of England," pp. 1–112 in
The Agrarian History of England and Wales, Vol. 4, *1500–
1640,* edited by Joan Thirsk (Cambridge, 1967).

Low Countries and North Sea Coastal Area

H. I. Keuning, "Siedlungsformen und Siedlungsvorgang. Einige
Gedänken über die Entwicklung der ländlichen Siedlungen in
den niederländischen Sandgebieten," *ZAA.* 9 (1961), 153–68.

Heinz Stoob, "Landausbau und Gemeindebildung an der
Nordseeküste im Mittelalter," pp. 365–422 in *Die Anfänge
der Landgemeinde und ihr Wesen,* Vol. 1; Vorträge und
Forschungen, Vol. 7 (Konstanz, 1964), 382–400. Henceforth
this collection will be referred to as *Landgemeinde* [Konstanz
colloquium].

Johanna M. van Winter, "Die Entstehung der Landgemeinde in
der Holländisch-Utrechtschen Tiefebene," pp. 439–45 in
Landgemeinde [Konstanz colloquium], Vol. 1; Vorträge und
Forschungen, Vol. 7 (Konstanz, 1964).

Adrian E. Verhulst, "Die Binnenkolonisation und die Anfänge
der Landgemeinde in Seeflandern," pp. 447–60 in *Landgemeinde* [Konstanz colloquium], Vol. 1; Vorträge und Forschungen, Vol. 7 (Konstanz, 1964).

France

Marc Bloch, *French Rural History. As Essay on Its Basic Characteristics,* translated by Janet Sondheimer (Berkeley, 1966),
pp. 26–30 and 35–63.

George T. Beech, *A Rural Society in Medieval France: The
Gâtine of Poitou in the Eleventh and Twelfth Centuries;* The
Johns Hopkins University Studies in Historical and Political
Science, series 82, no. 1 (Baltimore, 1964), pp. 37–41.

Bernard Bomer, "Paysages ruraux entre Val-de-Loire et vallée du
Loir," pp. 68–78 in *Géographie et histoire agraires* [Nancy
colloquium].

André Bouton, *Le Maine. Histoire économique et sociale des
origines au XIVᵉ siècle* (Les Mans, 1962), p. 340.

Louis Chaumeil, "L'origine du bocage en Bretagne," pp. 163–86
in *Hommage à Lucien Febvre; Eventail de l'histoire vivante*

offert par l'amitié d'Historiens, Linguistes, Géographes, Econo-mists, Sociologues Ethnologues, Vol. 1 (Paris, 1953).

Paul Flatres, "Les structures rurales de la frange atlantique de l'Europe," pp. 193–202 in *Géographie et histoire agraires* [Nancy colloquium].

Guy Fourquin, *Les campagnes de la région Parisienne à la fin du milieu du XIIIe siècle au début du XVIe siècle;* Publications de la Faculté des Lettres et Sciences Humaines de Paris, Série "Recherches," Vol. 10 (Paris, 1964), 59–76.

Central Europe

Wilhelm Abel, *Geschichte der deutschen Landwirtschaft vom frühen Mittelalter bis zum 19. Jahrhundert;* Deutsche Agrar-geschichte, Vol. 2, 2d ed. rev. (Stuttgart, 1967), 67–95.

Bruno Benthien, *Die historischen Flurformen des südwestlichen Mecklenburg; eine Studie zum Problem Dorf, Feld und Wirt-schaft, zugleich ein Beitrag zur Entwicklungsgeschichte der ländlichen Siedlungen im Bezirk Schwerin;* Veröffentlichungen des Mecklenburgischen Landeshauptarchivs in Verbindung mit der Staatliche Archivverwaltung, Vol. 1 (Schwerin, 1960), esp. map, p. 106.

Ingomar Bog, "Die wirtschaftlichen Trends, der Staat und die Agrarverfassung in der Geschichte Hessens," *ZAA* 18 (1970), 185–96.

Karlheinz Filipp, "Binnenkolonisation und Agrarlandschafts-genese der Nordostpfalz," *ZAA* 18 (1970), 36–42.

Herbert Helbig, "Die Anfänge der Landemeinde in Schlesien," pp. 89–114 in *Landgemeinde* [Konstanz colloquium], Vol. 2; Vorträge und Forschungen, Vol. 8 (Konstanz, 1964).

Barthel Huppertz, *Räume und Schichten bäuerlicher Kultur-formen in Deutschland. Ein Beitrag zur Deutschen Bauern-geschichte* (Bonn, 1939), map x.

Helmut Jäger, *Entwicklungsperioden agrarer Siedlungsgebiete im mittleren Westdeutschland seit dem fruhen 13. Jahrhundert;* Würzburger geographische Arbeiten; Mitteilungen der Geo-graphischen Gesellschaft Würzburg, Heft 6 (Würzburg, 1958).

Paul Kläui, "Genossame, Gemeinde und Mark in der Inner-schwiez mit besonderer Berücksichtigung des Landes Uri," pp. 237–44 in *Landgemeinde* [Konstanz colloquium], Vol. 1; Vorträge und Forschungen, Vol. 7 (Konstanz, 1964).

Anneliese Krenzlin, *Historische und wirtschaftliche Züge im Siedlungsformenbild des westlichen Ostdeutschland unter besonderer Berücksichtigung von Mecklenburg-Vorpommern und Sachsen;* Frankfurter Geographische Hefte, 27–29. Jahrgang (Frankfurt a. M., 1955), pp. 14–58 and maps.

Karl Lechner, "Entstehung, Entwicklung und Verfassung der ländlichen Gemeinde in Niederösterreich," pp. 107–62 in *Landgemeinde* [Konstanz colloquium], Vol. 1; Vorträge und Forschungen, Vol. 7 (Konstanz, 1964).

Gerhard Oberbeck, "Das Problem der spätmittelalterlichen Kulturlandschaft—erläutert an Beispielen aus Niedersachsen," *Geografiska Annaler* 43 (1961), 236–42.

Kurt Scharlau, "Flurrelikte und Flurformengenese in Westdeutschland. Ergebnisse, Probleme und allgemeine Ausblicke," *Geografiska Annaler* 43 (1961), 264–75.

———, "Gewannflurforschung in Hessen," pp. 29–52 in *Langemeinde* [Konstanz colloquium], Vol. 1; Vorträge und Forschungen, Vol. 7 (Konstanz, 1964).

Walter Schlesinger, "Bäuerliche Gemeindebildung in den mittelelbischen Länden im Zeitalter der mittelalterlichen deutschen Ostbewegung," pp. 212–74 in his *Mitteldeutsche Beiträge zur deutschen Varfassungsgeschichte des Mittelalters* (Göttingen, 1961), pp. 222–56.

Gunther Wrede, "Probleme der Siedlungsforschung in der Sicht eines Historikers," *Geografiska Annaler* 43 (1961), 313–20.

Northern and Eastern Europe

Johann M. Bak, "Zur Frühgeschichte ungarischer Landgemeinden," pp. 403–17 in *Landgemeinde* [Konstanz colloquium], Vol. 2; Vorträge und Forschungen, Vol. 8 (Konstanz, 1964).

Z. R. Dittrich, "Die Frage der slawischen Agrarverfassung in mittelalterlichen Böhmen und Mähren," pp. 387–402 in *Landgemeinde* [Konstanz colloquium], Vol. 2; Vorträge und Forschungen, Vol. 8 (Konstanz, 1964).

Kåre Kveseth, "Die Gemeinschafts- und Gemeindebildung des norwegischen Landes Hedmark in der Eisenzeit und im Mittelalter," pp. 325–78 in *Landgemeinde* [Konstanz colloquium], Vol. 2; Vorträge und Forschungen, Vol. 8 (Konstanz, 1964).

Walther G. E. Maas, *Zur Siedlungskunde des Warthe-Weich-sellandes; sozialgeographische Betrachtungen;* Wissenschaft-liche Beiträge zur Geschichte und Landeskunde Ost-Mittel-europas, no. 52 (Marburg/Lahn, 1961), pp. 19–34.

Hans Patze, "Die deutsche bäuerliche Gemeinde im Ordensstaat Preussen," pp. 149–200 in *Landgemeinde* [Konstanz collo-quium], Vol. 2; Vorträge und Forschungen, Vol. 8 (Konstanz, 1964).

Anna Rutkowska-Płachcińska, *Sądeczyzna w XIII i XIV wieku; przemiany gospodarcze i społeczne* (Wrocław, 1961), 8–90.

Reinhard Wenskus, "Kleinverbände und Kleinräume bei den Prussen des Samlandes," pp. 201–54 in *Landgemeinde* [Kon-stanz colloquium], Vol. 2; Vorträge und Forschungen, Vol. 8 (Konstanz, 1964).

Josef Žontar, "Der Stand der Forschung über die südslawische ländliche Ordnung," pp. 419–41 in *Landgemeinde* [Konstanz colloquium], Vol. 2; Vorträge und Forschungen, Vol. 8 (Kon-stanz, 1964).

2

The Persistence of English Common Fields*

DONALD N. MCCLOSKEY

Equity and Efficiency

With its three great fields planted in a communally regulated
rotation of crops, its common meadows and wastes, and its mixture of holdings in hundreds of strips less than an acre each,
the common or open-field system in all its variants had, by 1700,
characterized the agriculture of northern Europe for centuries.
In England, as elsewhere, it had never been universal, and had
from an early date been subject to erosion, giving way by agreement among the tenants and by compulsion from the landlords
to compact enclosure. Yet in 1700 a broad north-south swath of
England from the North Sea across the Midlands to the Channel
still exhibited the system in a more or less complete form. A
century and a half later, five thousand-odd separate acts of
Parliament and perhaps an equal number of voluntary agreements had swept it away, transforming numerous and vague
usufructs over scattered plots in the open fields into unambiguous
rights of ownership to consolidated and fenced holdings, free of
village use and village direction.

The open-field system in the Middle Ages and enclosure in
modern times have long been among the handful of central concerns of British economic and social historians. It is odd, therefore, that the intimate relationship between the two has been
slighted. The reasons for the persistence of communal agricul-

* I have inflicted earlier versions of this and related work on an embarras-
singly large number of my colleagues, too numerous, indeed, to mention here.
I thank them for their comments, and pledge more explicit acknowledgment
when the work appears in extended form.

ture in England for so long a time, after all, must be related
logically to the reasons for its eventual dissolution. A system of
agriculture that for centuries retained its major features, however
much altered in detail, must have had powerful justifications,
as must have had the expensive and unsettling procedures for
transforming it into a system of modern farms. Nonetheless,
historians of the medieval agricultural community have concentrated on the one set of justifications and historians of the enclosure movement on the other, and the two have been permitted to live their intellectual lives, as it were, in isolation.
It is often argued—to give one small example of the advantage
to disciplined reasoning gained from treating them together—
that the enclosure movement of the late eighteenth century was
the result of a rise in the price of grain, especially during the
Napoleonic Wars. Yet if this is true, as it may well be in part,
one must ask why earlier rises and falls in the price of grain,
of which there were of course many over the history of the open
fields, did not produce comparable results. Again, it is often
argued that the enclosure movement was motivated by the desire
of powerful landlords to expropriate the birthright of the peasantry. Yet if this is true—and the next essay shows that it is doubtful—one must ask why landlords waited in most cases until the
eighteenth century to expropriate. It may be possible in these
particular instances to reconcile the logic of the open fields with
that of the enclosures, but the difficult and neglected task is to
reconcile them on all points simultaneously; that is, to provide
a consistent body of reasoning that rationalizes both the persistence and the dissolution of open fields.

Another odd feature of the historiography of open fields and
enclosures is that it has been concerned almost exclusively with
the effects of agricultural organization and reorganization on
equity, rather than on efficiency—on the balance of social classes,
rather than on the allocation of resources. In his study of English
open fields, George Homans, in the manner of Maitland and
Vinogradoff, was chiefly concerned with "the elaborate arrangements whereby the economic equality of the villagers' holdings,
class by class, was assured" and with "the hierarchy of social
classes which went with the classes of holdings." [1] In their study

---

[1] George C. Homans, *English Villagers of the Thirteenth Century* (Cambridge, Mass., 1941), p. 206.

of English enclosures, the Hammonds, in the manner of Marx and Tawney, declared that "we are not concerned to corroborate or to question the contention that enclosure made England more productive. . . . Our business is with the changes that the enclosures caused in the social structure of England."[2] This emphasis on equity rather than on efficiency is readily defended in an individual scholar, but less so in an entire body of scholarship, because it leaves the impression that the organization of agriculture was either an unimportant factor in the standard of life in the English countryside or a factor whose impact is obvious, neither of which is on the face of it correct.

This essay and its sequel take the first step in bringing the study of open fields and of enclosures closer together, and in righting the balance between considerations of equity and efficiency, by examining the change in the efficiency of English agriculture attributable to the enclosure of open fields. The subject is difficult—indeed, one purpose is to show that it is considerably more difficult than has been supposed—and this preliminary journey through the logic and the evidence cannot be expected to yield very many definite conclusions. It does, however, uncover a good many unsuspected snares.

The Goths and Vandals of Open-Field Farmers

The initial question to be asked is, how efficient were the open fields? The question presupposes that it is useful to speak of "the open fields" as a single phenomenon, despite the enormous body of scholarship documenting their variety and flexibility. It is convenient, nonetheless, to begin with the simplest textbook characterization, for nothing essential to the argument depends on variations in the system. The usual assumption is that the creation by enclosure of simple, one might say "modern," property rights in land would expose agriculture to market forces tending to make it efficient, in the economic sense of producing the largest attainable satisfaction for given inputs of land, labor, and capital. If it is to be maintained that enclosure increased efficiency, therefore, it must be shown that the earlier system was not efficient.

2 J. L. and Barbara Hammond, *The Village Labourer* [London, 1948, a reprint of the 4th (1927) edition], Vol. 1, 19.

Historical opinion has for the most part accepted the judgment of contemporaries, sixteenth-century opponents of enclosure as well as eighteenth-century enthusiasts, that the open-field system was indeed inefficient. An examination of the underlying evidence on the whole justifies this opinion, if not the exaggerated language in which it was sometimes expressed. The root cause of the inefficiencies was the excessive scattering of each peasant's land. Under the textbook version of the open-field system, with a wheat-barley-fallow rotation among the three great fields of the village, each peasant's holding was divided into three approximately equal parts, allocated among the three fields, instead of being consolidated, as efficiency in farming would seem to demand, into one. In 1635 in the village of Laxton, Nottinghamshire, for example, John Freeman, a typical tenant, held 29.6 acres in the open fields, of which 33 percent was in West Field, 31 percent in South Field, and 35 percent in Mill Field.[3] He held, in addition, two enclosures of 3.4 and 7.3 acres, and town land of 1.6 acres, out of his total acreage in arable land of 42.1 acres—a fact that makes the point that by this date (and earlier) even nominally open-field villages were partially enclosed. Nonetheless, most of his land was scattered among the three fields. Worse still, within each field his holdings were split into dozens of scattered plots, ranging in size down to fragments of an acre. His 2.4 acres of meadow land were split into seven separate plots, his 29.6 acres of arable land into forty-four plots, of which three-quarters were smaller than an acre, and half smaller than half an acre.

Freeman's plots tended, however, to cluster together within a few broad bands across the face of the open fields, making their effective number considerably less than forty-four. The point is general: the evidence from maps in other open-field villages also suggests that the number of plots reported in lists of ownership and tenancy is usually well above the effective number. When, for example, one foreign half-acre strip separates three of Christian Coxe's in Llancadle, Glamorgan in 1622, it is clear that for most farming purposes the three count, although they were not counted, as one. No doubt Coxe and his neighbor could

[3] C. S. and C. S. Orwin's classic study, *The Open Fields* (Oxford, 1938), reproduces the "booke of surveye" for Laxton in 1635, from which these figures are compiled.

have traded land to eliminate the small inconveniences of the lack of contiguity; no doubt, too, it mattered little whether or not they did. Determining the effective number of plots is necessarily somewhat arbitrary, but it does not follow that one must therefore adopt the equally arbitrary and less illuminating criterion that one nominal plot is to be counted as one effective plot. For example, if one adopts for Coxe's holding the criterion that a collection of plots is to be counted as one when no piece is separated from another by more than one foreign piece and no part of any piece is outside a radius of 150 yards from the center of the effective plot, Coxe's twenty-seven distinct nominal plots are reduced to twelve effective plots.[4]

The lists of nominal plots are misleading for another reason as well, namely, as M. M. Postan put it, that "the pattern of actual economic occupation of land might differ very widely from that of official tenancies."[5] Subleasing and absentee ownership were common early and late in the history of the open field, and both obscure the nature of the typical operating farm. A peasant who held directly of the lord 20 acres might take subleases on 15 more from other peasants, renting out 5 of his own, to form a larger, relatively consolidated farm of 30 acres that would appear nowhere in the records. The evidence for this must be indirect, but it is persuasive. In Eversholt, Bedfordshire, in 1764, for example, there were 59 holdings of less than 50 acres, yet of these fully 33 were holdings of non-residents, who could not themselves have been operating their lands as farms.[6] And holders were often widows or, on occasion, minors, any of whom could be expected to have rented out their land. It is apparent that one cannot lean too heavily on the legal records of holdings (which are, until modern times, the only records) in describing the pattern of farming.

Making all due allowances for these doubts, however, the typi-

---

[4] The map for Llancadle is reproduced on pp. 504–505 of Margaret Davies, "Field Systems of South Wales," chapter 11 in A. R. H. Baker and R. A. Butlin, *Studies of Field Systems in the British Isles* (Cambridge, 1973). Coxe was a copyholder of thirty-nine acres.

[5] Postan's introduction, p. lix, to C. N. L. Brooke and M. M. Postan, *Carte Nativorum, Publications of the Northamptonshire Record Society* 20 (1960). Compare Edward Miller, *The Abbey and Bishopric of Ely* (Cambridge, 1951), p. 133.

[6] George H. Fowler, *Four Pre-Enclosure Village Maps, Quarto Memoirs of the Bedfordshire Historical Record Society* 2, pt. iv (1936), 37–53.

cal peasant farm appears to have consisted of some dozen or more effective plots scattered about the open fields, and this arrangement was costly. The most obvious cost, given much emphasis in the literature on modern cases of scattering, is the time spent moving from one plot to another in performing farming tasks on one's property, such as plowing. But the importance of this time spent has probably been exaggerated. When plowing was done jointly, as it sometimes was, there would be little loss on this account, for the entire area serviced by one plow would then be equivalent to a large consolidated plot, with no time wasted traveling. And it was often the case that a plot was typically one day's plowing (one or two-thirds of an acre), in which case, since the team of oxen or horses would in any event be brought back to the village at night to be fed and housed, there would be no travel other than the inevitable daily trip from the village to the land and back.[7] Other tasks, such as harrowing, weeding (which was especially important for the root crops that came into general use in the eighteenth century), hauling manure, cleaning drains, and harvesting, would still involve some excess travel, except in the unlikely event that each happened to require an integral multiple of the number of days required for plowing each plot.

It is relatively easy to show, however, that even in the most unfavorable case this cost of scattering is small. In studies of scattering in Europe after World War II, the excess travel involved in scattered plots has sometimes been calculated from the sum of the distances from the village to each plot and back, one commuting trip, as it were, for each plot.[8] This procedure, which yields impressively large travel distances, is misleading because the distances are the result of the nucleation of villages, not of scattered holdings of land: a consolidated holding, if it were

[7] See the Orwins, *Open Fields*, pp. 35–36, 43, 126–27.

[8] For example, Kenneth Thompson, *Farm Fragmentation in Greece: The Problem and Its Setting, with 11 Village Case Studies* Center of Economic Research, Research Monograph Series #5 (Athens, 1963), p. 29. Thompson uses the sum of one-way trips, but the criticism is the same. Compare Michael Chisholm, *Rural Settlement and Land Use: An Essay in Location* (London, 1962), pp. 43–66. His examples of the costs of scattering are usually examples of the cost of nucleation, such as that of moving manure from the farmyard to the field or of moving the crop to the barn. He uses the villages of La Mancha, Spain, as cases in point. Although these are very large villages, with long average trips to the fields, the holdings are not scattered.

located (as it would have to be) the same average distance from
the village as the scattered plots, would require the same daily
commute. Nucleation, a response to the desire for mutual aid
and protection, was in large part independent of scattering,
although scattering would have reinforced nucleation by reducing to some degree the relative advantage of dispersed homesteads over clustered ones. In the usual case, in which scattering
is not itself the main cause of nucleation, the relevant distance
is that traveled from plot to plot in tasks that require less than
a full day's work.

With the plots scattered over the relatively small area of
English villages, this distance would be small, even if it were
not true that a peasant's holding tended to cluster in a few
limited areas. If an average day could accommodate labor on as
many as four plots, for example, there would be three trips between plots to be made each day. If John Freeman's forty-four
nominal plots, to take the extreme case, were scattered over the
entire area of Laxton in such a way as to maximize the distance
between his plots, he would in three trips have to travel on the
order of only 1.1 miles each day in addition to his normal
commute from the village.[9] The degree to which this upper-
bound estimate overstates the amount of time wasted traveling
between plots may be judged by the average of only .14 miles
between each of Freeman's plots and the one closest to it in
Laxton's South Field, in which they were scattered more than in
the other two fields: this distance implies an average walk of
less than half a mile in the course of visiting four in a day.[10]

[9] This is an approximation to the solution of a difficult problem. The
problem is to find the locations of plots in a village, perhaps a village of
some convenient shape that can nonetheless approximate actual village shapes
(such as a rectangle or a circle) such that the distance travelling from plot
to plot is maximized. The special solution given here supposes that the area
of Laxton (about 6 square miles, larger than most villages) can be approxi-
mated by a 3.28 mile × 1.82 mile rectangle, and that Freeman is constrained to walk on a grid of squares .36 miles on a side, like an American
middlewestern street plan, in visiting his property. His property (in forty-
five rather than the correct forty-four plots) is imagined to be located at
each of the street corners, as it were, in the 9 × 5 grid. A route through
four contiguous plots, then, would require three trips of .36 miles each, for
a total of 1.1 miles per day.

[10] This estimate of the average distance between plots was derived by
marking off Freeman's plots on the map of South Field, using the guide to
the strip numbers (both the map and guide are given in the Orwins, *Open
Fields*). The scale of the map was inferred from the acreage of the field.

Again, on the eve of the enclosure of Goldington, Bedfordshire, in 1852, before which a good deal of consolidation had already taken place, one typical farmer held 103 acres in the open fields, scattered in only 7 or 11 plots (depending on how one counts close plots).[11] In the field in which they were least consolidated he had five, each about 5 acres, more than enough, one would suppose, to fill a day in most agricultural tasks, and certainly in plowing. Each of the five was about three hundred yards from its nearest neighbor. At one yard per second, a relaxed pace, each trip between plots would therefore take only five minutes, or, if as many as four of these large plots were to be visited, only fifteen minutes a day. It is evident that it was not the waste of time in traveling from one plot to another that inspired the enclosure of Goldington.

Nor was it here or elsewhere the waste of land in unploughed strips, or balks, between plots, a feature of the system that seems at first obviously inefficient. There is an ongoing dispute over the prevalence of balks, although there is little doubt that at least in some places they did exist: B. K. Roberts reports that in south Warwickshire, for example, they were commonly a yard or so wide between plots, which were themselves ten yards or so wide.[12] The 10 percent of the land occupied by them, however, was not merely an expensive form of fencing or access way. Indeed, a balk commonly occurred between two plots even if they were owned by one person, their use being, as G. Whittington put it in describing them in Scotland, as places "onto which were thrown the stones frequently turned up by the plough. The balks in fact were the drainage lines into which the crowns of the ridges shed their water."[13] Furthermore, balks could be and were mown for hay, and animals grazed on them. In short, the net loss of output, if any, was far below the percentage of the land allotted to them.

The less obvious but probably more important sources of inefficiency in the system of small and scattered, and therefore intermingled, plots are neighborhood effects. If Tom did not

---

[11] Frederick G. Emmison, *Types of Open-field Parishes in the Midlands* Historical Association Pamphlet Series no. 108 (London, 1937).

[12] B. K. Roberts, "Field Systems of the West Midlands," in Baker and Butlin, *Field Systems*, pp. 197–98.

[13] G. Whittington, "Field Systems of Scotland," in Baker and Butlin, *Field Systems*, p. 543.

keep the drains clean on his plot, Jack's plot was flooded. If he did not weed carefully or destroy molehills and anthills on his plot, Jack's was infected. If he was careless in turning his plow or making a way to his crop, Jack's crop was crushed. There are neighborhood effects under any organization of land, but they are greatly increased by holding land in small, scattered plots, an arrangement that increases the average propinquity of one man's land to others'.[14] The significance of neighborhood effects is that they reduce the incentive to apply the optimal amount of labor to the land, for if the fruits of Jack's labor are spoiled, his incentive to cultivate his crop is attenuated. The fruits could be dissipated in the tangle of mutual damages, with no one benefiting, or they could merely be stolen: the difficulty of policing property rights as complex as those that characterized open field agriculture was a constant temptation to theft of crops or land. Because the theft of a small medieval sheaf of grain was easy, for example, elaborate precautions were taken to keep people out of the fields at night, and to make sure that they carried off their crop only by day in conspicuous carts. Because the boundaries of plots were long and numerous, the theft of a furrow was also easy. The standard illustration of these points has long been the confession of Avarice in *Piers Plowman:*

> So I gather by guile the goods that I covet,
> By day and by night, busy everywhere.
>
> If I plant or plow I pinch so narrowly
> That I fetch a furrow or a foot's swathing
> From my next neighbour, and gnaw his half acre.
> If I reap I over-reach, or tell the reaper privately
> To seize for me with his sickle what was sown by another.[15]

The standard illustration of furrow stealing might just as well be a case in Castor, Northamptonshire, in which before the very late enclosure of 1898, "there was one spot in the common fields were two neighbors kept a plough each continually, and as fast

[14] In Joan Thirsk, ed., *The Agrarian History of England and Wales,* Vol. 4, *1500–1640* (Cambridge, 1967), Thirsk remarks that even when land was "freed of the burden of common rights, few men owned ring-fence farms. . . . On the contrary their land lay in scattered bits and pieces, and their neighbour's bad or indifferent farming touched them nearly," p. 162.

[15] H. W. Wells, trans., *The Vision of Piers Plowman* (New York. 1945). passus XIII, lines 390–96.

as one ploughed certain furrows into his land, the other ploughed
them back into his." [16] Whatever the cause, the lack of correspondence between effort and reward and the devices to make
them correspond more closely were costly. The usual formula in
the preamble to parliamentary enclosure acts in the eighteenth
century asserted that in open fields the plots "lie inconveniently
dispersed and intermixed, and in their present situation are
incapable of improvement," and a propagandist for enclosure
identified the source of the improvement to be expected from
their consolidation: "Whatever tribute of fertility the grateful
earth bestows as the reward of honest industry and good
management redounds solely to . . . [the occupier's] own
advantage." [17]

The local law, enforced by peasant custom or the lord's court,
could and did intervene in a variety of ways in the tangle of
intermixed plots, assigning part of a bundle of property rights
to one man, part to another. The very existence of these elabo-
rately detailed village bylaws is testimony to the severity of the
neighborhood effects. An alternative explanation for bylaws, that
they were framed to protect peasants against their own inclination to fall below certain minimum standards in farming, is
not plausible, for the village community and the lord's court
interfered with the activities of a peasant only when these had
an impact on the activities of others.[18] The bylaws marked the
boundaries of rights where they conflicted, otherwise leaving men
to their own devices. In addition to his claim to the crop from
his own land (aside from tithes), for example, the peasant was
assigned the right to prohibit trespass by men or animals on
his growing corn.[19] On the other hand, there was a large class of

[16] Gilbert Slater, *The English Peasantry and the Enclosure of Common
Fields* (London, 1907), p. 15.

[17] Henry Homer, *Nature and Methods of Ascertaining Specific Shares of
Proprietors Upon the Inclosure of Common Fields*, 2d ed. (Oxford, 1769),
p. 11, spelling modernized.

[18] The best discussions of village bylaws are contained in Warren O. Ault's
many works on the subject, notably "Open-Field Husbandry and the Village
Community, a Study of Agrarian By-Laws in Medieval England," *Transactions of the American Philosophical Society*, n.s. 55 (October 1965), and a
shortened and revised version of this, *Open-Field Farming in Medieval
England* (London, 1972), on which the assertion in the text is based. Thirsk
finds some merit in the alternative explanation (*Agrarian History*, p. 163); as
did E. C. K. Gonner, *Common Land and Inclosure* (London, 1912), p. 34.

[19] Bylaws of Laxton given in the Orwins, *Open Fields*, pp. 172–81, provide

well-defined rights over his property placed in the hands of others, rights known in the Roman law as, appropriately, "servitudes." Some of his plots may have served during certain weeks of the year since time beyond memory as roads to other men's plots, or as places for them to turn their plows. Again, by virtue of holding certain plots, he may have been required to repair the fences around the common field or to clean the communal drains; because one man's land led to another's in the open field, the effects of poor fencing or draining spilled over onto neighboring land, and stiff fines were necessary to induce each to contribute his labor to the prevention of the nuisance.

The most important servitude of the land in the open field was that it was open to common grazing at certain times of the year, after the crop was harvested, or when the field as a whole lay fallow. It is likely that the growing scarcity of pasture caused this practice. As population grew, the waste and meadow shrank in relation to the arable land, making the stubble of the arable valuable for grazing.

The grazing could be common or private. If private grazing were to be feasible, some method of preventing animals from wandering off one's property would be necessary, but the costs of fencing a scattered holding were very high. The costs of fencing even the relatively consolidated holdings created by the enclosure movement of the eighteenth century were high—as is shown later, a quarter of the value of a year's crop was a typical figure—and the costs of fencing a holding such as John Freeman's, scattered in 44 plots (albeit nominal, not effective, plots), would have been higher than that for a completely consolidated holding of the same size by a factor of eight or nine. Only two sides of a plot need be fenced, for the neighbors will fence the rest. Therefore, the distance to be fenced on a completely consolidated square holding of A acres would be $2\sqrt{A}$. When the A-acre holding is scattered into N small plots, the plots must be

---

good cases in point. The Leet Court decreed in 1789, for example, "that if any one have one or two sheep that are common trespassers in the cornfield he shall pay for every offense 1d. or forfeit 3s. 4d" and "that none make a way up or down William Pinder's Acre at the top of the West field." A reading of these and others confirms the assertion of F. Pollock and F. W. Maitland in *The History of English Law Before the Time of Edward I*, 2d ed. (Cambridge, 1898), Vol. 2, 145, that "the most elaborate and carefully worded of the private documents that have come down to us are those which create or regulate pasture rights and rights of way."

elongated into strips to accommodate the plow team. If the length
of these strips is ϕ times their width, it can be shown that each
of the N plots required $(1+\phi)\sqrt{\dfrac{A}{\phi N}}$ in fencing, implying that
the ratio of lengths to be fenced on the scattered holding to that
on the consolidated holding is $\frac{1}{2}\sqrt{N}\left(\dfrac{1+\phi}{\sqrt{\phi}}\right)$. For Freeman's

holding of 44 strips (N = 44), supposing, as the map of his holding
indicates, that $\phi = 5$ (that is, his strips were on average five times
longer than they were wide), this ratio of fencing costs is 8.9.
Even if he were able to make agreements with his immediate
neighbors to fence larger areas in squares and to graze communally within the fences, as was sometimes possible, the ratio
would be substantial. If he were able to allocate his 44 plots by
threes into 15 such partial enclosures, for example, the ratio of
costs would be $\sqrt{15}$, or 3.9. When the costs of land taken up by
the fencing itself and of land shaded from the sun are added to
the account (offset to some degree by the advantage of sheltering
crops and livestock behind the fences from destructive winds),
it is not surprising to find that scattered holdings were rarely
fenced. Communal grazing, for all its inefficiency, was the better
of two inefficient alternatives.

Tethering of animals was possible, and for this reason Marc
Bloch rejected scattering as a sufficient explanation of communal
grazing, declaring that it "arose first and foremost from an attitude of mind, from the notion that once land became unproductive it was no longer capable of individual exploitation." [20]
But tethering was largely confined to horses, with elaborate restrictions required even for some of these, namely, mares with
a foal.[21] Oxen were seldom tethered, and sheep could not be.
Tethering, moreover, would result in either inefficient grazing of
the plots or repeated retetherings. And tethering is asymmetrical
in its effects, unlike fencing: a fence protects my crops from your
animals as well as your crops from mine, giving us both an
incentive to build and repair the fence; tethering, however, only
protects your crops from my animals, leaving your crop dependent on my altruism or on the force of law for protection. In

[20] Marc Bloch, *French Rural History* (Berkeley and Los Angeles, 1966;
first published in French in 1931), p. 46.
[21] Ault, *Open Field Farming*, pp. 43–44; Thirsk, *Agrarian History*, p. 165.

any case, tethering, like the fencing of scattered holdings, was the exception, and common grazing on unfenced fields the rule.

One direct cost of this arrangement was uncontrolled breeding and endemic livestock disease, despite bylaws directed at both. The pathetic condition of beasts raised on common grazing regularly aroused the scorn of agricultural writers from the sixteenth century on. Another cost was the overuse of land, for if no one faced a price for failing to restrain his use of the land, everyone would put out too many sheep or cattle, crushing the seed and impacting the ground beyond the ability of the land to recover in the next season. To suppose that overstocking was by itself a very important loss, however, is to suppose, contrary to fact, that villagers took no steps to reduce this loss. As with the other inconveniences of the open fields, village law intervened, limiting with increasing rigor as population grew the number of animals a man could put on the stubble to a traditional "stint," often in rough proportion to the quantity of land he occupied in the fields. To be sure, enclosed holdings would have produced self-interested husbanding of the land superior to the stint's crude check on inefficiency. If the stint proved too crude, however, the village could allow the stinted rights to be bought and sold, as it sometimes did. Gilbert Slater reported in 1907 that in the village of Eakring (near Laxton), which survived as an open field late enough for him to visit it, the village meeting decided each year how many sheep could be pastured on the stubble and other common pastures, then auctioned the rights to the highest bidders, distributing the proceeds to the occupiers of village homesteads (the original owners of the rights).[22]

The logic of the overgrazing argument is not in any case compelling. Although cogent enough when applied to permanent pasture, the land in question was not permanent pasture, but fallow land, annually stirred by the plow if animals impacted it, and refreshed with new grain (and weed) seeds if animals crushed them. Therefore the arable lands lying fallow, which formed the bulk of the grazing (as distinct from hay) for animals in a fully developed open-field village, could not have been overgrazed, in the sense of that the land would not recover the following year. From this perspective the development of an elaborate stint and the frequent complaints that it was being

[22] *English Peasantry,* p. 12.

violated by peasants with ambitions to become full-time graziers can be seen primarily as a problem of equity (how much grass for his livestock will there be this year for Jack compared with that for Tom and Simon), not of efficiency (how much grass for their livestock will there be this year for Jack, Tom, and Simon together).

If the direct costs of common grazing were small, the indirect costs—resulting from the necessity for communal rules of cropping—were large. Common grazing on a peasant's fallow lands implied that he was constrained by communal rules on the timing and character of his planting and harvesting, for it would be futile for him to plant a crop when others had decreed that the field in which his plots lay was to be open to foraging cattle and sheep. All crops had to be planted, cultivated, and harvested within each field on a uniform schedule, especially as the very scattering that made common grazing desirable also made it desirable to have systematic arrangements for access to the plots. The presence of a nearby reserve of waste land for grazing, as in the fenland of the Holland division of Lincolnshire, would make common grazing and therefore common cropping unnecessary: the absence of any "urgent necessity to graze the stubble when the fens afforded such luxuriant pasture," Joan Thirsk argues, explains the absence of bylaws on communal cropping there. In the fens of the Kesteven division or of the Isle of Axholme in Lincolnshire, however, the arable land was not so fragmented by fenny ground; the fallow land was more valuable, and there were, therefore, communal rules of cropping and grazing.[23] In the sparsely and tardily settled forest regions of England, grazing on the stubble was often not necessary, although limitations on the use of the king's forest or the scantiness of grass shaded by trees sometimes made it so.[24] Even when grazing on the stubble was necessary, the village could complicate its rotations or permit neighbors to put temporary fences around their furlongs, as was common in the East Midlands and many other places from the earliest times.[25]

[23] Thirsk, "Field Systems of the East Midlands," in Baker and Butlin. *Field Systems,* pp. 252–53.

[24] *Ibid.;* Robert, in Baker and Butlin, *Field Systems,* p. 211; and see, on the poor quality of wooded pasture in the thirteenth century and its higher value for timber, David Roden, "Field Systems of the Chiltern Hills and Envirows," in Baker and Butlin, *Field Systems,* p. 327.

[25] Thirsk, in Baker and Butlin, *Field Systems,* pp. 258–62.

Although the communal rotation might have this flexibility, by comparison with enclosed land held in severalty it necessarily limited the ability of men to exploit unusual features of themselves or of their soil. A man with exceptional knowledge of root crops, or with soil able to yield three rather than two grain crops between fallowings, was discouraged from exploiting these advantages. As a sixteenth-century rhymester of agricultural improvement put it, referring to the illegality of taking more than the normal number of successive crops from land in regions of open fields (or "champion country"), where the commoners' decision as a group was law:

> Good land that is severall crops may have three,
>> in champion countrie it may not so bee:
> Ton taketh his season, as commoners may,
>> the tother with reason may otherwise say. . . .
> There common as commoners use,
>> for otherwise shalt thou not chuse.[26]

This analysis of the system's inefficiencies gives some indication of their importance. In view of the vigorous attempts to offset the inefficiencies with bylaws and changes in village routine, it would be surprising if the loss were extremely large—as large, say, as a quarter of output—notwithstanding the intemperate language of contemporary critics of the system. It will be shown in the next essay, in fact, that in the eighteenth century, on the eve of full enclosure, the barbaric practices of what Arthur Young called "the Goths and Vandals of open field farmers" reduced output by around 13 percent. And the loss was no doubt lower in open fields in their prime than in open fields on the verge of being enclosed. If such a loss is not enormous, neither is it negligible. The analysis, in any case, confirms the hypothesis that scattering was the root cause of whatever loss occurred: scattering, with its attendant inefficiencies, implied common grazing, with more inefficiencies, and scattering and common grazing together implied communal cropping, with still more.[27]

[26] Thomas Tusser, *Five Hundred Pointes of Good Husbandrie* (1580), edited by W. Payne and S. J. Heartage (London, 1878), pp. 50, 141; spelling somewhat modernized. T. E. Scrutton used this quotation in *Commons and Comon Fields* (Cambridge, 1887), p. 115.

[27] This conclusion fits well with recent views on the evolution of open fields, expressed, for example, in Baker and Butlin's "Conclusion" to their *Field Systems*. They argue that full-blown open fields were the end product

The Shrine of Equality

The inefficiencies of the open field system have presented historians with a puzzle: Why did it persist? The puzzle is relevant here because one must know the reason for its persistence to understand its dissolution in enclosure. With a miserably low and precarious standard of living, it is hardly credible that peasants would throw away 10 percent of their crop without some compensating advantage, yet the inefficiencies appear at first to amount to precisely that. It is not convincing to suppose, as some have, that peasants were simply indifferent to the gains from more efficient organization. Folke Dovring's otherwise illuminating treatment of modern fragmentation of farms, for example, is marred by this supposition: "It has always been noted that fragmentation means waste of time and draught power. As long as manpower was in excess supply, this could be tolerated up to a point." [28] But if other factors of production besides labor were wasted by the open-field system, as they surely were, or if the marginal product of labor were above zero, as it surely was, the open fields led to lost output, which would require some compensating advantage. And one need not rely on general arguments such as these in rejecting the premise that an excess supply of labor explains open fields. It has already been shown that the cost of travel between plots, which underpins the argument, was in any case trivial. Furthermore, the notion that labor time was considered valueless is doubtful. The simplest and most persuasive test involves determining whether labor was used with no concern for its value in other occupations, such as commuting from the village. It was not. Michael Chisholm, among others, has presented ample evidence, following von Thünen and the many geographers after him who have made the same point, that even in regions with an alleged surplus of labor, the labor-intensity of crops varies inversely with the dis-

---

of population growth in the face of scattered plots; the historical sequence being from shifting cultivation to an infield-outfield system (partly shifting, partly permanent), to a permanent field system with abundant waste for grazing, to, finally, a permanent field system with grazing on the fallow and communal cropping.

[28] F. Dovring, *Land and Labor in Europe in the 20th Century*, 3d rev. ed. (The Hague, 1965), p. 53. See also his "The Transformation of European Agriculture," chapter 6 in H. J. Habakkuk and M. Postan, eds., *The Cambridge Economic History of Europe*, Vol. 6 (Cambridge, 1965), especially pp. 626–31.

tance from the village. If it were true that "human time saved in one process of cultivation adds nothing to the general welfare . . . all the territory would be farmed at the same level of intensity." [29]

Nor is it convincing to argue simply that peasants tolerated the inefficiencies of the open fields until they were forced to change by the improvements of the agricultural revolution, for which enclosure was "necessary." M. A. Havinden and others have emphasized that open-field villages could and did introduce floating meadows, pasture land within fields of growing crops, clover, turnips, and other innovations.[30] Although this revision of the picture of technological stagnation in open-field agriculture drawn by hostile contemporaries has found its way into most accounts only recently, it has a long history: E. C. K. Gonner, for example, made the point in 1912.[31] Enclosure and changes in technique were of course connected, but not by a bond of mutual necessity.

It is easier to dispute explanations for the persistence and eventual disappearance of the open field than to construct them. Regional variation in the rate of enclosure is one obstacle to understanding. As Slater remarked in 1907, "the surprising fact is not that the common field system should gradually and quietly disappear in parish A, but that it should persist in parish B, until ended by the very expensive and troublesome measure of a special Act of Parliament." [32] The lack of progress in the last seventy years in solving this puzzle may be gauged by a similar remark by Joan Thirsk in 1964: "All countries in West-

[29] Chisholm, *Rural Settlement*, p. 64. He finds zoning to be especially plain in precisely those areas of modern Europe where the existence of surplus of labor is most plausible, that is, southern Italy (see his chapter 4).

[30] M. A. Havinden, "Agricultural Progress in Open-Field Oxfordshire," *Agricultural History Review* 9 (1961), 73–83. Compare W. G. Hoskins, *The Midland Peasant: The Economic and Social History of a Leicestershire Village* (London, 1957), pp. 231–33; and Thirsk, *Agrarian History*, p. 179. Dovring ("The Transformation of European Agriculture," p. 631), pointing to the introduction of modern techniques on severely fragmented land on the Continent down to the present, argues that "the allegation often made that land consolidation is a prerequisite of the use of modern crop rotations has not been borne out by experience, whatever damage fragmentation has done to the technical and economic efficiency of labour and capital."

[31] *Common Land*, p. 32. Gonner did doubt that root crops were easily introduced, but the work of Havinden and others has removed even this qualification.

[32] *English Peasantry*, p. 150.

ern Europe have the same problem to solve—they have all had experience of common-field systems existing side by side with enclosed farms." [33]

Since Slater wrote, there has been an increasing awareness of still another obstacle to understanding, also emphasized by Thirsk, namely, that open fields are not merely anachronistic relics of the distant past. Making use of recent German literature on the open fields, Thirsk points out that "it is possible to observe the gradual parcelling of rectangular fields into strips as late as the seventeenth and even the eighteenth centuries." [34] For an earlier period, as Thirsk argues, the less abundant English evidence is similar. In the thirteenth century Kent and Sussex had very irregular field systems, if any. By the sixteenth century, Kent was a county of enclosures, yet parts of Sussex had by then fully developed open fields, with communal cropping and grazing.[35] Evidence such as this casts doubt on the theory that the open field was a static system "consecrated by immemorial usage," as Gonner put it, whose rules "made conscious change well nigh impossible," [36] as it does on the related theory that the open field and its variants are to be explained as remnants of the racial pattern of settlement in Anglo-Saxon England. Conscious change was in fact quite possible, whether away from or towards a strict open-field regime. A striking German case in point is the land owned by the Abbey of Kempton in the Algäu region of southwestern Bavaria, on which consolidation, initiated by the peasants themselves, went forward by agreement from the middle of the sixteenth century on, three centuries before consolidation in neighboring regions of Germany had begun.[37]

Examples of the bewildering pattern of growth and decline in open fields need not be restricted to the eighteenth century and before, nor to one country. In 1928 Marc Bloch wrote in his celebrated essay on the comparative method in history that "we shall never arrive at a complete understanding of the English

[33] "The Common Fields," *Past and Present* 19 (December 1964), p. 3.

[34] *Ibid,* p. 10. There are other examples of new open fields in early modern times in eastern Europe and, more striking still, in New England (these however, disintegrated in the second generation of settlement).

[35] Alan R. H. Baker, "Field Systems of Southeast England," in Baker and Butlin. *Field Systems,* pp. 428–29.

[36] *Common Land,* p. 35.

[37] Alan Mayhew, *Rural Settlement and Farming in Germany* (London, 1973), p. 187.

open field system, the German *Gewanndorf,* or the French *champs ouverts,* by examining England, Germany or France alone." [38] His call for comparative work, unfortunately largely unheeded, was broadened still further by Joan Thirsk in 1966: "we may also learn something from the study of peasant cultivation in present-day Asia, Africa, and South America, where examples abound of intermingled strips." [39] Indeed we may. Down to the present, farms in many parts of the world remain or have become in the course of a few generations severely scattered. In the early 1960s Folke Dovring estimated that "at least one-third, and probably over half, of the agricultural land in Europe would need re-allocation or consolidation in order to do away with the technical disadvantages of bad layout, including among these the constraint to conform with neighbours in farming operations." [40] In 1969 the Organization for Economic Cooperation and Development delivered a similar judgment on southern Europe, reporting that in Spain, for example, the average number of separate plots per farm in 1962 was 14 and in Germany in 1960, 10, in both cases roughly a third of the farms having 10 plots or more.[41] The average number of plots per farm here is less than the nominal number in England under the open field system, but in isolated instances in modern Europe it has approached or exceeded it. In Czechoslovakia in 1938, for example, the median number of plots per farm was 30, and in Portugal in 1940, 26.[42] Around 1950, in parts of Greece many farms consisted of 50 to 100 plots each, and ten years later the situation was similar.[43] In a backward part of Ireland in the

[38] "A Contribution Towards a Comparative History of European Societies" in Marc Bloch, *Land and Work in Medieval Europe* (London, 1967), selected translations by J. E. Anderson from *Mélanges Historiques* (1966), p. 70.

[39] Thirsk, "The Origin of the Common Fields," *Past and Present* 33 (April 1966), 143.

[40] Dovring, "The Transformation of European Agriculture," pp. 630ff.

[41] Organization for Economic Co-operation and Development, Agricultural Policy Reports, *Agricultural Development in Southern Europe* (Paris, 1969), pp. 18, 83.

[42] Dovring, *Land and Labor,* p. 40. He gives some twenty cases, ranging upwards from Belgium's 6.8 plots per farm in 1950.

[43] Euthymios Papageorgiou, "Fragmentation of Land Holdings and Measures for Consolidation in Greece," pp. 543–48 in Kenneth H. Parsons, R. J. Penn, and P. M. Raup, eds., *Land Tenure: Proceedings of the International Conference on Land Tenure and Related Problems in World Agriculture held at Madison, Wisconsin, 1951* (Madison, 1956). Part 17 of this volume (pp. 535–64) is entitled "Consolidation of Fragmented Holdings" and con-

1960s the average holding consisted of 60 scattered plots.[44] Nor are scattered holdings confined to Europe. They occur in Africa and in Latin America.[45] And in Asia they are ubiquitous: noting their prevalence in Formosa, Korea, Japan, India, Pakistan, Thailand, and Indonesia, the Asian Agricultural Survey Team of the Asian Development Bank reported in 1969 that "The basic cause of operational inefficiency on small farms is the poor farm layout. . . . A farm of one hectare may be divided into more than a dozen small fields." [46]

In most of these cases scattering is treated as an unmitigated evil, as a source of inefficiency, and an obstacle to progress on a par with sacred cows and too numerous feast days, which must be rooted out, if necessary by compulsion, before agricultural development can proceed. Yet it has never been satisfactorily explained why peasants are so often opposed to consolidation if, as is commonly supposed, it would raise output with no impairment of other goals. Since the English example of the eighteenth century, followed closely by Sweden and France, one government after another in Europe and elsewhere has passed laws designed to eliminate scattering by persuasion, by subsidy, or by force, and it would be difficult to explain their painfully slow achievement of success if consolidation were so unambiguously advantageous. The Dutch reallotment act of 1924, amended in 1938 and later, made consolidation compulsory if favored by either a majority of the landlords or a preponderance of the land voted by its owners,

---

tains, besides Papageorgiou's piece, reports on scattering and enclosure in modern France, the Netherlands, and Japan. Thompson's *Farm Fragmentation in Greece* is a detailed study of the Greek case. See also Bernard O. Binns and others, *The Consolidation of Fragmented Agricultural Holdings*, Food and Agricultural Organization of the United Nations, Agricultural Studies #11 (Washington, D.C., 1950) for studies of scattering in Denmark, France, Ireland, and Switzerland.

[44] John C. Messenger, *Inis Beag. Isle of Ireland* (New York, 1969), p. 27. "Inis Beag" is a pseudonym.

[45] For example, among the farmers of east central Tanzania "the ideal pattern is to hold a number of scattered fields planted with several crops" (T. O. Beidelman, *The Karugu. A Matrilineal People of East Africa* (New York, 1971), p. 18). And see Oscar Lewis, *Life in a Mexican Village: Tepoztlán Restudied* (Urbana, Ill., 1951), p. 120.

[46] Asian Development Bank, Asian Agricultural Survey Team, *Asian Agricultural Survey* (Seattle, Wash., 1969), p. 645. See also Setsuro Hyodo, "Aspects of Land Consolidation in Japan," pp. 558–59 in Parsons, *Land Tenure*, and Oscar Lewis, *Village Life in Northern India* (Urbana, Ill., 1958), pp. 104–107.

and provided generous subsidies (all the costs incurred, for example, if the attempt to consolidate failed). Yet in the early 1950s consolidation of plots in the Netherlands was far from complete.[47] The first of many general consolidation acts in Germany was Hannover's in 1848, yet to this day farms in many parts of Germany are scattered.[48] Official concern with scattering, embodied at the state level in a series of consolidation acts, is half a century old in India, yet the problem (for so it is viewed) remains.[49]

What we may learn, then, from the ubiquity of scattered plots and from the tenacity with which peasants have clung to them—for eight or nine centuries in parts of Europe—is that scattering must have some powerful advantage to offset its admitted drawbacks. The many advantages that have been proposed in the literature have one feature in common: in the background they all assume that an absence of markets among peasants in grain, in labor, in cattle, in grazing rights, or in land made the given advantage achievable only by scattering.

Consider, for example, one of the less important features of the open-field system as it is usually described, namely, the holding of approximately equal amounts of land by each villager in each of the three open fields. It requires some compensating advantage, because it presumably resulted in some loss of efficiency from scattering, however small. The usual explanation is that it was necessary to have land in all three fields because each year one of the three lay fallow: a peasant who held all his land in West Field would starve in the year in which the village decreed that it must lie fallow and open to grazing livestock. The plain statement of the argument is enough to reveal its weakness, for a peasant with a more consolidated holding could raise a larger crop in one year, sell the excess to his neighbors, and buy food with the accumulated sum in the year in which his land lay fallow. There is little doubt that a market in grain inside or outside the village existed in medieval times, and no doubt whatever that it existed in a highly developed form in modern times. In his study of *English Field Systems,* H. L. Gray

[47] Philine R. Vanderpol, "Reallocation of Land in the Netherlands," in Parsons, *Land Tenure,* pp. 548–54.

[48] Mayhew, *Rural Settlement,* pp. 178–99.

[49] S. K. Agarwal, *Economics of Land Consolidation in India* (New Delhi, 1971), pp. 5–12.

used the equality of holdings in the fields as a "crucial test"
for the existence of a two or three-field system of communal
cropping.[50] The difficulty with the underlying argument passed
through his mind, but he rejected it on the ground that "increased abundance the ensuing year could scarcely repair the loss
to a peasantry which probably lived close to the margin of
subsistence." It may be wondered whether this bit of illogic in
a seminal work on English field systems has biased the historical
picture of their geography. To establish the existence of communal cropping (although not the other features of the open
fields), evidence of roughly equal holdings in several fields may
be sufficient, but is surely not necessary. If a market in grain
existed, communal cropping could be sustained without equally
divided holdings, and their presence or absence becomes a test
only of whether such markets had developed. Without access to
a market, indeed, the observed irregularities in the putative
general rule of equally divided holdings imply implausibly large
variations in real income from year to year.[51]

One might argue that equal division of holdings among the
fields was necessary not to insure a crop every year, but to insure
that the peasant's work was spread over several years, equalizing
the marginal utility of leisure from year to year. The scattering
of plots within each of the open fields has been explained by
Charles Parain in a similar fashion: "At the outset, when each
plot needed at least a day's work, the scattering was rather more
advantageous than not. A single tenant's holding all on one kind
of soil would often require to be worked quickly, when the soil
was in the right condition, and harvested quickly. Plots with
different soils are ready for working at different times." [52] Again,
however, the argument is undercut if there was access to a market, in this case a market for labor. If peasants could arrange

[50] H. L. Gray, *English Field Systems* (Cambridge, 1915), p. 40.

[51] Thirsk ("The Common Fields," p. 21) observes that "The vast majority
of tenants' holdings did not consist of strips evenly divided between two or
more cropping units. The distribution was often highly irregular and
this fact has been a constant source of bewilderment to historians." One
explanation for this irregularity (aside from the possibility that peasants
held makeweight plots of enclosed land, as they often did), is that there
existed markets in food or, as is argued in the paragraph below, in labor.

[52] In M. M. Postan, ed., *The Cambridge Economic History of Europe*,
Vol. 1, 2d ed. (Cambridge, 1966), 138. I am indebted to Stephano Fenoaltea
for drawing my attention to this point.

to trade labor, as they did, or to work part time for wages, either
for another peasant on his land in crops or for the lord on his
demesne, they would be able to spread their work without at the
same time needing to spread their land. One might argue, too,
that since the right to graze livestock on the stubble or fallow was
often stinted in proportion to the amount of land a peasant occupied in a field, he would have to occupy land in all three fields
to insure adequate grazing for his animals in each year. But a
market could intervene here as well: grazing rights often could
be, and in fact were, exchanged, permitting him to arrange his
plots with an eye to efficient cultivation rather than a schedule
of grazing rights.

Another feature of the open-field system, common grazing itself, would have been subject to the same process of erosion by
self-interested exchange. It is sometimes argued that common
grazing was an obstacle to gradual enclosure on private initiative,
for each commoner would resist attempts to reduce by individual
consolidation and enclosure the amount of land available for
grazing. When grazing rights are stinted in proportion to land
holdings, however, this argument loses force. To be sure, a commoner is deprived of the use of another's land for grazing when
it is enclosed, but at the same time the number of cattle grazing
on the remaining common field is reduced in proportion, leaving
the acreage per head of livestock unchanged. In other words,
when rights to grazing are well defined and exchangeable, each
peasant can enter into a mutually advantageous exchange with
the village as a whole.

Nowhere is the potential erosion of inefficient arrangements
by market exchanges clearer than for the explanations of the central feature of the open fields, the scattering of plots. One or
another *deus ex machina*—common plowing, egalitarian in-
stincts, clearing of waste lands, partible inheritance—is lowered
into the action to scatter the plots, but when it has been lifted
back into the rafters, the question arises why its effects persist.
In 1883 Frederic Seebohm argued that the scattered plots were a
consequence of the large number of oxen required to pull heavy
medieval plows: one contributor to the team would get one
day's plowing, another the next, and so on, distributing the
inconvenience involved in very early or very late plowing of a

contributor's land evenly over the whole group.[53] Seebohm's argument, perhaps because of its attractive air of technological determinism, has proven remarkably hardy; recently, for example,
Warren Ault and M. M. Postan have adopted it as their explanation of scattered plots.[54] It presupposes, however, that peasants
did not rent oxen from one another, which is incorrect. Variations in the rental price of oxen could compensate a contributor
for a bad plowing date, a cheaper arrangement than tolerating
the inefficiencies of scattered plots. Furthermore, even if such a
rental market did not exist, it does not follow from a desire to
avoid inconvenience in plowing dates that the plots had to be
scattered, for if each was a whole day's plowing it would not
matter where they were located; they might as well have been
consolidated.

In any case, as Paul Vinogradoff pointed out a few years later
in his *Villainage in England,* Seebohm's argument implies that
the scattering and intermixture of plots would not occur in regions where small plows requiring few oxen were used, or on
holdings large enough to support a full team, neither of which
was the case.[55] He proposed an alternative explanation, which
for a time supplanted Seebohm's: "The only adequate explanation of the open-field intermixture . . . [is] the wish to equalize
the holdings as to the quality and quantity of land assigned to
[each peasant] in spite of all differences in the shape, the position,
and the value of the soil." [56] Lord Ernle concurred: "To divide
equally the good and bad, well and ill situated soil, the bundle of
strips allotted in each of the three fields did not lie together, but
was intermixed and scattered." [57] As did Maitland: "Who laid

[53] F. Seebohm, *The English Village Community* (London, 1883), pp. 113ff.
[54] Ault, *Open Field Farming,* p. 20; Postan, *The Medieval Economy and
Society: An Economic History of Britain 1100–1500* (Berkeley and Los
Angeles, 1972), p. 49. As Ault points out, joint plowing is never mentioned in
bylaws, although quarrels about joint agreements among two or three neighbors do figure in the proceedings of manorial courts.
[55] P. Vinogradoff, *Villainage in England* (Oxford, 1892), pp. 231ff.
[56] *Ibid,* p. 254. Compare his *The Growth of the Manor,* 2d ed. (London,
1911), pp. 175ff., where he examines and rejects the arguments that the
scattering of strips came about from the gradual bringing of the waste into
cultivation or from the operation of partible inheritance. He concludes that
"although this system was not by any means the best for furthering the
progress of cultivation, it was particularly adapted to the requirements of a
community of shareholders," p. 176.
[57] Lord Ernle (R. E. Prothero), *English Farming Past and Present,* 6th
ed., edited and introduced by G. E. Fussell and O. R. McGregor (Chicago,

out these fields? The obvious answer is that they were laid out by men who would sacrifice economy and efficiency at the shrine of equality." [58]

It is strange to find Vinogradoff, Maitland, and the rest assuming that communal pressures were powerful enough to produce equality, even when the equality is taken to be, as Homans put it, "economic equality . . . class by class." It is strange partly because it is false; even when they are grouped by social class, holdings were far from equal, at any rate by the time they can be measured. But it is strange chiefly because the purpose of these scholars was precisely to overturn the notion of an egalitarian village community with broad powers over the land of its members. Maitland, and many writers after him, insisted that from the earliest times—indeed, as a matter of Germanic custom—land was owned privately in a most thoroughgoing fashion: allotted in severalty, its fruits accruing to its owner alone, inheritable, and partible.[59] Maitland hesitated to attribute alienability to land, yet here the recent accumulation of evidence on the selling and leasing of peasant land discussed below is decisive. One is tempted to turn Maitland's acerbic characterization of the theory of communal ownership onto his own theory of scattered plots: "This theory has the great merit of being vague and elastic; but, as it seems to think itself precise, and probably owes some of its popularity to its pretence of precision, we feel it our duty to point out to its real merit, its vague elasticity." [60]

There are, to be sure, documented cases of egalitarian distribution and redistribution of land. In open-field villages otherwise individualistic, for example, meadow lands were often redistributed by lot each year. But, to anticipate a later argument, the random distribution of scattered claims to the hay was more likely to have been a species of insurance in the face of a variable crop (variable because the area and yield of the meadows varied with rainfall) than an incongruous intrusion of egalitarianism. The insurance achieved by dividing the land on harvest eve was cheap because in this instance there was no fear that villagers

1961), p. 25. Compare E. Lipson, *An Introduction to the Economic History of England,* 5th ed., Vol. 2 (London, 1929), pp. 63ff.

58 F. W. Maitland, *Domesday Book and Beyond* (London, 1960; first published 1897), p. 394.

59 *Ibid,* essay 2, chapter 6.

60 *Ibid,* p. 398.

would have neglected to supply their own effort in hopes of
getting a share of the fruits of someone else's labor, for hay grew
naturally, with no cultivation necessary. There are, too, occasional examples of the redistribution of arable land, although its
prevalence in the part of Britain where it has been thought to
have been common, Scotland, has been exaggerated.[61] The most
celebrated case of periodic redistribution, that of the Russian
peasant community from the eighteenth century on, is instructive, for it appears that it was indeed a modern development,
and that the redistributions were undertaken in response to a
heavy burden of taxation and rent imposed upon the village as
a whole. The redistributions, in other words, were not a result
of innate and immemorial village egalitarianism; on the contrary,
they were lately imposed by lord and state the better to collect
their rents and taxes, with the enthusiastic and sometimes violent
support of the poorer peasants.[62]

Viewed merely as a theory of the origin rather than of the
persistence of scattered plots, the egalitarian theory presents
problems well expressed in 1928 by George Fowler (a follower of
Seebohm in this matter): "I am not aware of any direct evidence
in support [of it]; and when one considers the handful of men
who first settled in each township, and the abundance of land
available, the theory seems to be unnecessary." [63] There would
be no point, he was arguing, to a strictly egalitarian distribution
of a free good. Viewed as a theory of the persistence, and not
merely the origin, of scattered plots, its difficulties are still
greater, and similar to those that afflict Seebohm's theory of
co-aration: scattering was an inefficient way of maintaining
equality, just as it was an inefficient way of avoiding the inconvenience of early or late plowing. A community bent on equality
might have chosen to simplify its task of equalizing the value
of allotments by merely distributing a bundle of plots in all parts

[61] Whittington, in Baker and Butlin, *Field Systems*, pp. 536–43. Arguing
that the term "runrig" by no means always implies periodic redistribution, he
notes that there exist only a handful of documented cases of redistribution,
most of them from northwest Scotland.

[62] G. T. Robinson, *Rural Russia Under the Old Régime* (New York, 1932),
pp. 12, 34–35, 274 (note 24); Jerome Blum, *Lord and Peasant in Russia from
the Ninth to the Nineteenth Century* (Princeton, 1961), pp. 509–23. There
is some hint in Whittington that the Scottish cases arose from similar
causes, namely, the cojoint tenancy common there, p. 542.

[63] Fowler, *Pre-Enclosure Maps*, pt. i (1928), p. 4.

of the village to each peasant, rather than by adjusting the size of a single consolidated holding to its quality.[64] Once random distribution had insured a rough equality among holdings with respect to the convenience of their location or to their drainage or soil qualities, however, each member of the village could benefit from exchanges of plots to achieve consolidation. Equality would not be disturbed, for the exchanges would have to be mutually beneficial for the peasants to engage in them voluntarily, yet in the long run efficiency would be increased. In other words, even if egalitarianism influenced the initial distribution of land, it did not require any particular subsequent allocation. A market in land—the prior development of a money economy is not necessary, although it would have reduced the costs of exchange—with different prices for different qualities would have permitted the consolidation of holdings.

The holdings of free men were involved in an active market from the earliest times, and where these dominated consolidation would have been easy. It is sometimes argued that the lord of the manor would have been reluctant to permit a reshuffling of land that might disturb obligations attached to holdings of villeins. But M. M. Postan has emphasized that this obstacle to the existence of a villein land market is somewhat hypothetical, although he admits that in some cases it carries weight. For instance, the lord faced the same sort of evasion of death duties that the Internal Revenue Service faces today, namely, transfers of dutiable property before death; in this case the lord had an interest in controlling sales.[65] And, like landlords during the Napoleonic Wars who forced enclosure as a means of renegotiating long leases when the value of land rose, the thirteenth-century lord wished to control subleasing that might deprive him of the advantage of the rising price of fresh leases. Postan concludes, however, that "the purpose of control was not to restrict, still less to destroy, the village market . . . [but] to profit from his villein's transactions." [66]

---

[64] Vinogradoff, *Villainage*, pp. 235ff. argues that this administrative convenience was important. He recognizes briefly the difficulty that subsequent exchanges would transform the system to one of consolidated plots, but dismisses it by appeal to the continuing strength of "the communal principle with its equalizing tendency."

[65] Postan's introduction to Brooke and Postan, *Carte Nativorum* p. xlvi.

[66] *Ibid*, p. xlviii. Compare Roden, in Baker and Butlin, *Field Systems*, p. 356.

From an early date villeins took advantage of the lord's willingness to permit transactions in land. That they did so is hardly surprising, in view of the changing amounts of land that a given peasant family would require over its cycle of youth and age or of poverty and prosperity.[67] Rosamund Faith, summarizing recent work on this phenomenon by herself and Postan, among others, argues that in open-field villages of the late fourteenth century, at least on the ecclesiastical estates whose records have survived in comparative abundance, "land changed hands rapidly and on a large scale. . . . The chief function of the manorial court began to be that of land-registry for the virtually free market in peasant holdings that had come into being." [68]

Even in the thirteenth century, Faith notes, "there is ample evidence of an active peasant land market," although she argues that the transactions at this early date, in contrast to the centuries of the Black Death and the decay of serfdom, were "predominantly small-scale, involving odd acres and plots, a process which only marginally affected the ownership and structure of the basic family holdings." [69] If scattered plots had no advantages to set against their inefficiencies, however, and if there was no continuing mechanism to scatter them, even such piecemeal purchases and sales of land would produce in time consolidated holdings, for a peasant would seize every occasional opportunity to buy plots contiguous to his existing ones and to sell plots far from them, or merely buy up land in one quarter of the open field. If he could not get exemption from communal rules of grazing and cropping, of course, consolidation might not be worth the considerable effort necessary to achieve it. Sometimes he could not, the difficulty being that the other commoners felt that his enclosure reduced the grazing left for their animals.[70] It is unclear why this was so, for, as was noted earlier, when each person's stint was proportionate to the amount of land he held in the open fields, withdrawal of some of it would have no effect on the

---

[67] Postan, *Carte Nativorum*, pp. xxxiv–xxxv; Thirsk, in Baker and Butlin, *Field Systems*, p. 260.

[68] R. J. Faith, "Peasant Families and Inheritance Customs in Medieval England," *Agricultural History Review* 14 (1966), 92.

[69] *Ibid*, p. 86.

[70] The roll of the manorial court of Aspley Guise, Bedfordshire in 1662, for example, has a long list of enclosers who are ordered to throw open their land (Fowler, *Pre-Enclosure Maps*, p. 34). Compare Ault, *Open Field Farming*, pp. 45–46.

remaining land available per animal. The difficulty may have been that stints were sometimes not proportionate to land held, but granted by virtue of having any holding in the common fields, of whatever size, or even having a certain house in the village, whether or not land was still attached to its ownership. An encloser who could continue to put out as many animals on the remaining open fields as he did before enclosing was clearly a menace. Be that as it may, mere consolidation had some advantage, and in some regions exemptions from communal rules were granted.[71]

That such favorable conditions did not by any means always result in enclosure is testimony to the existence of a motive for scattering other than initial egalitarianism. It is sometimes suggested, by what may be called the land-hunger hypothesis, that an active land market increases scattering, because a peasant would buy up scraps of land at every opportunity, regardless of their location; a similar suggestion is that he sold or granted bits of land to provide gifts for the church and for his friends, dower for his daughters, or prayers for his soul, leaving the recipients of the land with scattered pieces.[72] Occurring as they do in a context in which scattering is being criticized for its inefficiency, these suggestions have a serious flaw: free trade in land would enable peasants to achieve whatever pattern of holding they thought best for themselves, and if scattering was the result, then scattering, contrary to the premise of the argument, must have been considered to be desirable. If scattering was perceived by peasants as an evil, as it has been by most outside observers, then it was open to the peasants to reduce or eliminate the evil by mutually advantageous exchanges of land. The conclusion must be, in short, that one must either ignore the voluminous evidence of a peasant land market, or abandon the egalitarian theory of the persistence of scattered plots.[73]

[71] Thirsk, in Baker and Butlin, *Field Systems*, p. 260.

[72] Thirsk, *ibid.*, p. 268, uses this argument, as do many others.

[73] The Orwins are scornful of the egalitarian theory, labeling it the "schoolboy" theory and making the same point as the one made here, with less emphasis on the market mechanism involved (*Open Fields*, p. 2): "Why did the farmers . . . not occupy compact holdings . . . equalizing differences in the quality of the land, or in its accessibility, by adjustments in the respective sizes of the holdings or in the rent assigned to them?" Yet they too are puzzled by scattering, and arrive finally at an explanation based on community feeling, similar in spirit to the egalitarian theory.

Identical difficulties afflict another explanation of the scattering of plots, which replaced egalitarianism for a time, just as egalitarianism had replaced co-aration; namely, that they were scattered as a natural result of egalitarian distribution of new village lands acquired during the communal clearing of waste, each man who contributed equal effort to the common enterprise receiving a scattered and therefore equal holding. The seminal work on the subject, an article in 1935 by T. A. M. Bishop describing such a process in Yorkshire after the devastations of the Norman Conquest, emphasized that the clearings were not communal, but individual, a point that has sometimes been overlooked in subsequent presentations.[74] If the postulate of communal clearing is nonetheless adopted, the difficulties are merely pushed to a later stage. If a large area was involved in each clearing, and if the scattering of plots had no attraction other than its contribution to equality, it may be wondered why the land was not laid out in consolidated holdings, adjusting size to quality. If a small area was involved, making the process one of gradual accretions to the village land and a consequent gradual increase in the number of parcels held by each family, it may be wondered why exchanges of lands to consolidate holdings did not occur. And in fact they often did occur: otherwise it would be difficult to explain why peasants held their land in certain limited areas of the village, however scattered within these areas. In short, there must have been some recurring and rapid mechanism working against the tendency of a market in land and in other rights to eliminate inefficient arrangements of holdings, in which case it would be this mechanism, not communal clearing of waste or egalitarian feeling, that would be the cause of scattering.

Partible inheritance, by which a holding is divided among a number of heirs rather than passing as a unit to one heir or to one group of heirs working it in common, appears at first to be just such a mechanism. Its merits in providing a continuing rationale for scattering was recognized by Bishop, who made it the central element in his theory: furlongs "were originally cleared and cultivated by individuals," but were subsequently

[74] Bishop's article is "Assarting and the Growth of the Open Fields," *Economic History Review* 6 (1935). pp. 13–29, reprinted in E. M. Carus-Wilson, *Essays in Economic History*, Vol. 1 (London, 1954), to which subsequent reference is made.

"divided up by being shared among the heirs of the original assarters." [75] By 1964, when Joan Thirsk's article, "The Common Fields," stated the theory in full, the weaknesses of the alternatives had already made it the usual explanation of medieval scattering. It has long been the usual explanation for scattering in modern times. Folke Dovring, speaking of the nineteenth and twentieth centuries, concluded that "land fragmentation on the Continent has far from diminished in importance; on balance, it has worsened over the period dealt with here. This has been above all because of the increasingly consistent application of rules on free division of inheritance," that is, the rules embodied in the Napoleonic Code.[76] Bernard Binns, pointing out that free division of inheritance is a feature of Muslim and Buddhist law as well as of Continental law, reached a similar conclusion: "The most usual cause of excessive fragmentation may be briefly restated as the influence of a social structure that creates a too great demand for a limited area of land by a population completely dependent on the land under a system of private law and custom which encourages progressive subdivision, especially subdivision to maintain, by a meticulous similarity in each subdivision, a physical equality of shares in the original holding." [77]

To use this argument, a number of geographical anomalies must be explained. On a worldwide scale, the hypothesis must explain how it is that similar rules of partible inheritance or similar rates of population growth can yield dissimilar degrees of scattering. In the Gojjam province of Ethiopia, for example, partible inheritance is applied today in the most thoroughgoing fashion, with daughters as well as sons inheriting land from their mothers as well as from their fathers; in Germany during the Middle Ages, on the other hand, sons alone inherited land, and only from their father's line. Yet farms in the Gojjam province consist of few plots—something over four—by comparison with the ten or twenty effective plots and many more nominal plots of medieval open fields in Germany.[78] In England the chief

---

[75] Bishop, "Assarting," p. 35.

[76] Dovring, "Transformation of European Agriculture," p. 631.

[77] Binns, *Consolidation of Fragmented Holdings,* p. 18.

[78] The Ethiopian case is described by Allan Hoben of Boston University in an unpublished paper, "Social Anthropology and Development Planning: A Case Study in Ethiopian Land Reform Policy" (no date c. 1971); the German case is in Mayhew, *Rural Settlement,* pp. 27, 90, 131, 134, and *passim.*

anomaly is that partible inheritance prevailed not in the heartland of the open fields, the Midlands, but in the very region where scattering was least severe, namely, the Southeast.[79] Thirsk has suggested that partibility was more widespread than this at one time, and believes that at least in the East Midlands there is evidence of partibility causing scattering.[80] Yet in the five counties from Oxfordshire to Essex, in all of which open fields occurred, David Roden finds "no evidence of the large-scale fragmentation following partible inheritance," even in the thirteenth century.[81] In any case, to posit an original partibility that died out in later times is to sacrifice the chief merit of the argument: namely, that it gives a continuing rationale, generation by generation, for the persistence of scattered holdings, and is therefore partly immune to the criticism that a market in land would eventually rectify an inefficient system of agriculture founded in the distant past.

However these empirical difficulties are to be overcome, partible inheritance does at least appear in logic to imply scattering, if not exactly by the route that one would expect. A scattered holding could be formed only by joining parts of two or more initially separate holdings: if some of John Tailer's land passes by inheritance to his nephew, Richard Smith, who inherits land from his father as well, Richard will have a scattered holding, some plots being Tailer land and some Smith land. Partible inheritance was in the Middle Ages, as it is today in societies that practice it, usually a division of the patrimony among the sons. Customs that put daughters on an equal footing with sons appear to have been rare, and daughters acquired land—dowries did not usually consist of land—only in the absence of sons.[82] In

---

[79] Faith, "Peasant Families," esp. p. 84, reviews the evidence for this assertion.

[80] In "The Common Fields" and in her contribution to Baker and Butlin, *Field Systems.*

[81] In Baker and Butlin, *Field Systems,* p. 356.

[82] See Faith, "Peasant Families," p. 82, where daughters inheriting equally with sons is described as "an extreme form" of partible inheritance. Homans (*English Villagers,* p. 141) described dowers from fathers to daughters as "all in money, or houses, or livestock, or utensils, or clothes. This was probably the rule in the matter of marriage portions in the champion country of England. Dowers were not generally made in land, unless in the form of a grant of land for a term of years." Dower "at the church door," given by the groom to his bride as a guarantee of support should he die before she did, was in land, often a third share of the estate, but reverted to

the absence of any children, the holding was usually inherited by the brothers of the dead man, and in the absence of brothers by his sisters. Consequently, if all heirs in a village married and all families had at least one son in every generation, there would be no scattering. There would be no heiresses bringing land to their marriages, and no nephews or nieces of childless couples inheriting an uncle's land. That is to say, there would be no joining of initially separate holdings. Richard Smith, with two brothers, would inherit one-third of each of his father's thirty scattered plots, but would acquire no additional land from his marriage or from his uncles. He would have a smaller holding than his father (the penalty for being in a family with more than one son), but a holding with the same number of plots.

This reasoning belies the common assertion that rapid growth of population directly increases scattering through inheritance.[83] On the contrary, it would appear to reduce it. The two events that cause scattering under partible inheritance in its usual form—marriages that produce no sons and marriages that produce no children at all—are less likely, the faster the natural rate of increase of the population of a village. Marriages must produce more surviving children if population is in fact to grow, implying a lower frequency of childless or sonless marriages. And in the rare form of partible inheritance in which daughters inherit equally with sons, the rate of scattering is not affected one way or the other by the rate of population growth, for no matter how quickly or slowly population is growing, all women are heiresses who add the existing average number of plots per holding to their husband's plots, thereby doubling the average number of plots per holding with each passing generation. In short, the theory implies that the rapid population growth of the nineteenth and twentieth centuries or of the thirteenth and early fourteenth centuries would have had no direct tendency to increase scattering.

The usual growth of village populations before the demographic revolution was, of course, either slow or negligible, and under these circumstances partible inheritance can be a potent

---

the heirs of the dead husband at the widow's death or remarriage, and could not be sold (Homans, pp. 177–91).

[83] The writings of Joan Thirsk may be taken, once again, as the best of a large literature. On this point see Thirsk in Baker and Butlin, *Field Systems*, p. 268. The indirect effects by way of land hunger were discussed above.

force for scattering.[84] The best way to show that this is the case is to simulate the experience of a village with no population growth, inferring the rate at which initially separate holdings would be joined. Population growth, putting migration to one side in order to simplify the argument, depends on the distribution of completed family sizes. One distribution that yields no population growth and is consistent with what little is known about medieval population is shown in Table 2–1.[85] It is assumed here that everyone marries, that there are exactly a hundred males in each fresh generation of two hundred people, and *that all these take wives from within the village* (in regions of primogeniture, by contrast, the rule was "no land, no marriage" and many men had no land: this assumption cannot be used even approximately, therefore, to simulate the results of a rule of

Table 2–1.   A Distribution of Completed Family Size in a 200-Person Village that Yields 200 People with Each New Generation

Number of Children per Family	Number of Families	Number of Children Surviving to Marry from these Families
0	15	0
1	26	26
2	25	50
3	20	60
4	8	32
5	4	20
6	2	12
Total	100	200

primogeniture).   Because marriages with no children can be thought of as being no marriages at all, but merely pairs of

[84] Indeed, if there are enough marriages lacking sons, primogeniture can be a potent force for scattering as well, because the holding was usually divided among the daughters in the absence of sons (Homans, p. 123). A close study of such details of inheritance rules may provide a way out of the difficulty that the regions of England with the most severe scattering practiced primogeniture, not partible inheritance.

[85] The distribution is calculable, although not here calculated, from wills, in the manner of F. R. H. DuBoulay, *The Lordship of Canterbury* (New York, 1966), pp. 159–60. His sample of forty-five wills of men on the estates of the Archbishop of Canterbury in the fifteenth and early sixteenth centuries (a third of which, unfortunately for present purposes, were "gent." or "esq.") contains some 20 percent with no children and 32 percent with only one (compared with 15 and 26 percent in the example here).

unmarried men and women, this assumption is not critical to the result.

The first route by which partible inheritance creates scattering is by producing heiresses, who bring land to their marriages. Only in the absence of sons will daughters become heiresses. Thus, in the one-child families in the table, half of the 26 children will be heiresses, because the probability of a one-child family having no sons is .50. The probability of a two-child family having no sons is .25, and therefore 25 percent of the 50 children of these families will be heiresses. Proceeding in this fashion through all sizes of families yields a total of 35.8 heiresses on average (out of the total of 100 women to be married) in each generation. Since under partible inheritance all males in the village inherit land from their fathers, 35.8 percent of the 100 marriages will be heir-heiress marriages and the rest heir-non-heiress marriages. The heiresses bring the average number of plots per holding in the village (call it N) to their marriages, and their husbands bring another N plots. Therefore, the average number of plots per holding when the new holdings are formed will be $N^* = (.358)(2N) + (1.000 - .358)(N) = (1.358)(N)$. That is to say, the average number of plots per holding will increase on this account 35.8 percent per generation.

The other route by which partible inheritance creates scattering is through childless families, whose land reverts to the brothers of the husband on his death. In essence, the land of Edward Cadman, dying without children, reverts to his father's estate or, if Edward was an only child, to his grandfather's estate; this newly refreshed patrimony is then split among the heirs of his father or of his grandfather in the usual way. For the distribution of family sizes given in Table 2.1, the average number of children who are heirs for each family endowed with property and having children is 1.6.[86] If Edward Cadman's

---

[86] The calculations underlying this result assume that all the estates increased by Edward Cadman's death are shared by families that do in fact have at least one child. The assumption is surely justified at this remove: dropping it would only add other, more remote childless marriages to the calculations, and childless marriages are in any event uncommon in the distribution used here. The nature of the calculations can be made clear by considering a three-child family. There is a probability of 1/8 that such a family will consist of three sons (that is, three male heirs), 3/8 that it will consist of two sons and a daughter (two male heirs), 3/8 that it will consist of one son and two daughters (one male heir), and 1/8 that it will consist of

land reverts to his father's estate—that is, if Edward does have siblings (the probability of this event being .69 for the distribution of family sizes in the table, given that all the inheriting families have at least one child)—the new patrimony is subject to two applications of filtering down by inheritance before it reaches the next generation, and each successive application increases the number of heirs by a factor of 1.6 on average. If his land reverts to his grandfather's estate—that is, if he does not have siblings (the probability of this event being .306)—the patrimony is subject to three successive increases of the number of heirs by a factor of 1.6. Therefore, the total number of heirs in the next generation for each childless family is $.694(1.6)^2 + .306(1.6)^3$, or about 3. In the distribution of family sizes given in the table, 15 percent of the families are childless, which yields $3(15)=45$ holdings of N plots each descending indirectly to the next generation. By a similar logic as that for heiresses, therefore, the number of plots per holding increases on this account 45 percent in each generation.

In short, in each new generation of 200 people, 100 holdings of N plots are created by the 100 sons receiving a share of their patrimonies, 35.8 by the failure of male issue, and 45.0 by the failure of any issue, for a total of 180.8 holdings of N plots each. These are formed by marriage into 100 holdings, then, of $(1.81)(N)$ plots each on average. Partible inheritance under these circumstances increases the average number of plots per holding by 81 percent for each generation. In only six generations, or roughly 120 years, consolidated holdings of the first generation would be scattered in holdings of 35 nominal plots each. An effective number of plots of 10 or so would develop in only 80 years. The argument that scattering in the open fields can be explained by partible inheritance appears to be cogent.

Having examined the machinery of this argument in detail, however, it is now necessary to reject it—the first objection being that it is indeed mechanical. The difficulty is that once the machine has been set in motion, the hypothesis itself provides no brake on its motion. If partible inheritance is to explain scat-

---

three daughters (three female heirs). Weighting the number of heirs by the probability of its occurrence yields 1.875 heirs on average. A similar calculation is performed for each family size, and the results are weighted by the probability of occurrence of each family size (excluding zero-child families); this yields 1.6.

tering, it must also explain why scattering did not continue indefinitely, the 35 parcels of the example giving way to 81 percent more in the next generation, and so on, in a progression 35, 63, 114, 207, towards agricultural disaster. At the end of a long discussion of "The Role of Inheritance" at a conference held in 1951 on the subject of land tenure, during which one case after another of scattering in Europe and elsewhere was explained by appeal to a model of partible inheritance, Otto Schiller pointed out that the model is contradicted by the very fact to be explained, namely, *stable* amounts of scattering.[87] At the least, then, the model must be supplemented by some factor bringing the scattering to a halt, perhaps the increasing inefficiency of scattered plots, which becomes large enough at some point to make it worthwhile to incur the costs of consolidation through exchanging land.

The second, and more fundamental, objection is that the argument assumes that a holding is split among the heirs plot by plot, each of three brothers, for example, receiving one third of each of the thirty plots of their parents. If scattering itself had no advantages, however, one would suppose that the more sensible way of dividing the holding would be into three holdings of ten of the original thirty plots.[88] And if this method of dividing the inheritance is adopted, the model of scattering through partible inheritance collapses. If the number of plots is sufficient to permit equal portions, the division of holdings will never involve the division of individual plots. The total number of plots in the village as a whole will not, then, change from generation to generation. The average number of plots per holding will be equal to the unchanging number of plots in the village as a whole, divided by the number of holdings. If there is no population growth, the number of plots per holding will not change at all, regardless of what rule of partible inheritance is in effect—whether division among the sons or division among all the children. And if population is increasing, the average number of plots per holding will *decrease* at a rate equal to the rate of population growth.

This reasoning must be modified somewhat to take account of

---

[87] Parsons, *Land Tenure*, p. 573.

[88] Or "to settle the property on one of [two or more coheirs] or to sell it to another person," as was the practice in seventeenth-century Kent (Baker, in Baker and Butlin, *Field Systems*, p. 392).

an inability to divide a holding equally among the heirs when
the number of plots was inappropriate: a holding consisting of
one consolidated plot to be divided among three heirs, for example, would have to be split into three portions. Yet once a
modest degree of fragmentation had been achieved, well below
that actually observed in the English open fields, there would be
little further fragmentation on this account, and none at all if,
as seems reasonable, the slight inequalities of inheritances in
land were ironed out with direct payments in more fungible
assets, such as money or livestock. Even assuming that such
side payments were impossible, no more than one plot would
need to be split in each holding when the land passed to the
heirs; since any number of plots can be split into equal holdings
consisting of an integral number of plots plus some fraction of
a single plot.[89] In the hypothetical village constructed above,
whose population does not grow, there would be 100 such plots
(from the 100 holdings) to be split in each generation. The increment to the number of plots per holding would be the number of heirs per holding minus one: a holding of 10 plots with
three heirs, for example, would be divided into three holdings
consisting of nine of the original ten plus three thirds of the
original tenth plot, for a total of twelve rather than ten plots,
or an increase of two. Applying this reasoning to the hypothetical example constructed earlier, the average number of
heirs per holding being 1.81, 81 new fragments $(1.81-1.00=.81)$
would be created with each generation of heirs.[90] In other words,
supposing the land of the 100 families of the village to be consolidated to begin with, the number of plots in the village would
increase by 81 in each generation, in a progression 100, 181, 262,
and so on, and the average number of plots per holding 1, 1.81,
2.62, and so on. Such a mechanism could perhaps explain why a
consolidated holding was broken into three or four separate

[89] To simplify the analysis, it is assumed here that all holdings consist of
plots of equal size, or have at least one plot large enough to serve by itself
as a makeweight.

[90] This is the factor derived above by which the number of plots increases
in each generation under the simple model of partible inheritance. Incidentally, the most direct way of deriving it is to observe that the 85 families
(out of 100 total) that have children have on average 1.6 heirs, as was
shown earlier, and that the 15 who have no children have on average 3.0
heirs. Thus, there are $.85(1.6)+.15(3.0)=1.81$ heirs per holding on average
in each generation.

plots, but it cannot explain why it was broken into a dozen or more: it would take 14 generations with no reconsolidation— conservatively, 280 years—to reach the typical figure in medieval open fields of, say, 12 effective plots per holding by this route.

The issue, then, is whether each individual plot or the entire patrimony was divided among the heirs. A technique for resolving this issue has been applied to evidence from Gillingham, Kent in 1447 by A. R. H. Baker. Baker used a survey of the manor in that year to determine whether people with the same last name (presumably brothers or the widows of brothers, or perhaps paternal cousins) held contiguous plots. If they did, as he found was sometimes the case, it would suggest that each individual plot from the patrimony was divided; if they did not, as he also found was sometimes the case, it would suggest that the entire patrimony was divided.[91] Notwithstanding the ambiguity of this particular use, the method does provide a way of assessing the significance of the argument from partible inheritance. In Laxton in 1635, for example, the results are less ambiguous. Holders of land with the last name "Tailer" were the most common of the 45 or so last names in the Laxton survey, 14 Tailers having holdings ranging from ½ to 137 acres. Yet only 4 of the 14—Thomas Sr., Alexander, Hugh, and the Widow Tailer—had any contiguous plots in the open fields. Furthermore, the nominal plots held by these 4 that were contiguous to at least one of the others amounted to only 12.7 acres out of their total holdings in the open fields of 138 acres (excluding meadows and closes, as does the figure for contiguous plots), or only 9.1 percent of the total. Only two other families—Robert and Samuell Holbem, and John and Thomas Freeman—out of the 45 land-holding families (which included many families with multiple occurrences in the lists) held contiguous plots. The contiguous acreage for the Holbems was 1½ acres out of their total holdings (including closes) of 59 acres, and that of the Freemans 1½ acres out of 100 acres. Partible inheritance was certainly not a powerful force supporting the scattering of plots in Laxton, and yet the scattering persisted in full vigor for another three centuries after the survey of 1635.[92]

[91] A. R. H. Baker, "Open Fields and Partible Inheritance on a Kent Manor," *Economic History Review*, 2d ser. 17 (1964), 1–23, esp. pp. 8ff.

[92] All these figures are compiled from the book of survey and pp. 136–47 in the Orwins, *Open Fields*.

Until such methods are applied to a wide sample of English villages, we will not know whether individual plots in the open fields were split on inheritance frequently enough to provide a cogent explanation of scattering. One can, however, directly examine the logic of splitting. The usual rationale is that the splitting of individual plots was necessary to achieve perfect equality in the new holdings formed from the patrimony. As Thompson put it in explaining scattering in modern Greece, equality demanded the "punctilious apportionment of . . . land even at the price of excessive fragmentation." [93] Peasants accepted this Judgment of Solomon, it is argued, because, although costly, it was fair. At its root, then, the explanation of scattering based on partible inheritance, like the other explanations we have examined, depends on the premise that scattering was thought to be necessary to achieve equal qualities of holdings. And it is subject to similar objections, principally the objection that scattering is an inefficient way of achieving equality. In an atmosphere of mutual suspicion, to be sure, it might be difficult to divide the entire holding into new holdings without each heir claiming that another's was superior in some way. There is, however, an obvious solution to this difficulty, namely, to form approximately equal holdings without unwarranted scattering, and then to determine which heir got which holding by drawing lots. As was noted earlier, open-field villages commonly used this method in the annual allotment of meadow lands, and it was also used by villages in regions on the fringe of the open fields; in Scotland and in Russia, for example, where the plow-land itself was reallotted periodically. The method was hardly foreign to the peasant mentality. And if the modern Greek case can be used to support the assertion that sometimes division by lot was not in fact used, it can also be used to support the opposite assertion: in the village of Vasilika on the Boeotian plain, for example, this method is applied in a thoroughgoing fashion to the lands, the animals, the buildings, and the equipment of the patrimony.[94]

Finally, aside from all these preliminary difficulties, the argument from partible inheritance ignores the possibility of sub-

[93] Thompson, *Farm Fragmentation in Greece*, p. 36.

[94] Ernestine Friedl, *Vasilika, A Village in Modern Greece* (New York, 1965), pp. 60–64, "The Division of the Patrimony."

sequent exchanges of land. The historians of medieval agriculture in the southeast of England are especially sensitive to this point. Speaking of the tenure of land peculiar to Kent, "gravelkind," under which land descended by partible inheritance but could also be bought and sold with a minimum of the usual feudal restrictions, A. R. H. Baker argues that "the former produced fragmentation, but the latter made possible consolidation." [95] He is able to rationalize, therefore, the observed pattern in Kent of simultaneous fragmentation and consolidation: as F. R. H. DuBoulay put it, "the fragmentation of inheritance was liable to be changed or even reversed by the operation of the land market." [96] And as, over time, the markets both in land and in other products and factors of production in the open fields developed and became less expensive, the argument that inefficient arrangements could not long survive market erosion is strengthened.

Scattering as Behavior toward Risk

One explanation of the scattering of plots in the open fields that does stand up under scrutiny is that scattering reduced risk.[97] Although he did not marshal the evidence for the point, and leaned towards an explanation of scattering in terms of communal solidarity, Marc Bloch is exceptional among historians of the system in emphasizing the force of avoiding risk. The consolidation schemes encouraged by French governments in the eighteenth century, he argued, were frustrated not only by the conservative and distrustful attitude of the peasantry, but also by their concern "to reduce exposure to agrarian accidents . . . to a minimum by working plots scattered over the whole terrain." If the heavy wheeled plow of the open fields could explain the extreme length of plots in regions in which it was used, risk aversion could explain their extreme narrowness, and therefore their large number, even in regions in which a lighter plow was used: "If the plots were dispersed . . . everyone had

---

[95] Baker, "Open Fields and Partible Inheritance," p. 19.

[96] F. R. H. DuBoulay, "Partible Inheritance in Medieval Kent," unpublished manuscript, p. 18, quoted in Baker, "Open Fields and Partible Inheritance," p. 20.

[97] What follows is a radical condensation of a long paper on the subject, available on request, "English Open Fields as Behavior towards Risk."

some hope of avoiding the full impact of natural or human disasters—hailstorms, plant diseases, devastation—which might descend upon a place without destroying it completely." [98] Bloch's argument is occasionally echoed in the work of economists and, more commonly, of anthropologists. In Bangladesh (then East Pakistan) in 1970, farmers "were strongly opposed to consolidation since fragmentation of land holdings was their prospective protection against loss of crops due to natural disasters," especially flooding that would leave high land (a mere six to ten feet above the rest) untouched.[99] Scattering of plots by the Amhara farmer of Ethiopia "is highly desirable, . . . for by providing him with fields of different qualities it enables him to diversify his crops and reduce the risk of total crop failure." [100] And one can find testimony that the desire to avoid risk caused scattering in a wide variety of other anthropological studies—of the Hopi Indians, of the Karugu in Tanzania, and of the peasants in southwest Switzerland.[101]

In the English case the explanation passes the first and most elementary test applied to the explanations discussed above, namely, scattering does follow from its premises. The object was to hold a diversified portfolio of locations. The land of England is notoriously variable, even over the two square miles or so of the typical village, in underdrainage, in slope, in soil structure and chemistry, and in exposure to frost, sun, and wind, each type being sensitive in a different way to each different pattern of weather over the farming season. A part of the village with sandy soil on a rise would shed excessive rain, while one with clay soil in a valley would hold the scanty rain of a dry season; a place open to the wind would grow wheat likely to lodge if there were high winds and rain at harvest time, but free of mold in a generally wet year, while a sheltered one would be relatively immune from windy disasters, but less dry and more moldy on that account; and one plot could be hit—to name a few more of the risks from which an English peasant would want insurance—

[98] Bloch, *French Rural History*, pp. 233, 55.

[99] John W. Thomas (Development Advisory Service, Harvard), personal correspondence.

[100] Hoben, "Social Anthropology," p. 34.

[101] Melville J. Herskovits, *Economic Anthropology* (New York, 1952), p. 363, citing work by Beaglehole, Lowie, and Forde on the Hopi; Beidelman, *The Karugu*, p. 18; and Robert M. Netting, "Of Men and Meadows: Strategies of Alpine Land Use," *Anthropological Quarterly* 44 (1972), 134.

by flooding, fire, insects, birds, rust, rabbits, moles, thieves, hail, and wandering armies—while another close by would go free. Furthermore, a year of high prices for wheat could be a year of low prices for oats and barley, adding a price risk to the yield risk, and consequently a peasant would scatter his holdings among the three fields of the village. Under such circumstances, in short, it behooved the peasant to hold many types of land, reducing the variability of his income from year to year, albeit (in view of the inefficiencies of tiny scattered plots) at the cost of a smaller average income. The inefficiencies of the open fields were premiums on an insurance policy in a milieu in which agricultural yields were low and unpredictable, and in which the costs of a shortfall—at best crushing debt or malnutrition and its associated diseases, at worst starvation—were high.

These ideas can be given a precise expression. A peasant dividing his A acres into N plots, each of which had a variance of yield of σ^2 and a correlation of yield from year to year with all the other plots of R, would achieve a variance for his entire holding of $\frac{A^2\sigma^2}{N}[1+(N-1)R]$. That is, the larger N is, the lower the variance. The larger N, however, would reduce the average yield: the yield is at a maximum when the holding is consolidated into one large plot (N = 1), easy to visit, to guard, to work with massive implements, and the yield is at a minimum when the holding is scattered into many tiny plots (N = 100, say). A convenient mathematical form for this notion is that the expected total yield of a holding is $Ac\left(\frac{A}{N}\right)^\epsilon$. The parameter ϵ measures the inconvenience of small plots (more precisely, it is the elasticity of yield with respect to the average size of plots, A/N) and the parameter c measures the productivity of the tools, techniques, land, and labor in agriculture. The peasant sacrifices expected total yield from his land in exchange for a lower variance of the total yield by increasing the number of plots, N. Let r be the ratio at which he is willing to sacrifice bushels of expected yield (or, when prices are introduced into the analysis, shillings of expected income) in exchange for one bushel squared (that being its units) lower variance. It follows that the best N he can choose is

$$N=\left[\frac{r\sigma^2(1-R)}{\epsilon c}\right]^{\frac{1}{1-\epsilon}}A$$

The equation is in accord with common sense. When ϵ is small (as it was), and $1/(1-\epsilon)$ therefore close to 1, it is easy to see that the equation asserts that the best N will be larger, the larger are the valuation of insurance (r), the variance of yield on a typical plot (σ^2), and the acreage of the holding (A), and the smaller are the correlation among yields in the village (R), the inconvenience of small plots (ϵ), and the productivity of agriculture (c).

The equation is also in accord with the evidence. In particular, when the values observed in medieval English agriculture for the variables on the right-hand side of the equation are inserted into it, the equation produces the observed number of plots. The detailed proof of this surprising assertion is too involved to present here, but the logic of the result is straightforward enough. Consider, for example, a 25-acre holding, one-third of which lies fallow each year (A = 16.7), that was broken into a dozen effective plots (N = 8, because 4 of the 12 lie fallow), and that on consolidation would have experienced a rise in productivity of 8 percent (well below the value observed in the enclosure movement of the eighteenth century). It can be shown that these data imply an ϵ of around .02 and a c near 1.0 (when output per acre is taken to be 1.0, to set the scale). It can also be shown (chiefly from the records of medieval demesnes and of modern experimental farms) that on such a holding R = .3 and σ = .6 (when, again, output per acre is 1.0). It can be shown, finally, that r must have been in the neighborhood of .02. These estimates together imply a best N of 8.3 effective plots or so, startlingly close to the observed value of 8. The closeness is not especially significant. What is significant is that at, say, only 3 plots, there is a net advantage in having more plots, and at 20 this advantage has long been offset by reduced productivity. The explanation in terms of risk aversion predicts correctly not only that scattering would have existed, but that it would have existed to the approximate degree that, in fact, it did.

The explanation passes the second test as well: it is not as vulnerable to erosion by market exchange as are the alternative explanations. Whereas other explanations must contend with the ample evidence for markets in grain, labor, grazing rights, oxen, and land, the market for insurance was poorly developed. A modern farmer can hedge against price risks by selling forward in organized commodity markets, but even he does not usually have available an insurance contract for hedging against yield risks. The peasant in an open-field village had available still fewer market arrangements for insurance, which drove him, the argument avers, to insure himself by scattering his plots. Apparently (given their absence), markets in insurance were expensive, and so the device of scattering, so costly in output foregone, was protected from market erosion.

Some care should be taken to use a wide definition of "insurance." Even in the most primitive agricultural economies there are available, at least potentially, devices for spreading risk that need not entail scattered plots, as when one peasant buys a share of another's crop. Peasant partnerships in land were, in fact, common in the areas of partible inheritance, which may be one reason why these places (East Anglia, for example),[102] contrary to the usual argument that partible inheritance causes scattering, had from an early date less scattering than the Midlands. Where extended families prevailed (the Balkan *zadruga* or perhaps the subdivisions of the Celtic clan), these could provide insurance without scattered plots—at the cost, to be sure, of shirking by some members of the family. Common charity among neighbors could provide insurance as well, although the volume of sermonizing on charity in the Middle Ages is no doubt testimony to its scarcity. And just as the relationship of peasant with peasant could provide protection against risk, so too could the relationship of tenant with landlord, for the landlord might share the risk of variations in yield (and the rewards for bearing the risk) by extending loans in bad years (at the cost of bad debts), or by entering into sharecropping arrangements with his tenants (at the cost of supervision), as he did in parts of France. Sharecropping was not unknown in England, although it appears only fleetingly in the records because it had no status in feudal law.[103] In short, the evidence is mixed, but it may be concluded tentatively that in most circumstances scattering was a cheaper form of insurance than the available alternatives.

Finally, the explanation in terms of risk aversion passes the

---

[102] See Miller, *Abbey and Bishopric of Ely*, pp. 130, 134, speaking of freeholds in Norfolk and the Isle of Ely in the thirteenth century.

[103] Eric Kerridge, in *Agrarian Problems in the Sixteenth Century and After* (London, 1969), p. 52, gives examples from the seventeenth century, some in open field regions.

test of consistency with the timing and extent of open fields and enclosures. The Midland clays were always more sensitive to weather than the free-draining sands of eastern England; it is not surprising, then, to find the Midlands slower to enclose. The peasants of the southeast and perhaps of the coast generally, involved from an early date in the diversified economy of London and the northwest coast of the Continent, faced broader and therefore more stable markets for their crops than did peasants farther inland, and could diversify their personal portfolios more easily outside of agriculture; it is not surprising to find their lands enclosed early—if, indeed, they were ever open. Nor is it surprising to find enclosure spreading from the sixteenth century on, as wider areas were brought into the network of national specialization, or as the security of property and the depth of the local capital market increased.

In fact, to return briefly to the formal model, each of the terms in the equation for the best number of plots moved, on the eve of enclosure, towards reducing that number. The variability of yields, σ, was reduced from the seventeenth century on by the introduction of disease-resistant grains, by the control over drainage represented by floating meadows, and by more reliable crops for feeding animals. As the variability fell, the uniformity (R) rose, as did the average yield (c). These changes in technique and in the direction of investment, furthermore, often increased the inconvenience of small plots (ϵ): small plots made it necessary to engage in cumbersome negotiations with one's neighbors to float a meadow; and they made it more difficult to specialize in the rearing of livestock, as was permitted by the availability of cheaper fodder. Finally, the rise in income and the wider opportunities for diversification outside of agriculture reduced the value of diversifying inside it (r).

The interpretation of scattering as behavior towards risk, then, has much to commend it. It does not rely, as do the alternatives, on an assumption that peasants adopted unnecessarily inefficient means of achieving their objectives. Nor does it rely on an assumption that chief among those objectives was equality. Finally, although much remains to be done in testing its applicability to the history of English open fields in detail, it agrees with the grosser facts of that history. If the interpretation survives further tests, the history of the open fields will need rewriting, as a history not of simple villagers driven by motives of communal solidarity, but of calculating farmers driven by motives of survival in conditions of extreme poverty and extreme uncertainty. And the romantic version of English agricultural history, so long under scholarly attack—of communities of peasants whose love of equality permeated even their economic affairs, wrenched from the soil by the new and grasping forces of market capitalism—will need further rewriting.

Part Two

PRIVATE PROPERTY AND ENCLOSURE

3

The Economics of Enclosure: A Market Analysis

DONALD N. MC CLOSKEY

The Great Metamorphosis and Its Historians

"If in the agrarian history of Europe there is one really striking transformation," wrote Marc Bloch, "it is the one that took place in the greater part of England, from about the beginning of the 15th century up to the early years of the 19th—namely the great enclosure movement. . . . Everything about this great metamorphosis catches and holds our attention."[1] So it does, and everything about the age of parliamentary enclosure that consummated it has caught and held special attention. Making all due allowances for the continuity of enclosure from century to century—the continuity of history is an easy theme, for it is usually a true one—the special place of the last century of enclosure in the attention of historians is fully justified on many counts, among them the statistics on the share of England's land enclosed after 1700.

The statistics, to be sure, are flawed for many reasons: the detailed records relate to enclosure by private act of Parliament alone, and the area enclosed by agreement, which was very large, must be inferred as a residual; the base point for the residual must be uncertain estimates by contemporaries of the area open or enclosed before the age of parliamentary acts; some few of the acts, indeed, especially before 1760 or so, merely confirm earlier private agreements; how to treat the enclosure of waste lands, even when they are catalogued separately in the parliamentary

[1] *Land and Work in Medieval Europe: Selected Papers by Marc Bloch*, translated by J. E. Anderson (New York, 1969), p. 49.

records, is conceptually difficult, especially during the massive extension of cultivation in the Napoleonic Wars; even within a nominally open-field village a substantial portion of the acreage in 1700 may have been "anciently enclosed," and it is uncertain in many cases whether or not this acreage was included in the enclosure awards. For some counties the uncertainty of earlier estimates made by Gonner, Slater, and Gray before World War I on the basis of aggregate parliamentary records, travellers' accounts, and other national sources,[2] has been narrowed by local history in the style of J. D. Chambers and his students. The importance of voluntary enclosures, to take an early example, was confirmed in 1932 by Chambers' own finding that in eighteenth-century Nottinghamshire, 41 *percent of the land was enclosed by voluntary agreement, against* 25 *percent with parliamentary sanction.*[3] Until all the counties of England are treated in similar detail, however, or until a proper random sample of the histories of enclosure in the 8500 or so parishes of England is collected, the precise statistical dimensions of the last century of the enclosure movement will remain obscure. Nonetheless, through the statistical haze one can discern its crude outlines: out of the 24 million acres of useful land in England (excluding Wales), some 6 million acres were enclosed by parliamentary act and, much more speculatively, perhaps 8 million acres by private agreement after 1700.[4] That is, at least half the agricultural land

---

[2] E. C. K. Gonner, *Common Land and Inclosure* (London, 1912; reprinted with an introduction by G. E. Mingay, London, 1966); Gilbert Slater, *The English Peasantry and the Enclosure of Common Fields* (London, 1907); H. L. Gray, *English Field Systems* (Cambridge, Mass., 1916).

[3] J. D. Chambers, *Nottinghamshire in the Eighteenth Century* (London, 1932), p. 149. These figures refer to 1700–1800. Twelve percent of the land area of Nottinghamshire was enclosed before 1700, and 22 percent remained unenclosed in 1800.

[4] The acreage of agricultural land, including arable, meadow, pasture, and woods, is taken from the testimony of W. Couling to the Select Committee on Emigration (1827), quoted in Lord Ernle, *English Farming Past and Present*, 6th ed. (Chicago, 1961; a reprint with introductions by G. E. Fussell and O. R. McGregor of the 5th ed., 1936), p. 503. It agrees with the estimate for 1688 of King, quoted on the same page. The acreage enclosed by act is the estimate of F. Clifford in *A History of Private Bill Legislation*, Vol. 1 (London, 1885), p. 495. The acreage enclosed by agreement is an estimate (or, more candidly, a guess) by Gilbert Slater in a review of the Hammonds' *The Village Labourer* in *The Sociological Review* 5 (January 1912), 63–65. It is meant to apply only to the eighteenth century, and might be taken, were its foundation in fact indisputable, as a lower bound on the acreage enclosed by agreement over the entire period, 1700 to the present.

of England was enclosed in the eighteenth and early nineteenth centuries.

Such statistical proofs of the importance of eighteenth-century enclosure have not gone unchallenged. Eric Kerridge, estimating that only a quarter of the land remained to be enclosed in 1700 (leaving a still smaller share to be enclosed by the parliamentary procedures that became popular in the second half of the century), can stand as the most persuasive representative of the view that "the hoary fable of the supreme importance of parliamentary enclosure should be relegated to limbo." [5] Kerridge's estimate, however, includes Wales, as the one here does not. Furthermore, when we map out his evidence by farming region, it appears that on his own reckoning about 45 percent is the correct figure for England alone. The share of land still to be enclosed in 1700 is in any case a low estimate of the more relevant figure—output or employment on such land—because the land of the Midlands (where by all accounts the open-field system survived longest) was intensely cultivated. It might be argued that there is direct evidence of earlier enclosure on a large scale, especially in the sixteenth century, when, to recall another set of hoary fables, sheep ate men. There seems to be no compelling reason, however, to reject Edwin Gay's calculation (as many historians nonetheless have, following Tawney in this) that under 3 percent of the cultivated land of England was enclosed from the middle of the fifteenth to the beginning of the seventeenth century.[6]

The eighteenth century, then, in the second half of which Parliament added broad powers of compulsion to the tools available for dismantling the open-field system, is the preeminent century of English enclosure. In the eighteenth century agriculture was still a large part of English income, and one might expect that the spectacle of a large part of the nation's productive apparatus being transformed by enclosure would have inspired elaborate historical inquiries into its causes and its consequences for efficiency. Yet the literature on enclosures, like the literature on open fields, passes lightly over causes, and emphasizes the effects on equity to the neglect of the effects on efficiency. An emphasis on equity rather than efficiency, and a lack of curiosity

[5] *The Agricultural Revolution* (London, 1967), p. 24.
[6] E. F. Gay, "Inclosures in England in the Sixteenth Century," *Quarterly Journal of Economics* 17 (1903), 576–97.

about the causes of enclosure, was to be expected, perhaps, in the pamphlet war among contemporaries, but it was carried forward in the nineteenth century by British scholars such as Thorold Rogers and Arnold Toynbee, who were puzzled by the decline of the yeoman; and by continental scholars such as Wilhelm Hasbach and Hermann Levy who, viewing the scene from the perspective of agricultural societies with a large class of peasant landowners, were fascinated by the dichotomized English system of masters and men, and by the barbaric way in which it was achieved.[7] The barbarism was brought to the center of the stage by the Hammonds in *The Village Labourer*, first published in 1911.[8] Much of the literature on enclosures since then has concerned itself with rejecting or supporting their implied political message, and the great bulk of it has adopted their definition of the historical issue involved. Historians of the old and the new systems of agriculture have treated efficiency as a matter of improvements in agricultural technique, such as new crops and new methods of drainage, or of improvements in marketing. Changes in agricultural organization within the village have been discussed in detail in relation to changes in the social classes of rural England, but not to changes in output. Thus, when W. G. Hoskins describes peasant land sales in Wigston Magna, Leicestershire, in the late sixteenth century, he asks questions about the distribution of property by class, and not whether the inefficiencies of the open-field system were altered by the sale and exchange of plots; when he discusses the village's enclosure in 1764–66, his questions again concern the weight of various social classes in the proceedings and the impact of enclosure on their strength in the community, not whether enclosure affected the efficiency of agriculture.[9]

This is not to say that the effects of agricultural organization and reorganization on equity should be ignored—they are of

[7] Marx's chapter 27 in *Capital* (Vol. 1) is, of course, the *locus classicus*. W. Hasbach, *A History of the English Agricultural Labourer* (London, 1908) and H. Levy, *Large and Small Holdings* (Cambridge, 1911) used the pamphlets as sources intensively. It is therefore not surprising that they, like many other historians of enclosures before and since, fell into the mental categories of the pamphleteers, categories primarily of equity, not efficiency.

[8] J. L. and Barbara Hammond, *The Village Labourer*, 4th ed. (London: 1927), reprinted for British Publishers Guild (London, 1948), 2 vols., is the edition to which subsequent reference is made.

[9] *The Midland Peasant. The Economic and Social History of a Leicestershire Village* (London, 1957), pp. 115–30, 247–60.

interest in their own right; we will see too that understanding the distribution of the spoils is essential for estimating their size and their causes. But the emphasis on equity has produced an unbalanced view of the enclosures of the eighteenth century. Aside from summary judgments based on scant evidence that they were "important" or "unimportant," there have been no estimates of the impact of enclosures on national income, and little inquiry into the reasons they occurred.[10] Reorientation is in order.

Cutting the Gordian Knot: The Costs of Enclosure

The gradual decline of the riskiness of farming can explain, perhaps, why the dissolution of the English open fields occurred chiefly in the seventeenth or eighteenth century, rather than in the thirteenth or fourteenth. It cannot explain without supplement, however, why enclosure was especially intense in the second half of the eighteenth century, or why the intensity of enclosure varied from year to year or from village to village. For purposes of explaining the persistence of the open fields over many centuries it is natural to emphasize, as did the previous essay, the power of markets to erode inefficient arrangements. Each separate use of the market reduces the inefficiencies, and the summation over centuries of these small steps can be expected to eliminate them entirely. For purposes of explaining as relatively brief an episode as the enclosure movement of the late eighteenth century, however, it is natural, in contrast, to emphasize the limits on the market's power to erode inefficiency—the limits, that is, imposed by the costs of engaging in markets. Here there is no passage of centuries to reduce the costs to insignificance, only sixty years of intense effort in leaping over them. The open fields could be propped up for many years (if not for many

---

[10] The unsettled state of thinking on the issue of efficiency can best be illustrated by contrasting the opinions on it rendered in two useful summaries of the recent literature on agricultural change in the seventeenth and eighteenth centuries: E. L. Jones, "Editor's Introduction" in his *Agriculture and Economic Growth in England 1650–1815* (London, 1967), and Peter Mathias' discussion in his *The First Industrial Nation* (London, 1969). Jones: "Novel systems of husbandry thus account much more for the new 'responsiveness' of agricultural supply than do improvements in agrarian organization" (p. 12); Mathias: "Enclosure was quantitatively the most important single movement affecting land use because it made all other innovations possible" (p. 73). Neither looks deeply into the causes of enclosure.

centuries) when it was expensive to exchange land. Clearly, then, the costs of changing from one system of agriculture to another belong in an account of the enclosure movement.

The costs of enclosing open fields were tightly bound to the legal methods for achieving enclosure. If one reflects that enclosure was a mere reassignment of property rights in land, it becomes plain that there is no purely technological reason that an enclosure should have been costly; if imposed from without with no regard for equity, it could have been achieved overnight. By a stroke of his pen a conqueror can achieve the result of eliminating inefficiencies in an earlier social arrangement, on which a society of laws must spend many years and much labor. If two identical villages are enclosed, one by expropriation and the other by mutual agreement constrained by laws, and if voluntary and legally guaranteed exchange of services is permitted in both villages after the enclosures, the allocation of resources, aside from the effect of the distribution of income itself on allocation, will come to be identical in both. Technology and the amounts of physical and human resources available in the two villages being the same, the most efficient method of organizing agriculture in the two will be the same, and, consequently, whatever the distribution of ownership of the resources available, the owners will deploy them in the same way. The only difference in the aggregate incomes of the two villages, without regard to the distribution of incomes within each, will be that the enclosure under the law will have been a good deal more expensive. Legal constraints on enclosure for the purpose of preserving equity, then, had the effect of making enclosure more expensive than it need have been.

The legally constrained agreements in question varied in complexity and solemnity from temporary exchanges of land among a few peasants to full parliamentary enclosure. Each of the alternative routes to enclosure had its own special array of costs, increased by the notoriously clotted state of the law of land and contract before the reforms of the late nineteenth century, and, therefore, even as parliamentary procedures cheapened and became the prevalent form, the older alternatives continued to be used in many enclosures. Aside from the seizure of wastes by the lord of the manor under the Statutes of Merton and Westminster (to begin at the beginning), under the common law perhaps the oldest and most natural procedure was consolidation by the piecemeal exchange of land, each landowner slowly building up a more and more consolidated holding until enclosure was accomplished. An alternative to this method was a simultaneous agreement to exchange lands. Simultaneous exchange had the advantage over piecemeal exchange that it more rapidly achieved whatever gains were to be had from cultivating consolidated plots, but it had the disadvantage that it required one large transaction rather than several small ones. A peasant who entered such an agreement was taking the risk that his new and unfamiliar holding would be substantially worse than his old one, a risk he did not face if he built up a new holding slowly, testing each piece of land as it was bought.[11]

For either method, the common law put up many obstacles. One obstacle, which, it has already been argued, must on the whole have been relatively minor, was that the lord of the manor had the right (except by local custom in Kent) to permit or to prevent the exchange of lands among those who held lands of him.[12] It is not immediately obvious why this would have slowed enclosure, especially when the lord-vassal relationship acquired the character of a landlord-tenant relationship, as it did increasingly in early modern times; after all, the landlord stood to gain, or at least did not stand to lose, from any increased efficiency of his tenants. Yet the power to permit implies the power to charge a fee for permission, and when he was not constrained by tradition to charge only a nominal sum, the lord of the manor could extract some or all of the mutual gains from exchange for himself, and thereby discourage it.

The law raised obstacles to the exchange of land in more direct ways, as well. For the larger freeholders, the ingenuity of the

[11] The analysis of the choice between slow and rapid methods of enclosure is probably more complex than this simple argument suggests. This argument is at least capable of being rejected by the facts—it would be rejected, for example, if villages with uniform land were no more likely to enclose by simultaneous agreement than villages containing many different types of land; and if a rise in the interest rate had no tendency to increase the share of enclosure accomplished by rapid methods (the higher interest rate would tend to raise the relative advantage of direct, brief methods of enclosure).

[12] The Orwins, with many other students of the open fields, put a good deal of emphasis on this legal obstacle to enclosure, attributing the enclosed state of Kent to its absence there. *The Open Fields* (Oxford, 1938), p. 68. But see the discussion of the land market in the previous essay.

common law lawyers in protecting a family's estate for all time from the depredations of profligate members of the line had by the eighteenth century reversed earlier tendencies towards the freer alienation of their land. For the copyholders, the ambiguity of their title long discouraged them from exchanges, the more so as they shared with the freeholders, large and small, the burdensome expenses imposed on transactions in land by the law and by the lawyers.

Some enclosures would not be worthwhile if they could not be accomplished rapidly by simultaneous agreement, extinguishing communal rights in an entire village, and under the common law simultaneous agreement to enclose was difficult to achieve. All those who owned rights of any sort in the open fields had to be brought into the agreement for it to be a legally binding contract, for the law quite reasonably required that a man's consent be obtained before the community could meddle with his property. What was perhaps less reasonable was that another part of the common law simultaneously made it impossible for some— minors, for instance, or those with life interests in entailed estates—to give their consent. In the seventeenth century men eager to enclose increasingly called on the other law of England, equity, to help them out of this difficulty.[13] Much of the county of Durham, and parts of Lancashire and Cheshire, for example, were enclosed in the seventeenth century by recourse to the Courts of Chancery or Exchequer, where the agreements were cast in the form of a collusive suit by one party in the village against another. In 1666 a bill in Parliament affirming the binding force of enclosures ordered by equity courts failed, however, and this route to enclosure was partially blocked. In most counties it had only infrequently been traveled, and in the middle of the eighteenth century statute law—parliamentary procedures for enclosures—superseded it even more completely than the older common law procedures of voluntary agreement.[14] In 1795, a select committee remarked of collusive actions in Chancery, in its *Report on . . . the Means of Promoting the Cultivation . . . of the Waste* (p. 24), that "from the difficulty and expense attending such proceedings, they have been long disused." We do not know

[13] The most detailed study of this method of enclosure is E. M. Leonard, "The Inclosure of Common Fields in the Seventeenth Century," *Transactions of the Royal Historical Society* n.s. 19 (1905), 101–46.

[14] *Ibid.*, pp. 232–33; Gonner, *Common Land*, pp. 55–57.

whether the degeneration of proceedings in Chancery (on their way to the horrors of Jarndyce and Jarndyce),[15] or whether the opening of an alternative and cheaper route through statute law was responsible for the abandonment of the route through equity. In any case, increasingly during the eighteenth century enclosure became a matter for special parliamentary action.

A parliamentary statute to enclose had two related advantages over the procedures available under either equity or the common law. It had, first, the advantage of special solemnity and permanence deriving from its constitutional power to override much of the other law. A very early act, of 1725, confirming the enclosure of a village in Leicestershire, was sought because, in the words of the bill, "the Agreement of the said Parties to the said Articles can [not] be made absolutely valid and effectual to answer the purpose thereby intended without the Aid of an Act of Parliament."[16] Indeed, if the full force of the statute was not directed at extinguishing the pattern of rights prevailing under the open fields, not even a parliamentary act was capable of making good an enclosure. A case in point was described in the Buckinghamshire report to the Board of Agriculture. An agreement in a village to exchange lands was ratified by Parliament, but despite this precaution, apparently because the new allotments were not properly fenced and were therefore not fully legal enclosures, one of the villagers was able to destroy the agreement fourteen years later, quite legally, by putting his flock of sheep out to graze in the traditional season on his neighbors' fields planted in clover.[17] The full parliamentary procedures, then, were necessary to prevent one man from imposing on his

[15] Dickens wrote in *Bleak House* (Cambridge, Mass., 1956; first pub. 1853), pp. 2–3: "This is the Court of Chancery . . . which gives to monied might the means abundantly of wearying out the right; which so exhausts finances, patience, courage, hope; so overthrows the brain and breaks the heart; that there is not an honourable man among its practitioners who would not give— who does not often give—the warning, 'Suffer any wrong that can be done you rather than come here!' . . . Jarndyce and Jarndyce drones on. This scarecrow of a suit has, in course of time, become so complicated that no man alive knows what it means."

[16] "An Appeal for confirming Articles of Agreement . . . in the Township of Norton-juxta-Twisscross," quoted in G. R. Fay, *Great Britain from Adam Smith to the Present Day* (New York, 1928), p. 233.

[17] James' and Malcolm's *General View of the Agriculture of Buckinghamshire* (1794), p. 29, quoted in T. E. Scrutton, *Commons and Common Fields* (Cambridge, 1887), p. 120 and in Ernle, *English Farming*, p. 162.

fellow villagers a revival of the open fields whenever it suited his immediate convenience.

The second advantage of a parliamentary statute was that it eliminated the power formerly vested in each villager to block the agreement at the outset. The rule of unanimous agreement in the procedures under common law and equity would not have created difficulties if there had been market competition to set the terms of the agreement. If Jack and Tom fall to quarreling about the price at which to exchange wheat for leather, they have only to reflect that the other could easily take his business elsewhere, and to ascertain what price the other could get elsewhere, to end the quarrel and strike a bargain. Under the circumstances created by the rule of unanimity in an agreement to enclose, however, the sponsors of an enclosure of a village had nowhere to turn if one of the owners of common rights proved recalcitrant. That one man could veto the enclosure, both by virtue of the legal requirement that he agree, and by the threat he posed to the new arrangement by the potential exercise of his ancient and legal rights if the rest of the villagers concluded an enclosure without his agreement. With each man placed in a position of monopoly with respect to the village as a whole, each had an incentive to bargain for a large share of the spoils of enclosure in exchange for his vote in favor of it, and the amount he could in principle extract was limited only by the total gain to the village as a whole from accomplishing it. Under these circumstances, it is apparent that only universal altruism or strong social pressures to conform could prevent the negotiations from breaking down. And this obstacle to agreement would obtain even in the unlikely event that no proprietor, whether from a rational calculation of his advantage or from mere perversity, was opposed to enclosure.

The parliamentary procedures, in contrast, required only a majority, and therefore broke at once the monopoly power of the parties to an enclosure. The usual majority required in the early years of the procedures was four-fifths of the land of a village, voted by its owners. This formula was itself significant. Under both the common law and equity, an owner of any rights in the open fields, a category that included tenants owning long leases (sometimes even those owning yearly leases) and cottagers owning minor rights, such as that of gathering the gleanings of the harvest, was considered an interested party whose veto was final.[18] It was the elimination of the veto itself, however, that was the chief advantage parliamentary statutes had over procedures available in case law. The amount a man could extract from the sponsors of an enclosure was now limited by the substitutability of others' votes for his in achieving a majority. The transfer payments—or, in more direct language, bribes—required for an agreement, and the negotiating costs of fashioning an agreement, were sharply reduced at a stroke. As Blackstone put it, speaking of the tangle of legal restraints on property developed in equity or common law, "in these, or in other cases of the like kind, the transcendent power of parliament is called in, to cut the Gordian knot." [19]

Why the cutting of the knot was delayed until the middle of the eighteenth century is unclear. The power of Parliament was less than "transcendent" under the Tudors and Stuarts, and, coupled with the opposition of the executive on social grounds to the supposed depopulating effects of enclosure, this may have limited the use of the parliamentary route for a time. The first enclosure of arable land by act appears to have been in parts of the manors of Marden and Bodenham, Herefordshire, in the fourth year of James I, but the experiment was not repeated until the end of the seventeenth century, and did not become commonplace until the 1760s.[20] The tightening grip of the landed classes on the machinery of Parliament under the first two Georges very probably had much to do with the gradually increasing popularity of parliamentary enclosures in the years before 1760. Perhaps, too, increasing costs of the procedures under the common law and equity, as these bodies of law became progressively more complicated, and as the legal profession tightened its monopoly on their use, made the parliamentary route more attractive. The very fact that the parliamentary route became more popular indicates that for some villages, at least, its costs (including costs of delay and recalcitrance) were lower. In any case, with the intervention of Parliament in the middle of the eighteenth century, the effective costs of enclosure did fall substantially and suddenly.

---

[18] Leonard, "Inclosure," pp. 236–38.
[19] William Blackstone, *Commentaries on the Laws of England,* 8th ed. (1778), 2, 344–45.
[20] Leonard, "Inclosure," p. 232; Gonner, *Common Land,* p. 58

The effect of the fall in costs would not have been felt uni-formly, but would vary with the character of the village con-templating enclosure. Villages with many men, for example, would experience a greater fall than small ones. A large village is much more likely to contain at least one recalcitrant villager than a small one. The introduction of a majority rule sharply reduces the importance of the difference in population, at least as it relates to the likelihood of failure in a vote on the enclosure. (Indeed, if the likelihood of recalcitrance is low, whether from the great profitability of enclosure, from altruism, or from fear of reprisal, the likelihood of failure to get a majority in a vote might be expected to be slightly higher for a small village than for a large one.) [21] One would expect on this count, therefore, to see more large enclosures after Parliament perfected its methods than before.

The effective population of villages was reduced in parlia-mentary procedures by the limitation of the franchise to free-holders, but it probably remained true, as it had been before, that larger villages were on balance more costly to enclose. To be sure, some costs—the fixed element in the fees to commis-sioners and, in the case of parliamentary enclosure, fees to parliamentary officials as well—were constant for any enclosure, of whatever size, and therefore lower per acre for a village of many acres. When such a village had many men, a large popula-tion would lead on this account to lower, not higher, costs. And some costs were probably more or less constant per acre, such as surveying and fencing. The costs of locating and buying out (or coercing) recalcitrants, however, would be higher in a large village than in a small one, as would be the costs of arbitrating the welter of claims. A larger bargain, involving more bargainers, is more expensive than a smaller one. In any event, historians

---

[21] The reasoning here is somewhat naive, leaving to one side as it does the question of how the shift from unanimity to majority will affect the strategic behavior of the villagers in casting their votes, but it is nonetheless suggestive. It depends on a binomial model of the probability of ayes and nays. If the fraction of recalcitrants is as low as 15 percent among the population of voters in all villages, under the rule of unanimity villages of ten voters will on average vote to enclose 20 percent of the time they are presented with the choice, but villages of twenty voters only 4 per-cent of the time. On the other hand, under the rule of a four-fifths majority, the ten-voter villages (assuming for simplicity equality in the holdings of each voter) will achieve enclosure 82 percent of the time and the twenty-voter villages 83 percent of the time.

have long assumed that the balance of costs favored small villages; it has served as part of the explanation, for example, of the early enclosure of the West country, the Welsh border, and Scotland, all regions of small villages, in sharp contrast with the Midlands.[22]

The costliness of large size is significant here because it is one of the characteristics easiest to measure among those that affect the costs of enclosure (among them the social strength of the large landowners, the native cooperativeness of the freeholders, the extent to which the village was already partly enclosed, and the cost of fencing in the region). A full study of the causes and consequences of eighteenth-century enclosure would use village size as one of the explanatory variables in a statistical explanation of how costs varied from one village to the next. "Between the idea/ And the reality/ Between the motion/ And the Act/ Falls the Shadow," says the poet, and in this exploratory essay the idea of isolating influences on the costs and benefits of enclosure statistically must remain in the shade. The bare idea, however, disciplines thinking. The costs of physically altering the face of the village varied from region to region with the cost of materials and labor—fencing costs, for example, would vary with the cost of hedging materials or of stone for walls. The specialists in the services of enclosure, such as lawyers, surveyors, and commissioners, were no doubt mobile over wide areas, but to the extent that they were not, some variation in their contribution to costs could be measured. This could be combined with the other variables to help disentangle the effects of costs from the effects of benefits on a region's rate of enclosure.

The extent of old enclosure in a village is still another such variable, for the closer a village was to an enclosed state, the less complex and expensive would have been the completion of the enclosure. In the limiting case in which a very few landlords

---

[22] See, for example, H. G. Hunt, "The Chronology of Parliamentary Enclosure in Leicestershire," *Economic History Review*, 2d ser., 10 (1957), 265–72: "[W]here the number [of proprietors] was small the surveyor had less work to do in making their 'particular survey' and the commissioners had fewer claims to deal with, the redivision of the land was much less complicated, and the expense of obtaining the proprietors' consents would also normally be less." Cf. Gray, *English Field Systems*, pp. 153, 407; Chambers, *Nottinghamshire*, p. 142; J. H. Clapham, *An Economic History of Modern Britain*, Vol. 1 (Cambridge, 1939, reprinted 1964), p. 23; Hoskins, *Midland Peasant*, p. xiv; F. G. Emmison, *Types of Open-field Parishes in the Midlands*, Historical Association, Pamphlet no. 108 (London, 1937), pp. 11–12.

owned all the land in the village, voluntary enclosure under the common law would have been cheap. The records of parliamentary enclosures are less informative on this point than they are on the size of villages, but, like information on the size of villages, information on the extent of old enclosure has the advantage that it applies to a specific village rather than to a more or less vaguely defined region of the country; when it is available it provides a more delicate instrument with which to dissect costs.

There are good reasons, then, to expect that the costs of enclosure varied across regions at any one time, and it is perhaps possible to exploit this variation to separate the influences on the rate of enclosure of a village's costs from that of its benefits. There are equally good reasons to expect that the costs varied through time in any one region. In both voluntary and parliamentary enclosures, for example, the costs of surveyors and fencing would vary from time to time. The most important variable cost, however, arose because all enclosure involved present costs in expectation of future benefits. That is to say, the rate of interest is relevant to the costs, as to the returns, of an enclosure.

T. S. Ashton put great emphasis on variations in the rate of interest as a cost factor in the explanation of the cyclical variations of investment in the late eighteenth century, and his observation that there is a good correlation in particular between the percentage yield on consols and the rate of enclosure has become a standard point in the literature. Later discussions have generally raised Ashton's point only to reject it, for two reasons. The first—given credence, indeed, by the way Ashton expressed himself in framing the hypothesis—is that landlords sponsoring an enclosure did not always have to borrow money or, what is equivalent, to sell assets to finance it.[23] The possibility of financ-

---

[23] T. S. Ashton, *An Economic History of England: The 18th Century* (London, 1955), p. 41: "The large proprietor might meet this [large expenditure on an enclosure] out of his own resources. . . . But this would usually involve a sale of assets. . . . Or he might seek a mortgage." In commenting on Ashton, J. D. Chambers and G. E. Mingay, in their *The Agricultural Revolution* (London, 1966), p. 82, use his admission of the possibility of self-financing to attack the relevance of the rate of interest: "Now it is possible that much enclosure was financed by borrowing on mortgage, and it is true that [the interest rate would then be relevant]. . . . But it seems probably . . . that a large proportion of enclosure, especially that promoted by large landlords, was financed not by borrowing but out of current estate income."

ing the enclosure out of current income, however, is irrelevant
to the issue of the importance of the interest rate. If the sponsors
chose to spend current income on an enclosure they would not,
it is true, face future outlays of cash for interest payments; but
they would forego future income by choosing not to invest in
alternative projects, projects whose rate of return can be expected to run parallel with the yield on consols. Self-financing,
in other words, has an opportunity cost, and this cost is proportional to the prevailing rate of interest.

The second reason for objecting to giving the interest rate
a central place in a discussion of the costs of enclosure also rests
on a misapprehension of what is germane to the decision to
invest. The objection is that the correlation between the yield
on consols and the rate of enclosure breaks down during the
Napoleonic Wars, a great many enclosures being undertaken
then despite a high interest rate.[21] Ashton pointed out that even
if the rate of interest rose, the sharp rise in the relative price of
agricultural products, which would increase the benefits of enclosure, could well have offset the rise in costs. But a more
fundamental response is available, namely, that it is not the
money rate of interest that measures the real opportunity cost
of an investment, but the rate of interest corrected for the expected rate of inflation in the general level of prices. A commit-
ment to pay £5 per year in future years for the right to use
£100 now is a very satisfactory arrangement indeed for a bor-
rower if the rate of inflation is 5 percent a year, for the real
rate of interest in that case is zero: since his £100 of borrowed
capital will be worth £105 next year from the effect of inflation
alone, he can meet the interest payment next year by selling off
£5 of it and can keep whatever real fruits the capital bears for
himself as a clear gain. From their experience in the 1790s
Englishmen had very likely come to expect a rate of inflation in
the neighborhood of 2 or 3 percent per year by 1800, and in
fact such an expectation was confirmed by the experience of the
next decade.[25] Under these circumstances the money rate of in-

24 Chambers and Mingay, p. 83, make this point, as do others who have
commented on Ashton's hypothesis.
25 Rates of annual growth within this range are characteristic of the price
indices of E. B. Schumpeter and E. W. Gilboy, and of A. D. Gayer, W. W.
Rostow, and A. J. Schwartz from 1790 to 1799, given in B. R. Mitchell,
Abstract of British Historical Statistics (Cambridge, 1962), p. 469-70). The

terest of around 5 percent corresponded by 1800 to a real rate of
interest of 2 or 3 percent, which is at least as low as the rates
prevailing during the earlier burst of enclosures in the late 1760s
and early 1770s. In short, the interest rate does appear on the
face of it to have been a significant influence on the costs of enclosure. It does belong with other variables, therefore, in a statistical study of the variation of those costs over time.

The costs of interest foregone, fencing, surveying, and so on,
were incurred in any enclosure, whether it was achieved by act
of Parliament or by agreement under the common law. Little is
known—or, given the paucity of records, directly knowable—
about how the other costs of enclosure, such as legal fees, organizational effort, and bribes to recalcitrants, varied from year to
year in proceedings under the common law. For parliamentary
enclosures, however, voluminous records of many of these costs
were generated by the legal and customary requirements of dis-
closure to public view of each step in the proceedings. The course
of the debate over the bill to enclose a particular village, the
large fees paid to parliamentary functionaries (although some,
no doubt, were secret), and the terms of the act that finally
emerged are more or less knowable from the records of Parliament itself and from published reports of its activities. In a few
cases the daily account books of the commissioners, appointed by
name in the act to supervise the enclosure, have survived. At
least before 1800, at about which time the custom of providing
it appears to have died out in some places,[26] a detailed statement
of the costs of surveying, the expenses of the commissioners' activities (including ample provisions of wine to speed their de-
liberations), and the like was often appended to the final award
of new properties. And the award itself, sometimes containing a
detailed field map or a statement of allotments of property by
the amount of each and the name of the recipient, survives in the
county record office or the parish chest for about two-thirds of the
villages enclosed by act.[27]

---

very high prices of the first two years of the new century are excluded from
these calculations purposely, to achieve estimates biased to the low side.
The rates of growth from 1802 to 1813 are similar in magnitude.

[26] Cf. W. E. Tate, "The Cost of Parliamentary Enclosure in England
(with special reference to the County of Oxford)," *Economic History Review*
2d ser., 5 (1952), 264, on Oxford and Lincolnshire.

[27] The estimate of two-thirds surviving is W. E. Tate's, in *The Parish
Chest: A Study of the Records of Parochial Administration in England,*

The records suggest that the parliamentary procedures were progressively simplified and cheapened. The expenses of the commissioners were a substantial portion of the recorded total, and it is therefore significant that the number of commissioners specified in the acts fell during the second half of the eighteenth century from a dozen or so to three or four.[28] An act of 1773 (13 Geo. III. c.81) reduced and standardized the majority required to set in motion the parliamentary procedures from four-fifths to three-fourths of the number and value of the acreage in a village, voted by its owners. The acts came to specify the date by which the award was to be promulgated, in order to meet the frequent complaint that the commissioners, taking on the responsibility for too many enclosures at once, dallied at their work on each and prolonged the period of uncertainty between the act and the award. The commissioners gradually became a professional class, and could be expected to have become more proficient as their experience broadened; the name of any given commissioner recurs many times in different acts.

The experience of Parliament itself, particularly in the first period of substantial parliamentary enclosure in the 1760s, no doubt had a similar cumulative effect on the ease with which a bill was made law.[29] It is true that not until 1836 (6 and 7 Wm. IV. c.115), well after the period of massive enclosure, was a truly general act for enclosure passed, under which the special appeal to Parliament for each was eliminated. Before that time each act of enclosure begged special exception from the law of property, as did each act of incorporation from the law of contract before the Joint Stock Companies Act of 1856. Repeated attempts were made during the seventeenth and eighteenth centuries to pass a general enclosure act, but Parliament chose to retain its power of detailed intervention into each of the thousands of private bills. As Maitland put it, "The mass of the statute law made in

---

3d ed. (Cambridge, 1969), p. 271. Some six thousand awards resulted from the forty-seven hundred or so parliamentary acts.

[28] W. E. Tate, *The Enclosure Movement* (New York, 1967), published in England as *The English Village Community and the Enclosure Movement* (London, 1967), p. 49.

[29] Gonner (*Common Land*, pp. 63, 65) disputes this, arguing from the fullness with which one Henry "Horner" described the procedures both inside and outside Parliament in 1761, that they were perfected before this time. The matter awaits statistical resolution. Incidentally, the author of *An Essay on the Nature and Methods of Ascertaining Specifick Shares . . .* was Henry Sacheverell Homer, and his book was first published in 1766.

the 18th century is enormous . . . [and] bears a wonderfully empirical, partial and minutely particularizing character. In this 'age of reason,' as we are wont to think it, the British parliament seems rarely to rise to the dignity of a general proposition." [30] The so-called General Enclosure Act of 1801 (41 Geo. III. c.109) was resisted by fee-takers inside and lawyers outside Parliament, as well as by the Church of England, which suspected that the value of its tithes was threatened by the act. Its passage was a victory for the improving spirits on the Board of Agriculture, but only a partial one: the requirement that each enclosure be approved by Parliament was retained. Among other simplifications, however, the framers of the bills for enclosure could now draw on forty standard clauses, and affidavits were now accepted in lieu of the physical presence of the signatories to a petition. The act provides a test of the sensitivity of the rate of enclosure to changes in its cost, and, true to expectations, a spurt of enclosures, particularly of waste lands, followed it. Each of the improvements in parliamentary procedures can be examined in this fashion, inserted together with the other influences on costs into a statistical analysis of their progressive reduction.

It may seem peculiar, however, to argue that the costs of parliamentary enclosure were reduced, in view of the plain evidence in the literature on enclosure that the expenditure per acre rose dramatically in the late 1780s and after. In Warwickshire, whose experience was by no means unusual, J. M. Martin found that the public costs—that is, the costs of securing the act, paying the commissioners and surveyors, and fencing the allotments of the tithe owners—rose sixfold from the earliest to the latest enclosures, and especially after 1790.[31] An adequate allowance for the inflation of the Napoleonic Wars would reduce the sharpness and extent of the rise somewhat, particularly as the commissioners and other specialists in enclosures would have reaped economic rents from the increased demand for their services.[32] Yet the rise would still be substantial.

---

[30] F. W. Maitland, "English Law" in *Encyclopedia Britannica*, 11th ed.

[31] J. M. Martin, "The Cost of Parliamentary Enclosure in Warwickshire," *University of Birmingham Historical Journal* 9 (1964), reprinted in Jones, *Agriculture and Economic Growth in England*, to which subsequent reference is made. Compare W. E. Tate, "The Cost of Parliamentary Enclosure," and H. G. Hunt, "The Chronology of Parliamentary Enclosure in Leicestershire," *Economic History Review*, 2d ser., 10 (1957), 265–72.

[32] Homer remarks in his *Nature and Methods*, 2d ed. (1769), that enclosures

As useful as this evidence is in providing a quantitative *explicandum* for an inquiry into the determinants of costs, however, it is not directly relevant to discovering how the cost curve moved. As Martin and the others who have documented the rise in costs have pointed out, the recorded costs rose not because an enclosure of given complexity had become more expensive, but because progressively more complex enclosures were undertaken as they became more profitable.[33] There is direct evidence of this increasing complexity in the widening interval between the date of the act to enclose and the actual award. In Tate's list of parliamentary enclosures in Nottinghamshire, for example, it is around two years in the 1760s and 1770s, but rises to six years by the 1790s and 1800s.[34] Each year's delay contributed directly to the real costs of enclosure by reducing the incentive to conserve one's soil, which on the morrow might become someone else's, and by a variety of other costs of disorganization. These costs of delay, incidentally, neglected in studies of the costs of enclosure, could be quite large. With yields of, say, 2½ quarters of wheat an acre on lands in such crops constituting half the acreage in any year, and prices of forty shillings a quarter, a loss of output from the overworking of land soon to be enclosed of as little as one-fifth for one year would add ten shillings to the other costs, which Martin reckons at something over forty shillings an acre before the inflation of the Napoleonic Wars. What is to the point here, however, is that a long interval is indicative of a complex, and therefore, costly, enclosure: an enclosure of a large village with many land owners and other claimants to ancient rights, and with many parcels of land severely scattered and intermingled. A typical enclosure in 1810 was not the same as one in 1770. Whatever the relevance of the rising cost to issues of equity, in particular to the issue of the burden on the small landowners, then, it is not relevant to the issue of how the costs of parliamentary procedures changed. To make progress on the latter

---

"have the temporary Effect of raising the Markets of the several Parties employed in carrying them into Execution" (p. 109).

[33] Cf. Martin, "Cost," pp. 133ff; and Hunt, "Chronology," p. 269: "Many enclosures involving very high costs were postponed till later in the eighteenth century . . . when market conditions were more favourable."

[34] W. E. Tate, *Nottinghamshire Parliamentary Enclosures, 1743–1856*, Record Series of the Thoroton Society, Vol. 5 (1935), *passim*. Compare Martin, "Cost," p. 135, where he speaks of an interval of one year during the early enclosures in Warwickshire rising to four or five years in the late eighteenth and early nineteenth centuries.

issue one must have information on the changing costs of an enclosure of unchanging specifications, and the observed costs do not directly provide this information; the observed increase in costs is a reflection of the increase in benefits, not of an increase in costs for a given enclosure.

A Plain Enough Case of Class Robbery

The argument being developed here speaks of costs and benefits, and presupposes that when benefits exceeded costs for a project to enclose, enclosure was undertaken. An enclosure, however, was not an investment by one man incurring the costs and receiving the benefits himself, but an investment by an entire community. The redivision and improvement of the community's land was regulated by a few commissioners, who acted together, in the words of Arthur Young, as "a sort of despotic monarch, into whose hands the property of a parish is invested, to recast and distribute it at pleasure among the proprietors; and in many cases without appeal." [35] True, he went on to observe, "if more cautious methods were resorted to . . . the work of an enclosure would be spun out through half a century," as indeed it was in the case of enclosure by gradual purchase and sale. Yet bold methods, wielded by commissioners appointed by the lord of the manor and owners of the tithes, presented ample opportunities for the redistribution of wealth from the poor to the rich. A bill in Parliament sponsored by a group of the larger landowners of a village, enacted into law by what in this period may be considered an executive committee of the landed class, and carried to its conclusion in an award formulated by commissioners who might reasonably be expected to be the agents of that class, had great potential for damaging the men trapped in its machinery. E. P. Thompson's pronouncement on this issue could serve as a motto for the many contemporaries and historians who have felt that the damage was severe: "Enclosure (when all the sophistications are allowed for) was a plain enough case of class robbery." [36]

[35] Arthur Young, *A Six Months' Tour Through the North of England* (London, 1770), Vol. 1, 226, quoted in the *General Report on Enclosures* to the Board of Agriculture (London, 1808), p. 61. The Act of 1801, by the way, contained provisions for appeal, among other restrictions on the power of commissioners.

[36] E. P. Thompson, *The Making of the English Working Class* (New York,

This judgment on the equity of enclosure would require no comment in an inquiry into its effects on efficiency and its causes were it not that the incentive to enclose could have been affected, at least theoretically, by the distribution as well as by the size of the spoils of enclosure. Wilhelm Hasbach's observation on the contemporary and retrospective assessments of enclosure is to the point here: "Those who look at the matter from the stand-point of production will not see that the economic changes have their ethical and social dangers. And the representatives of the ethical and social side fail to recognize or estimate the economic advantages." [37] This is true, and a balanced examination of either issue requires not a mere alternation of the two perspectives, setting the loss in equity against the gain in efficiency, but a mingling of them. The large landowners may have gained more from enclosure than the small, yet the increase in efficiency may have permitted all classes to gain something. Similarly, enclosure may have at all times and places raised the efficiency of agriculture, yet the method of sharing the costs and benefits may have varied from year to year and from village to village in such a way that an expectation of equal social benefit in two villages would produce an enclosure in one and a continuation of the open fields in the other. In other words, a mere shift in the distribution of the costs and benefits, with no change in their size, could have prompted an enclosure.

An ideally equitable enclosure would be one in which villagers were assigned shares of land of value proportionate to the value of their rights in the open fields. No one could be made worse off under such an arrangement, assuming that the costs of enclosure left a net social gain in efficiency to be distributed among the new property owners. The critics of enclosure have in mind two deviations from this ideal, and it must be asked whether these would have so shifted the burden onto the poor as to alter substantially the size of the net benefits accruing to the rest of the community.

The first is that those with vague rights in the open fields sometimes lost all claims on the fruits of enclosure; a valuable right was extinguished with no compensation. Squatters on the

1963), p. 218. See also the Hammonds' account of Arthur Young's disillusionment with the way enclosure affected the poor (*Village Labourer*, Vol. 1, 78–80).

[37] *English Agricultural Labourer*, p. 162.

commons and waste of the village were often treated in this fashion, and on occasion some part of the usufruct of the commons and waste owned informally by other classes in the village also vanished through disallowance of the claim before the commissioners, to reappear as part of the wealth of landowners generally. The question is whether in a substantial number of cases enclosure would have failed to go forward had equitable compensation for the loss of these ill-defined rights been required. It is difficult to answer this question. Ill-defined rights are, by the very meaning of the phrase, illusive and uncountable, consisting in this case of the right to take a few bits of fallen wood from the waste, or of the advantage of a location close to the commons on which a cow could be grazed. Without an elaborate accounting here, it is perhaps justifiable to draw the provisional inference from the descriptions of these rights in the literature that the answer to the question is, no: enclosure would not have been retarded by just compensation, because before enclosure the rights were of low total market value, however large a part they formed of the meagre living of those who claimed them.

The second deviation from the ideal, about which the interminable historical debate on the decline of the English yeoman has centered, is that the shares of land allotted in lieu of common rights were too small to bear the heavy costs of enclosure. It is generally agreed that allocation of land itself to small and large owners was reasonably equitable, and that therefore, aside from minor variations in the quality of soil, the small man might expect his just share of the increased efficiency from consolidated holdings.[38] To acquire the land, however, he was committed by law to fence it at his own expense within a specified short interval after the enclosure award. With an agricultural technology that depended heavily on the raising of livestock together with crops, an enclosure without fencing to prevent the livestock from wandering onto another man's land would be pointless. The cost of fencing per acre of allotment would vary inversely with the number of acres fenced; to be perhaps overly precise, assuming roughly similar rectangular plots, it would vary in-

---

[38] Note that it is land *owners*, large and small, who figure in this half of the tale of class robbery. At another remove, though worthy of further study, is the issue of whether new economies of scale in farming, unexploitable in open fields, reduced the value of small *tenants'* capital and managerial skills relative to that of large tenants.

versely with the square root of the number of acres in the plot. The cost of fencing per acre would be about three times larger for a plot of ten acres than for one of a hundred acres.[39] Fencing was a substantial part of the total costs of enclosure. J. M. Martin, in his largely successful attempt to rebut W. E. Tate's contention that enclosure costs were too low to damage the small landowners, puts them at half of the total, the rest being public expenses (fees for lawyers, commissioners, surveyors, and parliamentary officials, costs of new roads, and so forth) incurred up to the time of the award.[40] The costs of fencing weighed heavily, then, and especially heavily on the recipients of small allotments, who were driven by their disproportionate burden to a choice between a large mortgage on their property, if they could get it, and sale.

Although consistent with the alternative view that the small

[39] For rectangular plots with the longer side ϕ time larger than the shorter side, and assuming that only two sides were fenced by one person, trivial manipulations yield the expression

$$K \frac{1+\phi}{\sqrt{\phi}} \left(\frac{1}{\sqrt{A}} \right)$$

for the cost per square foot of a plot of A square feet, where K is the cost per linear foot of fencing (which is assumed constant over all plots, and which includes hedging and common drains as well). The result is insensitive to deviations from similarity in the rectangles of large and small plots, as can be shown by inspecting the ratio of the expressions for two dissimilar plots (that is, for two plots with different values of ϕ). Nor is it sensitive to reasonable deviations from rectangularity, although a more elaborate expression is needed to show this. The formula here is a special case of the formula developed in the previous essay to exhibit the effects of the number of plots (N) on fencing costs per holding (namely, the special case $N = 1$, expressed per acre of holding). It should be noted that new holdings, particularly large ones, were not completely consolidated. This would somewhat reduce the contrast in fencing costs between large and small holdings.

[40] Martin, "Cost," especially p. 141, where he collects his estimates of 22 shillings per acre for the public expenses and 24 shillings per acre for fencing, hedging, and drains on the edges of allotments. Martin's estimate of fencing costs is based on the cost of fencing tithe allotments (which were a public expense). It can be confirmed by inserting the costs of fencing per foot (about 6d., with sizeable regional variations: see Hammonds, *Village Labourer*, Vol. 1, 93n.) into the formula developed in footnote 39, simultaneously lending credence to the formula itself. The average allotment in Warwickshire enclosures was about 63 acres; J. M. Martin, "The Parliamentary Enclosure Movement and Rural Society in Warwickshire," *Agricultural History Review* 15 (1967), 23. For a square plot ($\phi = 1$ in the formula), this implies that the two sides fenced would total 3320 feet, which would cost 1660 shillings (at 6d. a foot), or about 26 shillings per acre enclosed on the average allotment (close to Martin's estimate of 24 shillings).

landowners' hurt was negligible, the relatively small amount of complaint against parliamentary enclosure in the eighteenth century (contrasted, say, with the uproar against common law enclosure in the sixteenth) is not decisive evidence. In 1912, the year after the first publication of the Hammonds' impassioned attack on the equity of enclosure, Gonner remarked with much truth that "when the gravity and delicacy of the task undertaken by the [enclosure] commissioners is considered, the existence of complaint against them is not astonishing. It is rather a matter for wonder that the complaints were not far louder and more universal," [11] a theme to which W. E. Tate later directed his prodigious labors on the records of enclosure.[42] Yet, to use Albert Hirschman's vocabulary, industrialization, improved transport, and a general quickening of the pace of economic life in the late eighteenth century would have provided the poor with opportunities for "exit" from a village newly hostile to their interests that would have made an attempt to acquire "voice" relatively less attractive, however much parliamentary enclosure damaged them.[43] That voluntary enclosure occurred alongside parliamentary enclosure in the late eighteenth century is also consistent with the rosier picture of the fate of small landowners, although again it is hardly decisive, for similar reasons: the damage could be great, yet the opportunities for complaint limited by the coercive powers of the larger landlords, and the opportunities for escape relatively attractive.

There is, however, a less easily corrected flaw in the picture of expropriation, which depends on exactly when during a parliamentary enclosure a small landowner would choose to sell out (or, if stronger language seems warranted, was compelled to sell out by his economic circumstances: the language differs but the observed behavior is the same). If he sold out only after he had fenced his plot, his wealth would indeed be reduced by the inappropriateness of small plots to the new circumstances of

---

[41] Gonner, *Common Land,* p. 82.

[42] For example, his "Members of Parliament and the Proceedings upon Enclosure Bills," *Economic History Review* 12 (1942), 68–75; "Parliamentary Counter-Petitions During the Enclosures of the Eighteenth and Nineteenth Centuries," *English History Review* 59 (1944), 392–403; "Opposition to Parliamentary Enclosure in Eighteenth Century England," *Agricultural History* 19 (1945), 137–42; and "Members of Parliament and their Personal Relations to Enclosure," *Agricultural History* 23 (1949), 213–20.

[43] As suggested by Eric Jones in the concluding essay of this volume.

agriculture. The large landowner who bought his plot but had not paid the onerous costs of fencing it (a sunk cost, and therefore no part of its price) would be better off, and in anticipation of this result would have been more eager for enclosure. In the extreme case, of course, a fenced plot of three roods might be of little use to him. He would have to tear down the fences and build new ones to incorporate such pitiful scraps into a profitable farm. This, however, would merely reduce the price he and the other landowners would be willing to pay for the scraps, adding a gratuitous social loss of having to rebuild the fences to the burden on the poor.

If the small landowner sold his allotment before he fenced it, however, the result is very different. The price that the larger landowners would be willing to pay would in this case be the present value of the net return from future crops minus the amount that it would cost to fence the purchased land along with their other land. Since the land is more productive in an enclosed than in an open state, the price the large landowners would be willing to pay (and would be compelled to pay if they compete with each other) would in fact be above what they would be willing to pay for the same land before enclosure. There is in fact a good deal of evidence that landowners did possess this minimum degree of foresight. F. G. Emmison's summary in 1937 of the evidence for Bedfordshire is a good example of how narrowly the best historians have missed the significance of the evidence. He reports that a "cursory examination of Bedfordshire documents revealed evidence in eight parishes of strong buying of strips and common-right cottages by the chief owners during the years before enclosure," interpreting it as an effort to avoid opposition to enclosure by early purchase. It does not occur to him that the evidence is also consistent with a successful attempt by small landowners on the other side of the market to avoid the hurt of enclosure by early sale. He reports, too, that "shortly after enclosure some of the survivors undoubtedly sold their allotments," arguing that the costs of fencing and the fixed costs of commissioners weighed heavily on the small men. Although he does not recognize that exactly when they sold out "after enclosure" is critical, he nonetheless sees that the motives to sell out included "the enhanced monetary value of newly

allotted land over open-field land." [44] If the large bill for fencing and commissioners did not take the small landowners by
surprise, in short, their land would have participated in the net
benefits of enclosure, and the final result of parliamentary enclosure would have been the same as enclosure by agreement.

There may not have been inequities in parliamentary enclosure, then, making it difficult to argue that the opportunity of
the rich to impose inequities on the poor, rather than the gain in
efficiency to be achieved, motivated enclosure. Still, small landowners sometimes opposed enclosure, and one may ask why. It
is occasionally suggested that open-field agriculture conferred
unique advantages on them, such as more than their share of
manure on their land when livestock grazed in common. It is
uncertain that small landowners did in fact have a lower ratio of
livestock to land than large, as is assumed in this particular
argument. If they valued the manure highly, they could in any
case invite their neighbors to feed their livestock on the newly
enclosed plot. And opposition by the poor to enclosure is a
world-wide phenomenon, even in agricultures less dependent on
animal fertilizers than English agriculture in the eighteenth
century. A more general explanation of their opposition is an
alleged reluctance to part with particular pieces of land, farmed
by their fathers and their grandfathers before them. This behavior can be given a narrowly rational interpretation. A small
landowner entering an agreement to enclose exposes himself to
the risk of getting a worse allotment than he had before, as was
argued earlier, even if there is an overall increase in efficiency,
and if the mechanism for reallotment has on average no systematic bias against small owners as a class. Given the administrative limits to precise adjustment of the new allotments to the
value of the old, he might prefer to bear those ills he had
(namely, the inefficiencies of open-field agriculture) than fly to
others that he knew not of. A man with a larger portfolio of
land, by contrast, would be exposed to less risk, even aside from
any direct influence over the terms of the enclosure that he might
have as a rich member of the village. And, in accord with the
reasoning of the previous essay, the small landowner might op-
pose forced consolidation of his land that would leave him
exposed to accidents of the market and the weather.

[44] Emmison, *Types of Open Field Parishes,* pp. 10–11.

Even if enclosure inflicted damages on small landowners, however, the advantage to the large landowners from inflicting them can be shown to be so small that it seems unlikely that the rate of enclosure was substantially altered by the potential for doing so. This is the decisive point. The facts on which the point rests are by no means novel. In 1928 George Fowler, noting that in a village in Bedfordshire enclosed in 1804, 98.3 percent of the cultivated land was owned by large owners, remarked that "the reader may well wonder where can be the large class of small-holders whose lamented disappearance is attributed to the Parliamentary Enclosures. The answer is that, in Oakley, as in many other places, he had almost vanished before these Enclosures were made." [45] In a recent survey of research into the issue over the last half century, Gordon Mingay estimates that by 1780 only 11 to 14 percent of the land was owned by the small owner-occupiers of Sweet Auburn.[46]

J. M. Martin's statistics on 125 parliamentary enclosures in Warwickshire can illustrate the point in more detail.[47] Allotments under 50 acres were fully 71 percent of the total number, and their average size was only 12.7 acres; that is, a sizable majority of the landowners were small, and from their point of view the potential damage from the costs of fencing was great: according to the formula developed earlier, the per-acre costs of fencing a 12.7-acre allotment would have been 59 shillings, greater than the costs of fencing a 71.5-acre allotment (the average size of those between 50 and 100 acres) by a factor of about 2.4.[48] To assess the advantage to be gained by the larger landowners from inflicting this damage, however, the relevant statistic is that the small allotments were so small that they made up only 14.5

---

[45] G. H. Fowler, *Four Pre-Enclosure Village Maps, Quarto Memoires of the Bedford Historical Records Society* 2, pt. i (1928), 10.

[46] G. E. Mingay, *Enclosure and the Small Farmer in the Age of the Industrial Revolution* (London, 1968), p. 31.

[47] J. M. Martin, "Parliamentary Enclosure Movement," p. 23. These statistics refer only to those enclosures that involved at least some common field; enclosures of waste alone are excluded.

[48] A 71.5-acre allotment must be accounted "large," so far as the cost of fencing is concerned, for it would have been only 39 percent more expensive per acre to fence than one of 132 acres (the average size for those between 100 and 200 acres). If the figure of 6 d. per foot of fencing mentioned above is used in the formula, the cost per acre for a square 12.7 acre allotment would be (as noted) about 59 shillings, for a 71.5-acre allotment 25 shillings, and for a 132-acre allotment 18 shillings.

percent of the total acreage of the village. Consequently, even
if these acres could be bought at a price that gave the buyers a
clear gain of as much as, say, 25 percent of the price that would
have obtained under equitable conditions, the fruits of the
expropriation would increase their total wealth very little. If
the smaller landowners in Warwickshire held 14.5 percent of the
village land, the larger held 85.5 percent. Supposing that all the
small landowners sold out after fencing (which is incorrect) at
the 25 percent discount (which is high), and that the only form
of wealth large landowners held aside from their own land was
the money needed to buy the land of small landowners at the
discount (which is an understatement of their wealth), the net
percentage increase in the wealth of large landowners arising
from the forced sale would be $(.25)(14.5)/[(85.5)+(.75)(14.5)]$, or
only 3.8 percent. It will be shown later that rents were doubled
by enclosure. This increased value of the land of large landowners would have increased their wealth, calculated on the same
basis, by $(2.0)(85.5)/[(85.5)+(.75)(14.5)]$, or 177 percent. The increase in wealth due to the greater efficiency of enclosed holdings
(on which higher rents could be charged and paid) is over forty
times that due to the partial expropriation of small landowners.
In other words, however much the small landowners themselves
were hurt by forced sale of their land, it appears most improba-
ble that the opportunity for hurting them influenced to any
substantial degree the rate of enclosure, much less that this
opportunity was its sole purpose.

The introduction of a bill or the passage of an act to enclose
was often delayed for many years inside and outside Parliament,
and one might be inclined to take this as evidence that an
enclosure inequitable to the small landowners was difficult to
achieve. Quite the contrary, however; it appears more likely that
the major source of delay was the adjustment of equity among
the larger landowners; for example, the adjustment of the share
to be allotted to the lay or ecclesiastical impropriators when
tithes were commuted into land.[49] Under parliamentary procedures, the ordinary landowner was deprived of the veto he

[49] The point is sometimes made that the poor were made worse off by
having to pay, as part of the assessment on all landowners, for the fencing
of the impropriators' allotments. But their share in the land would be
higher on that account, because the impropriators would in the absence of
an allowance for fencing demand a higher share.

possessed under the common law, but the impropriators of the tithes and the lord of the manor were not. Because Parliament, especially the House of Lords, was anxious that the Church of England should suffer no wrong from an enclosure, the opposition of the impropriators was sufficient to stop a bill. The lords temporal in Parliament were equally attentive to the terms of commutation of mineral and other rights owned by the lords of the manors. Each possessing a veto, then, the major interests were set to bargaining over the division of the spoils, and it is more likely, therefore, that the opportunity for redistribution among the rich—rather than what was from the point of view of the rich a trivial opportunity for redistribution away from the poor—and the costs of delay springing from this opportunity help to explain the timing of enclosure.

The Benefits of Enclosure

The discussion has so far considered only the costs of enclosure. There remain the benefits. Some historians of enclosure have attributed a part of its growing popularity to an increase in rationality, a new spirit of commercialism, or the like; that is to say, to a realization that there were indeed benefits to be had. To some extent, no doubt, men had to be taught that enclosure was beneficial, by witnessing successful enclosures in neighboring villages or by reading the arguments of improving pamphleteers; and to some extent, although this seems a good deal more doubtful, they may have had to be taught by events to value profitable transformations of their way of life. At some point, to account perhaps for phenomena that less speculative factors cannot explain, this hypothesis may have some use. Its use in any but this residual role is limited, however, by the paucity of its observable implications. It could conceivably be made more fruitful by specifying precisely how the spirit of commercialism or rationality spread, by region and by social class, for example. But in its present underdeveloped form it is consistent with any pattern of enclosure, and being consistent with any, is capable of being rejected by none. A hypothesis that cannot be put in jeopardy by facts is not an attractive one with which to begin.

It is sometimes argued, again, that a change in the relative price of, say, livestock and grain or of labor and land prompted enclosure. This class of argument especially excites the imagination of economists, but it is flawed. In its most popular version, indeed, it has fundamental defects; it asserts that allocation was rigid in open fields (which, as was pointed out in the previous essay, is doubtful), and that therefore any change in prices that indicated a reallocation would set men thinking about enclosure as a way around the rigidity (which in half the cases does not follow, unless the allocation before the change was the best attainable, a premise that fits poorly with the initial one of rigidity).[50] A more sophisticated version asserts that the rigidity of open fields made a prospect of repeated changes in technique in the future a reason for enclosure, and that such a prospect had entered men's minds in the eighteenth century.[51] Still another asserts that the eighteenth century brought economies of scale unexploitable in open fields.[52]

The approach taken here is to suppose that the benefits varied from year to year and from village to village, and that when the benefits exceeded the costs—or, to acknowledge the importance of distribution, when they did for those who had the power to set the machinery in motion—a village was enclosed. In any one year after enclosure the social benefit from the enclosure was the value of the increased output achieved. That is to say, it was the product of the price of agricultural output and the increase in output. What motivated men to enclose was not, of course, the benefit for one year alone, but the expectation of a stream of yearly benefits; to explain the timing of an enclosure, therefore, the benefit, like the cost, must be discounted back to the year in which it was set in motion. A fall in the interest rate, by increasing the value of distant returns relative to near costs, would prompt enclosures. The prices relevant to the decision to invest are the prices expected to obtain in the future (not those that actually obtained—the two would be identical only if men's expectations were always fulfilled). It is supposed, then, that the

[50] R. H. Buchanan, for example, uses such an argument to connect the opening of trade with England with Irish enclosures in the eighteenth century, in his "Field Systems of Ireland" in Alan R. H. Baker and R. A. Butlin, eds., *Studies of Field Systems in the British Isles* (Cambridge, 1973), pp. 605, 618, and *passim*.

[51] This was suggested to me by Axel Leijonhufvud of the University of California at Los Angeles in private correspondence.

[52] Hermann Levy, *Large and Small Holdings* (Cambridge, 1911) put forward this argument, as did Leonard, "Inclosure," p. 237.

rate of enclosure was governed by the present discounted value of the net expected benefits, and that the capital value of the social gain is to be calculated from the present discounted value of the net actual benefits.

These are familiar notions. It is a commonplace, for example, that the decision to enclose hinged on expectations. Expectations on the course of future prices can be given a concrete representation by making them depend on statistics of present and past prices, on the reasonable assumption that this is the information farmers in fact used to assess their prospects. Past runs of wet or dry weather could be included as well, the test of their influence, as that of past prices, being how much they contribute to the statistical explanation of the timing of enclosure. It is a commonplace, too, that the prices of agricultural output are relevant to explaining the timing and that, in particular, their sharp rise during the Napoleonic Wars had much to do with the spurt in enclosure. It is perhaps less of a commonplace to emphasize that what matters is not the absolute rise in prices but their rise relative to the costs of enclosure. The benefits of enclosure and therefore the amount that men are willing to pay for their accomplishment may rise, but may nonetheless be offset by a rise in the costs from a general inflation of prices, or from an inelasticity in the supply of commissioners, lawyers, surveyors, and others who found much of their employment in enclosure. Indeed, the rise in the price of wheat, which is sometimes considered by itself sufficient to explain the enclosures of the Napoleonic Wars, is less impressive, although still substantial, when it is compared with the rise in other prices.[53] To use a fruitful analogy, the rate of enclosure depends on both demand and supply, not on demand alone.

Prices are one component in the demand for an enclosure, the increase in physical output another. If the loss of efficiency from the open field system were not so difficult to measure, it

[53] "Other prices" are meant in this case to stand as a rough proxy for the costs of enclosure. The model of investment used here is a knife-edge one, because it supposes that any excess of benefits over costs, however small, will inspire an enclosure. A more realistic model would admit that large excesses are more potent than small ones. If this emendation proves its worth in future statistical work, it will imply another: since £1000 of benefit net of costs is the same amount in real terms as £2000 of benefit net of costs if the general price level has doubled between the two, the benefit itself will have to be deflated by the general price level

would be possible to specify the source and magnitude of the expected increase in physical output and to relate it to the varying conditions of soil, weather, major crops, and tenurial arrangements. Unfortunately, what is known directly about the loss of efficiency and the gain to be expected from eliminating it is only qualitative. It is known, for example, that, other factors held constant, enclosure for pasture was more beneficial than enclosure for tillage. Henry Homer's formulation in 1776 has not been greatly improved upon by later historians: "Land, which requires to be Kept in Tillage, is less incommoded by the Open Field State, than that which is fit for Pasture or Dairy. . . . These . . . Inconveniences which affect the Property of every Open Field . . . vary in Degree in almost every Parish, according to the Nature of the Soil, the Regulations or Bye-Laws which prevail, and other Circumstances." [54] The vagueness of this formulation would be no obstacle to quantitative analysis if there were statistics on the agricultural output of villages before and after enclosure, but in general there are not. Although yields per acre do appear to have increased during the eighteenth century, it is difficult to decide by how much, and still more difficult to allocate the increase in any detail to specific regions or times. [55]

The value of the increased output in a village, however, had to accrue in the first instance as income to its occupants, and this fact provides a way around the lack of information on output. An enclosure increased the value of all factors of production by increasing the output to be shared among them. Labor and capital were mobile, and therefore the increase in their productivity would reveal itself in an increase in their employment, not an increase in their price, for if labor and capital were paid more

[54] Homer, *Nature and Methods*, p. 8. Compare the similar emphasis put on the pasture-arable distinction by Gonner (*Common Land*, p. 37), Chambers (*Nottinghamshire*, pp. 150–54), and Hunt ("Chronology," p. 270).
[55] There is wide disagreement on the magnitude of the increase, if "disagreement" is quite the right word to use for a difference of emphasis on an issue that all writers confess is very much in doubt. For wheat yields alone, Chambers and Mingay (*Agricultural Revolution* pp. 34ff) follow Phyllis Deane and W A. Cole, *British Economic Growth 1688–1959* (Cambridge, 1964), pp. 62–75 and the earlier work by G. E. Fussell, "Population and Wheat Production in the Eighteenth Century," *History Teachers Miscellany* 7 (1929), in putting the increase at only 10 percent for the entire century. On the other hand, Ashton (*18 Century*, p. 51) follows the suggestion of M. K. Bennett, "British Wheat Yield per Acre for Seven Centuries," *Economic History* 3 (1935), 12–29, that the increase was a third in the second half of the century alone.

after an enclosure, more would flow into the village, and continue to flow until the previous wages and returns obtained. It is difficult to find evidence on the increase in the amount and value of employment of capital and labor after enclosure. For land, however, the situation is very different, both theoretically and evidentially. The value of land was made higher by the direct increase in its productivity arising from enclosure, and by the indirect increase arising from the larger amount of complementary labor and capital employed. Since land is an immobile factor of production, the higher value of it would reveal itself entirely in a rise in rents: clearly, land cannot flow from one village to another in response to a higher return. The rise in rent after an enclosure, therefore, can be used as an estimate of the increase in output attributable to the enclosure.

An economist might be inclined to object to the use of the increase in rent as an estimate of the increase in output on two grounds. First, it ignores the output spent in wage and interest payments to increase the employment of other factors of production, and would seem therefore to be merely a lower bound on the increase in output. So long as these other factors of production are in highly elastic supply to the individual village over the period during which the increase in rents is observed, however, the objection is irrelevant, because the payment to the increased factors is matched by their opportunity cost elsewhere. Output is increased in the enclosed village by the value of the fresh employment, but it is reduced elsewhere in the economy by the same amount, as these factors are withdrawn from their former employment. Only the increase in rent on land represents a net increase in the productive capacity of the economy.[56] Second, an economist might object on the grounds that the estimate ignores the effects of enclosure on the rest of the economy. Enclosures considered as a group, he might argue, increased the demand for labor and capital in the economy at large and increased the supply of agricultural products, inducing national movements in the prices of factors and products that would make the increase in rent a mere lower bound on the true increase in national income. Once again, however, the objection is irrelevant, in this case because enclosures are not being con-

[56] I am indebted to Axel Leijonhufvud for clarifying my thinking on this point.

sidered as a group when the increase in rent is measured. In each year only a trivial portion of the land of England was newly enclosed, however nontrivial was the result of sixty years of enclosure. Therefore, the increase in rent observed in the year or two after the enclosure of a village is trivially biased by the impact of all enclosures taking place in those years. The typical increase in rent is a good estimate of the typical increase in output.

What is significant about this reasoning is that the magnitude of the rise in rents after the enclosure of a village is comparatively easy to observe. The assessments for the poor rate and the land tax are relevant sources, as are the extant accounts of the landlords and farmers themselves. Contemporary pamphlets, manuals of farming practice, the country reports to the Board of Agriculture, papers in the *Annals of Agriculture,* and so on, estimate increases in rents even when they do not estimate the increases in output from enclosure or the loss of output from the open fields. The advice William Marshall, a well-known writer on agricultural subjects, gave in 1804 to those contemplating purchasing land is typical:

> Among the circumstances which influence the marketable value of lands . . . their state with respect to inclosure is a matter of great consideration. Open lands, though wholly appropriated, and lying well together, are of much less value, except for a sheep walk or a rabbit warren, than the same land would be in a state of suitable inclosure. If they are disjointed and intermixt in a state of common field, or common meadow, their value may be reduced one third. If the common fields or meadows are what is termed Lammas land, and becomes common as soon as the crops are off, the depression of value may be set down at one half of what they would be worth, in well fenced inclosure, and unencumbered with that ancient custom.[57]

Other contemporaries, and later historians assessing their testimony, concur with Marshall in putting rents after enclosure at roughly double what they were before enclosure.[58] In short, the

[57] W. Marshall, *On the Landed Property of England* (1804), pp. 13–14 (italics deleted).

[58] The figure has long pedigree. In his *Book of Husbandry* (1598) Fitz-herbert writes "by the assent of the lords and the tenants every neighbour may exchange land with another. And then shall his farm be twice so good in profit to the tenant than it was before" (quoted in Ernle, *English Farming,* p. 65, spelling modernized). Over a century and a half later Homer gives a

increase in rent is known in a general way, can sometimes be ascertained in detail for individual villages, and can be used as an estimate of the increase in the value of output from enclosure.

The evidence of the increase in rent is not perfectly free of extraneous elements, and requires careful interpretation. Any fortuitous influence on rent from variations in the price of agricultural output occurring at the same time as an enclosure must be removed, although it is not difficult to do so. It is more difficult to correct for the influence of agricultural improvements made at the same time as an enclosure, but neither related to it causally nor included in its costs. The simplest solution would be to look only at the increase in rent in those enclosures that were not accompanied by extraneous improvements. This is, however, costly in its waste of evidence: a more economical solution would be to attempt to remove the influence of the improvements directly.

Still another difficulty is that rents before an enclosure might not measure the true value of the land because of long leases entered into during an earlier period of low agricultural prices. Without persistent, unanticipated movements in agricultural prices, one would expect the rents even on long leases to reflect economic rent in a rough way. Leases need not be literally annual for the fulfillment of this expectation, or at any rate so Smith, Ricardo, and the rest believed in using short leases as the basis of their analyses of English rural society in the late eighteenth century. During the Napoleonic Wars, however, there did occur persistent, unanticipated inflation. Since leases were annulled by enclosure, the increase in rent might to some extent reflect a mere adjustment of the rent to an appropriate level rather than any real increase in productivity. In other words, the enclosure would present an opportunity for the landlord to repudiate the bad wagers he had made in earlier years that prices would not rise.[59] The significance of this effect depends on

---

doubling of rents as a typical result of enclosure (Homer, *Nature and Methods*, p. 64). Citations giving this order of magnitude of increase could be multiplied indefinitely. Compare Chambers and Mingay, *Agricultural Revolution*, p. 85.

[59] In a period of falling prices, of course, the effect is reversed. The rent before enclosure would be higher than the true value of the land, the change in rent would therefore be an understatement of the true rise in its productivity, and the landlord's incentive to promote an enclosure would be attenuated.

the length of leases in a village subject to an enclosure and the course of prices in the years preceding it. If long leases were common, an allowance should be made for their effect in the explanation of the rate of enclosure. The cycle of enclosure during the inflation of the Napoleonic Wars and the subsequent deflation, in short, may have been to some extent a product of the opportunity enclosure provides for the redistribution of income between a tenant with a long lease and his landlord. But as long as the prevalence of long leases can be estimated, the adjustment in the reasoning is not difficult to make.

With these reservations, then, the observed increase in rent can serve as an estimate of the increase in output. It can play the same role in the analysis of the demand side of enclosure as the costs will play in that of the supply side. In other words, its variation can be related in a statistical way to variations from year to year in prices and interest rates, and from village to village in the factors influencing the potential increase in output; just as the variations in the cost of enclosure can be related to the cheapening of parliamentary procedures and to differences in the sizes of villages. The complete model would bring the two together and isolate the causes and consequences of enclosure.[60]

The Benefits Net of Costs

Some of the foregoing information can be used in a brief and crude experiment that may illustrate the promise of the argument as a whole: let us ask the question, using money magnitudes typical of the midpoint of the enclosure movement, what was the order of magnitude of the increase in national income attributable to enclosures? If rents doubled on the 14 million or so acres of land enclosed after 1700, assuming as a low estimate that they earned typically a rent of 7 shillings an acre before

---

[60] There is a peculiarity of the model that is worth mentioning here. Once a village is enclosed it cannot be enclosed again. It permanently drops out of consideration. If one arrayed villages from the most to the least suitable for enclosure, the most suitable would be selected first, and thereafter only conditions (of price, interest rates, etc.) still more favorable to enclosure would in fact result in one. As the array of villages is, as it were, used up, the conditions for an enclosure become progressively more stringent. To use another analogy, the model—and the reality to which it refers—works on a ratchet principle.

enclosure (this before the inflation of the Napoleonic Wars), the increase in the value of agricultural output would be around £4.9 million each year.[61] Only opportunity costs need be subtracted from this total (although they affect the rate of enclosure, bribes necessary to get an agreement to enclose from recalcitrant landowners and from parliamentary officials do not detract from its social benefit), and on the basis of Martin's estimates these may be put at around £2 an acre. If they were put higher it would matter little for the results, because to convert this capital sum into a stream of income comparable to the yearly increase in rent it must be multiplied by an interest rate. Conceding that the rate on consols, typically well under 5 percent, is a riskless rate and therefore too low, one might still doubt that the relevant rate would be much above 10 percent. The 14 million acres enclosed, then, would result in a stream of income foregone of $(£2)(14 \text{ million})(.10) = £2.8$ million each year. If, therefore, one had the temerity to ignore the many necessary qualifications in view of the argument of this essay, the net gain to national income could be put at around £2.1 million a year. Considering that the components of the calculation were chosen to yield a lower bound, this is a respectable order of magnitude for a mere shift in the distribution of property rights, some 1½ percent of national income (England including Wales, which is not included in the numerator) and 3½ percent of agricultural income in 1770.[62] To put the matter another way, the return to enclosure was fairly high: an expenditure of 40 shillings an acre yielded an increased rent to the landlord of 7 shillings an acre in each year following, for a rate of return of about 17 percent per year.[63] And to put it still another way, relevant to the analysis in the previous essay of the choice between open and enclosed

[61] There is no clear consensus on what was, in fact, the typical rent before enclosure. Chambers and Mingay (*Agricultural Revolution*, p. 85) use a figure of 7 shillings for a comparable period. One would want rents on land in open fields, whereas this estimate refers to all land. It is biased upward by including enclosed (and therefore presumably more valuable) land, but biased downward by including rough pasture land and waste.

[62] The income estimates, based on Arthur Young's, are given in Deane and Cole, *British Economic Growth*, p. 156.

[63] In this form the calculation has a long history. For example, Slater, *English Peasantry*, p. 263, summarizing Arthur Young's calculations in 1799; Tate, "Cost of Parliamentary Enclosure," p. 265; and, most recently, G. E. Mingay, *English Landed Society in the Eighteenth Century* (London, 1963), p. 183.

fields when the costs of moving from one to the other are to be neglected, a village was roughly 13 percent more productive in an enclosed than in an open state; the increase in output was about 7 shillings an acre on land in 1770 with an output of about 50 shillings an acre.[64]

Whether or not these crude calculations can be improved upon by the more refined ones proposed earlier remains to be seen. The refinements require more information, particularly a usable sample of the enclosure histories of a good number of villages, complete with their topography and soil types, their size, their tenurial arrangements, and estimates of the cost and benefits of their enclosures. The constraints on the drawing of such a sample are many, for the records are often incomplete even when they have survived. What can be claimed at this point, to use an apt metaphor, is that the ground has been cleared, to some degree plowed and harrowed, and once it is seeded and cultivated the harvest of historical insight can be great.

[64] The output is the Deane and Cole estimate of agricultural income divided by 24 million acres. Agricultural income is relevant because agriculture used few inputs from other sectors of the economy: income will be much the same as gross output. The inclusion of Wales in the income biases it upward, and the estimate of productivity change downward, but probably relatively little; Wales was poor and small. The reported figure is simply

$$7 \Big/ \left[\frac{(50 + 57)}{2} \right].$$

4

Enclosures and Depopulation: A Marxian Analysis

JON S. COHEN AND MARTIN L. WEITZMAN

From the fourteenth to the nineteenth century, the enclosure of open fields, waste, and common lands in England has provided inexhaustible topics for controversy. From its earliest beginnings, this shift in the organization of landed property away from communal and towards private regulation attracted ardent advocates and equally fierce critics. One of the most controversial issues has been its relation to an observed or imagined depopulation of many rural localities.[1] Depopulation was debated from pulpits, through pamphlets and books, in the chancery, and in the courts, especially during Tudor and Stuart times, but the charge was levied again in the decades of the Industrial Revolution. Deserted villages, penniless vagabonds, and squalid, overcrowded squatter settlements were attributed by many to the abridgment of labor in agriculture that followed enclosures.

Even in so rich and varied a scholarly and popular literature, it is impossible to find a clear statement of the precise economic reasons why enclosures did or did not cause depopulation. The purpose of this paper is to demonstrate by simple economic analy-

---

[1] Many of the numerous writings on the enclosures in England contain discussions of their demographic effects. We have found particularly useful the detailed consideration of the subject in the following standard references: E. C. K. Gonner, *Common Land and Enclosure* (London, 1912); R. H. Tawney, *The Agrarian Problem of the Sixteenth Century* (New York, 1967); J. D. Chambers, "Enclosures and Labour Supply in the Industrial Revolution," *Economic History Review* 2d series, Vol. 5 (1953); Joan Thirsk, *Tudor Enclosures* (London, 1959); G. E. Mingay, *Enclosure and the Small Farmer in the Age of the Industrial Revolution* (London, 1968); E. Kerridge, *Agrarian Problems in the Sixteenth Century and After* (London, 1969).

sis that the enclosing of an estate necessarily led to the abridgment of labor on that land. While such an approach must over-
look many of the complexities of the history, it does allow us
to focus sharply on the basic economic forces that underlay enclosures. Since our concern is primarily with these economic
forces, we feel that our approach, derived from economic theory,
is the proper one to adopt in the present context.

Two features of the discussion must be emphasized at the
beginning. From an economic viewpoint, the physical acts of
enclosing—the hedging, fencing, or ditching—were not important by themselves, although they often accompanied what *was*
important. The essence of enclosures was the conversion of the
ownership of land from communal to a private basis. For our
purposes, enclosures are best viewed as a shift in the management
functions, decisions, and rewards from the traditions and politics
of village and manor to landlords and tenants functioning in the
environment of a market economy. To the extent that engrossing and consolidation accomplished this change, they must be
considered forms of enclosure.[2] Since the parliamentary enclosures after 1760 in many cases granted official sanction to what
had in fact already occurred, this analysis concentrates on the
enclosure movement between the end of the fifteenth and the
middle of the eighteenth centuries in England. Most of what is
said, however, is of a general validity, and may prove useful in
the examination of enclosures at other times and in the open-
field areas on the continent.

Very little economic literature exists that attempts to specify
formally the allocative and distributive features of an economy
typified by communal regulation of land. To understand the
economic consequences of a shift from such a system to a regime
of private property, such specification is necessary. Our model
of medieval agriculture is based on the following abstractions
from medieval reality: (1) rents are not profit-maximizing;
(2) land is regulated communally; and (3) a strong tendency
exists among villagers to move about, so as to equalize returns

---

[2] Thirsk in *Tudor Enclosures,* 19, and in "Enclosing and Engrossing" in
J. Thirsk, ed., *The Agrarian History of England and Wales,* Vol. 4, *1500–
1640* (Cambridge, 1967), 200–202, suggests that enclosure must be distinguished
from engrossing and consolidation. But from an economic point of view,
they would appear to be the same thing.

per family both within and between villages.[3] Given an economy on this model, the analytical apparatus necessary to understand the link between enclosures and depopulation in a region is presented in the next section of this essay. If the conditions of the analysis are fulfilled, then enclosures must cause a reduction in labor used on the land. Two other subsidiary but extremely valuable insights emerge from this analysis. First, rents must increase on newly enclosed estates. Second, there is good reason, based on strict production considerations, for a landowner after enclosure to shift crop mix away from grain and other products of arable husbandry, towards pasture. In the second and third sections of our study a brief examination is made of the historical material on enclosures in the light of the analysis. The results are not conclusive, but they suggest that more attention may be paid to the supply side of the wool trade, and that depopulation has been a frequently misunderstood issue.

The Model

The objective of our model is to make a first approximation of the impact of enclosures on labor requirements on the land in a typical open-field village. In spite of the complex patterns of land use and crop mixes, it is possible to make some general statements about aggregate production in such a village. To simplify our analysis, let us measure inputs and outputs in value equivalents, implicitly assuming that we have resolved all index number problems with adding up the various inputs and products. Although we know that villages frequently brought new lands into cultivation by clearing some of the surrounding wastes, we assume for simplicity that the land available to a village is fixed.[4] This involves no loss of generality, and allows us to consider all inputs and outputs per unit of land.

[3] Our conception of the medieval society closely resembles that of classical writers such as Vinogradoff, Maitland, Pirenne, and Bloch. As examples, see: P. Vinogradoff, *Villainage in England* (Oxford, 1892); F. W. Maitland, *Domesday and Beyond* (Cambridge, 1897); H. Pirenne, *A Social and Economic History of Europe* (New York, 1937); M. Bloch, *Feudal Society*, Vol. 1 (Chicago, 1961); and *French Rural History* (Berkeley and Los Angeles, 1966).

[4] Much of our knowledge of the communal aspects of medieval agriculture comes from the records of clearing operations in which most villagers participated, and from which all participants derived an equal share of the newly cleared land. On this see, among others, W. O. Ault, *Open Field Farming and the Village Community* (Philadelphia, 1965), p. 6 and *passim;*

Table 4–1.　Output and Labor Coefficients for Sheep and Wheat
　　　　　　　　Production

	Pasture	Arable
Value of output per unit of land	α_p	α_a
Amount of labor per unit of land	β_p	β_a

To begin with, assume that two products and production
processes are open to the villagers: sheep on pasture land, and
wheat production on the arable land.[5] Table 4–1 exhibits symbols for output and labor coefficients associated with each process.
On the basis of the technical aspects of the two processes, we
can postulate that less labor per unit of land is required for
sheep pasture than for arable husbandry, and that output per
worker is higher in sheep raising than in arable farming. That is,

$$\beta_p < \beta_a$$
$$\frac{\alpha_p}{\beta_p} > \frac{\alpha_a}{\beta_a}$$

We want to construct an aggregate production function for the
village. For every amount of labor, this function gives the corresponding maximum attainable output. The aggregate production function reflecting the pasture and arable processes is shown
as the curve OO in Figure 4–1. The total product curve of the
village is made up of straight lines, because we have so far limited
the analysis to two processes between which the marginal product
of labor is constant. More than two processes were available to a
village, of course. Aside from sheep and wheat, there were dairy
husbandry, other cereal crops, and various vegetables, all of
which represented additional options, either separately or in
combination, open to the villagers. Each of these processes can
be described in terms of their output and labor coefficients which,
we can assume, fall somewhere between the two extremes of sheep
raising and wheat growing. For example, dairy farming required
more labor per unit of output than sheep husbandary, but less
than wheat growing. Output per unit of labor was less for dairy
farming than for sheep, but more than for wheat. If we con-

R. H. Hilton, "Medieval Agrarian History" in R. B. Pugh, ed., *The Victoria History of the Counties of England: The History of Leicestershire,*
Vol. 2 (London, 1954), p. 156 and *passim.*

[5] This kind of approach is identical to that used in modern activity
analyses; in this case we associate each process with a different good.

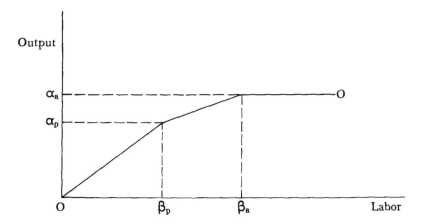

Labor Figure 4-1: Aggregate Production Function for Two Processes

tinue to increase the number of processes, we can eventually describe aggregate production with a fairly smooth curve OO as in Figure 4-2, rather than with a series of straight line segments, as in Figure 4-1. It must be remembered, however, that underlying the smooth total product curve for the village are identifiable processes associated with different outputs and mixes of input.

This analysis provides the necessary framework for an examination of the transition from communal to private regulation of property. To highlight the economic features of this change, we first consider a system of pure communal property, in which no obligations are paid to a local lord, and contrast this with a system of pure private property, where workers are hired to maximize profits.[6] Later in the analysis we will introduce nominal rent payments into the communal situation, but will demonstrate that this in no way alters the essential results of the pure case.

[6] We would argue that a strong spirit of community prevailed in the open field areas of England and that this created some tendency towards an equalization of output shares. Many scholars have noted this tendency; among others, Vinogradoff, *Villainage in England*, pp. 236-38; Bloch, *French Rural History*, pp. 45-48; Maitland, *Domesday and Beyond*, p. 337.

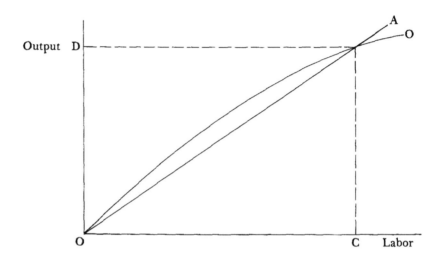

Figure 4-2: Aggregate Production Function for Many Processes

In Figure 4–2 the slope of the straight line OA represents the average output per man in the village when there are OC villagers. Suppose that, as a rough approximation, the output per man in this free village without a lord produces a standard of living equivalent to that throughout the economy. The nature of communal property, intervillage migration, and other forces exist that push in this direction. Taking the prevailing standard of living as a wage rate, the profit-maximizing position in this village lies at the point where the marginal product of labor is equal to the prevailing wage, that is, point E in Figure 4–3. In the pure communal village, where no one has the right to exclude others from participation in production, such points are unattainable. But at a particular moment in time, a potential landlord perceives that he can pay each villager at the prevailing standard of living (the slope of OA), make this equal to the marginal rather than the average product, and drive rent up to some substantial share of the total product. To realize maximum rent, the enclosing lord must be able to reduce the number of peasants on the land. These results are shown in Figure 4–3.

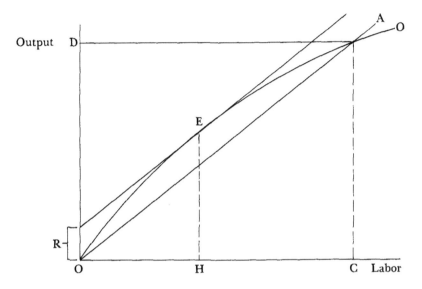

Figure 4-3: Rent Maximization and Depopulation: The Pure Case

The landlord, when he encloses the village, moves back along the *aggregate production function from A to E; he collects a rent* equal to OR, and reduces the number of peasants on the land by CH. This is an unavoidable result of enclosure.

This analysis raises two fundamental issues that we can treat only briefly here. First, what determined the timing of enclosure; and second, why was enclosing the land a *necessary condition* to maximize income from it? From our point of view, the enclosure movement was motivated by each potential landowner's desire to maximize profits from his estate. This wish for profits represented a break with medieval values in which a lord measured his wealth not so much by the income from his land as by the number of men under his command.[7] A variety of forces must have played a role in creating the proverbial greedy and covetous landowner, who makes his first appearance towards

[7] Marc Bloch's observation for France holds equally well for England: "Many a Frankish king and French baron if asked what his land brought in for him would have answered like the Highlander who said 'Five hundred men'" (Bloch, *French Rural History*, p. 72).

the end of the fifteenth century. We can only speculate that the Tudor peace, long-term trade expansion, religious changes, and a new military technology were important factors, among others, behind this metamorphosis.

For the most part, it was impossible for a potential landowner to raise rents without enclosing. In medieval England, neither lord, freeman, nor villein had clear title to his land; all estates, large or small, were held "of someone." [8] They all lacked the two privileges associated with private property: the right to alienate land and the power to exclude. Indeed, the whole concept of "ownership" was alien to medieval society, and the word does not appear in medieval legal documents. Whereas social relations in the modern world tend to be dominated by concepts of ownership, income, rent, and profit, the ruling principles in medieval society were lordship, tenure, and service. [9] The payments due a lord from his tenants were fixed by custom, and were immutable within the traditional context. By the operation of "enclosure" such customary rules were abolished, and owners gained clear title to land, giving them the right to use it as they wished. Some case studies of the early enclosures indicate that lords initially attempted to raise the level of customary rents without abolishing commons and common rights and controls, but eventually resorted to enclosure to bring about the desired increase in their incomes. [10]

It may be objected to this argument that manorial lords of open field villages did in fact receive, without enclosure, a variety of rent-like returns. But the array of dues, duties, services, and various rent payments made by a medieval tenant to his lord did not represent economic rent in the modern sense. The very

[8] Pollock and Maitland make clear the need to distinguish between feudal and modern land law (F. Pollock and F. W. Maitland, *History of English Law* (Cambridge, 1968), Vol. 1, 237 and *passim*). See also A. W. B. Simpson, *An Introduction to the History of Land Law* (Oxford, 1961), p. 44.

[9] R. B. Smith, *Land and Politics in the England of Henry VIII* (Oxford, 1971), p. 43.

[10] L. A. Parker's story of an enclosure at Cotesbach is extraordinarily rich in detail and insights. (L. A. Parker, "The Agrarian Revolution at Cotesbach, 1501–1612," in W. G. Hoskins, ed., *Studies in Leicestershire Agrarian History* (Leicester, 1949). See also Hilton, "Medieval Agrarian History," especially pp. 194–95.) While it does not matter analytically which group or class did the enclosing, in fact the large landholders (the aristocracy, the gentry, the new class of merchant-estate owners, and a few wealthy peasants) did it, and the copyhold villagers were expelled.

preconditions that would have made profit maximization a feasible objective were for the most part absent from medieval society. Institutions to enforce contractual obligations were nonexistent. Profits were not the only factor that determined how land was used. Factors markets, especially for land and labor, were not present.[11] Both custom and the political pressure of a peasantry kept economic rents below their profit-maximizing levels. The situation requires only a trivial modification of the analysis already made, illustrated in Figure 4–4. A traditional or "feudal" rent R is consistent with the use of OM peasants working the land. To increase rental income from R to R' while paying workers at the going rate (slope of HK), the lord must cut back the number of peasants on the land. Profits are maximized at the point where ON workers are employed, because production at this point yields the highest rent obtainable on a competitive market for labor, land, and the product. The cutback in workers reduces agricultural output, but it lowers labor costs even more. The lord need not exclude peasants if they agree to pay the new rent R', but this is tantamount to a reduction in their standard of living below that prevailing in open-field agriculture (shown by the slope of HK in Figure 4–4). So "excess" labor would leave the enclosed rent-paying villages to seek employment elsewhere.

An obvious consequence of enclosures, then, is that rents on newly enclosed estates will rise. This is the purpose of enclosures, and the source of rural depopulation in a newly enclosed region.

[11] M. M. Postan's attempt to demonstrate the existence of a widespread land market in medieval England on the basis of a very small sample from some East Anglican manors [M. M. Postan in "Introduction" to M. M. Postan and C. N. C. Brooke, eds., *Carte Nativorum* (Oxford, 1960)] has been questioned by P. R. Hymans in "The Origins of a Peasant Land Market in Britain," *Economic History Review* 23 (April, 1970). Pollock and Maitland warn us that the right to alienate land was an unsettled issue throughout the Middle Ages, so that it would be an error to argue that land markets were efficient allocators of this factor (Pollock and Maitland, *History of English Law,* 346). Even Kosminsky, whose purpose is to demonstrate, in good Leninist fashion, the rise of a kulak class of peasants in England by the late medieval period, is reluctant to say more than that capitalist relations were present in embryonic form on certain small manors. See Kosminsky, *Studies in the Agrarian History of England in the Thirteenth Century* (Oxford, 1956), p. 228 and *passim*. A similar case can be made concerning labor markets. As in all traditional peasant societies, land and labor had unique positions outside of the market place. Occasional transactions hardly constitute efficient markets.

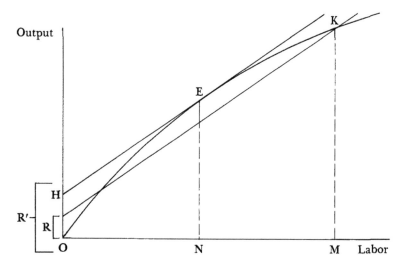

Figure 4-4: Rent Maximization and Depopulation:
The Case with Nominal Rents before Enclosure

Small wonder that contemporary observers associated a greedy,
rack-renting lord with a dwindling peasantry. A less obvious
though equally important result of enclosure is a movement along
the aggregate production curve to a less labor-intensive process.
If the coefficients presented at the beginning of this section are
correct, the analysis establishes a strong presumption that enclosures will lead to some conversion of land from arable to pasture.
In this context, it was the profit-seeking landlord who propelled
enclosures forward; the shift from arable to pasture occurred as
a consequence, rather than as a cause, of the movement. Sir
Thomas More said that it was the sheep that "ate men." Our
analysis indicates that Marx was not wrong in seeing under the
sheep's clothing the wolfish landlord.

Enclosures and Depopulation

The data on enclosures and depopulation in agriculture before
the end of the eighteenth century are inadequate to confirm or
to contradict the conclusions of our model. Surely depopulation

was often alleged, and it made enclosure a burning political and social issue. The frequent peasant uprisings in the sixteenth and seventeenth centuries were violent testimony to the discontent that enclosure caused.[12] Pamphleteers, preachers, poets, and philosophers made eloquent denunciations of enclosure precisely because it seemed to deny men their rightful heritage in the land.[13] The English crown, under the Tudors and early Stuarts— concerned with the peace and strength of the realm—took steps to halt those enclosures where depopulation appeared to be the likely result.

Analysis by contemporaries and by recent historians has noted, indeed, the relation between enclosure, sheep farming, conversion of arable land to pasture, and depopulation, attributing the latter to the fact that sheep require fewer laborers than grains and other field crops.[14] As Eric Kerridge notes, conversion from arable to "up and down husbandry" also led to a shrinkage of villages and a degree of agricultural depopulation.[15] Similarly, Kerridge notes that consolidated farms did abridge labor and quotes Joseph Lee, a seventeenth-century contemporary: "Let it be granted that our lands lying nearer together require fewer servants; are any bound to keep more servants than are needed for business; or may they not cast how to do the same business with less labor."[16] W. G. Hoskins, in his study of the Midland peasant, observed that, "Enclosures and engrossing in many areas seem to have forced people into unenclosed, unengrossed villages

[12] Some discussion of these issues can be found in J. Thirsk, *Tudor Enclosures.* Also see P. Ramsey, *Tudor Economic Problems* (London, 1965). W. E. Tate, *The English Village Community and the Enclosure Movement* (London, 1967), pp. 65–66 and *passim,* comments briefly on the demands of the peasants in these riots. It was primarily the uprising in 1607 that focused attention on enclosures (J. Thirsk, *Tudor Enclosures,* p. 11). In the same volume, Thirsk points out that in the Tudor period it was recognized that sheep alone were not deemed the sole cause of depopulation, nor were sheep masters considered the only ones responsible for enclosures.

[13] Thirsk, "Enclosing and Engrossing" devotes several pages to the pamphlet literature on enclosures.

[14] Modern statements on the issue take more or less the same position. See *ibid.,* and Thirsk, *Tudor Enclosures.* This theme runs through most discussion of the early enclosures. See among others, E. K. C. Gonner, *Common Land,* and R. H. Tawney, *Agrarian Problems,* pp. 177–230.

[15] Kerridge, *Agrarian Problems,* p. 121.

[16] Joseph Lee, cited *ibid.,* p. 126. Kerridge makes similar observations elsewhere. See, for example, E. Kerridge, "Agriculture, 1500–1793," in R. B. Pugh, ed., *The Victoria History of the Counties of England: A History of Wiltshire* (London, 1959), p. 54 and *passim.*

like Wigston . . . the consolidation of farms was depriving a great number of small peasants of acquiring some land." [17] The few detailed studies of enclosure invariably note a fall in the peasant population on newly enclosed estates.[18] But there is little emphasis in any of the literature of the basic economic point: that enclosures always caused a movement along the total product curve, and inevitably expelled peasants from the newly enclosed estates.

Further evidence favoring an economic analysis of enclosure lies in the fact that rents seemed to have risen on all newly enclosed estates. Enclosure in the sixteenth and seventeenth centuries was usually a last rather than a first resort to increase the rental value of an estate. Various expedients, such as a beneficial lease that set stiff entry fines but left unchanged the customary rent payments, were devised to push up rents without having to confront directly the rule of custom.[19] These tactics were only partially successful. "The most obvious and most common form of direct improvement was enclosure by which all surveyors were agreed it was possible to increase the value of arable and pasture by 50 percent. . . . Once consolidated and enclosed, the demesne could be let in blocks of 100 acres or so to substantial farmers from whom a substantial rent could be expected. Most great lords of whom adequate records survive were carrying out such enclosures in the early seventeenth century." [20] It was commonly agreed by most contemporaries of the early enclosures that they raised the return on land at least 50 percent.[21] Even parliamentary enclosures, particularly the

[17] W. G. Hoskins, *The Midland Peasant* (London, 1965), pp. 214–15.

[18] See, for example, Hilton, "Medieval Agrarian History," pp. 194–95; L. A. Parker, "The Agrarian Revolution at Cotesbach"; E. M. Leonard, "The Enclosure of Common Fields in the Seventeenth Century," in E. M. Carus-Wilson, ed., *Essays in Economic History*, Vol. 2 (London, 1962).

[19] It was often difficult for a lord to bring about even this alteration in tradition. See L. Stone, *The Crisis of the Aristocracy: 1558–1641* (Oxford, 1965), p. 308; Hoskins, *The Midland Peasant*, pp. 104–106.

[20] Lawrence Stone, *The Crisis of the Aristocracy*, p. 323. Unfortunately, Kerridge's attempt to demonstrate that aggregate rents rose rapidly between 1540 and 1640 is not entirely satisfactory. (E. Kerridge, "The Movement of Rents, 1540–1640," *Economic History Review* 2d series 1 (1953). See Stone, *The Crisis of the Aristocracy*, p. 327 and Cohen and Weitzman, "A Marxian Type Model of Enclosures," Working Paper 118, Department of Economics, Massachusetts Institute of Technology, footnote 46, for criticism of Kerridge's analysis.

[21] Ramsey, *Tudor Economic Problems*, p. 25; Gonner, *Common Land*, pp. 302–303.

ones that transformed those villages that maintained a strong communal character, raised the rental value of land.[22] "On average it can be estimated that rents perhaps doubled; the land-owner's gross return on his investment was probably between 15 and 20 percent, but higher where much waste was enclosed." [23] These findings tend to confirm this aspect of our analysis. We would expect rents to increase in real terms as land is enclosed and open-field villagers are displaced.

Enclosures and the Wool Trade

The enclosure movement was a continuous process, carried forward by a desire to maximize profits from commercial agriculture. Those interpretations that regard the movement as a series of separate episodes, each one mechanistically determined by different external forces, are basically misleading. The commonest example of this sort of historical argument is the one that maintains enclosures between about 1450 and 1550 were caused by a rise in the demand for wool. The rise in demand for wool, it is contended, led to an increase in the price of wool relative to the price of corn, which encouraged landowners to convert from arable to permanent pasture. Compact fenced farms provided better grazing land for sheep than unenclosed fields, so enclosure was a natural consequence of this shift in demand. Since pasture required less labor than arable land, villages were destroyed and peasants were eased off the land.

In one form or another this is the most familiar, the oldest, and the most widely accepted explanation of the Tudor enclosure movement.[24] Some modern scholars have indirectly raised doubts about its validity, however, Peter Ramsey notes that there were two active periods of enclosure in Tudor England: at the very beginning and the very end. The first corresponds with the supposed rise in the demand for wool, but at the end enclosure for pasture continues, even though price trends were unfavorable to

[22] See, for example, J. M. Martin, "The Parliamentary Enclosure Movement and Rural Society in Warwickshire," *Agricultural History Review* 15 (1967), 29–30.

[23] J. D. Chambers and G. E. Mingay, *The Agricultural Revolution* (London, 1966), p. 84.

[24] The most explicit modern version is that of P. J. Bowden in "Movements in Wool Prices 1490–1610," *Yorkshire Bulletin of Economic and Social Research* 3–4 (September 1952) and *The Wood Trade in Tudor and Stuart England* (London, 1962).

wool.[25] Lawrence Stone observes that enclosures raised the rental value of most estates. The period he investigates postdates the supposed rise in the demand for wool.[26] On the basis of detailed regional studies, Eric Kerridge concludes that enclosures for the most part led to a form of up and down husbandry, and only occasionally to a complete conversion to permanent pasture.[27]

On close examination, the available price and output data do not suggest so close a relation between sheep and enclosures.[28] Indeed, no systematic trend in the relation between wool and grain prices appears between 1450 and 1550. A regression run on P. J. Bowden's data shows that wool prices declined relative to those of grain.[29] English exports of unfinished woolen cloths did indeed rise between 1450–1550. The data on exports, more reliable than most for that period, demonstrate a marked upward trend. But we must not focus exclusively on demand, neglecting the strong push that came from the suppliers of wool, the enclosing landlords. The enclosing of land—we repeat—always led to a shift along the total product curve towards a less labor-intensive process, which in some cases caused a conversion from arable to pasture. The quantity of wool demanded increased as the supply of wool rose. The situation was undoubtedly complex, and no monocausal explanation is sufficient.[30] The tendency to focus on demand alone has, however, created an inaccurate account of the connection between enclosures and the wool trade. It is possible to argue with only slight exaggeration that the enclosure movement gave rise to the wool trade rather than the reverse.

[25] Ramsey, *Tudor Economic Problems*, p. 30.

[26] Stone, *Crisis of the Aristocracy*, p. 323.

[27] Kerridge, *Agrarian Problems*, p. 124.

[28] J. F. Wright, "A Note on Mr. Bowden's Index of Wool Prices," *Yorkshire Bulletin of Economic and Social Research* 7 (September 1955), and S. Pollard, "A Second Note on Mr. Bowden's Wool Prices," *ibid.*, both note this fact.

[29] The regression of the form $P_w/P_g = a + bt$, run for 101 years (1450–1550), yielded a negative b coefficient with a t statistic greater than 3. P. J. Bowden's data are contained in the "Statistical Appendix," Tables I and V, in Thirsk, *Agrarian History*.

[30] We have not treated in this paper, among other issues, the price revolution, the devaluation of English currency between 1500 and 1550, or the supposed rapid population increase, all of which must figure in any complete account of enclosures. They are unrelated to the point we are trying to make here, but for discussion of them see Cohen and Weitzman, "A Marxian Type Model of Enclosures."

One further word of evidence is in order. In the parliamentary enclosures of the eighteenth and nineteenth centuries, Chambers and Mingay have observed a rise in labor requirements and an actual increase in the agricultural population.[31] Yet Eric Kerridge contends that, even in essentially arable areas in the seventeenth century, depopulation occurred where farms were enlarged or consolidated without undergoing legal enclosure. Many parliamentary enclosures, then, may have been mere formalities in areas where estates had already been engrossed and consolidated. There is even reason to believe that parliamentary acts enclosed some land that was in fact already enclosed.[32] Everywhere where common rights were extinguished, very small-scale cultivators or holders of livestock declined in number. This is not to say that new techniques introduced prior to or accompanying enclosure might not offset the tendency to cut back on labor, shifting the total product curve upward. In the decades around 1800, this would suffice to explain the impressions of Chambers and Mingay. But there is no evidence that such shifts occurred in the sixteenth or seventeenth centuries.[33]

We have tried to show, through the use of a theoretical framework, that enclosure, stripped down to its underlying economic features, always exerted an influence in the direction of depopulation. Similarly, we were able to demonstrate that this result was closely bound to the increase in rental value of newly en-

[31] J. D. Chambers makes this a main point in "Enclosures and Labor Supply in the Industrial Revolution." Chambers and Mingay observe: "It should be emphasized that in the eighteenth century, with the exception of the late innovation (and only gradual adoption) of the threshing machine, the improved methods of farming were not labor-saving (although it is probable that the labor required per unit of output was reduced). And insofar as enclosure encouraged better farming and expanded acreage it may have greatly increased the supply of rural employment." (Chambers and Mingay, *The Agricultural Revolution*, pp. 98–99.) The supporting evidence for these conclusions is not detailed. Chambers and Mingay deal with the connection between enclosure and the disappearance of the small farmer, the supply of labor to industry, and the abridgment of labor on newly enclosed estates. These three issues must be separated, since they are fundamentally different. (See Cohen and Weitzman, "A Marxian Type Model of Enclosures.") While many of their observations are valid, therefore, such as that parliamentary commissions tended to operate fairly, they are unrelated to whether enclosing an estate led to a reduction in the number of peasants working on that estate.

[32] E. Kerridge, *The Agricultural Revolution* (London, 1967), p. 51.

[33] Kerridge, "Agriculture, 1500–1793," p. 46. Hoskins makes a similar point in *The Midland Peasant*, p. 249.

closed estates. Finally, it was shown that enclosure was accompanied by a shift from a more to a less labor-intensive production process. This framework allowed us to explain and emphasize economic aspects of the movement not apparent in contemporary comment or the historical literature.

The implications of this study extend beyond the historical case of England. Many present-day peasant economies in less-developed countries have common property features that closely resemble those of medieval open-field villages. The transition to commercial agriculture in these areas will provoke social problems similar to those that plagued England in the sixteenth and seventeenth centuries. The model presented can be extended to show that enclosures lead to highly complex economic changes—changes that are technically progressive, since they give rise to greater efficiency and specialization, but are simultaneously socially disastrous to labor, since in themselves they produce, by inexorable economic logic, an initial and appreciable decline in the standard of living of peasants and so of the working population as a whole.

Part Three

PEASANTS AND INDUSTRIALIZATION

5

Agriculture and Peasant Industry in
Eighteenth-Century Flanders.

FRANKLIN F. MENDELS

Well before the coming of modern industrialization in the nineteenth century, a large section of the population of Flanders was
involved in industrial occupations. A large export-oriented linen
industry—outside the framework of the city or factory—had
developed in the countryside during the seventeenth and eighteenth centuries to complement agricultural production on many
farms. Of the 600,000 inhabitants of East Flanders in 1800, more
than 100,000 adults and an undetermined number of children
were spinning flax, while another 22,000 adults were engaged in
weaving linen, mostly on a part-time basis.[1] This essay will discuss the impact of industry on agrarian organization and agricul-

* This paper has greatly benefited from the contributions made by Iris
Mendels and Lutz K. Berkner. It is based in part on material contained in
my unpublished dissertation (University of Wisconsin, 1969) for which
support was received from the Population Council and the University of
Wisconsin. This work has since been supported by USPHS Grant HD 05586,
and by grants from the UCLA Research Committee. Of course, I alone am
responsible for views expressed here.

I have followed the Anglo-American custom concerning Flemish place
names. When an English translation does not exist, the French version, if
available, is used.

[1] G.-Ch. Faipoult, *Mémoire statistique du département de l'Escaut*, Paris,
1805, edited by Paul Deprez (Ghent, 1960), p. 165. I would like to acknowledge my debts to the foundations laid in the published and unpublished
research of Professor Paul Deprez, of the University of Manitoba. I hope my
footnotes will reflect this adequately. I should also mention that the rarely
cited but superb piece by Professor Jan Craeybeckx, "De agrarische wortels
van de industriële omwenteling" [The Agrarian Roots of the Industrial
Revolution], *Revue belge de philologie et d'histoire* 41 (1963), 398–448,
anticipated some of my thoughts.

tural growth in Flanders in some of its spatial, economic, and demographic dimensions.

Industry

Producing linen had become the principal industrial activity in Flanders by 1800. The older woolen industry, which was the basis of Flemish industrial preeminence during the Middle Ages, had almost entirely vanished. Other industries, such as leather, paper, brick, glass, beer, gin, and linseed oil, although not negligible, were devoted only to the needs of the local population, and employed relatively few people.

Linen production was largely a rural activity. In Ghent, Bruges, Lille, Courtrai, and other cities, linen production stagnated or declined in the eighteenth century, while production in the rural hinterland increased. The number of looms in rural Vieuxbourg doubled from 4,976 to 8,868 between 1730 and 1792 [2] but decreased in Ghent from 400 to 300 between 1700 and 1780 (Figure 5-1). Although Ghent was declining as a center of manufacturing, it was becoming a more important commercial center. The number of pieces brought to the Ghent market doubled between 1700 and 1780 (Figure 5-2), and while there were only 39 linen manufacturers in the city in 1792, there were 69 merchants who dealt primarily in goods produced in the countryside.[3] The growth of rural industry is also attested in the probate inventories (*staten van goed*). They show a steady increase in the percentage of households that owned looms or

[2] Louis Varlez, *Les salaires dans l'industrie gantoise. II, L'industrie de la filature du lin* (Brussels, 1904), p. xxii; H. Coppejans-Desmedt, "De Gentse vlas industrie vanaf het einde van de XVIIIe eeuw tot de oprichting van de grote mecanische bedrijven (1838)," *Handelingen der Maatschappij voor Geschiedenis en Oudheidkunde te Gent* (HMGOG hereafter), new ser. 22 (1968), 179–202.

[3] "Tabelle van de getauwe bevonden binnen de naerschreven parochien, . . . 1792," edited by D. Berten, *Coutumes des pays et comté de Flandre, quartier de Gand, VII, Coutumes du Vieuxbourg de Gand* (Brussels, 1904), pp. 97–98; Paul Deprez, "De Kasselrij van de Oudburg in de XVIIIe eeuw," (Ph.D. dissertation, University of Ghent, 1960), p. 63. Source for Figures 5-1 and 5-2: J. Bastin, "De Gentse lijnwaadmarkt en linnenhandel in de XVIIe eeuw," HMGOG, new ser. 21 (1967), 131–62.

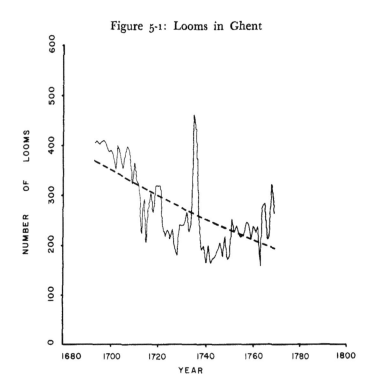

Figure 5-1: Looms in Ghent

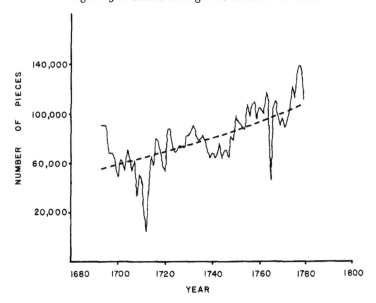

Figure 5-2: Pieces Brought to Market in Ghent

Table 5-1. Incidence of Spinning Wheels and Handlooms in Lede
            and Ertvelde

	1656–1705 [a]	1706–1755	1756–1795
Number of Inventories			
Lede	259	378	439
Ertvelde	292	237	221
Percentage with Spinning Wheels			
Lede	68	80	80
Ertvelde	77	77	85
Percentage with Handlooms			
Lede	43	48	50
Ertvelde	31	30	47
Percentage with Spinning Wheels and Handlooms			
Lede	33	39	41
Ertvelde	23	25	42
Percentage with Spinning Wheels or Handlooms			
Lede	83	90	91
Ertvelde	85	81	90

a Ertvelde, 1642–1705
Sources: J. de Brouwer, *Geschiedenis van Lede* (Lede, 1963), p. 246; A. de Vos,
    Geschiedenis van Ertvelde (Ertvelde, 1971), p. 456.

spinning wheels in the eighteenth century.[4] By the end of that
period, that proportion had become very high indeed (Table
5-1), reaching 90 percent in some cases. The proportion of households that owned a loom or a spinning wheel was much higher
than the proportion of heads of households who were classified as
weavers or spinners in the census.[5] This reflects the extent to
which the linen industry provided an income supplement.

The value of the annual output of linen cloth in the first
years of the nineteenth century amounted to 25.7 million francs.
In East Flanders the value of the production of linen cloth was

[1] Deprez, "Kasselrij," p. 74; A. de Vos, *Geschiedenis van Ertvelde* (Ertvelde,
1971), p. 456; J. de Brouwer, *Geschiedenis van Lede* (Lede, 1963), p. 235;
de Brouwer, *Geschiedenis van Impe* (Ghent, 1958), pp. 70–71; de Brouwer,
"Zo groeide Hofstade," *Tijdschrift van de Heemkundige Vereniging "Het
Land van Aalst"* 10 (1958), p. 20; de Brouwer, "Bijdrage tot de geschiedenis
van Denderleeuw," *Tijschrift van de Heemkundige Vereniging "Het Land
van Aalst"* 12 (1960), p. 30.

[5] In Ertvelde almost a half of the households had a loom at the end of the
eighteenth century, but there were only fifty-three weavers, or 7 percent of
the heads of household in the labor force. De Vos, *Ertvelde*, p. 717.

roughly equivalent to one-half of the value of the potato harvest, or one-third of the value of the harvest of all cereals.[6] Only a fraction of this linen cloth was consumed regionally. It was estimated in the department of West Flanders that local consumption amounted to 16 percent (1.2 million for a production of 7.3 million francs).[7] Only the production from the area of Courtrai and from southern Flanders was exported to France, and the principal market for the rest of the Flemish linen industry during the seventeenth and eighteenth centuries was Spain and her American colonies.[8] The *presillas* were used for packing coffee and indigo, the *brabantes* were used for the clothing of negro slaves, for packing, and for draperies, and the striped and checkered cloth (*toiles rayées and toiles à carreaux*) were used in making mattresses, drapes, and clothing for negro slaves.[9]

In the Spanish and Spanish-American market, Flanders competed with other large and growing European exporters. The Irish, Scots, Bretons, Dutch, Saxons, Silesians, and Russians were striving to improve their position, and, judging from the production and trade statistics, were successful.[10] Flanders thus had a significant place in the world market but essentially remained a price-taker: it was faced with an elastic demand for its linens at a world price it could not affect. On the contrary, the pros-

[6] These figures refer to year IX (1801–1802): East Flanders, 10.5 million francs; West Flanders, 7.3 million francs; South Flanders, 7.9 million francs (arrondissements of Bergues, Hazebrouck, and Lille), Dieudonné, *Statistique du Département du Nord* (Douai, 1804) vol. 2, 216; C. Viry, *Mémoire Statistique du département de la Lys* (Paris, 1804), p. 174.

[7] Viry, *Mémoire Statistique.*

[8] Natalis Briavoinne, *Mémoire sur l'état de la population, des fabriques, des manufactures et du commerce dans les provinces des Pays-Bas depuis Albert et Isabelle jusqu'à la fin du siècle dernier*, Académie Royale de Belgique, Mémoires Couronnés, 14 (Brussels, 1840); H. Coppejans-Desmedt, *Bijdrage tot le studie van de gegoede burgerij te Gent in de XVIII^{de} eeuw*, Verhandelingen van de Koninklijke Vlaamse Academie voor de Letteren, Wetenschappen en Schone Kunsten van België, [VKVA hereafter], 14 (Brussels, 1952).

[9] C. van Hoobrouck-Mooregem, *Exposition des produits de l'industrie du département de l'Escaut reçus à la mairie de Gand, à l'occasion du passage du Premier Consul en cette ville en Thermidor an VI* (Ghent, 1803). Rijksarchief, Ghent.

[10] J. G. van Bel, *De linnenhandel van Amsterdam in de XVIIIe eeuw* (Amsterdam, 1940), p. 49 and *passim*. Figures showing the impressive growth of the Irish and Scottish linen production are available in John Horner, *The Linen Trade of Europe* (Belfast, 1902). For other references, see Franklin Mendels, "Industrialization and Population Pressure in Eighteenth-Century Flanders," Ph.D. dissertation, University of Wisconsin, 1969.

perity of its merchants, farmers, wage laborers, and landlords was affected by the world price, and many contemporaries were quite aware of this.[11]

The income of a large part of the Flemish population, particularly the peasantry, had thus come to depend on the vagaries of international trade. For many—probably most—of the peasants in question, working in the linen industry was a part-time activity. The weavers and spinners took up their instruments only at times when agriculture did not demand their labor. Essentially, weaving and spinning were winter activities. In a full working day (5 A.M. to 8 P.M.), 5 to 6 els, that is, about 4 to 5 yards, of average quality linen cloth could be woven.[12] Thus it took 12 to 15 days of full-time work to weave one standard "piece" of 75 els (about 60 yards). On the basis of the census of 1792, 12 pieces of linen were calculated as the average output of an operating loom in the industrial villages near Ghent,[13] which means that the weavers worked an equivalent of 140 to 200 days per year.

According to the same source, each loom occupied one weaver, four spinners, and one and one-half other auxiliary workers, who could be children. In a household of this size and composition (a self-contained production unit), 5 els of linen could be obtained by working full time for one day. For this quantity, 3.75 pounds of flax were needed. Unless a peasant spinner grew it himself, the flax cost him 26 groten in the market at the middle of the century, while the final product (5 els of ordinary linen cloth) had a sales price of 60 groten. A full day's work for a five-person household could thus bring an income of 34 groten. This sum was very low, even compared with the average wage of unskilled workers, which was 20 groten per day in the winter.

---

[11] For comments by a Ghent merchant, see those quoted by J. Lefèvre, *Etude sur le commerce de la Belgique avec l'Espagne au XVIIIᵉ siècle*, Académie Royale de Belgique, Mémoires, Coll. in-8°, 2d ser. 16 (Brussels, 1922), p. 179. Paul Deprez has found a relationship between fluctuations in seignorial rents and conditions in the linen market. Deprez, "De inkomsten van het Land van Nevele," *Bijdragen tot de geschiedenis der Stad Deinze en van het Land aan Leie en Schelde*, 32 and 33 (1965 and 1966), 45–75 and 55–72.

[12] A. J. L. van den Bogaerde, *Proef op de Aanmoediging en uitbreiding der linnenweveryen in Oost-Vlaanderen, gevolgd an de tienjarige optelling van al de op de markten van Oost-Vlaanderen verkochten lynwaeden* (Ghent, n.d. [c. 1825]).

[13] "Tabelle van de getauwe, 1792."

The daily income of a five-person household engaged in linen work was thus less than the wage of two unskilled workers.[14] The family probably persisted in producing linen because it could not earn more elsewhere. As we shall see, winter wage employment was very hard to find, and a family needed cash to supplement the insufficient food that could be extracted from the land it rented. In this sense, the colonial linen trade served as a vent for a surplus resource which, in Flanders, was a seasonal labor surplus.[15]

Most of the labor force engaged in the linen trade was of the kind described above: family labor with very low opportunity cost. But there were also landless wage workers and servants involved in the industry and receiving income from it. These were not usually employed directly by a merchant-manufacturer since, in Flanders, the peasants owned their tools until the nineteenth century, and merchants were therefore not directly engaged in production. Rather, these laborers worked during the dead season for cloth-working peasant families that, owing to their size or composition, did not possess the correct mix of labor inputs. The wages they could earn in this way were always comparatively low. In 1765, they amounted to four-fifths of the winter wages of other unskilled rural workers.[16] In 1800, the wages of a full-time adult weaver were 0.94 francs per day in the countryside, and 1.26 francs in the city, compared to 1.36 for the urban tailor and 1.81 for a mason.[17] The alternative to low-paying winter weaving was unemployment, which was heavy in Flanders (and with which the numerous urban charitable institutions were unable to cope). Fifteen percent of the population of Ghent was on relief in 1772,

[14] Mendels, "Industrialization," pp. 200ff., based on J. F. D. Lichtervelde *Mémoire sur les fonds ruraux du Département de l'Escaut* (Ghent, 1815), pp. 114–15; Georges Willemsen, "Contribution à l'histoire de l'industrie linière en Flandre," HMGOG 7 (1906), 255; Paul Deprez, "Prijzen te Sint-Niklaas-Waas," in Charles Verlinden, *et al.*, eds., *Dokumenten voor de geschiedenis van prijzen en lonen in Vlaanderen en Brabant (XV–XVIIIᵉ eeuw)* (Bruges, 1959), pp. 121–23.

[15] This concept was popularized by H. Myint, "The 'Classical' Theory of International Trade and the Underdeveloped Countries," reprinted in Myint, *Economic Theory and the Underdeveloped Countries* (London, 1971), pp. 118–46.

[16] Willemsen, "Industrie linière," p. 229; Deprez, "Oudburg;" Denise de Weerdt, "Loon en levensvoorwarden van de fabrieksarbeiders, 1789–1850," in Jan Dhondt, ed., *Geschiedenis van de socialistische arbeidersbeweging in Belgie* (Antwerp, 1960), pp. 71–73.

[17] Archives Nationales, Paris, F20 139 (1801–1802).

when the government opened the first "modern" European prison, a thick-walled workshop where the inmates paid for their upkeep by working linen. Fourteen years later (1786), 20 percent were on relief in Ghent (9,480 out of about 45,000). For East Flanders, 57,000 persons were said to be on relief in 1801 in a population of 600,000.[18]

Poverty and unemployment thus coexisted with the form of industrial growth described above. This was not because industry produced impoverishment. Rather it appears on first analysis that an already impoverished population was forced to turn to industrial by-occupations to save themselves from destitution. In 1733 an observer wrote of Wasquehall, South Flanders, that the inhabitants were becoming "too numerous for all to apply themselves to agriculture; three-quarters of the inhabitants of the countryside are now occupied in manufacturing, with which they can pay their taxes and maintain their families, who would be reduced to mendicity without this help."[19] The relationship between agriculture and industry was more complex, however, than is implied by this statement. As we shall see, agricultural technology in fact permitted some degree of labor intensification. But before one can attempt to analyze the relationships between this industrial growth and the agricultural sector, the spatial distribution of the linen industry must be examined (see Figure 5-3).

The linen industry of Flanders was confined to the interior of the region; it was bounded on the west by the maritime strip along the English Channel. For instance, the area *(Métier)* of Furnes near the coast had 19,396 persons in the labor force in 1697, only 60 of whom (3.1 percent) were engaged in the textile industry. A century later (1796) there were still only 5.0 percent.[20]

[18] P. C. van der Meersch, "De l'état de la mendicité et de la bienfaisance dans la province de Flandre Orientale, 1740–1850," *Bulletin de la Commission centrale de statistique* 5 (1853), 25–268; Paul Bonenfant, *Le problème du paupérisme en Belgique à la fin de l'Ancien Régime*, Académie Royale de Belgique, Mémoires, Coll. in-8° (Brussels, 1934), pp. 33ff.

[19] In Victor Prévôt, "L'industrie linière du Nord de la France sous l'Ancien Régime," *Revue du Nord* 39 (1957), 214.

[20] In the polders proper, they were only 1.1 percent. D. Dalle, "De bevolking van de stad en van de Kasselrij Veurne in 1796," *Album Archivaris Jos. De Smet* (Bruges, 1964), p. 130; Dalle, "De volkstelling van 1697 in Veurne-Ambacht en de evolutie van het Veurnse bevolkingscijfer in de XVIIe eeuw," *Handelingen van het Genootschap voor Geschiedenis te Brugge* 40 (1953), 95–130 and 41 (1954), 18–54.

Figure 5-3: Map of Flanders

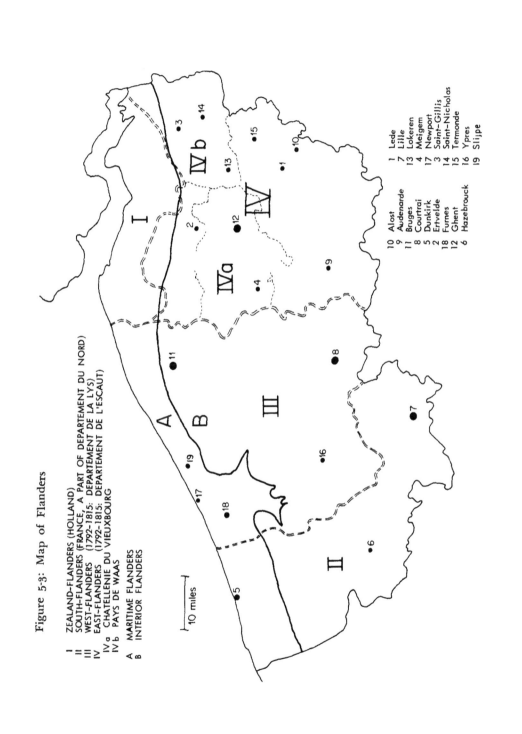

I   ZEALAND-FLANDERS (HOLLAND)
II   SOUTH-FLANDERS (FRANCE, A PART OF DEPARTEMENT DU NORD)
III WEST-FLANDERS (1792-1815: DEPARTEMENT DE LA LYS)
IV   EAST-FLANDERS (1792-1815: DEPARTEMENT DE L'ESCAUT)
IVa CHATELLENIE DU VIEUXBOURG
IVb PAYS DE WAAS

A   MARITIME FLANDERS
B   INTERIOR FLANDERS

10 miles

10	Alost	1	Lede
9	Audenarde	7	Lille
11	Bruges	13	Lokeren
8	Courtrai	4	Meigem
5	Dunkirk	17	Newport
18	Ervelde	3	Saint–Gillis
2	Furnes	14	Saint–Nicholas
12	Ghent	15	Termonde
6	Hazebrouck	16	Ypres
		19	Slijpe

Indeed, the hinterland of Furnes (and Ypres) had shed its old woolen industry by the end of the seventeenth century, almost precisely when other areas of Flanders were acquiring international significance in linen production.[21]

The industrial interior was bounded on the east by the flax-growing Pays de Waas and the hinterland of Termonde, with their markets in Saint-Nicholas, Lokeren, and Termonde. "The Pays de Waas and the area of Termonde do not have a large linen manufacture. The thousand to fifteen hundred looms there do not merit much consideration when in a single village of the Châtellenies of Vieuxbourg, Alost, Courtrai or Audenarde, there are more than a thousand." [22] A number of spinners and only a few weavers worked there; but the flax harvest was large, larger than the quantities consumed domestically by the linen industry. Indeed, a handsome surplus of more than one-fourth of the total output was sent abroad in normal years.[23] This commercial flax production was supplemented by the limited amount that peasants could grow on their own, and by the production that originated in the maritime areas.[24]

Finally, the degree of industrialization in the southeast of Flanders, particularly the area immediately east of Audenarde, is difficult to ascertain. The proportion of weavers in the labor force appears to have fallen in the second half of the eighteenth century, but there is some doubt as to the quality of the data used by De Rammelaere in establishing this fact.[25]

To summarize, the linen industry was located in the interior. Its labor was local, its raw materials mainly came from the northeast (Pays de Termonde and Pays de Waas). It must nevertheless be remembered that every village of the industrial area did not have a large number of weavers. One can easily find in the local censuses of the Revolutionary period areas where two

[21] E. Coornaert, *La draperie-sayetterie d'Hondschoote (XIV–XVIIIe s.)* (Rennes, 1930); D. Dalle, "Pogingen tot het héropbeuring van de wolnijverheid te Veurne (15de–17de eeuw)" (Ghent, 1960), pp. 77–86.

[22] Text of 1765 quoted in Willemsen, "Industrie linière," p. 291.

[23] Mendels, "Industrialization," pp. 192ff.; Willemsen, "Industrie linière," pp. 255, 269, 281; P. Lenders, s.j., *De politieke crisis in Vlaanderen omstreeks het midden der achttiende eeuw* VKVA 25 (Brussels, 1956).

[24] P. J. Bouman, *Geschiedenis van de Zeeuwschen landbouw in de negentiende en twintigste eeuw* (Wageningen, 1946), pp. 17–18.

[25] G. De Rammelaere, "De beroepsstructuur van de plattelandse bevolking in Zuidoost-Vlaanderen gedurende de 18e eeuw," *Tijdschrift voor sociale wetenschappen* (Ghent) 4 (1957), 225–43.

almost contiguous villages had entirely different occupational structures. For example, the village of Balegem southeast of Ghent had as many weaving household heads as there were farmers, while neighboring Lemberge did not shelter a single weaver or spinner.[26]

Land and Labor in Maritime Flanders

There is a counterpart to the spatial distribution of industry in the spatial organization of Flemish agriculture. The lack of rural industrial development in the maritime strip was related to the development there of a commercial agriculture with large, up-to-date farms and a scattered and sparse population. This is in contrast to the agriculture and settlement pattern of the interior, which was marked by subsistence peasant agriculture, small farms, and a very dense population.

Maritime Flanders is a strip of polders (land reclaimed from the sea and below sea level), bordered by a fringe of dunes that extends from Artois through Zealand-Flanders to the Scheldt. Its soil, reclaimed between the ninth and nineteenth centuries, consists of a layer of heavy loam resting on a sandy foundation in the subsoil. In contrast to the rest of Flanders, it is extremely fertile and able to support soil-exhausting crops. Its dense fabric, however, requires very sturdy, heavy, and costly ploughs and other implements pulled by teams of horses. The nature of the soil thus required a large amount of fixed capital.[27] This region, not surprisingly, was one of large capitalistic farms, a region of *grande culture* (Table 5–2). It produced wheat, butter, and cheese for sale in foreign as well as domestic markets. Some of the land in the dunes or along the dikes and highways, however, was fragmented and owned or rented by peasants and part-time agricultural workers. In contrast to the rest of Flanders, a large proportion of the soil was held by successful farmers, who employed a large number of agricultural laborers or servants, or

[26] Results of a study of the family and social structure of these two villages and others will appear shortly.

[27] Viry, *Mémoire;* J. N. H. Schwerz, *Anleitung zur Kenntnisz der belgischen Landwirtschaft* (Halle, 1808–1811), Vol. 3, 123ff.; Emile de Laveleye, *Essai sur l'économie rurale de la Belgique* (Paris, 1875), p. 25; Raoul Blanchard, *La Flandre* (Paris, 1906); M. A. Lefèvre, *L'habitat rural en Belgique* (Liège, 1926).

Table 5–2. Size of Farms, Polder Area, Métier of Furnes, 1697

Hectares	Number of Farms	Percent of Farms
20 and above	14	28.6
15–19	5	10.2
10–14	13	26.5
5–9	14	28.6
Less than 5	3	6.1
Total	49	100.0

Source: D. Dalle, "De bevolkstelling van 1697 in Veurne-Ambacht en de evolutie van het Veurnse bevolkingscijfer in de 17e eeuw," *Handeligen van het Genootschap voor Geschiedenis, Société d'Emulation, te Brugge* 90 (1953), 97–130.

both. Almost 38 percent of the labor force was classified as wage workers in 1697 in the métier of Furnes.[28] It was an agrarian structure similar to the English style.

Maritime Flanders was never as densely settled as the rest of the region. The maritime section of the department of Escaut (Zealand-Flanders) had a density of 53 persons per square kilometer in 1800, compared to 191 in the rest of the department.[29] The maritime arrondissement of Dunkirk had a density of 117 at about the same date, while the area around Lille in the interior had 272.[30] Similarly, maritime Furnes had 71, but Courtrai in the interior had 200.[31] The population density of the whole region was high (West Flanders, 115; Nord, 141; East Flanders, 165; as opposed to England and Wales, 45; France, 50; the Netherlands, 60; Belgium, 88), but the aggregate statistics conceal the marked contrast between maritime and interior Flanders. The density was extreme in the interior, and there was a marked internal differentiation of high and low-density zones. As a consequence of the sparse local population, the large farms depended on migrant labor to meet the seasonal needs of agriculture. Wages in the maritime areas were reputed to be higher than in

[28] In Lede (interior), there were 6.2 percent in 1796. De Brouwer, *Lede*, p. 240; Dalle, "Bevolking 1796," p. 130.

[29] Faipoult, *Mémoire*, p. 30.

[30] Dieudonné, *Mémoire;* and Raoul Blanchard, *La densité de la population du département du Nord au XIXe siècle* (Lille, 1906).

[31] J. Peuchet and P. G. Chanlaire, *Description topographique et statistique de la France* (Paris, 1811), Vol. 17.

the rest of Flanders, as one would expect under such conditions.[32] In the maritime region, however, there was little permanent immigration of surplus labor from the rest of the country; in fact, there is evidence of measures taken by the local authorities to prevent this from happening.[33]

The population growth of villages in the maritime region was generally slower in the eighteenth century than in interior villages. In sample areas taken from the maritime region of Furnes, population only increased from 6,600 to 9,600 persons between 1700 and 1800.[34] In other areas the population completely stagnated, while villages a few miles away, situated in the sandy zone, experienced rapid growth. A prefect once wrote that the death rate was higher in the very low and humid areas of the polders, where the climate tended to be unhealthy.[35] But other literary evidence links the slow population growth to late marriages and widespread celibacy. The marriage and migration patterns are related to the persistence of large commercial farms.[36] Since it would have been uneconomical to divide them, because the soil required heavy ploughs that were only practical on large plots,[37] the farms remained unfragmented and all the farmers' sons could not become farmers in turn. They had to enter into other occupations or migrate. Little is known about emigration, but it is my hypothesis that it differed in the mari-

[32] Archives Nationales, Paris, F20 435 Lys; Rijksarchief Ghent, Escaut 1636 (1805); Thomas Radcliff, *A Report on the Agriculture of Eastern and Western Flanders* (London, 1819), p. 192; D. Dalle, *De bevolking van Veurne-Ambacht in de 17ᵉ eeuw*, VKVA 49 (Brussels, 1963), 100.

[33] Whereas Deprez shows evidence of the construction of cabins in the sandy areas of the interior, Dalle has shown the stiff resistance on the part of the local authorities to such construction, as witnessed by regulations and prohibitions in the course of the eighteenth century. Deprez, "De boeren"; Dalle, *Veurne-Ambacht*, pp. 83–88. Similarly, for Zealand-Flanders, see M. T. Boerendonk, *Historische studie over den Zeeuwschen landbouw* (The Hague, 1935), pp. 322–24.

[34] Dalle, *Veurne-Ambacht*, p. 180.

[35] Faipoult, *Mémoire*, pp. 29–30.

[36] Viry, *Mémoire*, p. 50; Abbé Mann, *Mémoire sur les moyens d'augmenter la population et de perfectionner la culture dans les Pays-Bas Autrichiens*, Mémoires de l'Académie Impériale et Royale des Sciences et Belles Lettres 4 (Brussels, 1783), p. 171.

[37] It would have been impossible for small farms to share in the use of ploughs because it was the practice to enclose the fields with ditches, hedges, bushes, or rows of trees. C. Petit, "Clôtures et forme des champs en Belgique," *Bulletin de la Société Belge d'Etudes Géographiques* 12 (1942), 125–222; F. Dussart, "Les types de dessin parcellaire et leur répartition en Belgique," *ibid.*, 30 (1961), 21–65.

time regions from the experience of the interior, where no such curbs to fragmentation existed.

Land and Labor in the Interior

The interior of Flanders experienced a comparatively high average population growth rate in the eighteenth century. In spite of very slow growth in the first two or three decades, the population doubled by the end of the century. (The population of England and Wales only increased by 55 percent, that of Holland by 10 percent.) The population density of the Flemish interior was comparatively high in 1700—it had already been high in the Middle Ages in comparison with the rest of Europe—and the trends in the eighteenth century only served to increase the contrast. It has already been noted above that, on first analysis, demographic pressure directly promoted rural industrialization. This is supported by the fact that those sections of the countryside where population growth was curbed did not industrialize. But it is premature to speak of demographic "pressure" until one has learned more about the agricultural response to population changes.

First, the rapid population increase created incentives both to clear new land and to reduce the amount of fallow. The former seems to have been undertaken by bankers, financiers, the nobility, and church landowners.[38] It is impossible to say how much of this took place in the course of the eighteenth century. We do know that toward the end of this period, woods, marshes, and heaths added up to approximately one seventh of the total surface of the department of East Flanders,[39] and a later inquiry expressed pessimism about the possibility of further reclamations.[40]

[38] Viry, *Mémoire*, pp. 26–27; G. G. Dept, "Note sur le défrichement dans le comté de Flandre au xviiie siècle," *Bulletin de la Société Belge d'Etudes Géographiques* 3 (1933), 120–29; H. Coppejans-Desmedt, "Economische opbloei in de Zuidelijke Nederlanden," in J. A. Van Houtte *et al.*, eds., *Algemene geschiedenis der Nederlanden*, Vol. 8 (Antwerp, 1955), 266; P. J. Bouman, *Zeeuwsche landbouw*, p. 14.

[39] Faipoult, *Mémoire*, p. 149.

[40] By 1820, in the Province of East Flanders (now amputated of most of Zealand-Flanders) 250,000 out of 275,000 hectares were productive. Algemene Rijksarchief, The Hague, Nationale Nijverheid N 3394b. Rapport sur le défrichement des terres au Ministre de l'Industrie Nationale, 1820; and Observations sur le défrichement des terres incultes, des landes, et des bruyères de la Flandre Orientale, 1819.

The possibilities of reducing the amount of fallow land had been almost exhausted, too; a famous trait of Flemish agriculture, which impressed foreign visitors so much in this period, was farming without fallow.[41] Instead, farmers used long and complex rotation sequences, including an occasional year under clover, and made use of various types of manure purchased at the market, such as the refuse from gin distilleries.

Besides expanding the total area under cultivation, the number of farms increased in the interior, particularly among the smallest sizes (Table 5–3). The village of Lede, east of Ghent, approximately doubled its population between 1701 and 1791 (from ca. 1300 to ca. 2600 persons), but the number of its smallest farms more than doubled. The same was true of neighboring Saint-Gilles (Table 5–4). It is possible both that small tenures were further divided, and that some large blocks were split up by their owners. (In Tables 5–3 and 5–4, note the decrease in farms above 10 hectares).[42] It would appear that population growth

[41] Richard Weston, *A Discourse of Husbandrie used in Brabant and Flanders shewing the Wonderful Improvements* . . . (London, 1652), in the University of Wisconsin, rare books collection; Paul Lindemans, *Geschiedenis van de landbouw in Belgie*, Vol. 1 (Antwerp, 1952), 117ff.; Bernhard H. Slicher van Bath, "The Rise of Intensive Husbandry in the Low Countries," in J. S. Bromley and E. H. Kossman, eds., *Britain and the Netherlands* (London, 1960), pp. 130–53.

[42] In Meigem, a sandy village west of Ghent, the number of small farms did not increase as rapidly, although the population also doubled. Paul Deprez, "Uitbatingen en grondbezit in Meigem (1571–1787). Een methodologisch artikel," HMGOG, new ser. 10 (1956), 159–65; see also C. De Rammelaere, "Bijdrage tot de Landbouwgeschiedenis in Zuid-Oostvlaanderen (1570–1790)," HMGOG, new ser. 16 (1962), 21–40; de Brouwer, "Denderleeuw," p. 42; de Brouwer, "Hofstade," p. 32; and de Brouwer, "Impe," pp. 76ff.

Table 5–3. Size of Farms, Lede

Hectares	Number			
	1695	1701	1751	1791
20 and above	4	5	4	3
10–19	20	23	11	5
5–9	15	23	28	43
2–4.9	85	88	120	120
1–1.9	73	82	122	131
0.3–0.9	86	74	76	121
less than 0.3	130	52	89	169
Total	350	345	450	472

Source: J. de Brouwer, *Geschiedenis van Lede* (Lede, 1963), p. 219.

Table 5-4. Size of Farms, Saint-Gilles

Hectares	Number	
	1691	1797
15 and above	5	4
10–14	21	5
5–9	38	45
1–4	95	180
0.6–0.9	12	21
less than 0.6	19	105
Total	190	360

Source: M. Bovyn, *St-Gillis bij Dendermonde in 1571–1800* (Ghent, 1958).

was directly responsible for the fragmentation, but this relationship was in fact mediated by the land tenure system. Tenancy was more common than proprietorship among small as well as large farms, both in the interior of Flanders and in the maritime region. In Meigem, for instance, of the 111 holdings counted in 1765, 79 were held in tenancy, 11 were owned by their occupiers, and 21 were mixed. Of the 11 that were held in proprietorship entirely, none was larger than 4 hectares, while all of the 6 farms that were larger than 25 hectares were farmed by tenants. Tenancy was thus the usual form of land tenure, and the more so among the larger farms.[43] The same was true in the maritime area.[44] The exception to this Flemish pattern was found along the eastern border of the interior, where peasant proprietorship was predominant.

In Lede, which belonged to this area, of the 350 holdings counted in 1695, 63 were held in tenancy, 253 were owned by their occupiers, while the others were mixed.[45] The eastern boundary of the area of proprietorship has been mapped by Paul Deprez, but his source was not indicated.[46] It shows the Pays de Waas, the Pays de Termonde, and the Pays d'Alost to

[43] Paul Deprez, "De boeren in de 16de, 17de, en 18de eeuw," in J. L. Broeckx *et al., Flandria Nostra* (Antwerp, 1957), Vol. 1, 141–42. Also, I. Delatte, "L'évolution de la structure agraire en Belgique de 1575 à 1950," *Annales du Congrès de la fédération archéologique et historique de Belgique, Tournai, 1949* (Brussels, 1951), Vol. 1, 480–88.

[44] D. Dalle, "Landbouwbedrijven in het Iperse in 1695," *Handelingen van het Genootschap "Société d'Emulation" te Brugge* 101 (1964), 240–47.

[45] De Rammelaere, "Zuid-Oostvlaanderen," pp. 38–40; de Brouwer, *Lede,* p. 208.

[46] Deprez, "De boeren," p. 142.

the south of Audenarde as the areas of ownership. Much of this area of peasant proprietorship does not seem to have been heavily industrialized, but the tantalizing correlation breaks down when one remembers that the Pays d'Alost (where Lede is located) had many weavers and spinners.

But the Pays d'Alost differed in one other respect—it was the only area of Flanders where open fields still prevailed. The fields were divided there into minuscule strips, sometimes no larger than 30 by 300 feet [47] (about one-tenth of a hectare). In fact, in Lede there were 27 "farms" in 1695, 28 in 1701, 46 in 1751, and 106 in 1791 that were smaller than one-thirteenth of one hectare.[48] Within the same Pays, however, there coexisted large blocks of land tilled by wealthy farmers.

The causes for such differences in both the ownership and layout of land probably could not be found in soil conditions. They lay, rather, in the conditions and period of initial settlement in the Middle Ages.[49]

The number of peasant proprietors may have increased slightly in the course of the eighteenth century.[50] Some writers have, in fact, explained the astounding increase in land prices by attributing it to the peasants' strong taste for proprietorship, even if there purchases were accompanied by great indebtedness, made possible by the development of a mortgage system.[51] Although peasant demand undoubtedly helped drive up the price of land, there were other reasons as well. Much of the land in Flemish villages was owned by landlords from neighboring cities. Jan Frans Hopsomer, a bourgeois of Ghent, owned one-fifth of the surface of Meigem.[52] Jacobus F. Maelcamp, another Gentenaar, was worth 70,000 gulden in real property at the time of his second marriage, and his possessions were spread over thirty-four different localities in Flanders. His rental income was estimated at 6654 gulden [53] for a rate of return of 9.5 percent at the time of his death in 1741.

[47] Dussart, "Dessin parcellaire," p. 36.

[48] De Brouwer, *Lede*, p. 219.

[49] A. E. Verhulst, *Histoire du paysage rural en Flandre* (Brussels, 1966).

[50] Deprez, "Meigem;" Hubert van Houtte, *Histoire économique de la Belgique à la fin de l'Ancien Régime* (Ghent, 1920), pp. 405ff.

[51] van Houtte, pp. 509-10. See also Deprez, "De hypothekaire grondrente in Vlaanderen gedurende de 18de eeuw," *Tijdschrift voor Geschiedenis* 79 (1966), 141-49.

[52] Deprez, "Meigem," p. 169.

[53] Coppejans-Desmedt, *Gegoede Burgerij*, pp. 117-19.

Such handsome returns on land did not persist. As is shown
in Table 5–5, the price of land increased much faster than land
rents in the interior, driving down the rate of return to 1.5

Table 5–5. Prices, Rent, and Population

	1690–99	1700–09	1730–39	1750–59	1790–89
Interior					
1) Price of Land	1.26	1.00	1.34	2.57	10.22
2) Rent of Land	0.69	1.00	1.02	1.02	2.31
3) Rate of Return on Land	3.6%	6.6%	5.0%	2.6%	1.5%
4) Price of Rye	1.67	1.00	0.78	0.85	1.10
5) Price of Linens	1.13	1.00	0.79	1.28	1.96
6) Population	n.a.	1.00	1.16	n.a.	1.67
Maritime Area					
7) Rent of Land	1.11	1.00	1.30	1.07	1.89
8) Price of Wheat	1.32	1.00	0.76	0.91	1.19
9) Population	n.a.	1.00	1.01	n.a.	1.30

Sources:

1) Land prices from the area of Nevele; Paul Deprez, "De boeren in de 16de, 17de, en 18de eeuw," in J. L. Broeckx *et al.*, *Flandria Nostra* (Antwerp, 1957), Vol. 1, 144. Base 1700–1709=100.

2) Land rents from the same as (1); *ibid.*, p. 147. Church and poor administration property.

3) Rent÷price, from the data for (1) and (2).

4) Ghent *mercuriale*. Base 1699–1708=100, 1709 being extraordinarily high, in Charles Verlinden *et al.*, *Dokumenten voor de geschiedenis van prijzen en lonen in Vlaanderen en Brabant, XVe–XVIIIe eeuw* (Bruges, 1959), pp. 64–65.

5) Linen prices in Spain deflated by the Spanish/Flemish silver price ratio, in Earl J. Hamilton, *War and Prices in Spain, 1651–1800*, (Cambridge, Mass., 1947), pp. 34, 53, 77, 233ff., and Verlinden, *Dokumenten*, p. 21.

6) Sample taken from villages in the neighborhood of Ghent. Source: Franklin Mendels, "Industrialization and Population Pressure in Eighteenth-Century Flanders," Ph.D. dissertation, University of Wisconsin, 1969, p. 144. 1696–1705, 1716–1745, and 1786–1795.

7) Rent from the polder village of Slijpe. Church and poor administration property. Base 1700–1709=100. Verlinden, *Dokumenten*, pp. 237–38.

8) Wheat is a more representative product than rye in the polders. Mercuriale of Newport. Base 1699–1708=100. Verlinden, *Dokumenten*, pp. 67ff.

9) Sample taken from ten villages in the neighborhood of Furnes by D. Dalle, *De bevolking van Veurne-Ambacht in de 17^e eeuw*, Verhandelingen van de Koninklijke Vlaamse Academie voor de Letteren, Wetenschappen en Schone Kunsten van België 49 (Brussels, 1963), 24–25, 227. Years: 1693, 1704, 1735, 1794.

percent in the 1780s. Mortgage rates fell continuously from an average of 6 percent at the beginning of the eighteenth century to 4.5 percent toward the end.[54] If the principal source of the increase in land prices had been peasant demand, one would have expected mortgage rates to rise as well, because peasants were presumably the ones who had to borrow in order to purchase land. But in reality they fell. This suggests that the supply of loanable funds increased faster than the demand for them from the so-called land-hungry peasantry. This in turn suggests that the urban merchants, manufacturers, and magistrates who injected money in the mortgage market were also responsible for most of the increase in land prices.

Why did these land purchasers allow the rate of return on their landed investment to fall so low, lower even than what they could earn on mortgages? The reason was that this form of investment paid nonmonetary dividends in the form of security and prestige. Land rents also increased, although less than land prices. The fact that they increased faster than food prices, however, could be explained by a combination of an increase in population, land-saving agricultural changes, the development of the linen industry, and land fragmentation. Finally, land rents did not increase as fast in the maritime area as in the interior because of a slower population increase, fewer land-saving agricultural changes, the lack of development of a rural industry, and barriers to land fragmentation.

The rapid fragmentation of the land could have been induced by the prevalence of an egalitarian system of inheritance customs.[55] However, the latter probably had more effect on transfers of land titles among absentee owners than on their tenants. It is often forgotten that the legal rules of inheritance deal with the

[54] Deprez, "Hypothekaire grondrente." New estimates of land rent based on a much larger sample than previously used confirm Deprez' figures. See F. de Wever, "Pachtprijzen in de streek rond Gent (18e eeuw)," in Verlinden, *Dokumenten* 3 (1972), 222–86. See also de Wever, "Pachtprijzen in Vlaanderen en Brabant in de achttiende eeuw. Bijdrage tot de konjunktuurstudie," *Tijdschrift voor Geschiendenis* 85 (1972), 180–204 (this article came to my attention after the final draft of this paper was written). My thanks to Vernon Ruttan and J. Verhelst for their critique.

[55] *L'agriculture belge*, Congrès International de Paris, 1878 (Paris, 1878), p. xxxiii; Jean Yver, "Les deux groupes de coutumes du Nord," *Revue du Nord* 35 (1953) and 36 (1954); Félix van de Walle, *Le régime successoral dans les coutumes de Flandre* (Lille, 1902); E. M. Meijers, *Het Oost-Vlaamsche erfrecht* (Haarlem, 1936); *Het West-Vlaamsche erfrecht* (Haarlem, 1952).

ownership of real property and not its rental, and that therefore they should not be expected to affect the subdivision of the land in an area of tenancy if the owners live away from the villages. It is true that, in one of the rare concrete descriptions of Flemish succession practices, subdivision of the land among the offspring when the parents are deceased is mentioned.[56] A contrast is noted between the polder areas, where such practices never occur, and the interior, where they do. The study in question deals, however, with the Pays de Waas, which is precisely an area of ownership. If, therefore, the old Flemish inheritance customs could have had an effect on the evolution of the countryside, it would have been in the eastern border, where peasant ownership predominated.

Elsewhere, that is in most of Flanders, economic-demographic rather than legal causes must be sought. Fragmentation was ultimately caused by population growth, but it came about through the response of landlords to the price mechanism. The fragmentation of the land was a market phenomenon—the result of the fact that higher unit rents could be drawn from small holdings than from the large ones in the interior.[57]

Small self-contained family units with no wage labor only sought to maximize output, even if the marginal productivity of labor was thereby driven to very low levels.[58] When marginal productivity fell low enough, mostly in the winter, they started their seasonal textile occupation. Large holdings, on the other hand, required wage labor, and would not continue operating to the point where the marginal productivity of labor was lower than the set wage. Output per hectare on large holdings was therefore lower and commanded lower unit rents as well, as shown in Figure 5–4.

Although the interior of Flanders stands out as an area of

[56] Prosper Thuysbaert, *Het Land van Waes. Bijdrage tot de geschiedenis der landelijke bevolking in de XIXe eeuw* (Courtrai, 1913), pp. 70–71.

[57] Benoit Verhaegen, *Contribution à l'histoire économique des Flandres* (Louvain, 1961), I, 127ff.; De Laveleye, *Essai sur l'économie rurale de la Belgique* (Paris, 1875), pp. 51–52; Guillaume Jacquemyns, *Histoire de la crise économique des Flandres* Académie Royale de Belgique, Mémoires, Coll. in-8°, 26 (Brussels, 1929), 233; S. Seebohm Rowntree, *Land and Labour. Lessons from Belgium* (London, 1911), p. 49.

[58] Except that one would expect them to interrupt their efforts when the utility of this (small) marginal income became smaller than the gain in utility obtainable by taking some rest instead. This takes effect once the family is past the subsistence level.

Figure 5-4: Annual Rent per Hectare of Arable Land

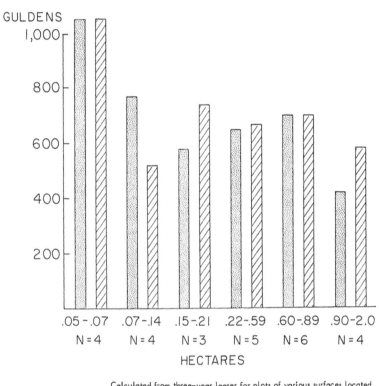

Calculated from *three-year leases for plots of various surfaces located in Vieuxbourg:* Sint-Maria-Leerne, Poesele, Vinkt, Meigem, and Landegem. (Published in Paul Deprez, "Pachtprijzen in het Land van Nevele (17e en 18e eeuw)," in <u>Dokumenten</u>, *I, 181ff)*

1730

1746

great fragmentation, the statistics show that many large plots remained in commercial operation, and must have been able to generate surpluses. If we follow the productivity and diet estimates made by the Prefect Faipoult and recently by Vandenbroeke, it would seem that two-thirds of one hectare were sufficient to feed a family of five on the diet that prevailed at the end of the eighteenth century.[59] If this was so, one farm family in

[59] Chr. Vandenbroeke, "Cultivation and Consumption of the Potato in the 17th and 18th Century," *Acta Historiae Neerlandica* 5 (Leiden, 1971), 38 (translated from *Tijdschrift voor Geschiedenis,* 1969).

four in Meigem, one in three in Saint-Gilles, and one in two in Lede, would have had to purchase food at the market. These numbers represent *minimum* estimates of the proportion of farms that needed supplementary, nonagricultural sources of income, for one must add rent and taxes to the minimum subsistence requirement. In fact, the probate inventories for Lede show that in the period 1786–1795, 88 percent of households had spinning wheels or looms.[60]

Another response that can be related in many ways to the growth of population, to the spread of industry, and to the fragmentation of the land is the progressive diffusion of the potato in the course of the century. It first appeared near Bruges in 1709, and spread rapidly to the small farms of the interior;[61] but there was little or no trade in potatoes until much later. The peasants grew this crop for their own consumption as an inferior substitute for rye, which could then be sold in the market for the cash they needed to pay their rising rents. In 1801, about 14.5 percent of the surface planted with food crops in East Flanders was given to potatoes. (According to a recent article, this figure would represent the maximum ever reached there.)[62] In Flanders, as in many other European regions, the potato played an important role in changing the balance between population and the means of subsistence, for the weight yield per hectare of a potato crop was ten times larger than that of land planted with bread cereals. It is easy to exaggerate this development, however. The nutritive value of potatoes is five times smaller than that of rye or wheat for a given weight. Assuming no change in caloric consumption per capita and no increase in the land effectively under cultivation, we may estimate that the population increase allowed by the substitution of potatoes for rye and wheat would have been not more than 14.5 percent [63] in the eighteenth century.

In reality, the population of Flanders almost doubled in that century and, furthermore, toward the middle of this period the region became a net food exporter for the first time since the

---

[60] De Brouwer, *Lede*, p. 245.

[61] Mendels, "Industrialization," pp. 130ff.

[62] Faipoult, *Mémoire*, pp. 104–105; Chr. Vandenbroeke and W. Vanderpijpen, "De voedingsgewassen in Vlaanderen tijdens de xviiie en xixe eeuw (1700–1846)," *Revue Belge d'Histoire Contemporaine* 2:2 (1970), 47–82.

[63] Since an acre planted with potatoes can support twice as many people as an hectare planted with wheat, a 100 percent substitution theoretically allows a 100 percent population growth, and so forth.

Middle Ages.[64] So even though Flanders was already very advanced in its agricultural techniques in 1700, other changes must have taken place besides the spread of the potato. Knowledge of improved rotation cycles probably spread. In the village of Lede for example, only 3.6 percent of the probate inventories from the early seventeenth century mention clover on the field. This grew to 56.8 percent in the late seventeenth century, and peaked at 84.8 percent in the late eighteenth century.[65]

The food surplus produced by Flanders and exported to other provinces and countries did not entirely originate in the maritime area. The calculations in Appendix 5.1 lead to the conclusion that the maritime area of East Flanders produced a theoretical food surplus (above human minimum consumption, but not counting animal consumption, or input into food industries such as beer and gin) which was equal to 64 percent of total output. The theoretical surplus from the interior was 26.5 percent. Although the relative sizes of these surpluses cannot be checked against independent evidence, their sum (33.6%) can, and seems realistic.[66] It might seem paradoxical that the interior of Flanders could generate a food surplus, although much evidence points to population pressure in this region. But the surplus most probably originated from the large capitalistic farms that coexisted with the small holdings. Furthermore, some of it may even have come from peasant farms, in spite of the fragmentation taking place at the time. The existence of a surplus is not incompatible with other evidence pointing to low standards of living, nor is impoverishment impossible in the midst of agricultural progress and industrial expansion.[67] The engine of this growth was the pressure of rising debts and rents, which ultimately can be traced back to demographic pressure,

[64] Hubert van Houtte, *Histoire économique,* pp. 255ff.; Chr. Vandenbroeke, "De graanpolitiek in den Oostenrijken Nederlanden," *Revue Belge de Philologie et d'Histoire* 45 (1967), 369–87.

[65] The same source reveals a growth of turnip cultivation and a decline of beans. De Brouwer, *Lede,* pp. 232–33.

[66] Faipoult, *Mémoire,* p. 107, finds 43 percent and W. Vanderpijpen 25 percent (after animal and industrial consumption). "De landbouwstatistiek in Vlaanderen onder het Frans bewind," *Revue Belge d'Histoire Contemporaine* 2:2 (1970), 43.

[67] Bonenfant, *Paupérisme;* J. Craeybeckx, "De arbeiders voor de industriële omwenteling," in J. Dhondt, *Arbeidersbeweging,* pp, 27ff; Craeybeckx, "De arbeiders in de XVIIᵉ en de XVIIIᵉ eeuw," in *Flandria Nostra* 1, 281–328; Deprez, "Evolution démographique et évolution économique en Flandre au 18ème siecle" (Contribution to the Third International Conference of Economic History, Munich, 1965), mimeographed.

mediated by the existing system of land ownership and distribution.

The progress of agriculture and the growth of industry can be related in one more way. Innovations in Flemish agriculture had both a labor-using and a seasonal bias. It was noted by a contemporary that on one acre of a Flemish farm, wheat demanded 25 man-days of work, while rye required 21 man-days. But the potato patch required 77 man-days per acre, of which 50 were needed for the deep digging and repeated ploughing necessary to cultivate this crop. When flax was grown, the requirement was 82 man-days for pulling the weeds.[68] While the new crops undoubtedly increased employment per acre, thereby facilitating the reduction of the size of family farms, they also reinforced the seasonal peaks of employment and accentuated the winter slack.

Flax cultivation also had high seasonal labor peaks, since weeding and harvesting required a large number of workers within a few days. A flax stalk that has become ripe very quickly becomes over-ripe, resulting in a considerable deterioration in the quality of the fiber. In the eighteenth century 12 to 15 adult workers could harvest one hectare of flax in one day. The flax crop covered 14,000 hectares of land in East Flanders alone, requiring 170,000 to 210,000 man-days of labor within a very few days of the calendar.[69] As other crops came to maturity and competed for the same labor in the same season, there was a shortage of labor at certain times of the year. For big farmers this was a reason to hire servants and laborers on half-year contracts, long before the peak season, to insure their harvest labor.

In summary, during the eighteenth century, the aggregate amount of land under cultivation did not keep up with the increase in the number of farm households. Households of roughly constant size had to live on holdings of diminishing dimensions. This was made possible by the increased output per acre and rising labor intensity. Labor intensity did not rise evenly across the annual cycle, however, and this provided periods of slack during which nonagricultural activities, above all the linen industry, could be carried out.

[68] Lichtervelde, *Mémoire* (1815).
[69] Calculated from Faipoult, *Mémoire*, pp. 26, 36–46, 104; Ph. Vandermaelen, *Dictionnaire géographique de la Flandre Orientale* (Brussels, 1834), p. 121; and Institut d'Etudes Economiques et Sociales des classes moyennes, *Le lin* (Brussels, 1951), p. 23.

Summary and Conclusion

The economic history of Flanders from the late seventeenth to the late eighteenth century adequately fits what I have called elsewhere a phase of "proto-industrialization"—a period of rural industrialization with simultaneous bifurcation between areas of subsistence farming with cottage industry and areas of commercial farming without it.[70]

The linen industry was only a by-occupation for the Flemish countryside, a subsidiary income for an essentially agricultural population. Yet it is striking how much the story of its organization and growth is intimately connected with other aspects of the agrarian economy in the eighteenth century. I have tried to show that its spread resulted from forces that can be traced back ultimately to population pressure. Rural industry, like the diffusion of the potato and of new agricultural techniques, permitted the multiplication of people on the land through the fragmentation of farms. Without it, such a rate of natural increase of population as was experienced in Flanders would have necessitated emigration to cities or other regions.

But this is only one side of the coin, for the rate of natural increase of the Flemish population was not determined exogenously. Elsewhere I have shown that in rural-industrial areas, improvement in the relative price of linen produced surges in the number of marriages.[71] Rural industry itself thus helped to accelerate the rate of population growth. It not only permitted population growth, but actively promoted it. The role of cottage industry was therefore perverse in the sense that it perpetuated the dismal pressures that had first induced its penetration into the countryside. As long as an outlet was readily found for the output of the cottage industry, this dismal high-pressure equilibrium remained feasible. It was destroyed in the nineteenth century, when competition from machine-made yarn and cloth and from the new urban cotton industry threw the Flemish rural economy and society into a dreadful crisis.[72]

---

[70] Mendels, "Proto-Industrialization: The First Phase of the Process of Industrialization," *Journal of Economic History* 30 (1972), 241–261.

[71] Mendels, "Industrialization," chapter 5; Mendels, "Industry and Marriages in Flanders before the Industrial Revolution," in Paul Deprez, ed., *Population and Economics, Proceedings of Section 5 (Historical Demography) of the IVth Congress of the International Economic History Association, 1968* (Winnipeg, 1970), pp. 81–93; Mendels, "Proto-Industrialization."

[72] G. Jacquemyns, *Histoire de la crise économique des Flandres;* A. de Vos,

Appendix 5.1 Estimated Food Surplus in 1804

The surface of the polder zone in East Flanders (at the time when this province included Zealand Flanders) was 65,300 hectares; that of the interior, 292,400 hectares. The former had a population of 34,750 persons (1805), the latter, 558,750.[73] Assuming that the diet was the same for the inhabitants of both areas, 0.618 liter of grain per person per day and 1.3 kg. of potatoes were consumed.[74] If the yields in quintals per hectare were also the same, that is, 33 for wheat, 36 for rye, and 347 for potatoes,[75] a family of five needed for subsistence 0.47 hectares of wheat *or* 0.44 hectares of rye and 0.10 hectares of potatoes.[76]

To feed the polder zone at subsistence level, one would therefore need to have 695 hectares planted with potatoes and 3,266 hectares with wheat (or 3,058 hectares of rye). Assuming that no rye was grown there and that wheat and potatoes together constituted the same proportion (28.3 percent) of total land surface as devoted to food crops in the province as a whole, approximately 3,695 hectares should have been planted with potatoes (20 percent of foodcrop surface assumed) and 14,783 hectares with wheat (80 percent assumed).

The difference between the estimates of consumption needs and of crops production is an excess of 3,000 hectares for potatoes and 12,000 for wheat. Theoretically, the exportable proportion of output was therefore 64 percent. In the interior 558,750 inhabitants would have needed 11,175 hectares of potatoes and 52,522 hectares of wheat (or 49,170 hectares of rye). It was estimated, however, that 16,521 hectares were planted with potatoes, 17,378 hectares with wheat, and 49,229 with rye. The surplus produced here was therefore approximately equal to the output of 22,000 hectares, or 26.5 percent.

"Bloei en verval der plaatselijke Handweefnijverheid te Evergem (1794–1880)," HMGOG new ser. 13 (1959), 113–62.

[73] Faipoult, *Mémoire,* p. 30.
[74] Vandenbroeke, "The Potato," p. 38.
[75] Faipoult, *Mémoire,* p. 107; Vandenbroeke, "The Potato," p. 37.
[76] Vandenbroeke, "The Potato," p. 38.

6

Peasant Demand Patterns and Economic
Development: Friesland 1550–1750*

JAN DE VRIES

What role did the peasant as a consumer play in European
economic development? Many historical investigations have af-
firmed the importance of agricultural production as a precondi-
tion or concomitant condition of industrial growth, but what of
peasant demand? To the extent that this question is even considered, the response is usually to dismiss peasant demand as an
unlikely economic stimulus. What active market role can one
expect of "the conservative, homosociologicus peasant, the market insensitive, immutable, unpersuadable peasant, the kin-
bound, caste-bound, contented peasant"? [1]

A widely held view ascribes to peasants the striving for a target income, "set at a conventional level by a combination of
social and economic criteria—the critical or approving behavior
of friends, neighbors, and kin and the amount of reciprocity
which they are prepared to give according to what they themselves have received." [2] Such a peasant household, suddenly
faced with an increased income, would cut back its productive
efforts in the future, since less effort would now suffice to attain

* This study was made possible by financial support from the Humanities
Research Center of Michigan State University. Among those whose helpful
comments have improved this study I wish to acknowledge Stanley Brandes,
Paul David, Donald McCloskey, and A. M. van der Woude—without, of
course, implicating them in the remaining errors.

[1] Raj Krishna, "Models of the Family Farm," in C. R. Wharton, ed.,
Subsistence Agriculture and Economic Development (Chicago, 1969), p. 186.

[2] Robert Firth, "Social Structure and Peasant Economy: The Influence of
Social Structure upon Peasant Economies," *ibid.*, p. 36.

the target income. And if an increased income were spent, "the experience of nineteenth-century France shows us that a middle and rich peasantry is about as uninviting a market for mass manufactures as may be found and does not encourage capitalists to revolutionize production. [Peasant] wants are traditional; most of its wealth goes into more land and cattle, or into hoards, or into new buildings, or even into sheer waste, like those gargantuan weddings, funerals, and other feasts which disturbed continental princes at the turn of the sixteenth century." [3]

The peasant, then, is enmeshed in "compact social relations of self-contained communities," and is pulled from the ideal of self-sufficiency by market forces only to the extent that they permit him to purchase certain "traditional" goods. "The market is held at arm's length." [4] The peasant, so defined, cannot be an agent of economic development; he is an obstacle to it.

These explanations do not seem satisfactory. When we turn our attention back to the peasant as producer, we cannot help but observe that peasant agriculture in many areas has specialized and successfully engaged in market production. Such a transformation cannot be understood independently of demand patterns. In an economic organization dedicated to supplying its own needs, production decisions are integrally related to consumption decisions. Therefore, peasant specialization cannot be understood simply as a production response to market stimuli; it is also a response to peasant wants and needs. For commercial production to be more than simply a marginal activity superimposed on a self-sufficient household economy, demand patterns must shift. Home-produced and consumed goods can give way to specialized market production only when the peasant household's consumption also shifts to goods produced outside the household. The following schematic representations of peasant household economy should make this clear.

Figure 6–1, the self-sufficient household, requires no explanation. We wish only to call attention to the fact that nonagricultural production plays a very important role in such a household. The peasant cannot be understood simply in the role of cultivator.

[3] E. J. Hobsbawm, "The Crisis of the Seventeenth Century," in Trevor Aston, ed., *Crisis in Europe, 1560–1660* (Garden City, 1967), p. 27.

[4] Robert Redfield, *Peasant Society and Culture* (Chicago, 1956), pp. 45–46.

Figure 6-1: Self-sufficient household

leisure	non-agricultural	agricultural	production
			consumption

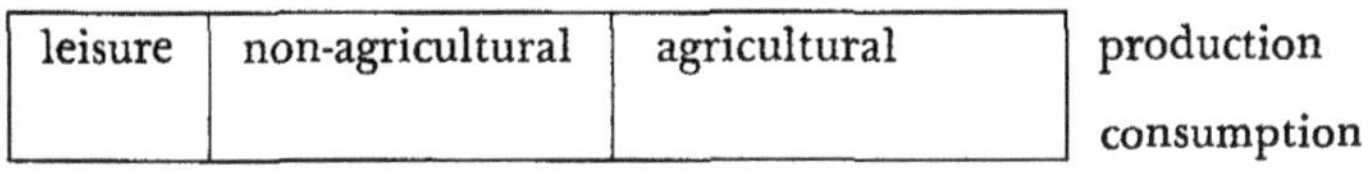

Figure 6-2: Self-sufficient household with marketed "surplus"

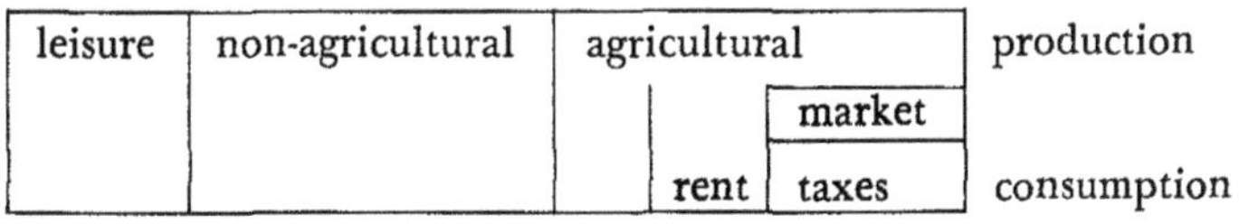

leisure	non-agricultural	agricultural		production
			market	
		rent	taxes	consumption

Figure 6-3: Specialized, commercialized household

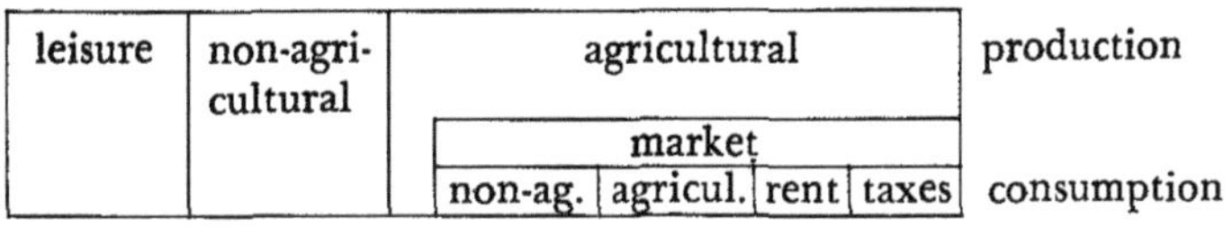

leisure	non-agri-cultural	agricultural				production
		market				
		non-ag.	agricul.	rent	taxes	consumption

These figures are predicated on assumptions which should be made explicit. Increased agricultural production and, hence, increased labor time devoted to agriculture, requires a reduction of the time devoted to other activities. Many studies suppose the chief trade-off is between labor (in agriculture) and leisure. (See, for instance, Ester Boserup, *The Conditions of Agricultural Growth*.) Our analysis holds that the most important trade-off is between labor in agriculture and labor in the home provision of crafts, maintenance, transportation, and fuel. The importance of these non-agricultural activities in the peasant household economy is demonstrated in many anthropological studies. See also, A. V. Chayanov, *The Theory of Peasant Economy* (Homewood, Illinois, 1966).

In Figure 6–2 the household enters the market to gain the means to pay taxes. One could add the payment of some monetary rent and the purchase of small amounts of such goods as salt without altering the basic fact that market activity is "tacked on" to a basically self-contained production and consumption system. The marketed output is "surplus" in the strict sense of the word. Many peasant-based economies have developed regions of specialized production and interregional trade on the basis of such a marginal market involvement. While the flow of traded goods may be strategic for an urban governing or religious class, these goods form but a small fraction of total output, most of which does not enter the market. With the bulk of the peasantry isolated from the market as consumers, the potential market for traders and "industrialists" is confined to a tiny minority of the population.

Because such a large portion of the population is, from the perspective of the market, inactive in an economy portrayed by Figure 6–2, a further development of specialization, one in which the production schedule of the peasant household is transformed, is crucial to economic development. Only then does specialized production penetrate deeply into the overall economy,[5] trade becomes more than a superficial activity, and—crucial to our argument—only then does a large portion of the population enter the market as significant consumers. Figure 6–3, which portrays a market-dependent peasant household, is not simply an exaggeration of Figure 6–2. On the contrary, production for the market entails a complete reallocation of labor time (in the typical case, an increase in food production at the expense of handicrafts and domestic maintenance activities), and a complete alteration in the demand pattern of the household. Goods previously produced at home are now purchased; services provided for oneself are provided by specialists; certain consumption habits inevitably change altogether, since the market offers goods made by different methods, new goods, and new relative prices to replace those implicit in home production.

Are peasant households prepared to undergo such a transformation in their way of life, and, if so, under what conditions? Hymer and Resnick have examined this question through a formal model, the "Z Goods" model,[6] in which they conclude that peasants will reduce home handicraft production for food specialization and, concomitantly, replace home-produced goods with manufactures in consumption if the manufactured goods are highly desired and considered superior to the home-produced "Z Goods" that they must replace if specialized production is to proceed. Improved prices for food producers and improved

[5] The industrial sector in this phase of economic development has recently been singled out for investigation. See Franklin Mendels, "Proto-industrialization: The First Phase of the Industrialization Process," *Journal of Economic History* 32 (1972), 241–61.

[6] Stephen Hymer and Stephen Resnick, "A Model of an Agrarian Economy with Nonagricultural Activities," *American Economic Review* 59 (1969), 493–506. The chief characteristics of the "Z Goods" model are presented in Appendix 6–1.

agricultural productivity have much less effect; they can speed the process of specialization, but, by themselves, only reduce the effort devoted to agricultural production that suffices to meet financial obligations and acquire basic commodities.

We return, through this analysis, to the subject of peasant tastes (and of the capacity of a manufacturing sector to produce superior commodities). We have established that peasant demand patterns not only determine what is consumed, but influence what is produced in the agrarian sector. What demand patterns can one expect of peasants?

A Case Study

We will shed light on this question through an historical investigation of peasant consumption in the Dutch province of Friesland in the two centuries between 1550 and 1750. This region experienced agricultural specialization, thoroughgoing commercialization, and increased farm income in the century and a half after 1500. At the beginning of the sixteenth century it had long since ceased to be a self-sufficient economy. It is, in fact, unlikely that self-sufficiency ever characterized this livestock-raising region. But Friesland's market involvement attained a wholly new level of magnitude during the sixteenth and early seventeenth centuries. The subregions of the province became more sharply distinguished from one another: some became devoted to arable production, some to livestock breeding, and most to dairy production. The volume of butter and cheese marketed in the province increased until the mid-seventeenth century, and price trends in the Dutch Republic indicate that dairy farmers enjoyed a long-term improvement in their terms of trade. This trend is evident in Figure 6–4, which shows the amounts of rye and woolen cloth that could be purchased with the income gained from the sale of a fixed quantity of butter during the sixteenth and seventeenth centuries. The substantial investment of capital in new, larger farm buildings, land reclamation, drainage improvement, and transportation facilities in the first two-thirds of the seventeenth century, together with the developments mentioned above, supports the view that real farm income increased substantially.

In the late seventeenth and early eighteenth century conditions

Figure 6-4: "Terms of trade" of butter and rye prices (base years 1530–1544) and butter and woolen cloth prices (base years 1625–1629), in five-year averages.[a]

[a] Source: N. W. Posthumus, *Inquiry Into the History of Prices in Holland* (London, 1946, 1964).

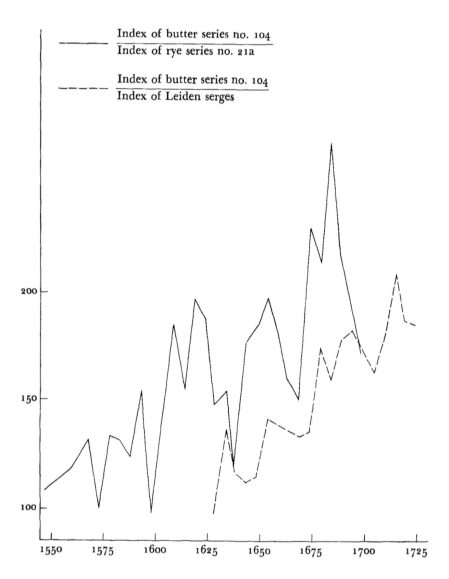

became less favorable for agricultural prosperity. Dairy prices
weakened, while rents and, particularly, taxes remained at their
old levels or increased. Early eighteenth-century epizootics and
a troublesome dike rot also contributed to the reduction of agricultural profits.[7]

What happened to peasant demand during this long period of
agricultural change? Did the range of goods, their quantity, and
their place of manufacture change? What impact did peasant
demand have on the nonagricultural sector of the economy?
These are the questions we wish to answer. We can hope to do
so because of the existence of two sources: one, the *Quotisatie
Cohieren,* is an occupational census of 1749 that will be considered later; the other is the *Weesboeken* (Orphan books). These
documents include notarized inventories that record in abundant
detail the possessions of Friesian peasants who died leaving
minor children (under twenty-five years of age). They exist in
great profusion for the seventeenth and early eighteenth centuries. The earliest rural inventories date from 1550; we are
unable, therefore, to describe the transformation from its beginnings. Nevertheless, the existing records are a gold mine of
information, which usually list all movable property and outstanding debts and credits, and which occasionally describe the
real property and the monetary values of each possession as well.
The thousands of inventories deal with all rural dwellers whose
estates were worth the trouble and expense of a notarized inventory. The very poorest people are excluded, but peasant
farmers, as well as most craftsmen, boatmen, rural merchants,
and so forth, are included in the *Weesboeken.*

This study examines 512 inventories drawn mainly from two
central Friesian *grietenijen* (jurisdictions): Leeuwarderadeel,
which includes fourteen hamlets in 62 square kilometers; and
Hennaarderadeel, with twelve hamlets in 59 square kilometers.
To provide a contrast between subdistricts of distinctly different
agricultural structures, we have also examined inventories of
Barradeel, a coastal arable district; Idaarderadeel, a dairying and
breeding district; and Ooststellingwerf, a higher-lying district in
the southeastern corner of Friesland with a less commercialized

---

[7] For sources and details see Jan de Vries, *The Dutch Rural Economy in
the Golden Age* (New Haven, 1974), pp. 174–92.

agricultural structure, a condition it shared with most of the eastern provinces of the Netherlands.[8]

Tables 6–1 through 6–10 summarize the inventory data for forty-one selected commodities. An attempt to distinguish among different economic classes has been made by dividing the households into three groups: those possessing ten or more milk cows, those possessing under ten, and those possessing none. In a predominantly livestock-raising province, this seems a useful criterion for distinguishing the overall economic status of households. By grouping the inventories in this way, the averages reflect real changes in the possessions of economic classes rather than changes in the proportion of different economic classes recorded in the *Weesboeken*. The households without livestock, unfortunately, consist not only of craftsmen and poor persons, but also of government officials, innkeepers, pastors, and other persons who make this category too heterogeneous to be of great value. Moreover, in the sixteenth century the *Weesboeken* recorded the presence of too few nonagricultural households to permit statistical analysis.[9]

For each commodity, the tables show two things: they present the average quantity found in all inventories that record its

[8] The *Weesboeken* are deposited in the Rijksarchief, Leeuwarden, Archieven der Nedergerechten. Those used in this study are: Barradeel, no. 30, Vols. 1–8; Hennaarderadeel, no. 5i, Vols. 1–10; Idaarderadeel, no. 10j, Vols. 1–15; Leeuwarderadeel, no. 1m, Vols. 1–43; Ooststellingwerf, no. 9f, Vols. 1–3; Wonseradeel, no. 6s, Vols. 28–32.

[9] The following table indicates the size of the inventory sample for each period and class:

		Milk cow herd			
Grietenij	Period	Ten and over	Under ten	Zero	Total
Hennaarderadeel	1550–62	24	17	1	42
Leeuwarderadeel	1566–74	25	35	1	61
Leeuwarderadeel	1583–99	51	21	10	82
Idaarderadeel	1614–21	16	5	2	23
Leeuwarderadeel & Wonseradeel	1616–41	43	25	15	83
Ooststellingwerf	1631–47	——18——		1	19
Hennaarderadeel	1646–54	22	11	7	40
Barradeel	1651–55	9	12	0	21
Leeuwarderadeel	1677–86	24	23	3	50
Barradeel	1679–92	——16——		0	16
Idaarderadeel	1690–1702	——19——		7	26
Leeuwarderadeel	1711–50	18	19	12	49
Total		232 53	168	59	512

presence, and they give the percentage of inventories that record the presence of the commodity. The significance of the latter statistic varies among the commodities. In most cases concerning dairy equipment, bedding, linens, clothing, and furniture— goods possessed by nearly all households—the percentages serve only to indicate the exhaustiveness of the inventories. The percentages are usually below 100 percent because of unexplained omissions, because the notary is content to record simply "some" or "several" of a good, or because the good is disposed of outside the orphan settlement. This last case accounts for the unsatisfactorily small percentage of inventories that fully record clothing. In the case of wagons, boats, plows, curtains, *schoorsteen kleden* (fireplace mantel cloths), chests, and obvious luxury commodities, the percentages are intended to give a rough idea of how widespread was the possession of the commodity. In certain instances where aggregation was impossible, only the percentage of inventories recording the presence of the commodity is given.

The use of inventories—a stock—to describe demand—a flow —requires that certain assumptions be made about depreciation rates. Since our aim is to estimate the trends in demand rather than the actual volume of demand, we need only be concerned about changes that might occur in the depreciation rates of the various goods to be considered. In the period under examination the techniques of production experienced no profound change. We therefore believe it reasonable to assume that no changes in quality influenced the depreciation rates. On the other hand, changes in taste, particularly in the standards of appearance that peasant households wished to maintain in their dress and home furnishings, may well have influenced the depreciation rates. It is conceivable, for example, that a more fastidious peasantry discarded its linen goods more rapidly in the course of the seventeenth century. We must be mindful of this possibility in interpreting the inventory evidence presented below.

The Findings

FARM EQUIPMENT

There are few sudden departures in the record of farm equipment holdings; rather, this sector is characterized by a gradual increase in certain, usually expensive, items, plus an increase in items that indicate the production capacity of the farm. On most farms the costliest pieces of equipment were wagons and boats. The tables show them to become gradually more numerous and more general in the course of the seventeenth century, although a closer analysis in Table 6–11 shows that the increase was mainly confined to the areas of livestock specialization [Hennaarderadeel and the southern half (Zuidertrimdeel) of Leeuwarderadeel].[10] With an average value of 35 gulden in the seventeenth century, a doubling of the average number of wagons on a farm had a considerable impact on the total value of farm equipment. In the mid-eighteenth century, the most prosperous peasants began acquiring another vehicle, the chaise. These pleasure vehicles were even more costly than the farm wagons.

The possession of a plow, the principal criterion of one's place on the social and economic scale in many parts of Europe, did not count for much in Friesland. Plows hardly ranked among the more costly farm implements listed in the inventories (five to fifteen gulden was common in the mid-seventeenth century), but more significantly, fewer and fewer households possessed them at all as most regions reduced their arable land in favor of livestock husbandry. The decline in plow ownership in Hennaarderadeel can be read from the tables. The Leeuwarderadeel percentages form a contradictory trend, but when the farms of this *grietenij* are divided between its two parts—the Noordertrimdeel, increasingly arable land, and the Zuidertrimdeel, increasingly dairy farms—the trends become clear. In the Noordertrimdeel, between 71 and 80 percent of all farm inventories record a plow from 1583 to 1750; in the Zuidertrimdeel the percentages fall from 67 percent in 1583–1599, to 57 percent in 1616–1641, and to 31 percent in 1677–86. In 1711–50, a period of recurrent epizootics, the percentage recovers to 44.

In most of Friesland peasants specialized in butter production.

---

[10] Friesland never knew the customs of *corvée* or *spandienst*. The latter, the economic consequences of which are detailed by F. W. Henning in his *Dienste und Abgaben der Bauern im 18. Jahrhundert* (Stuttgart, 1969), required farmers to maintain wagons and horses to provide transport services to local lords. In the absence of such obligations, transport service in Friesland became a specialized undertaking. Teamsters and, particularly, bargemen swelled the populations of strategically placed rural centers. The record of the peasants' wagon and boat ownership should be interpreted in the context of a probable diminution of the self-provision of transport services.

Their production process required wooden *aden* (decreaming vessels), butter churns, of course, and cylindrical, copper cheese kettles in which the residual milk was heated to be made into a low-butterfat cheese. The inventories reveal trends in the ownership of these objects that reflect a gradual increase in the output of the dairies.

The *aden,* flat, oval, bowl-shaped vessels with square edges, held from twenty-five to thirty liters of milk. The separation process required two days. If these vessels were used nearly to capacity at some point in the course of the lactation cycle, an increased milk output per cow would require a larger stock of *aden.* The records of farms with ten or more milk cows show, in fact, a steady increase in the average stock of *aden* from 1.6 per milk cow in 1550–1562 to 2.0 in the mid-seventeenth century. On the smaller farms no such consistent trend is apparent, however, and we should probably resist reading too much into these figures.[11]

We can be more confident in interpreting the information on cheese kettles. Throughout the two centuries of our investigation, most households owned one of these costly objects, but the particularly informative inventories of Hennaarderadeel permit us to observe changes in their capacity, which rose steadily from an average of one-half *ton* in the mid-sixteenth century, to three-quarter *ton* in 1600, to one and one-quarter *ton* by the mid-seventeenth century. This growth helps explain the greatly increased value of cheese kettles (whose capacities are not recorded) from seven gulden in 1575 to sixty gulden in the mid-eighteenth century.

Finally, we can note that vats and pails became somewhat more numerous in the course of time. Metal pails came to supplement the wooden ones in the seventeenth century.

The inventories also permit us to follow the diffusion of a labor-saving innovation. Butter churning, a very labor-intensive activity, could easily require the services of several milkmaids on a large farm. A rising wage level for farm servants (their salary range, as recorded among the outstanding debts in the inventories, rose throughout the seventeenth century) would eventually stimulate demand for a labor-saving churning method. In the

---

[11] The recorded value of *aden* was: 1559, 4 stuiver; 1651, 10 stuiver; 1768, 20 stuiver. A 1768 inventory also recorded copper *aden* (they were normally made of wood) valued at 8 gulden apiece.

1660s the *karnemolen,* a mechanical, horse-powered butter churn, was patented. Its installation required considerable space in a reconstructed dairy. Tables 6–1 and 6–2 show how these *karnemolens,* costly, indivisible, and labor-saving, were adopted first on the largest farms, and only in the eighteenth century on a portion of the smaller farms.[12]

FARM BUILDINGS

The descriptions of farm buildings found in the inventories indicate that the "rebuilding of rural England" charted by W. G. Hoskins for the period 1570–1640 had its counterpart in rural Friesland. The farm structures used in the early sixteenth century were the linear descendants of the *oud Friese huis.* These structures, as described in old Friesian laws of the eleventh through fourteenth centuries, consisted of a one-room space for man and livestock, surrounded by wattle walls and decked with a thatched roof resting on beams. The fireplace was originally an open place on the floor, and smoke escaped through an opening in the roof. By the sixteenth century the living quarters had been separated from the stalls, and during the century a dairy room was often added as well.[13]

The average size of the medieval *oud Friese huis* appears to have been nine *vakken,* or sections of about two meters each, which marked the crossbeam intervals and conveniently marked off each cow stall. A nine *vak* house, thus, was about eighteen meters long by eight meters wide, the standard width of this method of construction. Such a structure could neither offer much storage space for farm products or hay, nor house a large herd. By the mid-sixteenth century the need for more space had forced the farmers to elongate their houses somewhat. The inventories of Leeuwarderadeel in 1566–1574 show the *oud Friese huis* to be universal, but the average length was now fourteen *vakken.* Almost half of the buildings described had separate milk rooms of two or three *vakken,* and many of the larger farms possessed a separate small building of three or four *vakken.*

[12] For a much more dramatic and consequential example of the diffusion of a labor-saving innovation, see the well-known article of Paul A. David, "The Mechanization of Reaping in the Ante-Bellum Midwest," in Henry Rosovsky, ed., *Industrialization in Two Systems* (New York, 1966), pp. 3–39.

[13] S. J. Fockema Andreae, E. H. ter Kuile, and R. C. Hekker, *Duizend jaar bouwen in Nederland,* Vol. 2 (Amsterdam, 1957), 210; S. J. van der Molen, *Het friesche boerenhuis in twintig eeuwen* (Assen, 1942), p. 40.

The process of elongation did not overcome the lack of storage space for bulky commodities, and in the late sixteenth century peasants experimented with other architectural types. Various new types evolved and spread, all possessing lofty barns that brought hay storage into the structure and including large milk rooms, dairy storage areas, and much more elaborate living quarters.

The new farm types can be traced back to the last decades of the sixteenth century. In Leeuwarderadeel the inventories of 1566–1574 describe only the old-style structures. The inventories of 1583–1599, however, describe two farms in a novel way: they record the presence of a *schuur*, or barn. In 1616–1619, 27 percent of the inventories record barns; in 1634–1641 the percentage rises to 64. In Hennaarderadeel, old-style buildings with an average length of twelve *vakken* monopolize the 1550–1562 inventories; a century later the only form of description to be found is *"huis en schuur"* house and barn). This transformation brought with it a shift from thatched to tiled roofs (over the inhabited portion of the buildings, at least), and a shift from wattle-and-daub to brick-wall construction.

This "rebuilding of rural Friesland," largely financed by peasants, cannot yet be quantified in terms of money, although it seems certain that its impact on the regional economy was considerable, particularly in the first two-thirds of the seventeenth century. We can be somewhat more precise with regard to the relative importance of farm equipment.

Farm inventories for the English counties of Nottinghamshire in 1559–1566 and Bedfordshire in 1616–1619 show the value of farm implements hovering between five and six percent of total movable property. In Sussex G. H. Kenyon determined the value of farm implements to be only four percent of the total in 1611–1659, but it rose thereafter to seven percent in 1660–1699 and nine percent in 1700–1744.[14] In Friesland, as can be seen in

14 P. A. Kennedy, "Nottingham Household Inventories," *Thoroton Society,* record series, Vol. 22 (1963). Our figure is drawn from the twenty inventories listing farm equipment for the period 1559–1566. The average value of equipment was £5.15, or 5.5 percent of total movable property. F. G. Emmison, "Jacobean Household Inventories," *Bedfordshire Historical Records Society* 20 (1938), 1–143. Our figure is drawn from the thirty-five inventories identified as belonging to yeomen and husbandmen. The average value of equipment was £7.17 or 5.9 percent of total movable property. G. H. Kenyon,

Table 6–13, wooden implements alone were valued at nearly ten percent of the total in the late sixteenth century, and rose to over seventeen percent by the early eighteenth century.

Peasant expenditures on buildings and equipment were clearly substantial, and must have acted as an important stimulus to the production of metal goods, brick, tile, and, particularly, wooden goods. These data are not in accord with the widespread belief that peasant investment rates were very low or nonexistent.[15]

HOUSEHOLD POSSESSIONS: TEXTILES AND CLOTHING

The textile industry was easily the largest in any preindustrial economy. For this reason, and because it acted as the "leading sector" in the English Industrial Revolution, the peasant demand patterns for textiles possess a special importance. This case study provides a good opportunity to observe textile demand in a period of increasing peasant income and, as Figure 6–4 makes clear, of improved terms of trade between dairy products and woolens. How did the demand for textiles respond to these conditions?

Blankets, never present in abundance, became less numerous in both large and small farm households. Bedsheets, relatively more plentiful, show no clear trend in the two centuries of our investigation. Tablecloths, washcloths, and chair cushions all declined in number in both large and small farm households. Altogether, the trend of textile ownership is surprising—indeed, perverse. How can we account for it?

The number of beds gives a clue. The inventories provide an unexpected source for the demographic history of the region. Historians have long suspected a decline in fertility and in house-

---

"Kirdford Inventories, 1611 to 1776, with particular reference to the weald clay farming," *Sussex Archeological Collections,* Vol. 93 (1955).

[15] For examples, see: M. M. Postan, "Investment in Medieval Agriculture," *Journal of Economic History* 27 (1957), 580; and T. W. Schultz, *Transforming Traditional Agriculture* (New Haven, 1964). Postan maintains that "the main reason [for very low investment rates] is not that potential sources of savings were insufficient, but that very little was actually saved: that the bulk of the profit was squandered, or that such savings as were made were not devoted to productive investment." Schultz explains the same phenomenon as it applies to modern peasants by insisting that the rate of return to investment in traditional agricultural capital is simply too low to attract savings. This study cannot topple such mighty generalizations. We must be content with the observation that in rural Friesland the savings of (mainly tenant) farmers did find its way into productive investment.

hold size between the early and late seventeenth century.[16] If the number of beds possessed by a household held some rough correspondence with the size of the households, we can read from Table 6–12 a sudden fall in household size in the mid-seventeenth century. Even if no correspondence between beds and people will be admitted, the decline in the number of beds is clear, and this of itself must have diminished the household demand for blankets and bedsheets—and most other linens, for that matter. When we calculate the number of blankets per bed, for instance, we uncover a remarkable stability. Other things being equal, a smaller household will possess fewer textiles. But other things were not equal; textiles were becoming cheaper, yet their ownership still declined.

The possession of clothing is of great interest to us, but here the inventories are weakest. The available figures are based on small percentages of the total inventories because the clothing of surviving family members was normally excluded from the notary's enumeration, and because the clothing of the deceased was often simply lumped together, unitemized, or otherwise disposed of uninformatively. The bewildering variety of terms in those lists that do exist add to the uncertainty of this part of the study. The available information for men's coats, trousers, socks, and hats, and for women's skirts is not sufficient to point to more than the possibility of a slight increase in the quantities owned over the two-century period. In the case of men's and women's shirts, however, we have more information; it shows a doubling of the average stock of shirts owned in the first half of the seventeenth century.

Waistcoats are of considerable interest since, in the course of the seventeenth century, it became customary to adorn them with silver buttons. Such waistcoats became *de rigueur* among reputable peasants, yet the tables show no increased ownership of waistcoats until the eighteenth century. Then the increase is considerable. Large farmers, who had owned an average of

[16] The most exhaustive and rewarding study of Dutch demographic history is to be found in the recent work of A. M. van der Woude, *Het Noorderkwartier* (Wageningen, 1972). With reference to an important rural district in North Holland, he is able to demonstrate a fall in household size after 1650. Friesian demography is discussed in J. A. Faber's *Drie Eeuwen Friesland* (Wageningen, 1972), but in the absence of suitable evidence he is able only to hypothesize a decline of fertility after 1650 (p. 90).

fewer than two for over a century, owned 2.6 in 1711–1750 and
4.3 in 1759–1785.

Many elements in the peasant costumes, which have taken
their place with windmills and tulips to symbolize the Netherlands to generations of people all over the world, were evolving
in the seventeenth and early eighteenth centuries. What impelled this development and what impact did it have on peasant
demand for textiles? The inadequacy of the clothing descriptions, unfortunately, prevents a satisfactory answer to these
questions.

One category of textile goods enjoyed an obviously increased
demand: curtains for windows (in contrast to bed curtains, which
were already widespread in the sixteenth century), and *schoorsteen kleden,* decorative cloths placed on fireplace mantels. But,
much as these goods tell us of the changing tastes and standards
of comfort in the peasant home, they can hardly have affected
aggregate textile demand very much.

All in all, peasant demand for textiles shows some important
but curious features. We can make a distinction between the
demand for woolens and that for linens; the former appears in
small and decreasing quantities, while the latter was present in
rather large and slightly increasing quantities. We do not know
whether this dichotomy was the result of relative prices, changes
in dowry customs, or other factors. When all textile products are
considered together, the most notable finding is the highly inelastic demand. In this case study, the demand for textiles can
be observed in a considerable range of income and relative price
conditions, but no positive demand response is evident in the
tables.

FURNISHINGS AND LUXURY GOODS

If increased peasant income was not spent on textiles, how was
it spent? The more widespread presence of curtains directs our
attention to the home interior and its furnishings. To these the
Friesian peasants paid a new attention, although this is not
readily apparent in the record of table, bench, and chair ownership. Here no noteworthy trends are in evidence. The significant change is hidden behind the statistical facade. Inventories
from the mid-seventeenth century began occasionally listing not
simply tables, but eight-sided tables, or round tables, and not

simply chairs, but chairs with side arms. A finer, more costly furniture was replacing cruder objects in the peasant interior.

This refinement is most clearly expressed in the case of chests. Sixteenth-century inventories rarely mention them. Instead, the *kist,* a trunk, and the *tresoor,* a low wooden box, provided storage space for linens and valuables. The great oak chest, sometimes eccentrically painted, often elegantly wrought, and costly, became a significant item in the early seventeenth century. By the end of the century it had taken its place as a characteristic part of the Dutch farmhouse interior.

Another transformation not apparent from the tables took place in the realm of tableware. Tin spoons, the chief eating utensil, became more numerous in the early seventeenth century, and glassware—mainly beer glasses and bottles—began to be listed with some frequency in the 1590s. Not until well into the seventeenth century, however, could many households be found with more than two or three glasses, and a like number of bottles. By the end of the century, households possessing a dozen beer glasses and decanters with silver stoppers were not uncommon. Still, the total value of these objects was small; more important was the change in plates, dishes, cups, and other crockery.

During most of the period of this investigation, tin bowls and dishes gradually found a place as a supplement to the more general wooden plates. The end of the seventeenth century brought a new development, in which both tin and wood gave way to earthenware and porcelain. Many eighteenth-century inventories identify dishes, cups, and saucers as delftware. (Earlier inventories never mentioned cups and saucers. Their presence is evidently related to the spread of coffee and tea drinking.) The inventories, which in earlier centuries rarely evaluated the pottery and glassware at more than a gulden or two, in the eighteenth century listed porcelain holdings worth from ten to thirty gulden. In the inventories of 1759–1785, no wooden and few tin plates were to be found; Delft porcelain replaced them, large farms averaging 19.8 dishes, and small farms 13.6. These figures exclude cups, saucers, odd pieces, and other types of earthenware.

A variety of other objects were introduced to the peasant home during the period of our investigation. Mirrors spread in the first century, and accumulated in the second. Clocks, unknown until the last decade of the seventeenth century, suddenly became ubiquitous in the more substantial households. One finds references to paintings in the seventeenth-century peasant inventories, but with only a few exceptions the notaries' valuations indicate that they were not oils. They were, rather, decorative boards and hangings. These objects, valued at a few stuivers apiece, became quite common by the mid-seventeenth century.

Most of these new, or more common, goods can best be understood as elements of urban culture whose introduction into a rural household signifies assimilation of urban cultural norms. The spread of books perhaps exemplifies this best. Even before the Reformation (which, of course, came to the Netherlands much later than elsewhere in Europe), a few inventories record the presence of *"Duytschen bybels."* After the Reformation the possession of bibles, testaments, psalmbooks, and songbooks became much more common, although never universal. More interesting still is the presence, beginning in the early seventeenth century, of secular works in peasant "libraries." Most notaries give the number of books, without bothering to list their titles, but those few who give complete information tell us of peasants in the early seventeenth century owning travel books and histories of Friesland and Amsterdam. The numerous presence of these volumes is the more remarkable when it is remembered that they were written in Dutch, which is not the native language of the Friesians. The religious works, when they were adorned with silver hinges and clasps, could be quite costly, but the entire libraries of most peasants rarely received a valuation of over four gulden.

Finally we turn to examine the luxury consumption *par excellence* of a peasant society: objects of silver and gold. Such objects functioned, of course, not only as consumer goods, but also as a store of value, a reasonably liquid form of wealth. And characteristic of a store of value is an extremely long depreciation period. If, for simplicity, we assume that gold and silver do not depreciate at all, and are passed through inheritance from generation to generation, an observed increase in peasant holdings would reflect an increased level of demand only when the *rate* of accumulation rises. On the other hand, a fixed level of gold and silver holdings would reflect a complete absence of demand. Unfortunately, the inventory data for these goods, for which a more sophisticated statistical analysis is required, are unsatisfactory.

The lists of gold and silver objects in the inventories defy aggregation into a single, comprehensive measure. Since most of them went to the widows or were otherwise disposed of, notaries usually neglected to place a value on them, and since a wide variety of goods is subsumed in the category, we can devise no useful method to compare the holdings over time. The one overall measure we have, the percentage of households possessing at least one silver object (excluding buttons), shows an erratic increase, but by no means does it tell the whole story.

Very few sixteenth-century inventories record more than a few silver objects, usually confined to rings, buttons, chains, and buckles. The only valuations given for this period were for 12, 19, 26, and 63 *goldguldens*. The inventories for the period 1616–1654 show the presence of a variety of objects worn and used by women: most frequently encountered was the *onderriem*, a waistband worn under the outer clothing, to which were fastened key chains, knife sheaths, and purses. Parts of all these objects might be made of silver. Other objects that were occasionally found include silver beakers, brandywine decanters, little boxes, and pipes. These objects were of considerable value, and when added to the more common buttons and buckles could raise the total value of silver objects to well over 100 gulden.

By the early eighteenth century, prosperous peasants owned gold rings and buttons as well as a much-expanded inventory of silver objects. Silver buttons, now required on waistcoats and other outer garments, were owned by the dozen; silver spoons, conspicuously displayed on special wall racks, were also widespread, despite their cost of three to four gulden per spoon. Beakers, cups, mustard pots, decanters with silver stoppers, and other paraphernalia often ran to lists of three to four pages in the notarial inventories. The few overall evaluations given are usually over one hundred gulden; indeed, in north Holland, the average value of silver and gold owned by six large dairy farmers in 1733–1737 was nearly three hundred gulden.

An interesting development, which can be said to mirror the gradual accumulation just described, is the elaboration of the *oorijser*. The *oorijser* was originally an iron ring that encircled the head to bind the long hair of Friesian women. In the sixteenth century a few silver *oorijsers* are recorded, but they become common, in the inventories, only in the later seventeenth century. By the eighteenth century gold *oorijsers* are more numerous than silver. During this long period their shape also undergoes an evolution. From a slender silver band in the sixteenth century, they gradually grew in width until, in their final form (attained in the second half of the eighteenth century), they all but encapsulated the skull.[17] The eighteenth-century gold *oorijsers* were valued at from 60 to 105 gulden.

TOTAL VALUE OF MOVABLE PROPERTY

These various trends in the movable property of Friesian peasants can be summarized in monetary terms. Of the 512 inventories upon which this study is based, 122 record the value of the possessions. Table 6–13 presents this information in the basic categories employed by the notaries. Since the value of silver and gold was rarely, and that of the survivors' clothing only occasionally, recorded, our statistics are not complete: silver and gold are omitted, and the textile category is somewhat underestimated (by a consistent margin, we hope).

The basic trends can be read at a glance. The importance of glass and earthenware rose steadily, until their value is subsumed in the metals category. Thereafter the rise was probably even more rapid. Farm equipment, principally wooden goods, assumed an increasingly large proportion of the total value. When we turn to the categories that would appear to hold the most promise for industrial growth, metals and textiles, we uncover trends that may seem surprising. Metal goods—iron, copper, and tin—accounted for a roughly constant percentage of the total value (although the inclusion of glass and earthenware in the later periods must be taken into account), but textiles—woolens, linens, and clothing—declined steadily in comparison with the other categories.

Long-Term Trends

In our effort to identify changes in the structure of peasant possessions, we may have erred in exaggerating their importance. A doubling of the average number of tin spoons over a two-century period is obviously not sufficient to revolutionize the mining industry or the peasants' way of life. Moreover, many

---

[17] The historical evolution of the *oorijser* is displayed in the important silver collection of the Fries Museum, Leeuwarden.

goods remained as they had been in both quantity and quality. No technological revolution altered the context of peasant production and consumption. But *within this stable context the multiplicity of small, indeed trivial, changes in consumption constituted the physical expression of a changing peasant culture* that is worthy of our attention. The range of goods found in the peasant home gradually expanded, and these new goods were produced outside the peasant household by specialists. Our study cannot uphold the image of peasants striving for a target income, suspicious of novelty, and fearful of becoming dependent upon the market.

How many of the Friesian peasant's possessions were home-produced? This, of course, the inventories do not reveal, although *it is difficult to believe that many of the newly introduced goods* (i.e., oak chests, clocks, mirrors, silver beakers) could ever have been introduced into a self-sufficient household economy. The inventories do, however, list the petty debts left by the deceased: their analysis can give a general impression of the peasants' dependence on the market.

The most frequently encountered petty debts in the period 1550–1599 were, in order of frequency, for textiles, labor, bread, grain, shoes, smithwork, ironware, beer, and livestock. In the period 1616–1654, the list reads differently: bread, beer, "store goods" (which, of course, subsumed a wide variety of goods available in rural shops, a seventeenth-century novelty), textiles, ironware, shoes, smithwork, carpentry, labor. Also encountered in this period were debts to wheelwrights, wagonmakers, cabinet-makers, and fodder merchants. There were no references to purchased grain.

This investigation of petty debts does not rest on a sufficiently large base of inventories to warrant our making many inferences, but two things stand out quite clearly: first, home bread-making, which may have existed in the earlier period, to judge from the evidence of purchased grain, is no longer important in the later period, when 83 percent of the households examined owed money to bakers.[18] Second, the later period is characterized by a wider range of creditors, particularly fabricators of wooden goods.

[18] J. H. Knoop, the author of the *Tegenwoordige Staat van Friesland* (Leewarden, 1763), described the types of bread consumed in the province. He concluded his description with the following observation: "Here I must remark that, as in several other Netherlandish provinces, it is not the

What factors can account for the long-run trends in peasant demand uncovered by this study? Price movements are, unfortunately, not known for most finished consumer goods. It seems unlikely, given the absence of major technological changes, that most consumer goods became dramatically less expensive. In the one case where we know this did happen, with woolen cloth, the consumer response indicates that the price elasticity of demand was well below one.

Peasant income movements are not known in detail either, but it appears that income increased until the third quarter of the seventeenth century, and thereafter it suffered significant setbacks. Comparisons between households with large herds and those with small herds (our proxy for wealth), indicate that the richer households owned more of most goods. Here again, textiles were an exception. Distinctions between the textile holdings of households with large and small herds are difficult to make after we discount for the larger size of the more well-off households. Is this sufficient evidence that the income elasticity of demand was below one? With regard to other goods, it is ironic that many of the most costly additions to peasant inventories were made in the century after 1650, when rising income cannot be the chief explanation.

The evolution of peasant demand was guided by more profound factors than price and income alone. Although the evidence upon which this study rests hardly enables us to creep into the minds of the peasants, a cultural explanation seems to be warranted. We observed earlier that many of the new acquisitions represented urban culture and filtered down to the peasants, as it were, from their social superiors (if it is possible for a Friesian peasant to have a superior of any sort). Could the mid-seventeenth century decline in household size (imputed from the decline in bed ownership) have been partially caused by a desire to increase expenditure on luxury and status objects, which could only be accomplished, in this era, by reducing expenditures on the basic commodities (such as textiles) required by a large household? This is sheer speculation, we must confess, but it would be foolish to deny that these peasants possessed what

---

custom here for each—especially the farmer—to bake his own bread, as is the case in Germany and elsewhere, but rather each buys it at the baker" (p. 469).

we would call social aspirations that transcended the traditional peasant aspirations for land, livestock, and hoarded plate. Consider the demand for linens, as an example. Peasants in many areas have been observed to place great value on the ownership of a large stock of linens. The Friesian peasants seem to be no exception to the rule, but their increased income was not channeled in this direction. They apparently acquired a new vision of the good life.

In 1825, William Cobbett, in his *Rural Rides*, records his happening upon the auction of an English yeoman's farm. Here he could observe the changed consumption habits of a well-to-do farmer. His disgust for the farmer's new life style—as for so many things—knew no bounds.

> Everything about this farm-house was formerly the scene of *plain manners* and *plentiful living*. Oak clothes-chests, oak bedsteads, oak chests of drawers, and oak tables to eat on, long, strong, and well supplied with joint stools. Some of the things were many hundreds of years old. But all appeared to be in a state of decay and nearly of *disuse*. There appeared to have been hardly any *family* in that house, where formerly there were, in all probability, from ten to fifteen men, boys and maids: and, which was the worst of all, there was a *parlour!* Aye, and a *carpet* and *bell-pull* too! One end of the front of this once plain and substantial house had been moulded into a *"parlour"*; and there was the mahogany table, and the fine chairs, and the fine glass, and all as bare-faced upstart as any stock-jobber in the kingdom can boast of. And, there were the decanters, the glasses, the "dinner-set" of crockery ware, and all just in the true stock-jobber style.[19]

The parlor, which seemed to Cobbett so unnatural in a yeoman's house, and which he held to be a product of the economic evils wrought by the Napoleonic wars, was actually the result of a long-term development that we see unfolding already in seventeenth-century Friesland.

Demand Pattern and Occupational Structure

We have established that the peasants of our case study became specializing producers and, hence, market-dependent consumers.[20]

[19] William Cobbett, *Rural Rides* (Penguin edition, 1967), pp. 226–27.

[20] The account book of the Friesian farmer Rienck Hemmema, for the years 1571–1573, indicates that most of the grain and nearly all of the dairy

So little household labor was expended upon self-provision that even bread was purchased. We have also established that peasant demand characteristics were not static. New commodities came into vogue, and the composition of expenditure changed. We must now consider what impact peasant demand had on the nonagricultural sectors of the economy. The objects of our attention were, after all, not a tiny, well-off minority at the peak of the social pyramid. The agriculturalists whose wealth and demand characteristics we have described include almost all of Friesland's landed population: they were, if you will, a broad middle-class consumer group.

A 1749 occupational census, the *Quotisatie Cohieren*, which gives the occupation of each head of household, provides us with the opportunity to gauge the impact of peasant demand on the economy. This impact can be examined with special clarity in Friesland, since its economy possessed few other "export" sectors. Seafarers were numerous in several coastal cities and villages, and an important brick and ceramics industry flourished in the same area. But the inadequacy of the census data for these places forces us to exclude them in any event. Otherwise, a substantial

---

output of the farm was marketed. Although he grew wheat, Hemmema sold it and purchased rye to feed the household and servants. See: B. H. Slicher van Bath, "Een landbouwbedrijf in de tweede helft van de zestiende eeuw," *Agronomisch-Historisch Bijdragen* 4 (1958), 67–188; *idem*, "Robert Loder en Rienck Hemmema," *It beaken*, 20 (1958), 89–117.

In the mid-eighteenth century, the accounts of a dairy farm in Holland, kept by a trustee of orphaned children, show how thoroughly market-oriented agriculture had become. The table in Appendix 6.2 presents the average yearly income and expenditure during the period 1743–1749. This farm of about thirty hectares had a total value—real and movable property combined—of approximately 4600 gulden, an average annual income of 2840 gulden, and an average annual expenditure of 2654 gulden. The savings of approximately 200 gulden per year went to retire a 3000–gulden debt, over 1000 gulden of which had been incurred in the modernization of the farm house. All clothing was purchased, and the only foods that was both produced and consumed on the farm were the dairy products and most of the meat. The household purchased meal, bread, biscuits, beer, carrots, apples, peas, potatoes, and some meat.

One did not have to travel far, however, to find peasants whose contacts with the market were minimal. Until the mid-nineteenth century, farms on the sandy soils of the eastern and southern provinces could be characterized as follows: "[Their] cash income was very small, it sufficed to pay taxes and rents and was often gotten by the sale of hogs just before the due dates for these payments. Rents in shares or quantities of grain lasted until 1860 in these areas, and purchased goods often were bought via exchanges in kind." J. Baert, "De geldomzet in het boerenbedrijf van 1795–1940," *De Economist* 95 (1946), 599.

seasonal peat digging industry is the only important activity—
urban or rural—that did not ultimately depend on the income
of the agricultural sector; the bulk of the secondary and tertiary
sectors of the Friesian economy served local markets.

Table 6–14 presents the occupational structures of rural Friesland (eighteen of the thirty *grietenijen*), the capital city, Leeuwarden, and a summary of the ten smaller cities. Immediately
apparent is the sriking fact that in this agricultural province
farmers made up less than one-third of the rural population, let
alone the total population. When we add to these farmers their
live-in servants (not enumerated in the census) and the portion
of the common laborers who worked on the farms, the total
agricultural labor force becomes somewhat larger. (If we assume
that servants were relatively as numerous as the 1795 census
showed them to be—10.6 percent of the population—that two-
thirds of all rural servants worked on farms, and that half of
the common laborers worked on farms, agriculture would account
for 51 percent of the rural labor force and 37 percent of the
total provincial labor force.) The fact remains that the demand
of the farm sector supported—directly or indirectly—a very large
number of nonfarm workers.

This had not always been so. The early sixteenth-century
population of Friesland had been less urbanized, and the rural
population had been overwhelmingly attached to the land. A
good 70 percent of the total population derived its livelihood
directly from agriculture.[21] Over the two centuries covered in
this study, the Friesian economy remained firmly based upon
agriculture, but the agricultural labor force fell from around 70
to no more than 37 percent of the total. The economy grew
through the process of household specialization described at the
beginning of this essay. The peasant households' unfolding
demand characteristics gradually reduced the percentage of nonagricultural goods they provided for themselves, and supported
with increasing strength the development of a highly articulated

---

[21] See de Vries, *Dutch Rural Economy*, pp. 101–105. The urban population
in 1511 is unlikely to have exceeded a quarter of the total. As for the rural
population in that year, the *Aanbreng van 1511*, a land tax register, shows
that the rural industrial and trade centers (*vlekken*) had not yet taken shape,
and that the landless population in most *grietenijen* was very small. J. A.
Faber, in *Drie eeuwen Friesland*, feels justified in concluding that 70 percent
of the total population was directly dependent upon agriculture (p. 129).

occupational structure. The economy—both urban and rural—became richly endowed with skills and capital, although, significantly, the scale of industrial and service enterprise never evolved beyond the artisan workshop serving local markets.

Agricultural specialization in other regions and at other times has made those regions dependent upon distant, sometimes foreign, producers of manufactured goods.[22] In Friesland peasant specialization in the sixteenth and seventeenth centuries fostered the proliferation of nearby, small-scale suppliers. With the notable exception of the textile industry, which was all but nonexistent in Friesland, most other industries and services arose in both urban and rural areas to supply local demand. For every Leiden or Twente weaver and Delft potter filling orders for Friesland, there must have been dozens of local village and town craftsmen. Moreover, the trends in peasant demand displayed in Table 6–13 (stagnation in metals, decline in textiles, and expansion in wooden goods) could only increase the relative importance of local suppliers.

A Comparison

The Friesian demand pattern and occupational structure can be placed in perspective through a comparison with another region with a different economic structure.[23] The rural economy of

[22] See: Stephen Resnick, "The Decline of Rural Industry under Export Expansion: A Comparison among Burma, Philippines, and Thailand, 1870–1938," *Journal of Economic History* 30 (1970), 51–73; E. L. Jones, "Agricultural Origins of Industry," *Past and Present* 40 (1968), 58–71; Anton Maczak, "Export of Grain and the Problem of the Distribution of National Income in the Years 1550–1650," *Acta Poloniae Historia* 18 (1968), 75–98; Witwold Kula, "Un' Economia Agraria Senza Accumulazione, La Polonia dei secoli XVI–XVIII," *Studi Storici* 9 (1968), 594–622.

[23] The comparison of peasant inventories in this study is confined to different districts within the province of Friesland. Such records exist, of course, for other provinces. We have examined those of Holland and Utrecht, but they do not date from a sufficiently early time, nor are they sufficiently numerous, to permit the sort of study attempted here. An interesting selection of inventories drawn from all social classes at the time of the Dutch Revolt has been assembled by H. A. Enno van Gelder, *Gegevens betreffende roerend en onroerend bezit in de Nederlanden in de 16e eeuw.* Rijksgeschiedkundige Publicatieën, Vols. 140 and 141 (The Hague, 1972, 1973).

Similar inventories also exist for other countries. English historians have made interesting use of probated inventories, but chiefly to describe farm production methods and trends. See: Joan Thirsk, *English Peasant Farming*

northwestern Europe can be divided into a maritime region of highly capitalized, specialized producers, and a landward region where rural life is less market-oriented and the social structure more pervasively imprinted with a feudal heritage. Within the province of Friesland two *grietenijen* in the southeast corner, Oost and Weststellingwerf, shared many of the characteristics found in the adjacent, landward provinces.

A comparison of peasant inventories in Ooststellingwerf with those of maritime Friesland (in Table 6–15) shows a large gap separating the "standard of living" of the agricultural populations of the two regions. The more spartan existence of the Ooststellingwerf peasants is reflected in the value of their movable property: the average value of six inventories in the years 1631–1647 came to 371 *gold gulden,* or just over a quarter of the value of maritime region inventories of the same period.

This "standard of living" gap suggests that the region's social structure lacked the "middle-class" peasant demand that supported industrial and service occupations. The nearby province of Overijssel provides another indication of this same char-

(London, 1957); W. G. Hoskins, *Essays in Leicestershire History* (Liverpool, 1950); G. H. Kenyon, "Kirdford Inventories 1611 to 1776, with particular reference to the weald clay farming." *Sussex Archaeological Collections,* Vol. 93 (1955). For the use of inventories as a source of architectural history, see M. W. Barley, "Farmhouses and Cottages, 1550–1725," *Economic History Review* 7 (1955), 291–306; for their use in urban history, see Alan D. Dyer, *The City of Worcester in the Sixteenth Century* (Leicester, 1973). Several other works have published collections of inventories or summaries of inventory values: F. Steer, *Farm and Cottage Inventories in Mid-Essex* (Chelmsford, 1950); F. G. Emmison, "Jacobean Household Inventories," *Bedfordshire Historical Record Society,* Vol. 20 (1938); Margaret Cash, "Devon Inventories in the Sixteenth and Seventeenth Centuries," *Devon and Cornwall Record Society,* new ser., Vol. 11 (1966); P. A. Kennedy, "Nottinghamshire Household Inventories," *Thoroton Society,* record series, Vol. 22 (1963).

German inventories have been used, again, principally for the light they shed on farm production characteristics, by Walter Achilles, *Vermogensverhaltnisse Braunschweigischer Bauernhofe* (Stuttgart, 1965), and F. W. Henning, *Bauernwirtschaft und Bauerneinkommen im fürstentum Paderborn im 18. Jahrhundert* (Berlin, 1970).

In France, Pierre Goubert's *Beauvais et le Beauvaisis de 1600 à 1730* (Paris, 1960) makes use of peasant inventories. No effort has yet been made to use the inventories for interregional and international comparisons. The data available in the works cited generally do not suffice to make such comparisons, and we have resisted the temptation to do so here. But the records exist, and such comparisons seem to be called for to improve our understanding of the regional differences that affect the spread of industrialization in the eighteenth and nineteenth centuries.

acteristic. Here the bulk of the province (the districts of Twente
and Salland) formed part of the landward economic zone to
which Ooststellingwerf belonged, while a small area bordering
the Zuider Zee (the district of Vollenhove) shared the economic
characteristics of maritime Friesland, which it adjoined. **B. H.**
Slicher van Bath has analyzed the wealth tax levied in this
province in 1675. The tax fell on all persons with assets of at
least 500 gulden. Figure 6–5 presents the findings in the form
of a Lorenz curve. This cumulative measure of inequality shows

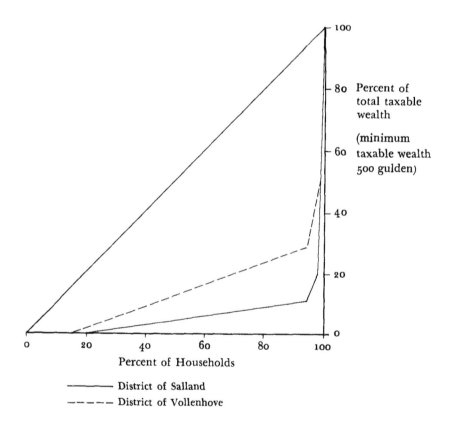

Figure 6-5: Wealth distribution in rural Overijssel, 1675
Source: B. H. Slicher van Bath, *Samenleving onder spanning*
    (Assen, 1957), pp. 255-258.

at a glance how the wealth-holding patterns of the two zones differ from one another. The extreme inequality of Salland (and the curve for Twente is almost exactly the same) indicates the absence of an economically specialized, highly capitalized peasantry.

The mid-eighteenth-century occupational structure of Oost and Weststellingwerf gives evidence of a lack of economic inter-dependence—that is, of the weak linkages—between the peasant households and the other economic sectors. Over half the households were agricultural in this corner of the province, and while rural maritime Friesland possessed one industrial worker for every two farmers, in Oost and Weststellingwerf the ratio was 1 to 3.5. The tertiary sector was also weakly represented. While farmers outnumbered those occupied in trade, transportation, and social services by less than 2 to 1 in maritime Friesland, in Oost and Weststellingwerf farmers were over 5 times as numerous. These contrasting ratios take on an added significance when one recalls that the maritime zone was studded with cities, whose populations also served rural markets, while Oost and Weststellingwerf were far removed from even the smallest urban settlement.

We can summarize the difference in rural occupational structure by calculating the population per practitioner of several occupations in maritime Friesland, Oost and Weststellingwerf, and (using the 1795 occupational census analyzed by Slicher van Bath) in Overijssel. These calculations, presented in Table 6–16, show an impressive difference in the average number of consumers supplied by the craftsmen of the two basic regions. These figures, and much of our preceding argument, would be of scant usefulness if the craftsmen were not primarily dependent on their crafts for their income. Should they prove to have been marginal farmers who sought to supplement their inadequate agricultural income with by-employments, then we must draw conclusions from Table 6–16 that are the opposite of what we intend to show. Since Goubert and Saint-Jacob describe seventeenth-century craftsmen in the Beauvaisis and in Burgundy as *"manouvriers* seeking additional means of livelihood," [24] we must

24 Pierre Goubert, "The French Peasantry of the Seventeenth Century: A Regional Example," in Trevor Aston, *Crisis in Europe,* p. 158; see also,

determine the true economic nature of rural craftsmen in Friesland and Overijssel before we can safely draw conclusions.

Concerning Overijssel, we possess no information that can
solve this problem. The 1795 occupational census records very
few joint occupations, but the presence of a larger cottar class
raises the possibility that just as these miserable households
added spinning and weaving as by-employments, so they may
have added carpentry, shoemaking, etc.

We are confident that this does not characterize the artisans
of rural maritime Friesland. Here the social structure did not
include a large cottar class, and the inventories of craftsmen,
storekeepers, and transport workers show these persons to have
been innocent of livestock and farm equipment. Here the craftsmen were as specialized as the peasants, and a numerous industrial population was less a symptom of rural overpopulation than
of high peasant demand.[25]

Conclusions

Peasant demand was not a negligible factor in the economic
life of early modern Europe. Ignoring it not only distorts our
knowledge of markets for industrial output, but removes from
view an important element in the determination of the supply
elasticity of agricultural output. Being content with a caricature,
on the other hand, can only result in a misspecification of the
historic and potential role of peasants in economic development.

The Friesian peasants of this case study by no means stand
for all peasants. It is likely that peasants in adjacent maritime
regions behaved similarly, but just a few dozen miles inland
peasant demand characteristics, as we have seen, differed sharply.

How did the Friesian peasants dispose of their income, which
apparently increased in the first century of our analysis? They

---

P. de Saint-Jacob, *Les Paysans de la Bourgogne du Nord au dernier siècle de
l'Ancien Régime* (Paris, 1960).

[25] The distribution of labor requirements in the course of the year undoubtedly contributed to the absence of farming combined with crafts in
rural Friesland. Types of farming with highly pronounced peak labor loads
lend themselves to combination with other employments during slack times.
The dairying and breeding economy of most Friesian districts was characterized by a more even distribution of labor demand. The considerable
capital investment needed to operate livestock farms must also have acted
to keep the farm and nonfarm populations separate.

avoided the trap of using their income to chase after parcels of land. While this might gain for some a bit of status and security, its net economic effect was to redistribute wealth and drive up land prices. Various local factors, including good tenure terms, made the peasants content to rent. They also avoided the purchase of superfluous horses, which observers of other European peasants have cited as a frequent drain on income.[26] Despite these economies, the expenditure on capital goods bulked large in the total peasant budget, and increased in importance during the two centuries after 1550. These expenditures supported much of the market for wooden goods.

The demand for consumer goods did not keep pace with producer goods. Conceivably, it also suffered from a high demand for gold and silver objects. It remains an open question whether the glittering hoards found in the inventories of later years, accumulated over generations of Republican peace and order, actually indicate an increase in the level of peasant demand. On thing is certain: in the early nineteenth century, no other provinces in the Kingdom of the Netherlands (which then included Belgium) could approach Friesland and its neighboring provinces of Groningen and North Holland in their per-capita number of gold and silver smiths.[27]

Expenditures for consumer goods did not command the bulk of the peasant budget, but they are not without interest. Not only did the Friesian peasants become highly dependent upon the market for every type of consumer good, but they did not fail to acquire new tastes that had important implications for their way of life. The most noteworthy trends uncovered in the study were the price and income inelasticity of demand for most textiles, and the apparent eagerness to acquire and accumulate goods that are normally associated with urban, or at least non-rustic, culture.

The peasants operated farms with strong linkages to other

[26] For an account of a farming region with an irrationally large number of horses per farm, see Walter Achilles, *Vermögensverhaltnisse*.

[27] The provinces with the largest per capita number of gold and silver smiths in the Kingdom of the Netherlands at the time of the industrial census of 1819 were, in order, Groningen, Friesland, and North Holland. The provinces with the smallest number were, in order, Drenthe, East Flanders, Namur, Hainault, Limburg, and Gelderland. I. J. Brugmans, ed., *Statistieken van de Nederlandse Nijverheid uit de eerste helft der 19e eeuw*, Rijksgeschiedkundige Publicatieën, Vols. 98 and 99 (The Hague, 1956).

sectors of the economy; they enjoyed, moreover, a relatively high
standard of living, and, over the years, added new goods to their
range of consumption. It is not far-fetched to speak of these
peasants as modernizing. Their economy became highly commercialized, thoroughly specialized, rich in skills, and well endowed with capital. By the mid-seventeenth century the rural
population was well educated (to judge from the many teachers),
mobile (to judge from the numerous canals and transport services), and receptive to urban culture.

They did not thereby revolutionize industrial production.
Small-scale, local producers appear to have been quite well suited
to satisfying the growing wants of this peasant population.[28]
None of the important changes in agricultural production or in
consumer demand traced in this study readied the economy for
the organizational and technical changes associated with modern
industry. Apparently it was possible for an economy to develop
satisfactorily in many ways and yet avoid industrialization. For
such changes we must turn our attention to regions (such as
Twente and Flanders) with a much less fortunate economic
history.

[28] This line of reasoning can, of course, be set on its head. The production
limitations of the nonagricultural sector, one might argue, channeled peasant
demand into certain fields. Had one placed a Sears Roebuck catalogue in
their hands, their consumption habits would have been entirely different.
We will refrain from such an exercise in counterfactual history. This recalls,
however, the conclusion of Hymer and Resnick that peasant supply elasticity
requires a manufacturing sector capable of supplying superior goods. To
judge from the growth of specialized output, a manufacturing sector without
appeal to the Friesian peasant was *not* a problem in this case study.

Appendix 6.1 Z-Goods Model

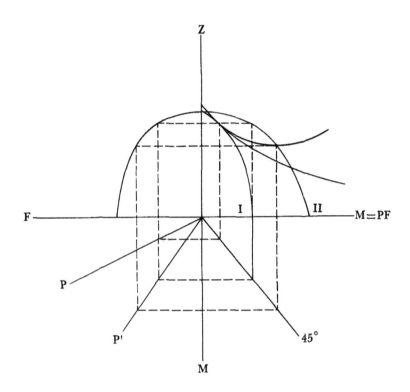

Source: Stephen Resnick, "The Decline of Rural Industry under Export
Expansion: A Comparison among Burma, Philippines, and Thailand, 1870–
1938," *Journal of Economic History* 30 (1970), 51–73; figure on p. 54.

Quadrant II shows a production possibilities curve between Z
(nonagricultural goods) and F (food production); quadrant III
shows the terms of trade between food and M (manufactures, or
nonagricultural goods produced outside the peasant household).
P' indicates more favorable terms of trade to the food producer
than P. Quadrant I shows the consumption possibilities curves
that correspond to the price relations (P=1; P'=2). Consumption takes place at the tangency of the consumption possibilities
curve and the (unshown) community indifference curve. The
successive tangency points derived by shifting the terms of trade
trace an offer curve.

The shape of the offer curve is directly related to the character of the household's marketed food supply curve. If the offer curve is shaped as in the dotted line in quadrant 1, better terms of trade for food producers will stimulate an increased food specialization and, consequently, an increased purchase of manufactures, but only to a certain point. Further price improvements encourage (through the substitution effect) continued increases in the demand for M (manufactures), it is true, but these price changes also increase real income, and as the income effect becomes more important the demand for Z (nonagricultural goods), and for leisure, reduces the household's marketed food production. The price changes would permit, after all, a smaller volume of marketed food to suffice in acquiring the manufactured goods wanted by the household.

A transformation of the production mix is possible only when the shape of the offer curve does not bend backward over a wide range (represented by the broken line). This can happen only when the manufactures are considered superior to home-produced goods (so the income effect on the demand for Z is negative). This study of peasant demand attempts, in effect, to determine the shape of the offer curve in a peasant economy. Was the demand for manufactured goods and specialists' services limited to fixed quantities of a few goods, or did it grow and expand when price and income changes permitted? The answer to this question would help one understand what sort of role peasants could play—as both producers and consumers—in the process of economic development.

Appendix 6.2 Accounts of a Dairy Farm in Holland

	in gulden	% of total income
Average yearly income, 1743–1749		
sale of dairy products	1842	64.9
sale of livestock, hides, etc.	537	18.9
sale of grain, straw, wood, etc.	388	13.6
rental of land and house	73	2.6
Total	2840	100.0
Average yearly expenditures, 1743–1749		
Farm operations		
purchase of livestock	264	9.3
farm inputs (hay, fodder, seed)	218	7.7
land rental	443	15.6
labor costs	340	11.9
maintenance	136	4.8
subtotal	1401	49.3
Household expenditures		
food and drink	205	7.2
clothing and shoes	155	5.4
general	314	11.0
subtotal	674	23.6
Taxes	579	20.4
Total	2654	93.3

Source: A. G. van der Steur, "Een Warmondse boerenboekhouding uit de tijd van de veepest (1742–1749)," *Leids Jaarboekje* 62 (1970), 161–87.

Appendix 6.3   Tables

Table 6-1. Farm Equipment. Wealth class: ten or more milk cows

Goods	Henn.* 1550–62	Leeuw.* 1566–74	Leeuw. 1583–99	Leeuw. 1616–41 Wons.* 1628–33	Henn. 1646–54	Leeuw. 1677–86	Leeuw. 1711–50
Wagons							
Average number [a]	0.92	1.83	1.70	2.00	2.00	2.90	2.42
Percentage [b]	75%	84%	82%	81%	91%	96%	100%
Average of all [c]	0.69	1.54	1.39	1.60	1.82	2.75	2.42
Boats							
Average number	1.05	1.00	1.00	1.14	1.10	1.10	1.20
Percentage	79%	68%	59%	65%	91%	71%	56%
Average of all	0.83	0.68	0.61	0.74	1.00	0.77	0.67
Plows							
Average number	0.97	1.00	1.00	1.04	1.00	1.30	1.10
Percentage	63%	72%	88%	74%	46%	54%	61%
Butter churns							
Average number	1.09	1.10	1.00	1.00	1.05	1.34	1.00
Percentage	92%	72%	83%	89%	100%	96%	100%
% with power churns	0	0	0	0	0	35%	72%

Aden (decreaming vessels)						
Average number	25.0	28.3	27.6	29.9	30.7	26.6	28.1
Percentage	96%	92%	92%	95%	100%	100%	94%
Per milk cow [d]	1.6	1.8	1.8	2.0	2.0	1.8	1.9
Cheese presses							
Average number	1.0	1.1	1.2	1.1	1.2	1.2	1.2
Percentage	79%	80%	90%	80%	100%	83%	100%
Cheese vats							
Average number	1.9	1.90	2.5	2.6	2.7	2.0	3.0
Percentage	96%	84%	95%	91%	100%	21%	95%
Wooden pails							
Average number	5.5	5.5	6.1	6.2	6.8	6.3	9.5
Percentage	79%	68%	88%	100%	96%	96%	95%
Cheese kettles							
Average number	1.0	1.0	1.0	1.0	1.0	1.0	1.0
Percentage	71%	12%	?	83%	100%	88%	?

* Henn.=Hennaarderadeel; Leeuw.=Leeuwarderadeel; Wons.=Wonseradeel.
[a] Average number of the article found in those inventories that record its presence.
[b] Percentage of all households that possess the article.
[c] Average number of the article owned by all *households*, whether or not they possess any.
[d] Average number of *aden* owned per milk cow.

Table 6–2. Farm Equipment. Wealth class: under ten milk cows

Goods	Henn. 1550–62	Leeuw. 1566–74	Leeuw. 1583–99	Leeuw. 1616–41 Wons. 1628–33	Henn. 1646–54	Leeuw. 1677–86	Leeuw. 1711–50
Wagons							
Average number	0.9	1.5	1.5	1.9	1.7	2.4	2.9
Percentage	59%	37%	48%	40%	27%	78%	77%
Average of all	0.59	0.57	0.71	0.76	0.45	1.91	2.26
Boats							
Average number	1.0	1.0	1.7	1.4	1.0	0.9	1.0
Percentage	82%	9%	14%	24%	46%	43%	32%
Average of all	0.79	0.09	0.24	0.24	0.45	0.39	0.32
Plows							
Average number	1.0	1.0	1.0	1.2	1.0	1.1	1.3
Percentage	35.3	31%	48%	44%	18%	70%	63%
Butter churns							
Average number	0.97	1.1	7.2	1.0	1.0	1.0	1.0
Percentage	88%	34%	63%	77%	100%	100%	68%
% with power churns	0	0	0	0	0	0	23%

Aden (decreaming vessels)							
Average number	14.9	18.5	14.9	12.0	13.5	11.8	16.0
Percentage	88%	37%	67%	80%	100%	100%	84%
Per milk cow	2.4	2.8	2.8	2.4	2.8	1.8	2.4
Cheese presses							
Average number	1.0	1.1	1.0	1.0	1.0	1.0	1.1
Percentage	48%	34%	63%	55%	82%	74%	79%
Cheese vats							
Average number	2.2	1.9	2.3	2.4	1.9	1.3	3.3
Percentage	88%	40%	69%	59%	91%	26%	84%
Wooden pails							
Average number	3.5	3.8	4.1	4.2	4.2	4.1	5.4
Percentage	59%	37%	81%	100%	100%	83%	100%
Cheese kettles							
Average number	1.1	1.0	?	1.0	1.0	1.0	1.0
Percentage	41%	6%	?	45%	46%	52%	16%

Table 6–3. Textiles. Wealth class: ten or more milk cows

Goods	Henn. 1550–62	Leeuw. 1566–74	Leeuw. 1583–99	Leeuw. 1616–41 Wons. 1628–33	Henn. 1646–54	Leeuw. 1677–86	Leeuw. 1711–50
Beds							
Average number	6.1	5.9	5.2	6.0	6.2	4.5	4.6
Percentage	100%	100%	98%	100%	100%	100%	100%
Blankets							
Average number	11.6	11.6	9.9	11.5	12.0	8.1	8.8
Percentage	100%	100%	90%	100%	100%	100%	100%
Average per bed [a]	1.9	2.0	1.9	1.9	1.9	1.8	1.9
Tablecloths							
Average number	6.5	6.5	5.7	6.2	6.6	3.9	3.1
Percentage	100%	96%	95%	94%	100%	83%	67%
Washcloths							
Average number	4.5	4.7	5.7	6.0	4.5	2.9	?
Percentage	71%	72%	90%	83%	91%	38%	?

Bedsheets							
Average number	41.3	34.3	24.2 [c]	37.4	45.6	31.6	30.6
Percentage	100%	96%	100%	95%	100%	96%	95%
Average per bed [b]	7.1	5.9	4.7	6.2	7.4	7.0	6.7
Chair cushions							
Average number	10.2	13.6	9.7	11.7	11.8	7.1	7.6
Percentage	67%	64%	88%	83%	82%	83%	72%
Table napkins							
Average number	12.0	9.2	11.2	15.5	8.0	6.5	6.3
Percentage	4%	24%	10%	40%	46%	33%	39%
Curtains							
Average number	?	5.0	2.2	3.0	2.6	2.9	4.1
Percentage	?	4%	33%	23%	59%	83%	89%
Schoorsteen kleden							
Average number	1.0	1.0	?	1.7	1.5	2.0	2.9
Percentage	8%	4%	?	31%	68%	79%	89%
Spinning wheels							
Average number	1.3	2.4	2.4	2.6	2.4	0	2.1
Percentage	17%	40%	53%	54%	96%	?	95%

[a] Number of blankets per bed.
[b] Number of bedsheets per bed.
[c] This number does not include *wytlingen*, a type of bedsheet included in the other averages.

Table 6-4. Textiles. Wealth class: under ten milk cows

Goods	Henn. 1550–62	Leeuw. 1566–74	Leeuw. 1583–99	Leeuw. 1616–41 Wons. 1628–33	Henn. 1646–54	Leeuw. 1677–86	Leeuw. 1711–50
Beds							
Average number	4.6	4.9	4.0	3.8	3.8	3.4	3.4
Percentage	100%	100%	100%	100%	100%	100%	100%
Blankets							
Average number	8.3	9.5	7.4	8.0	6.8	6.0	6.6
Percentage	100%	80%	100%	88%	100%	100%	95%
Average per bed	1.8	1.9	1.9	2.1	1.8	1.8	1.9
Tablecloths							
Average number	4.8	5.4	'4.0	4.5	3.9	3.9	3.2
Percentage	88%	40%	75%	77%	91%	61%	53%
Washcloths							
Average number	4.3	5.9	3.6	2.8	2.4	2.2	?
Percentage	65%	37%	69%	77%	64%	26%	?

Bedsheets							
Average number	20.5	25.6	15.6[a]	21.8	24.1	20.6	23.8
Percentage	100%	46%	100%	100%	100%	96%	100%
Average per bed	4.5	5.2	3.9	5.7	6.3	6.1	6.9
Chair cushions							
Average number	8.6	11.0	7.6	7.3	6.2	5.2	5.5
Percentage	65%	34%	81%	59%	55%	65%	53%
Table napkins							
Average number	0	10.0	0	5.3	14.0	5.0	6.8
Percentage	0	9%	0	14%	27%	17%	42%
Curtains							
Average number	?	0	3.0	1.0	1.0	2.6	5.2
Percentage	?	0	13%	9%	18%	74%	90%
Schoorsteen kleden							
Average number	0	0	?	1.2	1.2	1.5	2.4
Percentage	0	0	?	27%	46%	87%	74%
Spinning wheels							
Average number	1.0	2.2	1.9	2.0	2.0	?	1.8
Percentage	18%	14%	50%	45%	100%	?	79%

a This number does not include *wyllingen*, a type of bedsheet included in the other averages.

Table 6–5. Textiles. Wealth class: zero milk cows

Goods	Leeuw. 1583–99	Leeuw. 1616–41 Wons. 1628–31	Henn. 1646–54	Leeuw. 1711–50
Beds				
Average number	2.5	2.7	3.7	2.8
Percentage	80%	100%	100%	100%
Blankets				
Average number	5.6	5.7	7.3	6.2
Percentage	90%	100%	100%	92%
Average per bed	2.2	2.1	2.0	2.2
Tablecloths				
Average number	5.2	3.6	5.0	5.5
Percentage	50%	54%	86%	50%
Washcloths				
Average number	7.0	2.0	6.7	?
Percentage	25%	62%	43%	?
Bedsheets				
Average number	19.7	16.9	30.0	20.9
Percentage	100%	93%	100%	100%
Average per bed	7.9	6.3	8.1	7.5
Chair cushions				
Average number	6.2	6.9	9.9	6.7
Percentage	75%	100%	100%	50%
Table napkins				
Average number	17.7	7.7	23.7	21.6
Percentage	38%	23%	43%	67%
Curtains				
Average number	4.7	2.8	6.0	5.8
Percentage	39%	31%	14%	75%
Schoorsteen kleden				
Average number	?	1.3	2.7	2.0
Percentage	?	23%	43%	75%
Spinning wheels				
Average number	1.0	1.6	1.3	1.2
Percentage	25%	54%	86%	42%
Wagon				
Average number	1.0	0	1.0	2.0
Percentage	10%	0	14%	17%
Average of all	0.10	0	0.14	0.33
Boat				
Average number	0	0.7	1.3	1.5
Percentage	0	20%	43%	17%
Average of all	0	0.13	0.57	0.25

Table 6-6. Clothing. Wealth class: ten or more milk cows

Goods	Henn. 1550–62	Leeuw. 1566–74	Leeuw. 1583–99	Henn.[a] 1595–1600	Leeuw. 1616–41 Wons. 1628–33	Henn. 1646–54	Leeuw. 1677–86	Leeuw. 1711–50
Men's coats								
Average number	1.3	1.0	1.2	1.0	1.1	1.0	1.0	1.0
Percentage	17%	8%	25%	53%	49%	46%	46%	11%
Waistcoats								
Average number	1.9	1.0	1.3	1.4	1.6	1.3	1.6[b]	2.6
Percentage	29%	4%	40%	33%	26%	36%	61%	50%
Pants								
Average number	1.5	0	1.6	3.0	2.0	1.6	2.9	2.6
Percentage	8%	0	20%	13%	20%	50%	63%	44%
Pairs of socks								
Average number	2.0	2.0	1.8	2.5	1.9	2.3	2.5	2.4
Percentage	8%	8%	23%	13%	26%	27%	71%	50%

Pairs of shoes								
Average number	2.0	0	1.8	0	1.6	2.0	1.7	1.9
Percentage	4%	0	13%	0	14%	14%	42%	44%
Shirts								
Average number	5.3	6.8	7.0	7.0	11.9	16.6	18.3	14.3
Percentage	38%	20%	68%	53%	46%	50%	67%	67%
Hats								
Average number	1.0	1.0	1.7	1.5	2.4	4.8	1.9	2.0
Percentage	13%	4%	25%	27%	20%	50%	63%	50%
Women's skirts								
Average number	0	0	0	0	2.4	2.5	2.3	3.4
Percentage	0	0	0	0	14%	36%	13%	39%
Shirts								
Average number	4.5	4.0	3.1	8.0	10.1	11.6	18.2	12.3
Percentage	17%	12%	18%	27%	29%	41%	21%	50%

a The results of 15 Hennaarderadeel inventories are presented here. These inventories have not been sufficiently analyzed for general inclusion into this study. But since the clothing records are relatively good, they have been added to the other results.
b Of the inventories recording waistcoats, 76 percent record waistcoats with silver buttons.

Table 6-7. Clothing. Wealth class: under ten milk cows

Goods	Henn. 1550–62	Leeuw. 1566–74	Leeuw. 1583–99	Leeuw. 1616–41 Wons. 1628–31	Henn. 1646–54	Leeuw. 1677–86	Leeuw. 1711–50
Men's coats							
Average number	1.0	1.0	1.0	1.0	0.9	1.0	0.67
Percentage	18%	6%	6%	23%	55%	22%	11%
Waistcoats							
Average number	1.0	1.5	1.3	1.0	1.3	1.4[a]	2.5
Percentage	6%	6%	38%	28%	64%	52%	42%
Pants							
Average number	0	0	1.5	2.2	1.8	3.6	2.4
Percentage	0	0	25%	27%	46%	39%	37%
Pairs of socks							
Average number	1.5	2.0	1.2	3.0	2.3	2.5	2.4
Percentage	12%	8%	44%	9%	73%	52%	37%

Pairs of shoes							
Average number	0	1.0	1.0	1.0	1.8	1.5	1.7
Percentage	0	3%	13%	9%	55%	43%	32%
Shirts							
Average number	3.8	6.2	5.4	7.9	10.3	11.1	15.3
Percentage	35%	17%	63%	36%	73%	52%	58%
Hats							
Average number	1.0	1.0	1.0	1.0	1.3	1.9	1.4
Percentage	6%	3%	19%	14%	55%	57%	37%
Women's skirts							
Average number	1.0	0	0	1.3	3.3	3.8	3.3
Percentage	6%	0	0	7%	55%	22%	32%
Shirts							
Average number	0	4.5	5.0	5.3	8.9	9.7	9.3
Percentage	0	6%	13%	41%	73%	39%	37%

a Of the inventories recording waistcoats, 33 percent record waistcoats with silver buttons.

Table 6–8. Furniture and luxury goods. Wealth class: ten or more milk cows

Goods	Henn. 1550–62	Leeuw. 1566–74	Leeuw. 1583–99	Leeuw. 1616–41 Wons. 1628–31	Henn. 1646–54	Leeuw. 1677–86	Leeuw. 1711–50
Chests							
Average number	0	1.0	?	1.3	1.6	1.7	1.9
Percentage	0	4%	?	23%	64%	88%	95%
Tresoor							
Average number	1.3	1.1	1.1	1.2	1.0	0	0
Percentage	79%	67%	53%	17%	18%	0	0
Tables							
Average number	2.2	2.6	2.7	2.8	2.5	2.6	3.0
Percentage	100%	83%	100%	79%	100%	100%	100%
Benches							
Average number	2.7	?	4.4	4.2	2.4	4.0	1.7
Percentage	54%	?	85%	83%	82%	29%	83%
Chairs							
Average number	11.3	15.3	14.1	14.9	14.5	12.2	16.7
Percentage	100%	96%	100%	100%	100%	100%	95%

Mirrors							
Average number	1.3	1.0	1.0	1.3	1.4	1.5	1.6
Percentage	33%	8%	20%	74%	100%	92%	95%
Schilderijen							
Average number	0	?	0	0	3.6	3.0	4.8
Percentage	0	?	0	0	41%	29%	28%
Tin spoons							
Average number	12.0	12.3	15.4	21.6	22.3	20.0	20.7
Percentage	83%	76%	100%	98%	100%	96%	83%
Wood plates							
Average number	17.8	18.3	15.4	22.8	19.8	13.8	14.4
Percentage	33%	46%	85%	80%	100%	92%	78%
Tin plates							
Average number	12.0	12.0	9.3	9.8	7.3	6.5	6.0
Percentage	8%	13%	10%	49%	46%	8%	17%
Bibles & books							
Percentage	13%	4%	5%	29%	18%	42%	56%
Clocks							
Percentage	0	0	0	0	0	0	83%
Silver							
Percentage	33%	8%	14%	42%	68%	42%	72%

Table 6-9. Furniture and luxury goods. Wealth class: under ten milk cows

Goods	Henn. 1550–62	Leeuw. 1566–74	Leeuw. 1583–99	Leeuw. 1616–41 Wons. 1628–31	Henn. 1646–54	Leeuw. 1677–86	Leeuw. 1711–50
Chests							
Average number	0	0	?	1.0	1.0	1.4	1.6
Percentage	0	0	?	12%	36%	61%	90%
Tresoor							
Average number	1.1	1.1	1.2	1.0	1.0	0	0
Percentage	88%	28%	56%	23%	36%	0	0
Tables							
Average number	2.0	3.0	2.6	2.3	2.3	2.2	3.2
Percentage	88%	44%	100%	80%	100%	96%	95%
Benches							
Average number	2.0	?	3.6	4.3	2.3	2.0	1.6
Percentage	6%	?	88%	77%	64%	4%	58%
Chairs							
Average number	8.9	12.4	9.9	11.1	11.1	10.4	11.5
Percentage	94%	53%	100%	95%	100%	91%	90%

Mirrors							
Average number	0	1.0	1.0	1.0	1.1	1.3	1.8
Percentage	0	3%	13%	36%	91%	78%	90%
Schilderijen							
Average number*	0	?	0	0	0	3.5	3.7
Percentage	0	?	0	0	0	17%	16%
Tin spoons							
Average number	14.0	10.3	11.1	18.5	17.5	12.5	18.0
Percentage	18%	66%	86%	96%	100%	87%	84%
Wood plates							
Average number	6.0	16.0	12.7	15.8	13.3	11.4	9.0
Percentage	6%	22%	75%	86%	100%	78%	37%
Tin plates							
Average number	0	8.0	5.0	12.0	6.3	2.8	4.0
Percentage	0	9%	6%	5%	27%	17%	11%
Bibles & books							
Percentage	6%	0	0	32%	18%	17%	42%
Clocks							
Percentage	0	0	0	0	0	4%	58%
Silver							
Percentage	12%	0	14%	44%	73%	22%	58%

Table 6–10. Furniture and luxury goods. Wealth class: zero milk cows

Goods	Leeuw. 1583–99	Leeuw. 1616–41 Wons. 1628–31	Henn. 1646–54	Leeuw. 1711–50
Chest				
Average number	0	0	2.0	1.4
Percentage	0	0	29%	92%
Tresoor				
Average number	1.0	1.0	0	0
Percentage	13%	15%	0	0
Tables				
Average number	1.9	1.8	2.0	2.5
Percentage	88%	80%	100%	92%
Benches				
Average number	1.3	2.6	2.5	1.4
Percentage	88%	62%	57%	42%
Chairs				
Average number	5.3	10.5	11.0	11.4
Percentage	88%	100%	100%	92%
Mirrors				
Average number	1.0	1.7	1.3	1.4
Percentage	25%	23%	86%	100%
Schilderijen				
Average number	0	0	8.5	3.3
Percentage	0	0	29%	25%
Tin spoons				
Average number	12.8	16.3	13.1	9.6
Percentage	90%	100%	100%	100%
Wood plates				
Average number	14.4	19.9	17.0	29.0
Percentage	88%	62%	100%	25%
Tin plates				
Average number	15.0	6.0	8.0	4.3
Percentage	25%	23%	43%	33%
Bible & Books				
Percentage	0	23%	42%	75%
Clocks				
Percentage	0	0	0	8%
Silver				
Percentage	20%	7%	57%	58%

Table 6–11. Wagon and Boat Ownership

Period	Wagon ownership per farm household				
	Hennaarderadeel	Leeuwarderadeel noordertrimdeel	Leeuwarderadeel zuidertrimdeel	Idaarderadeel	Barradeel
1550–62	0.6	—	—	—	—
1566–74	—	1.4	0.6	—	—
1583–99	—	1.3	0.8	—	—
1602–19	—	—	—	0.6	—
1616–41	—	1.0	1.4	—	—
1646–54	1.4	—	—	—	3.1
1677–86	—	2.2	1.8	—	—
1676–1702	—	—	—	1.3	3.1
	Boat ownership per farm household				
1550–62	0.81	—	—	—	—
1566–74	—	0.33	0.50	—	—
1583–99	—	0.36	0.63	—	—
1602–19	—	—	—	0.33	—
1616–41	—	0.34	0.50	—	—
1646–54	0.80	—	—	—	0.15
1677–86	—	0.36	0.94	—	—
1676–1702	—	—	—	1.31	0.25

Table 6–12. Number of beds per household, according to wealth class

Grietenij	Period	Wealth class measured in size of cattle herd			
		ten and over	under ten	none	Total
Hennaarderadeel	1550–62	6.1	4.6	—	5.3
Leeuwarderadeel	1566–74	5.9	4.9	—	5.5
Leeuwarderadeel	1583–99	5.2	4.0	2.5	4.4
Hennaarderadeel	1595–1600	5.4	4.3	3.0	5.0
Leeuwarderadeel & Wonseradeel	1616–41	6.0	3.8	2.7	4.7
Hennaarderadeel	1646–54	6.2	3.8	3.7	5.1
Leeuwarderadeel	1677–86	4.5	3.4	—	3.9
Idaarderadeel	1676–1702	4.3	2.3	1.3	3.3
Leeuwarderadeel	1711–50	4.6	3.4	2.8	3.8

Table 6–13. Value of movable property of farm households in Leeuwarderadeel (in *goldgulden* of 28 stuivers)

| Period | Total | Livestock | Wooden Goods | | Textiles | Metals | Glass & stone-ware |
			Equipment	Household			
1583–99	838.09	545.04		94.9	156.17	41.16	0.19
1616–19	985.11	579.04		112.6	210.14	82.03	1.12
1634–41	1345.23	732.04	166.04	80.07	283.25	79.02	4.09
1677–86	1036.01	609.10	172.20	31.21	163.13	59.21	*
1711–23	1324.05	795.18	225.23	40.12	186.22	75.14	*
1759–85	1664.05	1093.12	345.00			225.13	

Value of movable property of farm households in Leeuwarderadeel, expressed in percentages of the total for each period

| Period | Livestock | Wooden Goods | | Textiles | Metals | Glass & stone-ware |
		Equipment	Household			
1583–99	65.0		11.3	18.7	5.0	0.1
1616–19	58.8		11.5	21.3	8.3	0.1

Period	Equipment	Household	Textiles	Metals	Glass & stoneware
1634–41	12.3	6.0	21.1	5.9	0.3
1677–86	16.6	3.0	15.8	5.8	*
1711–23	17.1	3.1	14.1	5.1	*
1759–85	20.7		13.6		

Value of movable property of farm households in Leeuwarderadeel, excluding livestock, expressed in percentages

Period	Total value minus livestock (in *goldgulden*)	Wooden Goods		Textiles	Metals	Glass & stoneware
		Equipment	Household			
1583–99	293.05	32.2		53.4	14.2	0.2
1616–19	406.07	27.6		51.8	20.2	0.4
1634–41	613.19	27.1	13.1	46.3	12.9	0.7
1677–86	426.19	40.5	7.2	38.3	14.0	*
1711–23	528.15	42.7	7.7	35.3	14.3	*
1759–85	570.13	60.5		39.5		

* Included under metals.

Table 6–14. Occupations of heads of households in Friesland, 1749

Occupational Categories	Eighteen Grietenijen		Leeuwarden		Ten small cities [a]	
	Number	%	Number	%	Number	%
Agriculture (primary)						
Agriculture	3959		126			
Fishing and hunting	145		7			
Subtotal	4104	33.7	133	4.1	333	5.0
Industry (secondary)						
Pottery, brick, glass	35		31			
Construction	385		207			
Wood and straw crafts	149		107			
Leather crafts	326		115			
Peat, mining [b]	72		—			
Metal industries	140		64			
Wagon and boatmaking	187		25			
Instrument making	25		27			
Textile trades	343		405			
Food preparation	288		203			
Subtotal	1950	16.0	1184	36.6	2744	41.1
Trade and Transportation (tertiary)						
Merchant activities	412		}199			
Retail activities	80					

Transportation	971		251			
Innkeeping	72		33			
Subtotal	1535	12.6	483	14.9	1961	29.3
Social Services (teritary)						
Liberal professions	51		207			
Education	121		32			
Government service	199		85			
Military	13		968			
Religious services	111		24			
"Well-to-do" persons	78		—			
Subtotal	573	4.7	1316	40.6	547	8.2
Common Laborers	3178	26.1	108	3.3	377	5.6
Charity	457	3.7	?		?	?
Unknown	391	3.2	16	0.5	724	10.8
Total "occupied"	12188	100.0	3240	100.0	6686	100.0
Retired, "old and poor"	106 }		416		?	
Widows	735 }					
Total households	13029		3654		—	
Total population	48068		14270		27344	

a Bolsward, Dokkum, Franeker, Harlingen, Hindeloopen, Ijlst, Sloten, Sneek, Staveren, Workum.

b The labor force engaged in peat digging is not identified in this occupational census. A sizeable portion of the common laborers was undoubtedly primarily engaged in peat digging.

Sources for columns one and two: Rijksarchief, Leeuwarden. Archief van de Rekenkamer, no. 14. "Quotisatie Cohieren van 1749"; column three derived from data in J. A. Faber, *Drie eeuwen Friesland*, Vol. 2, pp. 440–41.

Table 6-15. Inventories of farm households in Ooststellingwerf and maritime Friesland

Goods	Ooststellingwerf 1631–47	Leeuwarderadeel 1616–41 Wonseradeel 1628–31
Wagons		
Average number	2.0	2.0
Percentage	68%	66%
Average of all	1.43	1.30
Boats		
Average number	0	1.2
Percentage	0	50%
Average of all	0	0.60
Plows		
Average number	0.9	1.1
Percentage	53%	68%
Butterchurns		
Average number	1.0	1.0
Percentage	53%	84%
Percent with power churns	0	0
Decreaming vessels		
Average number	0	24.0
Percentage	0	90%
Per milk cow	0	1.9
Cheese press		
Average number	0	1.1
Percentage	0	70%
Wooden pails		
Average number	2.9	5.5
Percentage	53%	100%
Beehives		
Average number	15.6	0
Percentage	21%	0
Milk cows		
Average number	4.9	12.8
Horses		
Average number	1.5	2.7
Sheep		
Average number	32.0	1.7
Chests		
Average number	1.0	1.2
Percentage	6%	19%

Table 6–15. *Continued*

Goods	Ooststellingwerf 1631–47	Leeuwarderadeel 1616–41 Wonseradeel 1628–31
Tresoor		
Average number	1.0	1.1
Percentage	6%	19%
Tables		
Average number	1.3	2.6
Percentage	67%	79%
Benches		
Average number	2.5	4.3
Percentage	24%	81%
Chairs		
Average number	6.7	13.5
Percentage	94%	98%
Mirrors		
Average number	1.0	1.2
Percentage	11%	60%
Tin spoons		
Average number	9.6	20.5
Percentage	50%	97%
Wooden plates		
Average number	11.5	20.0
Percentage	44%	82%
Tin plates		
Average number	7.0	10.0
Percentage	28%	32%
Bibles & books		
Percentage	24%	30%
Silver		
Percentage	11%	43%
Beds		
Average number	3.3	5.2
Percentage	100%	100%
Blankets		
Average number	4.1	10.3
Percentage	89%	96%
Average per bed	1.2	2.0
Men's shirts		
Average number	6.3	10.5
Percentage	33%	42%

Table 6–16. Population per worker in selected occupations in rural Friesland and Overijssel

| Occupation | Population per worker in | | |
	Overijssel	O. & W. Stellingw.	Friesland
Carpenter	184	183	104
Shoemaker	298	153	153
Wooden shoemaker	852	—	*
Baker	553	556	318
Wagon and boatmaker	2483	1020	325
Smith	610	437	388
Teacher	1073	1530	401

* Wooden shoes, a hallmark of rural Holland, were apparently not widely worn before the eighteenth century. Since they must be considered an inferior substitute for leather shoes, the absence of wooden shoemakers in Friesland probably indicates a higher level of prosperity.

Part Four

AGRICULTURE IN THE WORLD ECONOMY

7

Organization and Change in Productivity in Eastern Prussia

ROBERT A. DICKLER

Investment Opportunities and Innovation

For about 100 years, starting in the mid-eighteenth century, European grain markets experienced a secular boom. According to Slicher van Bath, prices were steadily rising; wages advanced as well, but lagged behind the price rise from about 1750 to 1850.[1]

> High prices exercise a stimulating effect on rents and the purchase price of land. People who have made fortunes in trade and industry are more prepared, at this stage, to buy land and invest money in agricultural improvements, buildings, farmsteads, and backing reclamation and drainage schemes. This means that during a boom, cultivated area will expand. Money will more readily be invested in land reclamation and drainage schemes in that, as has been said, rising agricultural prices often coincide with increases in the quantity of money. There is plenty of capital and the rate of interest in the capital market is low.[2]

The research in price history on which this analysis is based clearly indicates widespread pressures for extension of cultivation for nearly a century. This fact provides a starting point for an examination of the economic impulses behind the agrarian reforms in East Elbian Prussia during the first decades of the nineteenth century.

---

[1] B. H. Slicher van Bath, *The Agrarian History of Western Europe*, translated by Olive Ordish (London, 1963), pp. 113–14.

[2] *Ibid.*, p. 116.

To see more clearly the relation between investment opportunities, the adoption of new techniques, and the need for restructuring agricultural organization, a reformulation of Slicher van Bath's argument in terms of a microeconomic theory of investment may be helpful.[3] In such a theory, the entrepreneur is assumed to derive utility not only from present and future consumption, but also from the size of his productive establishment.[4] Capital consumption then enters directly into the utility function. The demand for capital services may be obtained by first maximizing the utility function, subject to the production function and the intertemporal budget constraint of the entrepreneur; and then solving the system of equations derived from the first order conditions for a maximum. Since capital services are obtained by using up existing and newly acquired capital— past and present investment—current investment can be expressed as a dependent variable by suitable transformation of

[3] A theory based on profit-maximizing principles may seem inappropriate in the context of nineteenth-century Prussia. But van Bath also treats the Junker of the fifteenth century in the following manner: "The east German *Rittergutsbesitzer* (owner of a knight's estate) grew cereals for export to Western Europe and exploited his estate for profit. By every means permissible, or otherwise, he sought to enlarge the area under his control. *He exploited the peasants and tried to drive them from their land.* His estate was simply a plantation business concern, producing for the market." *Ibid.*, p. 157 (emphasis added). This assertion is, of course, diametrically opposed to Max Weber's view of the Junker: "Even then [in the course of the nineteenth century] was the estate predominately a form of communal economy which was patriarchically directed and ruled. . . . [N]ormally the agricultural worker was not vulnerable to pressure of pure economic exploitation. Confronting him was not an entrepreneur, but rather a territorial ruler in miniature. *The lack of a specific profit orientation of the lord and the* apathetic resignation on the part of the worker complemented one another and were the psychological supports for the traditional form of operations as well as the political rulership of the landed aristocracy." Max Weber, "Entwickelungstendenzen in der Lage der ostelbischen Landarbeiter," in *Gesammelte Aufsätze zur Sozial-und-Wirtschaftsgeschichte* (Tübingen, 1924), p. 474. Weber argued further that decadence and threat of displacement by the capital-rich bourgeoisie pushed the Junkers during the nineteenth century to become what was in the earlier centuries *not* their main occupation: entrepreneurs seeking a profit. How did the Junker respond to changes in world market conditions? "The typical lord of the manor continued to operate in a traditional way, *as if he were producing for the local market.*" *Ibid.*, p. 473 (emphasis added). Other than simply being an assertion that the Junker did not behave as if he maximized profits, and therefore utility, the economic meaning of this assumption is not intuitively obvious.

[4] L. R. Klein, "Notes on the Theory of Investment," *Kyklos*, Vol. 1 (1948), p. 101. The following sketch of the theory is based on this highly illuminating article.

the demand for capital services.[5] The demand for additional
capital (land and the means to improve land—drainage, reclamation, etc.) will depend on profits deflated by the price of capital,
relative price of consumer goods and capital goods, interest rate
(relative price of present consumer goods and future consumer
goods), and finally, the existing capital stock.[6]

The advantage of this formulation over Slicher van Bath's for
our present purpose is that it focuses attention on the fundamental importance of *relative* price movements in the determination of desired investment activities. Even with high interest
rates—provided they were constant—and with agricultural wage
increases lagging behind cereal price increases, continuing pressure would remain for higher levels of investment. In the framework of such a model, the stimulus to investment activity in
agriculture from the mid-eighteenth century to the mid-nineteenth century was derived from a "profit inflation" in northern
Europe.[7]

It will be recalled, however, that the Junkers' inertia during
this period is usually contrasted with the great interest in reform
and technical change that was displayed by monarchs, statesmen,
and a few enlightened landed aristocrats.[8] Two reasons may be
advanced to explain why many Junkers did not respond immediately to the investment opportunities. First, the necessary
new technology had not been proven for local conditions. In
this sense, experimentation with crop rotation on the state
domains was the beginning of agricultural extension in Germany.[9] The state undertook investment in knowledge, embodied
in human capital, while the peasants supported the model farms
with their taxes. But gestation periods for investments in knowledge are often several decades long. English experience was in-
applicable in many respects on the sandy soils east of the Elbe,
and original research in soil exhaustion was a long-run project
under nineteenth-century research techniques. Moreover, in-
vestors generally do not base decisions on current output and

---

[5] *Ibid.*, pp. 99–100.

[6] *Ibid.*, p. 102.

[7] For a useful critical discussion of this concept, see M. H. Dobb, *Studies in the Development of Capitalism* (London, 1946), pp. 235–38.

[8] Th. von der Goltz, *Geschichte der Deutschen Landwirtschaft*, Vol. 1 (reprint from the 1903 Stuttgart ed.; Aalen, 1963), p. 437.

[9] Wilhelm Abel, *Geschichte der deutschen Landwirtschaft* (Stuttgart, 1962), pp. 253–57.

factor prices, but rather on their anticipated movement. For
large investments to be sensitive to changes in the real wage,
anticipated price changes must be expected to be both large and
relatively permanent. The investments of which Slicher van
Bath speaks—reclamation, drainage, buildings—depend on expectations based on wage and price movements over a fairly
long period. The record of relative prices extending over a
decade or more may be considered relevant for an optimal
decision.[10] But the secular boom of the late eighteenth century
was not without short-term reversals. A slight decline in rye
prices occurred in German cities between 1780 and 1785, and this
may have put a damper on expectations formed on the basis of
experience from 1750 to 1780.[11] But after 1785, the price rise was
spectacular.[12] A secular boom with anticipated increases in
profits is revealed quite clearly in the prices of estates: they
tripled in Silesia and quintupled in Brandenburg over about a
fifty-year period without a single decade of price decrease, starting in 1750.[13]

The Napoleonic Wars at the turn of the century could not
easily reverse the changes in relative prices that had developed
over half a century. Nor did the crisis of the early 1820s discourage the many large estate owners who by now were convinced of
the merits of crop rotation. At the turn of the century, many
grain producers were still "bullish." [14] During this long-term
expansion of the European grain market, it was perhaps not too
difficult to persuade even a cautious *Rittergutsbesitzer* of the
merits of free markets in land.

The change in relative factor prices gave a stimulus to the
adoption of new crop rotations in order to achieve new output
levels.[15] By 1800, nearly all potentially arable land in most
provinces of the East Elbian Region was being used, as is evident
from Table 7–1. To extend arable land under the old technique

---

[10] Klein, "Notes on the Theory of Investment," pp. 103–105.
[11] Abel, *Geschichte der deutschen Landwirtschaft*, p. 310, figure 38.
[12] *Ibid.*, p. 310.
[13] *Ibid.*, p. 305.
[14] Von der Goltz, *Geschichte der Deutschen Landwirtschaft*, Vol. 2, p. 168.
[15] Folke Dovring, "The Transformation of European Agriculture," chapter
6 in *The Cambridge Economic History of Europe*, vi, edited by M. M.
Postan and H. J. Habakkuk (Cambridge, 1965), pt. 2, pp. 631–39. Heinz
Haushofer, *Die deutsche Landwirtschaft in technischen Zeitalter* (Stuttgart,
1963), pp. 44–49.

Table 7–1. Land Utilization in the East Elbian Region of Prussia, 1800–1907 (millions of hectares)

Year	Arable and Horticultural				Grass-lands	Agricul-tural	Forest	Other	Total
	Food Crops (1)	Fodder Crops (2)	Fallow (3)	Total (4)	(5)	(6)	(7)	(8)	(9)
1800	4.6	—	2.8	7.4	7.2	14.6	5.9	2.2	22.7
1840	5.9	.5	3.0	9.4	7.4	16.8	4.7	1.2	22.7
1861	7.9	.9	3.2	12.0	3.7	15.7	5.5	1.5	22.7
1883	9.2	1.1	2.1	12.4	3.7	16.1	5.3	1.3	22.7
1895	9.5	1.3	1.8	12.6	3.5	16.1	5.3	1.3	22.7
1907	10.1	1.4	1.1	12.6	3.4	16.0	5.4	1.3	22.7

Sources: Estimates based on official and semiofficial data obtained from Leopold Krug, *Betrachtungen über den National-Reichtum des Preussischen Staats, und über den Wohlstand seiner Bewohner* (Berlin, 1805), pp. 36–49; A. Lengerke *Beiträge zur landwirtschaftlichen Statistik des Preussischen Staates* (Berlin, 1847); A. Meitzen, *Der Boden und die landwirtschaftlichen Verhältnisse des Preussischen Staats,* Vols. 3–4 (Berlin, 1869), pp. 382–83 in Vol. 3 and Übersicht A in Vol. 4: *Preussische Statistik,* Vol. 246. Supplementary sources and methods rely principally on Siegfried von Ciriacy-Wantrup, *Agrarkrisen und Stockungsspannen: Zur Frage der langen "Welle" in der wirtschaftlichen Entwicklung* (Berlin, 1936), pp. 45–50, especially pp. 45–47; H. W. Finck von Finckenstein, "Die Getreidewirtschaft Preussens von 1800–1930," *Vierteljahresheft zur Konjunkturforschung, Sonderheft 35* (Berlin, 1934), p. 53; Finckenstein, *Die Entwicklung der Landwirtschaft in Preussen und Deutschland, 1800–1930* (Wurzburg, 1960), pp. 228–29; Josef Rybark, *Die Steigerung der Produktivität der deutschen Landwirtschaft im 19. Jahrhundert* (Berlin, 1905), p. 12.

of the three-field system would have required withdrawal of
land from sheep grazing at a time when the international wool
market was expanding.[16] Yet if yields were to remain constant
under the old technology, extension of cereal production required expansion of agricultural land. Given the institutional
constraints to transactions in land, increase in the Junkers' cropland often came about at the expense of the peasant cultivators'
agricultural land. But where institutional obstacles to massive
redistribution of holdings (*Bauernschütz*—peasant protection)
were operative, the Junker grain grower was compelled to think
in terms of land-saving technology.

Adoption of two new crops, potatoes and clover, made it possible to grow more food on a given amount of agricultural land.
The system of crop rotation, which used these crops, and the
improved three-field system, which incorporated potatoes, raised
the yield of arable land. Furthermore, there was no immediate
or long-term danger from labor scarcity. The land planted in
potatoes could support from two to four times the number of
persons previously sustained from the same plot of land under
grain.[17]

The lag in wages behind prices is attributed by Slicher van
Bath to population growth.[18] E. Boserup's argument that an
abundance of labor makes it profitable to invest in and use labor-
using techniques is, of course, consistent with this view.[19] Wage
determination on a manor, however, hardly fits the model of
wage determination in a perfectly competitive labor market.
Part of the lag in wages behind rising prices stemmed from the
monopsonist position of the local lord with respect to wage
laborers or day laborers (*Tagelöhner*), and his power over the
peasants. It is plausible to assume that the Junkers were eager
to feed the rural laborers potatoes, and convert the grain land
previously required to feed them to commercial cereal production. Rises in the level of investment then may have induced
population growth. Other new crops—clover and alfalfa—also

[16] Abel, *Geschichte der deutschen Landwirtschaft*, p. 293. This was primarily an English development after 1800, but the profitability of high-
quality wool production was well established before then.

[17] K. H. Connell, *The Population of Ireland, 1750–1845* (Oxford, 1950),
p. 93.

[18] Slicher van Bath, *The Agrarian History of Western Europe*, pp. 91–94.

[19] Ester Boserup, *Conditions of Agricultural Growth* (Chicago, 1965), pp.
102ff.

permitted a rise in total yields from a fixed quantity of agricultural land. Permanent rises in the cropping frequency for a given area are feasible only when soil nutrients can be restored without resorting to fallow. The new cover crops not only fixed nitrogen, but also provided a cattle feed that increased manure production.

A massive increase in the agricultural land under the Junkers' control was thus not required to produce an increase in the output of the estates. The existing institutionalized obligations, however, limited the scope of application of the new technology. The introduction of crop rotation required that the lord have a freer hand in the management of land resources. Control was necessary to consolidate holdings, and the gains from consolidation were increasingly apparent. Introduction of new technology on a large scale, then, required abrogation of existing village rights either by force or by legal means.[20]

[20] The present interpretation rejects the premise that land was relatively abundant in the East Elbian region at the time of the agrarian reforms. Assuming an abundance of land, however, historians have argued that the agrarian policies of the Prussian state were set in motion by the attraction of empty cultivable lands in the northeast. For example, the revised version of the now classic article by Gunther Ipsen presents quantitative evidence of land abundance: G. Ipsen, "Die preussische Bauernbefreiung als Landesausbau," in Wolfgang Köllmann and Peter Marschalck, *Bevolkerungsgeschichte* (Koln, 1972), pp. 154–89; originally published in *Zeitschrift für Agrargeschichte und Agrarsoziologie* 2 (1954), pp. 29–54. Ipsen makes use of land utilization data compiled by H. W. Graf Finck von Finckenstein, "Die Getreidewirtschaft Preussens von 1800–1930," *Vierteljahresheft zur Konjunkturforschung*, Sonderheft 35 (Berlin, 1934), p. 22. Ipsen takes notes of Finckenstein's underestimation of arable land, but his corrected figures still lie about 30 percent under the levels consistent with the official published estimates of Leopold Krug, whose data were accepted without serious reservation by August Meitzen in his authoritative reference work on Prussian agriculture, *Der Boden und die landwirtschaftlichen Verhältnisse des Preussischen Staats* (Berlin, 1871), Vol. 3, 382–83. Finckenstein's estimates were subjected to serious criticism by Siegfried von Ciriacy-Wantrup, who pointed out that according to Finckenstein, 40 percent of the total Prussian land area was waste (*unland*) in 1815, but that neither absolute figures nor adequate citations of sources and methods enable a reconstruction of this highly implausible figure. See Siegfried von Ciriacy-Wantrup, *Agrarkrisen und Stockungsspannen, Zur Frage der langen "Welle" in der wirtschaftliche Entwicklung* (Berlin, 1936), pp. 42–50. Neither Finckenstein, in his latter work, especially *Die Entwicklung der Landwirtschaft in Preussen und Deutschland, 1800–1930* (Wurzburg, 1960) nor Ipsen, who draws heavily on Finckenstein's data, takes note of Ciriacy-Wantrup's objections. Until Finckenstein's estimates and Ipsen's corrections can be justified explicitly, it would seem that the contemporary compilation by Krug better serves as a point of departure in the discussion of relative factor endowments in the various regions of central

Agrarian Reform and the Land Market

A free market in land was a fundamental institutional innovation embodied in the Royal Edict of October 9, 1807,[21] which was conceived by the progressive minister of state, Freiherr von Stein. The liberal philosophy of the Reforms was thereby given its formal legal articulation, but the question of the initial distribution of ownership of the resources was left open. Subsequent legislation of September 14, 1811, initiated and executed under the direction of Stein's conservative successor, Hardenburg, defined general procedures for "regulation" of the relations between lord and peasant, a process in which mutual privilege and obligation was to be replaced by a system of individual property rights.[22] After some further delay, the decisive Declaration of 1816, which Aereboe aptly termed the Reaction Edict, got down to specifics.[23] The terms of regulation were highly favorable to the lords. They were entitled by law to one-third of the peasants' hereditary possessions, and half of their nonhereditary possessions. Moreover, the declaration denied property rights to a major segment of the peasantry; those who could not harness a

Europe during the transformation of traditional agriculture. Further research is needed to provide substantiation of Ipsen's well-known and thought-provoking "Landesausbau" thesis, which asserts that the peasant emancipation enabled significant numbers of peasants to populate and improve the land, which otherwise would have lain waste. Before acceptance of the "Landesausbau" thesis is warranted, additional studies must resolve the difficulties of distinguishing between waste and fallow under low-intensity systems of cultivation, and the problems of ascertaining the numbers of landless laborers who assumed the work burdens of intensive cultivation. Thus relative land abundance need not be taken as a fact established by the widely cited works of Finckenstein and Ipsen, but rather as a key assumption open to question.

[21] Fuller English-language treatments of the impact of the Stein-Hardenburg reforms on the East Elbian region are available in the standard texts. See W. Bowden, M. Karpovich, and A. P. Usher, *An Economic History of Europe since 1750* (New York, 1937), pp. 273–81. Also, J. H. Clapham, *The Economic Development of France and Germany, 1815–1914* (Cambridge, 1963), pp. 37–46. In this section an attempt is made to supplement and update these works with pertinent quantitative results recently published by German and Polish specialists. The standard textbook treatment in German is now that of F. Lütge, *Deutsche Sozial- und Wirtschaftsgeschichte*, 3d ed. (Berlin, 1966), pp. 433–44. The monograph providing a synthesis of the vast literature on the subject is F. Lütge, *Geschichte der deutschen Agrarverfassung* (Stuttgart, 1963), pp. 169–97.

[22] F. Lutge, *Geschichte*, p. 196. See also Max Weber, *General Economic History*, translated by Frank Knight, (New York, 1927), pp. 104–105.

[23] Friederich Aereboe, *Agarpolitik: Ein Lehrbuch* (Berlin, 1928), pp. 151–52.

team (*nicht spannfähige Kleinstellen*) could not claim rights of ownership.[24] Thus, when the Ordinance of 1821 set down the administrative procedures for divisions and enclosure of the commons and for consolidation of holdings,[25] these peasants, by virtue of their inferior status under the law, were dispossessed of grazing land.[26] They were forced to remain legally dependent on the former lords and on the larger peasants and land holders. Not until the Ordinance of 1850 were property rights extended to this lowest group.

With the introduction of private property into the East Elbian Region, nearly a million hectares of peasant land were transferred to large estate owners, either through regulation or through the market.[27] This represents about 6 percent of the agricultural land of the region. Assuming that most of the commons enclosed were either arable or convertible into arable land, we may estimate that about 8 percent of the potentially cultivable land, and about 20 to 25 percent of the additions to arable land between 1800 and 1861 were derived from these transfers. The weakening of the "middle class" peasantry that resulted was the outstanding feature of the East Elbian "Prussian solution" [28] to the problem of transforming traditional agriculture. It was a solution determined in part by the initial conditions of enclosure,

---

[24] M. Weber, "Entwicklungstendenzen," p. 474.

[25] Von der Goltz, *Geschichte der Deutschen Landwirtschaft*, Vol. 2, 148–49. These pages provide clarification of the many different terms employed with reference to the legislation. Much confusion arises because two distinct activities—separation and consolidation—were usually, but not always, part of the same decision handed down by the commissions that executed the laws. Not only are many terms used for the same activity, but often one term is used to refer to these two activities.

[26] Aereboe, *Agrarpolitik: Ein Lehrbuch*, p. 151. Clapham, *Economic Development*, p. 48. Recall that the wool market was also beginning its four-decade rise.

[27] F. Lütge, *Deutsche Sozial- und Wirtschaftsgeschichte*, p. 443. Hans Mottek, *Wirtschaftsgeschichte Deutschlands*, Vol. 2 (Berlin DVW, 1969), p. 37, and the footnote, where the literature is cited. This is four times the loss noted by Bowden, Karpovich, and Usher, *An Economic History*, p. 278! Their figures and interpretation were probably derived from von der Goltz, Vol. 2, 189.

[28] Alexander Gerschenkron, "Agrarian Policies and Industrialization, Russia 1861–1917," in M. M. Postan and H. J. Habakkuk, *The Cambridge Economic History of Europe*, Vol. 6, *The Industrial Revolutions and After* (Cambridge, 1965), pp. 725–26.

which channeled most of the potential gains from technological advance to the landed aristocracy.[29]

From the outset, "free peasants" were saddled with the burdens of regulation. Of the million hectares transferred to the estates, 422,000 came as compensation for commutation of feudal services and dues.[30] Net sales by peasants amounted to another 100,000 to 200,000 hectares, in response to settlements that had imposed large cash obligations on them.[31] The remaining 300,000 to 500,000 hectares were bought and enclosed by lords and wealthy merchants when peasants ran into financial difficulties, as in the 1820s, when grain prices temporarily turned sharply downward.[32]

It was during this crisis that activity in the land market increased markedly. Wealthy prospective buyers borrowed in order to buy out at low prices those peasants who had been weakened by regulation and interest rates far above those that had been permitted under the policy of peasant protection in force before 1806.[33] Agricultural credit organizations rationed mortgages among the large holders;[34] local money lenders dealt with the peasants. According to Finckenstein,[35] the value of mortgage debt in the Eastern Region (excluding Saxony) rose from about 150 million marks to nearly 225 million marks between 1810 and 1830—a rate of increase of nearly 25 percent per decade, when the prices of holdings were falling well below prices of 1800.[36] Two observations support the view that the large owners borrowed to buy out the smaller. First, the increase in mortgages

---

[29] W. I. Lenin, "Das Agrarprogramm der Socialdemokratie in der ersten russischen Revolution von 1905–1907," in *Werke,* Vol. 13 (Berlin, 1963), p. 236.

[30] R. Berthold, H. Harnish, and H. H. Müller, "Der Preussische Weg der Landwirtschaft und neuer westdeutsche Forschungen," in *Jahrbuch f. Wirtschaftgeschichte,* 1970/IV, 286. Lütge, *Geschichte,* pp. 191–97.

[31] Lütge, *Geschichte,* p. 232.

[32] For details of the price movements, see Wilhelm Abel, *Geschichte,* p. 312 and figure 40. Lütge, *Geschichte,* p. 238.

[33] Max Sering, "Die innere Kolonisation im ostlichen Deutschland," *Schriften des Vereins für Socialpolitik* 56 (Leipzig, 1893), p. 66.

[34] *Ibid.,* p. 46. The crisis also led to a change of ownership of many large estates. See Finckenstein, *Die Entwicklung der Landwirtschaft,* p. 119. Finckenstein notes that only large estate owners were able to assume liabilities in the form of "Pfandbriefe." See especially Aereboe, *Agrarpolitik,* p. 521, where he argues that the rationing of credit was an important factor in the weakening of the peasantry.

[35] Finckenstein, *Die Entwicklung der Landwirtschaft,* p. 387.

[36] See Abel, *Geschichte,* p. 320.

rationed to large holders is approximately the value of 300,000 hectares of small holdings at 1810/1820 prices.[37] Second, provincial data bring out the correspondence between the increase in the mortgages of large holders and the weakening of the middle-sized peasantry through regulation. On the one hand, of the 420,000 hectares in compensation accruing to the lords, over half (220,000) were officially transferred in Pomerania (excluding Stralsund) and Posen.[38] On the other hand, of the increase of 75 million marks of debt for the East Elbian Region from 1810 to 1830, nearly 40 million originated in these two provinces.[39]

Against this background of government intervention and imperfection in the capital market, Sering's assessment of the results of transactions during the half century when the Reforms were implemented puts the region's first sustained experience with land markets in historical perspective: "they [the results of market transactions] do not give expression to a freely competitive relationship between the large and small scale operatives."[40] With no obligation to protect local peasants, enterprising estate owners were free to innovate and to use much of the village land in production for world markets. As one historian put it, the peasant emancipation in Prussia was also an emancipation of the lords.[41]

[37] In 1861, the median value of 1 hectare of bare land on a holding of 2–5 has. to 5–20 has. in most of the provinces of the region was between five and six hundred marks. See Friederich Aereboe, *Die Beurteilung von Landgütern und Grundstücken*, 2d ed. (Berlin, 1921), graphs presented in appendix. According to Sering, "Die innere Kolonisation," p. 67, the price of holdings bought by large estate owners doubled between 1830 and 1850. See also Abel, *Geschichte*, p. 320, which indicates an increase of roughly the same order of magnitude. Thus, as a first approximation, land prices in the 1820s could be set at about 250 marks per hectare. Dividing the increase in indebtedness (75 million marks) by the average price of a hectare of small holding (250/ha.) gives 300,000 ha., or the amount peasants sold the lords and merchants. While the average price may be questioned, there is striking agreement in the orders of magnitude between the quantity of land sold, estimated by Sering and cited by Lütge, *Geschichte*, p. 232, and the amount arrived at independently by using Finckenstein's mortgage values and extrapolated land prices.

[38] Berthold, Harnish, and Müller, "Der Preussische Weg," pp. 285–86.

[39] Finckenstein, *Die Entwicklung der Landwirtschaft*, p. 119.

[40] Sering, "Die innere Kolonisation," p. 63.

[41] Annemarie Wald, "Die Bauernbefreiung und die Ablösung des Obereigentums: Eine Befreiung der Herren," (*Historisches Vierteljahresschrift*, Vol. 28, 1934), p. 811, quoted by Lütge, *Geschichte*, p. 234, note 143.

Agrarian Reform and the Supply of Labor

The mobilization of human resources was intended in the Reform legislation as a counterpart to a free market in land. According to von der Goltz and Knapp, an unanticipated outcome of the reforms was the establishment of a class with little or no property and dependent on wages in money or kind for its maintenance.[42] By 1871 only two males out of five engaged in agriculture could be classed as "independent in ownership and occupation."[43] Slicher van Bath, however, argues that for centuries, the *Rittergutsbesitzer* consistently tried to "drive the peasants off the land,"[44] and that even from the beginning of the eighteenth century a growing class of *"freie Tagelöhner"* could be observed.[45] If such a development occurred, then it is not surprising that soon after the Reforms a class of landless laborers was in evidence. Their presence at this time was, in Lütge's words, "not so novel as Knapp claims."[46]

At issue here is not simply the dating of structural shifts from peasants to wage laborers in the manorial labor supply, but more importantly, the causal relationship between the Reforms and the development of a market for agricultural labor.[47] If the supply of landless laborers had experienced expansion for over a century, the accumulated labor reserve may have contributed heavily

[42] Von der Goltz, *Geschichte*, pp. 157ff, pp. 190–204. W. F. Knapp, *Die Bauernbefreiung und die Ursprung der Landarbeiter in alteren Teilen Preussens*, 2d ed (Munich, 1927). Max Weber, "Entwickelungstendenzen," p. 474, adheres to this position.

[43] For the seven provinces, the number of independent male owners ("selbständig in Besitz und Erwerb) was 459,192. The number of males engaged in agriculture, excluding male dependents, was 1,171,863. The first group composes 39.2 percent of the latter. Females were not included in the calculation because many were counted as dependents who were in fact workers engaged in agriculture, but not independent owners. *Preussische Statistik* 30, 238.

[44] Slicher van Bath, *Agrarian History*, p. 157.

[45] Friederich Engels, "Zur Geschichte der preussische Bauern," in Marx-Engels, *Werke*, Vol. 21 (Berlin, 1962), 242.

[46] Lütge ,*Geschichte*, p. 234.

[47] Interesting tentative hypotheses concerning the relation of institutional change to long-term shifts in labor market conditions were presented by M. H. Dobb, *Studies in the Development of Capitalism* (London, 1946), pp. 23ff. Other things being equal, excess demand leads to state intervention, excess supply to economic liberalism. Unfortunately, this theme is not developed in the discussion of the Prussian reforms in the East Elbian region (p. 241). Despite its liberal inspiration, the Prussian reforms involved a good deal of state intervention on behalf of the lords, as we have seen.

to the pressure for the Reforms.[48] In a period of expanding demand for grain and relatively inelastic supply of arable land, this reserve could be used profitably on a large scale only after further evictions and consolidation of holdings. Reform was feasible to the extent that labor supply was highly elastic. This was nearly certain if two necessary conditions were fulfilled:

1) relative abundance of labor,[49] and;

2) nearly landless labor compelled to work for wages.[50]

The vagueness of nomenclature and the incomparability of published statistics on rural population groups during the first half of the century necessitates extensive archival research before the influence of shifts in labor supply can be ascertained. At present, the reliable evidence is scarce. In an appendix to his splendid study of the labor market in Poland (including territories then under Prussian administration), Stanislaw Borowski presents estimates of the landless population for counties in the province of Posen for the years 1810, 1849, and 1861.[51] His figures, based on published and archival sources, are summarized for the district level in Table 7–2. The astonishing fact that emerges is that over half the population was dependent on income from wages even before the major pieces of legislation were enacted. Of all the heads of households (*Hauptpersonen*), between two-thirds and three-fourths were "mobile" in the sense that they were "unattached" to a plot of land (*Ackerlos*). Further research along these lines for the other provinces is needed before conclusions can be made about the prevalence of landless labor

[48] *According to one recent analysis,* "Under the impact of the French Revolution and of some interests of the State and especially because of demographic pressures, the rural population gained personal freedom in 1807–09 and economic freedom in 1811–23." Stanislaw Borowski, "Demographic Development and the Malthusian Problem in the Polish Territories under German Rule, 1807–1914" in Paul Deprez, ed., *Population and Economics: Proceedings of Section V of the Fourth Congress of the Economic History Association, 1968* (Winnepeg, 1970), p. 46.

[49] The role of population pressure as a stimulus for labor-using technological change and closely associated changes in the system of tenure has been examined empirically by E. Boserup, *Conditions of Agricultural Growth*.

[50] The existence of landless labor as a necessary condition in the context of the transition from feudalism to capitalism in the neighboring Baltic states of Russia was explored by V. Lenin, *Die Entwicklung des Kapitalismus in Russland* (German translation of the 4th Russian ed., Berlin, 1956), pp. 187–92.

[51] See Table 7–2 for reference.

Table 7–2. Changes in the Landless Population and Agricultural
Labor Force, Posen Province 1810, 1849, 1861

District	Total	Persons without a Holding	
		Number	Percent
Population (heads and households and dependents)			
Posen (District)			
1810	402,633	204,232	50.7
1849	644,542	360,732	56.0
1861	652,053	384,100	58.9
Bromberg			
1810	186,294	105,304	56.5
1849	359,131	192,809[a]	53.7[a]
1861	345,929	215,483	62.3
Labor Force (heads of households only)			
Posen			
1810	128,478	89,081	69.3
1849	195,435	147,376	75.4
1861	205,024	158,264	77.2
Bromberg			
1810	67,357	49,481	73.5
1849	90,519	67,149	74.2
1861	108,318	87,762	80.1

[a] Corrected for miscalculations and of probable misprints in source. Figures
given in source are 166,222 and 43.3 percent.

Source: S. Borowski, *Ksztartowanie sie rolniczego rynku pracy w Wielkopolscle
w okresie wielkich reform agrarnych, 1807–1860* (The Development of the
Market for Agricultural Labor in Great Poland at the time of the Major
Agrarian Reforms of 1807–1860), (Poznan, 1963), p. 623; Aneks 43.

in the region as a whole. Tentatively, one might assume that
conditions were similar in most of Pomerania.[52]

From Table 7–2, it can be ascertained that heads of households
and dependents increased more rapidly than the population as a
whole. In the district of Posen, the heads of households maintained a rate of increase of 18 percent per decade from 1810 to
1861. In Bromberg the rate was 20 percent per decade. Judging
from nineteenth-century standards of rate of natural increase,
these are very high rates for such a long period before the demographic transition, which probably began around 1860.[53] In the

[52] Clapham, *Economic Development*, p. 39.

[53] R. A. Dickler, *Labor Market Pressure Aspects of Agricultural Growth
in the Eastern Region of Prussia, 1840–1914: A Case Study of Economic-
Demographic Interrelations during the Demographic Transition* (Ph.D.
dissertation, University of Pennsylvania, 1975), chapter 2.

province of Posen the rates of natural increase in this period were not sustained above 10 percent per decade for long periods of time.[54] The numbers of heads of household were growing at around 15 percent per decade in both districts. Thus, the period was one of structural shifts. But how much greater was the rate of structural shift after the Reforms than before them? A mid-eighteenth century benchmark estimate for landless laborers would have shed considerable light on this question. What is clear is that something besides natural population growth was accounting for the growth of the landless population.

Another approach to the same problem would be to look at the growth of landless labor after the Reforms' work had been completed. If the legislation was partly responsible for bringing about the structural change, then deceleration of the growth of landless labor should be observable after all the peasantry had been "regulated," and hence relegated in part to landless status. In Table 7–3 it is seen that by 1851, the commutation of feudal dues and services was 98 percent complete in Posen. This implied that most of the peasant losses from compensation had been realized. From Table 7–2, it can be calculated that the average increase per annum in the number of landless laborers was even higher in 1849–1861 than it was during the previous period. Un-

[54] Borowski, "Demographic Development," p. 36.

Table 7–3. Index of Progress of Agrarian Reforms in the East Elbian Region of Prussia, 1851–1875

| Province | Cumulative Total of Service Abolished: Days of Team Labor | | |
	1851	1875	1851 as percent of 1875
East Prussia	207.9	209.1	99.4
West Prussia	169.6	178.2	95.1
Posen and Pomerania	2818.7	2877.6	98.0
Brandenburg	1159.8	1201.1	96.6
Silesia	1447.4	1599.4	90.4
Saxony	200.8	212.0	94.7
REGION	6004.1	6217.4	96.6

Source: Alfred Kotelmann, *Die preussische Landwirtschaft* (Berlin, 1853), pp. 293–94; Rudolph Berthold, *et al., Jahrbuch f. Wirtschaftsgeschichte* (1970/IV), p. 279.

less this reflects a lag in "selling out" as a result of weakening
from earlier compensation for commutation, these crude results
suggest that the Reforms do not appear to have exerted an independent influence in the province.

A similar development is apparent in Estonia, an area integrated into the same grain market as Prussia, and similarly
dominated by landlords of the Junker type for much of its early
history. Recent examination of census materials, archival sources,
estate and parish records,[55] and vital statistics from 1780 to 1850
have developed a much clearer picture of population movements
in the country. High death rates kept the natural increase low
at the end of the eighteenth century, but the rate of natural
increase speeded up after the turn of the century. The ac-
celeration has been attributed to better climate and smallpox
vaccination.[56] The analysis benefited from recognizing the role
of the death rate, but it is doubtful whether the rate was completely independent, especially at a time when the potato was
being introduced elsewhere in the Baltic Region. In fact, the
1840s were bad years not only for the Prussian peasantry, but for
the Estonian peasantry as well.[57] The demographic crises of
1845 and 1846 may indicate the presence of a nearly landless
class of workers similar to that of Eastern Prussia. A process of
consolidation had been proceeding during the second quarter of
the nineteenth century, after reforms early in the century.[58] The
parallels with Eastern Prussia are striking.

Even if one cannot assess the impact of the Reforms, it is clear
that obstacles to the formation of a labor market were being
removed well before 1807, the year of peasant emancipation. But
this may not have been the case in provinces where the royal
policy of peasant protection (*Bauernschütz*) had been successful.

[55] *Hans Kruusi, Essays in Honor of His 75th Birthday,* edited by J. Kahk
(Tallinn, 1966).

[56] S. Vahtre, "On the Dynamic Balance of the Population of Government
Estland at the End of the Eighteenth and in the First Half of the Nineteenth
Centuries," in *Kruusi, Essays,* pp. 56–83; summary, p. 230.

[57] J. Kahk, "Concerning the Condition of the Peasantry in the Estonian
Part of the Livonian Government in the Eighteen-forties," in *Kruusi, Essays,*
pp. 115–32; summary, p. 231.

[58] H. Ligi, "The Peasant Edicts of Estland in 1804 and the Peasant Obligations," in *Kruusi, Essays,* pp. 84–114; summary in German, p. 231. V.
Fainstein, "On the Consolidation of Peasant Lands by Estate Owners in the
Second Quarter of the Nineteenth Century," in *Kruusi, Essays,* pp. 133–45;
summary in German, p. 232.

If one views the early modern history of the labor market as the diffusion of wage labor, then regional variations are explainable in terms of standard economic theory. Success in using wage labor in one or two provinces may have exerted pressure on lords in other provinces to do likewise in order to remain competitive in world markets. Where peasant protection was enforced, repeal was necessary in order to introduce wage labor. One counter argument to the famous Knapp thesis is that the Reforms gave legal sanction to a movement of eviction and consolidation that had already contributed to the growth of the class of landless laborers. In view of the expanding grain market before 1800, this view has at least a certain plausibility.

Productivity Change and Consumption

We turn now to a brief description and analysis of the technological change that followed the reorganization of Eastern Prussian agriculture. Following the work of Hayami and Ruttan on Japan,[59] Table 7-4 exhibits a measure of the growth of labor productivity (Q/A) and breaks it down into two components: output per unit of land (Q/A) and land per worker (A/L). It appears that the implementation of new technology in Eastern Prussia before 1861 resulted in steady gains in output per worker. Table 7-4 shows an average rate of growth in labor productivity (gross output per worker) of 4.4 percent per decade in the first four decades of the century, and nearly 8.0 percent per decade from 1840 to 1861. Yields from agricultural land rose in both periods, especially after 1840. The amount of agricultural land per man declined in both periods, but land actually under plow, that is, arable land per man, declined only in the first period. The accelerating growth of yield of agricultural land was achieved in the second period partly through rising arable land per worker. The new technology was indeed labor-intensive (land-saving), but arable land was being extended faster than the work force as pasture was converted to tillage. Sometime around 1840, it would appear, pasture suddenly became relatively unprofitable.

One need only consult a basic text [60] to verify that this is

---

[59] Y. Hayami and V. Ruttan, "Factor Prices and Technical Change in Agricultural Development: The United States and Japan, 1880–1960," *Journal of Political Economy* 78 (1970), pp. 1115ff.

[60] Bowden, Karpovich, and Usher, *An Economic History,* p. 586.

Table 7-4. Aggregate Productivity Change and its Components, East
Elbian Region of Prussia, 1800–1840 and 1840–1861 (percent change, average per decade)

	1800–1840	1840–1861
1. Aggregate gross output		
Q/L	4.4	7.9
Agricultural land		
Q/A	12.9	21.3
A/L	−5.6	−9.3
Arable land		
Q/A	7.2	9.0
A/L	−3.9	4.3
2. Major crop production		
A/L	7.5	7.5
Q/A	13.5	1.9
A/L	−3.8	4.9
3. Cereal crop production		
Q/L	−2.8	4.3
Q/A	6.4	.4
A/L	−5.6	.0
4. Wheat and rye production		
Q/L	2.4	7.4
Q/A	5.1	4.4
A/L	−2.1	2.4
5. Potato production		
Q/L	168.2	13.8
Q/A	11.8	−24.0
A/L	125.0	55.6

Symbols: Q Gross agricultural output
            A Land, in hectares
            L Agricultural labor force (males 14–60)

Sources: Output and land input data obtained from sources given in Table
7-1. Labor input in agriculture based on census data: *Zeitschrift des Kgl.
Statistisches Büros*, 1861; Preussische Statistik, Vol. 5. Rural males in age
group 15–60 was used as an approximation to the male labor force in
agriculture.

exactly what occurred. The division and enclosure of the commons had earlier in the century removed a major obstacle to improved breeding. With private grazing, breeding could be developed rapidly, and the expanding market for merino wool
gave for a time an incentive to maintain pasture even in the
face of expanding grain markets. Changes in Germany's competitive position in the wool market disturbed this equilibrium.

In the 1820s Germany supplied England with half of her total imports of wool; in 1830, 27 million pounds, about 90 percent of the English market, came from Germany. Only one decade later, the German share of English wool imports fell to 40 percent (22 million pounds) and by 1860, the 10 million pounds exported from this area supplied only 10 percent of the English market. The number of sheep per unit of agricultural land grew at 34.0 percent per decade from 1816 to 1840 and 7.0 percent per decade from 1841 to 1873. This fairly rapid shift in emphasis from pasture to tillage reflected the comparative advantage of newly competing areas—Australia, Argentina, India, and other European countries—and is evidence of the region's integration into the world economy. It also strongly supports Slicher van Bath's view that the estate owners were operating with a view to profit.

The gains in productivity to be obtained by applying crop rotation and the opportunities in world markets created the initial pressures for improvement. As fallow was reduced, however, and soon after arable was extended, diminishing returns set in. A third factor affecting the mix of pasture and tillage was thus the yield from marginal cropland. Sections 2, 3, 4, and 5 of Table 7–4 make clear that there was a drastic decline in potato yields during the second period, while the rise in cereal yields was slowed. A slowdown occurred in land-saving technological change, as measured by the aggregate yield from arable land. If this decline in yield had been accompanied by a fall in the arable land-man ratio, a good case for "population pressure" might be made; but such was not the case. The fall in yield represented a shift in the demand for arable that magnified the change in relative prices associated with the opening up of competing wool suppliers overseas.

The principal conclusion is that land under major crops was being expanded faster than the number of male workers, a fact that lends support to a model of technological and institutional change induced by a demand for exports. In Table 7–5, it is seen that among the cereals, wheat and rye were expanding in output partly at the expense of barley (used locally for beer) and oats (used locally for horse feed and gruel). Increased specialization was accompanied by concentration in export crops. Specialization alone might be expected to come from population growth in the region, but specialization in export production suggests the operation of other more powerful factors.

Although historians generally accept that the potato was adopted in Prussia during the last half of the eighteenth century,[61] the data presented in Table 7–5 cast serious doubt on the validity of this position. In 1800, only 100,000 hectares, or .7 percent of the agricultural land, was planted in potatoes; by 1861, over nine times this amount had been planted. The number of hectares planted per male worker rose from .04 in 1800 to .31 in 1861. This order of magnitude of increase in absolute level of cultivation has its parallel in the Kingdom of Poland. According to Baranowski, in 1810, about 35,000 hectares were cultivated, and by 1860, approximately 279,000 hectares were under potatoes.[62] The potato may have been introduced widely in Central Europe as a result of the famine of 1770–1772, but its rapid rise in relative importance, that is, its adoption during the period of phenomenal increases in grain prices resulting from a shift in

[61] William Langer, "Europe's Initial Population Explosion," *American Historical Review* 69 (1963), pp. 1–17. Slicher van Bath, *Agrarian History*, p. 268: "By 1770 they came into general use," their quantitative importance is not estimated here.

[62] Bohdan Baranowski, *Poczatki I Rospowszechnienie Upranv Ziemwiakow na ziemiach srodkow'cj Polski* (Lodz, 1960), pp. 50, 64, 66.

Table 7–5. Agricultural Land Utilization, East Elbian Region of Prussia, 1800, 1840, 1861

Land Use Category	1800	1840	1861
	(millions of hectares)		
Agricultural land	14.6	16.8	15.7
Arable land	7.4	9.4	12.0
Major crops (cereals and potatoes)	4.1	5.1	6.7
Cereals	4.0	4.7	5.5
Wheat and rye	1.9	2.7	3.3
Potatoes	.1	.4	1.0
	(percent)		
Agricultural land	100.0	100.0	100.0
Arable land	50.7	56.0	76.4
Major crops (cereals and potatoes)	28.1	30.4	42.7
Cereals	27.4	28.0	35.0
Wheat and rye	13.0	16.0	21.0
Potatoes	.7	2.3	6.3

Source· See sources for Table 7–1.

Table 7–6. Trends in Specialization and Changes in Pattern of Consumption East Elbian Region of Prussia, 1800–1840

Province	1800	1840	Change	1800	1840	Change
	A. Grain Export [1]			B. Potato Adoption [2]		
East Prussia	37.2	47.8	10.6	8.0	50.5	42.5
West Prussia	41.6	56.8	15.2	10.8	79.0	68.2
Posen	48.1	63.7	15.6	20.6	148.9	128.3
Pomerania	41.6	49.2	7.6	21.0	51.3	30.8
Brandenburg	56.2	57.3	1.1	4.8	57.6	52.8
Silesia	46.8	51.0	4.2	8.0	34.6	26.7
Saxony	49.3	51.4	2.1	4.0	44.0	40.0
REGION	46.1	52.9	6.8	10.3	85.2	74.9
	C. Wool Export [3]			D. Pork Adoption [4]		
East Prussia	3.3	4.9	1.6	1.6	1.6	.0
West Prussia	5.7	8.3	2.6	1.2	1.4	.2
Posen	9.1	13.4	4.3	1.0	1.2	.2
Pomerania	6.7	12.6	5.9	.6	.7	.1
Brandenburg	6.9	8.5	1.6	.7	.7	.0
Silesia	5.4	6.5	1.1	.2	.3	.1
Saxony	7.0	8.2	1.2	.8	.9	.1
REGION	6.5	7.8	1.3	.8	.9	.1

[1] Wheat and rye output as a percentage of total cereal output.
[2] Potato output as a percentage of total cereal output.
[3] Sheep per cow.
[4] Pigs per cow.

Sources: August Meitzen, *Der Boden* Vol. 2, Übersicht D; otherwise as in Table 7–1.

export demand, must be seen as one of the most striking features of the region's agrarian history.

Highly perishable if exposed, not easily transported on the poor roads of the region, potatoes were used almost exclusively in the locality where they were produced. Knowledge of how much of the potato crop was used for food and how much for fodder is difficult to obtain, but some inferences may be drawn from trends in pig production. In Table 7–6, these inferences are made by means of some crude indexes. Changes in grain exports (panel A) are measured by the change in the share of the main export cereal grains—wheat and rye—in total cereal grain production. Panel C shows the varying importance of wool exports by changes in the sheep herd relative to cattle in the various provinces; panel D presents the same calculation for hogs. Panels B and D indicate that the expansion of potato output relative to cereals was far greater than the expansion of pigs relative to the stock of cows. If a drastic shift to pig-raising had occurred, there would have been a fairly pronounced increase in numbers of hogs relative to the size of dairy herds, which provided the other basic component of the diet, milk. This did not happen, and we must conclude that the increase in potato output over cereal (panel B) must have been an increase directed largely to human consumption.

It may be argued that the adoption of the potato represented the free decisions of small holders and landless laborers to respond to the rising relative price of grain. But it seems more likely that small holders and wage earners with a bit of land may have adopted the potato as the only way to avoid starvation, given the amount of land made available to them after the commutation of services and dues and the enclosure of the commons. In effect, the adoption represents the estate owner's monopsonistic position as an employer of labor in what could be viewed as a local command economy. The individual estate owner wished to maximize the amount of cereal surplus, given the amount of land under his control; potatoes took up less land per calorie, and every hectare planted in potatoes created a net release of grain land for the production of money crops.

The impact of potato consumption on nutritional standards depended on what was eaten along with it.[63] In the Prussian context, the question depends on whether the agricultural laborer and his family had gruel with or without milk. In his famous investigation for the *Verein für Sozialpolitik*, Max Weber noted the following about the changing rural diet:

> The earlier combination of cereals and dairy products constituted a guarantee that protein, fats and carbohydrates would be ingested in a relation corresponding to the needs of the body. The increased potato consumption supplied to a great extent the required carbohydrates. On the other hand, the intake of needed protein through increased meat consumption—the absolutely necessary correlate of reduced cereal consumption—is problematical. There exists a danger as a consequence of the characteristic peculiarity of the potato, that the necessary complementarities in each dimension will not be realized, that hunger will be stilled but that muscle power

[63] Connell, *Population*, pp. 121–62, especially pp. 151ff. R. N. Salaman, *The History and Social Influence of the Potato* (Oxford, 1949), pp. 258–62.

will not be reproduced; that by resorting to alcohol, the attempt is made to compensate for the deficiencies.[64]

Weber's comparison was based on the worker's midday meal on a typical manor in Silesia in 1790 and a hundred years later. Potatoes and water soup had replaced cereals and milk. The conversion had probably taken place by the mid 1840s, the so-called "Hungry Forties," which contributed to temporary depopulation of parts of Prussia and to populating parts of the United States. The prominence of the potato in the diet at this time was noted by Alfred Kotelmann, who carried out a survey of Prussian agriculture in the late 1840s: "It may well be that the nutrition derived from potatoes and gruel, from which the East Prussian worker almost exclusively lives and which comprises during weekdays his mid-day, morning and evening meals, is inferior to the nutrition which is contained in the foodstuffs— colonial wares, meat, vegetables, bread—which the generally better situated worker from Rhineland consumes."[65] The Russian economic historian, Kulisher, argued that the potato had become the food of last resort during periods of cereal scarcity in the latter part of the eighteenth century.[66] This is vague, but it could refer to the chronic scarcity which local laborers encountered in the face of growing export demand for the estate's grain production. At that time, the pioneer of the new "rational agriculture" in Prussia, Albrecht Thaer, issued a warning against heavy reliance on the potato during normal times because it was believed to cause many kinds of disease.[67] Yet it was just in "normal times" that the use of the potato could release land and labor, and permit improved crop rotations and a more productive use of land.

If the spread of the potato depended on the adoption of crop rotation, and the stimulus to adoption of crop rotation was the pressure of export demand on cereal prices, then an implied association exists between export expansion and potato adoption. The scatter of the cross-sectional data from panels A and B of

[64] Max Weber, "Die Verhältnisse der Landarbeiter in ostelbischen Deutschland," *Schriften des Vereins für Socialpolitik* 55, Vol. 3 (Leipzig, 1892), 776–78.
[65] A. Kotelmann, *Die Preussische Landwirtschaft* (Berlin, 1853), pp. 4–5.
[66] J. Kulisher, *Allgemeine Wirtschaftsgeschichte* (Berlin, 1929), Vol. 2, p. 57.
[67] *Ibid.*, p. 57, note 3.

Table 7–6 does not give any strong impression of such an association. If, however, the sample is stratified to exclude Brandenburg and Saxony, where the middle-class peasantry was considerably stronger, and where the cities were more developed,
then the scatter of the logarithms of the indices A (grain exports)
and B (potato adoption) shows a nonlinear monotonic positive
relationship. Posen, the province with the highest change in grain
exports, also has the highest index of potato adoption. The non-
conformity of Saxony is not surprising; where the middle-class
peasant was prosperous, his family ate cereals. In most of the
provinces east of the Elbe, the *Tagelöhner*, the "free laborer,"
fared much worse, and so did his family. During the period of
rapid growth in cereal production for export, the rise in output
per worker in the Eastern Provinces was accompanied by an increase in infant mortality.[68]

The argument of this paper may now be drawn together.
Starting in the mid-eighteenth century, a profit inflation created
incentives to extend grain cultivation and to adopt land-saving
(labor-using) technology in the East Elbian Region of Prussia.
Favorable shifts in the demand for grain tended to put pressure
on traditional institutional arrangements that made the supply
of land and the supply of labor relatively inelastic. The feudal
relation of lord to peasant broke down under this pressure both
before and after the Agrarian Reforms of 1807–1821. The
initiative for the Reforms may not have originated with the
Junkers, but once the Reforms were set in motion, it appears
that the lords and other large land owners had them adminis-
tered in such a way as to maximize profits in grain production
for export. After the Reforms, much land formerly used by
peasants for pasture and for production on their own account was
drawn into production for the world market. The middle class
of peasants was seriously weakened in the process. The growing
importance of the potato in the diet was a manifestation of the
peasantry's declining position, and of a lowering of its real income and consumption levels during the profit inflation.

[68] F. J. Neumann, "Pauperismus und Kindersterblichkeit," *Jahrbuch f.
Nationalökonomie und Statistik*, 3. F., Vol. 5, pp. 617ff.

8

Scale and Organization in French Farming, 1840–1880

GEORGE W. GRANTHAM

The survival of peasant farming was until very recently a distinguishing characteristic of French agricultural organization.
The persistence of a large number of small and poorly equipped
farms retarded the technical transformation of French agriculture
in this century, and has imposed substantial costs on French and
common market consumers by way of inefficient schemes of
income maintenance, mainly through subsidies and price supports. The most widely accepted explanation of the hardiness
of peasant farming in France stresses the wide distribution of
property that had emerged by the end of the eighteenth century
and the reluctance of French farmers to leave farming for other
occupations. While this interpretation is compelling enough in
its outlines, it fails to distinguish France from countries such as
the United States, where ownership of land at the beginning of
the nineteenth century was even more widely and evenly distributed, and where farming was still mainly oriented towards
assuring family subsistence. In this essay I consider some of the
special circumstances which in France sustained a system of small
subsistence farms, and even generated a final flowering of peasant
agriculture in the last part of the nineteenth century.

Peasant Property and Peasant Farms

Although the extent of peasant land ownership in the nineteenth
century will never be known with complete accuracy, the signs
of an extension of peasant modes of farming are unmistakable.

After reviewing the national statistics of landowning and modes of tenure, Labrousse concluded that the share of farm land controlled by peasants increased from about one-third at the beginning of the century to over one-half by its end.[1] The evidence for this hypothesis consists of the cadastral or land survey records and the national statistics of farms classified by size and mode of tenure.[2] The obstacles to inferences from these data are well known. The cadasters were carried out by commune, so that holdings in different communes by the same person appear in the statistics as separate properties. Even within a commune, the *côtes* or assessments were not always consolidated, and with the play of exchange and purchase over the years the discrepancy between the number of *côtes* and the number of property owners tended to rise over time, making it difficult to draw any conclusions about the state of land ownership from the numbers and size of assessed holdings.[3] The other comprehensive sources of data on ownership and farm size are the numbers reported in the decennial "censuses" of 1852 through 1892. These figures are even more difficult to interpret than the cadastral records, as they are the result of uncontrolled responses to census questionnaires sent to the communal administrations. The correspond-

---

[1] Ernest Labrousse, "The Evolution of Peasant Society in France from the Eighteenth Century to the Present," in Evelyn M. Acomb and Marvin L. Brown, Jr., eds., *French Society and Culture Since the Old Regime* (New York, 1966), pp. 48–51.

[2] See Statistique Générale de la France, *Statistique de la France, Statistique agricole décennale de 1852*, 2 vols. (Paris, 1858, 1860); *Statistique de la France, résultats généraux de l'enquête agricole décennale de 1862* (Nancy, 1868); Ministère de l'Agriculture, *Statistique agricole de la France (Algérie et colonies); résultats généraux de l'enquête décennale de 1882* (Nancy, 1887); and Ministère de l'Agriculture, *Enquête décennale de 1892* (Paris, 1897). The agricultural *enquêtes* are not censuses, as they did not proceed by direct enumeration on the farms, but were compiled from responses to questionnaires sent to rural municipalities as revised by canton and departmental statistical committees. The estimates of farm size and ownership were supposed to be checked against the communal land registers. The nonstatistical inquiries that are of interest are Ministère de l'Agriculture, *Enquête sur la situation et les besoins de l'agriculture, 1866–1872*, 38 vols. (Paris, 1867–1872), hereafter cited as the *1866 Enquête;* Ministère de l'Agriculture, Direction de l'Agriculture, Office des Renseignements Agricoles, *La Petite propriété rurale en France: Enquêtes monographiques (1908–1909)* (Paris, 1909); and Office des Renseignements Agricoles, *Enquête sur les salaires agricoles* (Paris, 1912).

[3] These problems and others are exhaustively treated by Alfred de Foville in *Le Morcellement, études économiques et statistiques sur la propriété foncière* (Paris, 1885), pp. 63–70, 74–88, 91–94.

ence that surrounds these censuses clearly shows that the *maires* often did not understand the questions about property and farm size, and simply refused to answer them.[4] Besides these evident measurement problems, there is a further question of whether farm size is a good index of farm types. A fifty-hectare *métairie* farmed by a man and three grown sons could be considered a peasant farm on the basis of its use of family labor; a ten-hectare vineyard employing hired workers could easily be termed a commercialized or "capitalist" farm.

With all the defects in the statistical record, it is nevertheless reassuring that historical opinion agrees with Labrousse's assessment.[5] Peasant farms, most of them concentrated in holdings of five to thirty hectares, were increasing in number down to the last decade of the century. The range of farm sizes open to family farming probably widened over the course of the century, as the improved draft implements and plow teams raised the area that could be cultivated by a given amount of labor, while rising crop yields lowered the amount of land needed to sustain a family at a given level of income.[6]

The broad outlines of the evolution of farm size as they appear in the published statistics of 1862 and 1882 are displayed in Tables 8–1 and 8–2. During this period of rapidly changing techniques and rising productivity, the number of small owner-occupied farms increased. Between 1862 and 1882 the number of farms between five and thirty hectares increased by 228,000 or 21 percent, while the number of holdings larger than thirty

[4] Enquête agricole décennale, questionnaires cantonnaux, 1862, Archives Nationales, Paris, F11 2697–2712.

[5] See, among others, Roger Thabault, *Education and Change in a Rural Community, Mazières-en-Gatine, 1848–1914*, translated by Peter Tregear (London, 1971), pp. 88, 147; Philippe Vigier, *Essai sur la répartition de la propriété foncière dans la région Alpine* (Paris, 1966), pp. 175–77; Paul Bois, *Paysans de l'Ouest; des structures économiques et sociales aux options politiques depuis l'époque révolutionnaire dans la Sarthe* (Paris, 1971), pp. 49–50; René Musset, *Le Bas-Maine, étude géographique* (Paris, 1917), pp. 371–73; Lucien Gachon, *Une Commune rurale d'Auvergne du XVIIIe au XXe siècle* (Clermont-Ferrand, 1939), pp. 100, 111; François-P. Gay, *La Champagne du Berry; essai sur la formation d'un paysage agraire et l'évolution d'une société rurale* (Bourges, 1967), pp. 144–45, 152–53; and Jesus Ibarrola, *Structure sociale et fortune dans la campagne proche de Grenoble en 1847* (Paris, 1966), p. 95. The consolidation of large capitalist farms at the expense of the peasantry is documented in Pierre Brunet. *Structure agraire et économie rurale des plateaux tertiaires entre la Seine et l'Oise* (Caen, 1960), p. 290.

[6] Labrousse, "The Evolution of Peasant Society," pp. 57–58.

Table 8-1. Number of Farms by Size, 1862 and 1882

Hectares	1862	1882	Change	1882 as Percent of 1862
1–5	1,815,558	1,865,878	50,320	103
5–10	619,843	769,152	149,309	124
10–20	363,769	431,335	67,556	119
20–30	170,744	198,041	21,297	116
30–40	95,796	97,828	2,032	102
40 and above	154,167	142,088	−12,079	92

Source: Ministère de l'Agriculture, *Statistique Agricole de la France, résultats généraux de l'enquête décennale de 1882* (Nancy, 1887), p. 173.

hectares declined. The number of owner-occupiers and full-time renting farmers increased by 400 thousand. The tables also show that the decline in the number of large farms was associated with a fall in the number of agricultural laborers. These movements can hardly have been unconnected. Taken together, they suggest that as large farms were broken down into small ones, at least

Table 8-2. Agricultural Labor Force by Status, 1862 and 1882

	1862		1882		
	Number (thousands)	Percent	Number (thousands)	Percent	1882 as Percent of 1862
Landowners					
Full owners	1,813	24.7	2,151	31.2	119
Part-renters	649	8.8	500	7.3	77
Part-share tenants	204	2.8	147	2.1	72
Part-time laborers	1,134	18.4	727	10.5	64
Total Landowners	3,800	51.7	3,525	51.1	93
Nonlandowners					
Renters	387	5.3	468	6.8	121
Sharecroppers	202	2.7	194	2.8	96
Laborers	869	11.8	753	10.9	87
Hired laborers and domestics	2,096	28.5	1,954	28.3	92
Total Nonlandowners	3,554	48.3	3,369	48.8	95
Total employed in agriculture	7,354		6,894		

Source: *Enquête décennale de 1882*, pp. 189, 192.

some of the laborers previously employed acquired land and became peasant farmers in their own right.

The nationwide surveys of agriculture of 1866, 1908, and 1912 support and extend the conclusions that emerge from study of the statistical record. In twenty-eight volumes of published testimony before the agricultural hearings in 1866 there is abundant confirmation of the hypothesis that agricultural laborers were acquiring land for their own use. Most witnesses deplored the loss of a free and formerly docile labor force, and perhaps exaggerated the extent of the drain, but the reports taken at regional capitals in every department are too consistent to be discounted. The following description of the reversion to subsistence farming in Aveyron is one of the more extensive commentaries.

> Many workers have succeeded in buying a house and a plot of land, which they cultivate bit by bit, turning the soil with pick and hoe and allocating their time so that the work is done at precisely the right moment. In this way they lavish innumerable days and refuse to work for others except when they have some time to spare. . . .
>
> The land is now perhaps better cultivated, as the soil is worked by hand; but one should not draw any conclusions from this fact that there has been any progress in tools, livestock husbandry or farming practice. For instead of increasing the amount of land in forage crops, which is the basis of any truly progressive agriculture; indeed, rather than keeping the amount of land in forage constant, these farmers plow the remaining small strip of meadow allotted them which, being too small to support even one animal, now constitutes the best arable land of their tiny holdings.
>
> This system supports a few more families than the old one did, but it no longer produces for the general market and it is slowly exhausting itself through lack of fertilizer as a result of the disappearance of the livestock. Even when it does manage to produce something, it is due to manual labor that absorbs the family's time and is not remunerative. Three-fourths of these families do not harvest enough corn to feed themselves and are thus obliged to buy more or less from the market according to the state of the harvest.[7]

In more fertile areas, such as the Beauce, small proprietors found it difficult to compete with large farmers and might be driven to work excessive hours to maintain themselves.[8] The

[7] *1866 Enquête,* Vol. 19, Aveyron, 212, 221–22.

[8] "The landholding laborers work at home and the extreme division of their holdings causes them to lose time, something which does not occur on a large farm. Given equal effort the small holdings produce much less than

witnesses also argued that the small peasant farmer produced too dearly to compete with other farms except in garden vegetables and poultry.[9]

The surveys of peasant property and rural labor markets that were conducted in the early twentieth century show that through much of France the surge of peasant ownership and farming patterns had not yet subsided. Using rather flexible definitions of small, large, and medium farms, which were aimed at isolating the small peasant farmer from larger enterprises, the ministry of agriculture found that the small farms were increasing their share of agricultural land and farm units in more than half of the departments.[10] Thus, far from bringing a slow disintegration of the peasant property that had been held at the beginning of the century, the period between 1800 and 1900 was one in which peasants held their own and even expanded their share of farm land and labor.

Some of the geographical variation in the evolution of farm size can be seen in Table 8–3, in which departmental movements have been averaged by broad regions. The expansion in the number of peasant holdings seems to have been most pronounced in western and southern France. In the plains surrounding Paris and stretching northeastward into Belgium, the large farms managed to hold their own, and sometimes to expand their share of land and farm units. One pattern that does not break through the regional averages is the distinction between cereal-producing regions, where farm sizes tended to move towards a unimodal distribution, and the hilly pastoral regions, where the movement was bimodal. One reason for the double movement of farms in the uplands of France may be the formation of large ranches from land previously held in common and,

medium or large ones. Nevertheless . . . the loss of time is made up by the considerable amount of labor furnished by an individual placed in these conditions. This labor is such—sometimes 20 out of 24 hours—that there is in fact an increase in production. But its excessiveness is perhaps one of the causes which have led part of the agricultural population to turn away from farming." *1866 Enquête,* Vol. 6, Eure-et-Loir, 361.

[9] *1866 Enquête,* Vol. 9, Allier, 193: "Small holders produce above all what they themselves consume. Their production does not enter into the general market." See also Vol. 5, Nord, 163; Yonne, Vol. 9, 467: "The small farmer produces too dearly to market anything but vegetables, fruits or fowl"; Vol. 17, Basses-Pyrénées, 218; Vol. 23, Vaucluse, 73: "The small proprietors, who are the most numerous, do not purchase industrial goods."

[10] Direction de l'Agriculture, *La Petite propriété rurale en France.*

Table 8-3. Change in Number of Farms by Farm Size, 1862–1882
(1862 = 100)

	Hectares					
	1–5	5–10	10–20	20–30	30–40	40+
Northeast	101	130	129	121	122	103
Normandy	101	115	121	117	115	103
Champagne	156	158	142	134	141	121
East	116	128	121	109	109	134
Brittany	108	117	116	108	100	82
West	141	150	100	83	92	91
Loire Plains	141	156	136	126	105	87
Massif Central	97	125	126	120	108	80
Southwest	105	122	107	115	105	99
Southeast	118	154	132	105	100	95

Note: The regional groupings of departments are as follows: *Northeast:* Nord, Pas-de-Calais, Aisne, Somme. Oise, Seine-et-Marne, Seine-et-Oise, Eure-et-Loir; *Normandy:* Eure, Seine-Inférieure, Calvados, Orne, Manche; *Champagne:* Ardennes, Meuse, Meurthe-et-Moselle, Marne, Haute-Marne, Aube, Yonne; *East:* Vosges, Côte-d'Or, Doubs, Jura, Haute-Saône, Saône-et-Loire, Rhône, Ain, Isère; *Brittany:* Ille-et-Vilaine, Côtes-du-Nord, Finistère, Morbihan, Loire-Inférieure; *West:* Sarthe, Mayenne, Maine-et-Loire, Deux-Sèvres, Vendée, Charente, Charente-Inférieure; *Loire Plains:* Loiret, Allier, Nièvre, Cher, Indre, Loir-et-Cher, Indre-et-Loire, Vienne, Haute-Vienne, Creuse, Corrèze; *Massif Central:* Puy-de-Dôme, Loire, Haute-Loire, Cantal, Lozère, Aveyron, Lot, Dordogne; *Southwest:* Tarn, Tarn-et-Garonne, Lot-et-Garonne, Haute-Garonne, Gers, Gironde, Landes, Hautes-Pyrénées, Basses-Pyrénées, Ariège; *Southeast:* Pyrénées-Orientales, Aude, Hérault, Gard, Bouches-du-Rhône, Var, Drome, Ardèche, Basses-Alpes, Hautes-Alpes, Vaucluse.

Sources: Statistique Générale de la France, *Statistique de la France; résultats généraux de l'enquête agricole décennale de 1862* (Nancy, 1868); *Enquête décennale de 1882.*

on the other hand, the breakup of arable farms into small plots in the more fertile sections of these departments. The difference in the response of landholdings between the cereal regions of northeastern and southwestern France seems better explained by differences in technological and economic conditions.

Technological Factors in the Agrarian Structure

The spread of peasant farming coincided with changes unprecedented for France in agricultural implements and farming practices. The fallow was swiftly replaced by meadows and root breaks between 1840 and 1880, and the harvest was almost entirely cut with the scythe by the 1870s. Threshing was done by machine outside the limited range where it could be carried out with rollers on an open floor. By 1880 mechanical reapers and mowers were beginning to harvest and mow grass in every part of France. Despite this, most observers agreed that progress was slower than it should have been, and that it was confined on the whole to the larger farms. French agriculture by 1880 exhibited what has come to be known as technological dualism. Ancient and modern techniques coexisted, and the old showed no tendency to be pushed aside by the new.

The simultaneous application of old and new techniques in an industry is a normal aspect of dynamic economic processes. Producers will adopt new techniques at different times because the ages of their equipment differ, and because technological information and experience are costly to acquire. It is not surprising, therefore, that during periods of rapid technological progress a gap should emerge between the most modern and traditional techniques. In agriculture, large farms modernized more rapidly, in part because their managers were better educated and had better access to technical information. Another reason can be found in the interaction between the agrarian structure and the state of agricultural technology. It is these latter that are the chief concern of this paper. The technical possibilities for factor substitution, combined with the differences in relative factor costs as between peasant and nonpeasant farms, helped to produce a divided agricultural organization.

Peasant farms and commercial farms form two clusters in the continuum of farm types that ranges from subsistence farming with family labor to specialized farming with hired labor. For us, the most important difference between peasant and capitalistic farms lay in the terms on which they obtained their labor. Under certain technological constraints small differences in relative factor costs can lead to wide variations in factor combinations and scale of operations. These variations can themselves reinforce the underlying institutions that encouraged them in the first place. Agricultural technology in the nineteenth century seems on the whole to have been quite compatible with a division of farms into two social and technological regimes. In the state of the art as it existed around 1850 it was possible for farmers to apply vast quantities of labor in farming without forcing its marginal product to decline rapidly. In economic jargon, the elasticity of substitution between labor and other factors was high. Small differences in labor costs as between farm types, therefore, could easily be translated into large differences in the labor-intensity of the techniques they used.

This excursus in the cloudy domain of production functions provides a basic hypothesis about the nature and consequences of technological change in nineteenth-century France. It is not possible to test the hypothesis of a high elasticity of substitution directly from the statistical record, but that there was a great ease in using labor for land and other factors is strongly supported by contemporary evidence and agricultural science.

The main physical basis for the easy substitutability of labor in agricultural production was the sensitivity of crop yields to careful tillage and weeding. In part this is because yields in 1850 were still very low outside the Paris region and Flanders— probably not more than eight to twelve bushels per acre on the average, or four to six times the amount sown.[11] At these levels even small absolute increases in output from better cultivation and more careful harvesting meant large proportional increases in production, and would therefore justify the expenditure of great amounts of labor in response to small differences in labor costs. The principal reason for low yields was that the land was poorly tilled. The inadequacy of tillage on peasant farms is a continuing theme in the technical and reportorial literature of the mid-nineteenth century.[12] In part, the condemnation of tra-

---

[11] Michel Morineau, *Les Faux-Semblants d'un démarrage économique: agriculture et démographie en France au xviiie siècle*, Cahiers des Annales, Vol. 30 (Paris, 1971), 24–31; William H. Newell, "The Agricultural Revolution in Nineteenth-Century France," *Journal of Economic History* 33 (December 1973), 697–731.

[12] See especially the reports by the inspectors of agriculture on departmental agriculture in the 1840s. Ministère de l'Agriculture, *Agriculture française, par MM. les Inspecteurs d'agriculture, d'après les ordres de M. le ministre de l'agriculture et du commerce, département de l'Isère* (Paris, 1843); *Haute-Garonne* (Paris, 1843); *Côtes-du-Nord* (Paris, 1844); *Tarn* (Paris, 1845); *Nord* (Paris, 1843); *Hautes-Pyrénées* (Paris, 1843); *Aude* (Paris, 1847); and O. Leclerc-Thouin, *L'Agriculture de l'Ouest de la France, étudiée plus spécialement dans le département de Maine-et-Loire* (Paris, 1843). For a fuller account of these factors in agriculture technology see George W. Grantham, *Technical and Organizational Change in French Agriculture between 1840 and 1880; An Economic Interpretation* (Ph.D. dissertation, Yale University, 1972), chapter 3.

ditional tillage continued the tradition begun when Duhamel de Monceau translated and interpreted Jethro Tull's *Horse-hoeing Husbandry* in the previous century, but it was also grounded in the observation that shallow and incomplete plowing left the fields poorly drained and weed-infested, requiring a fallow or root break before opening the ground to cereals. Commenting on the use of fallow in the strong clay soils of the Narbonnaise, the inspector of agriculture for Aude wrote that:

> in these strong soils, the fallow is the very best precedent for wheat. This is not only because wheat requires this costly expedient; but because with the implements at their disposal, the soil is ordinarily so badly plowed and the plowing is carried out at such inopportune times, that the seed is rarely sown in well-prepared beds. The fallow, therefore, is about the only way of obtaining a good tilth. The successive plowings which it receives and the action of the atmosphere on the earthy molecules, the breaking up of the sod, sowing carried out properly—these are the reasons which explain without difficulty the success of wheat after fallow.[13]

According to the report of the inspector for Tarn, the fallow was the "remedy *in extremis*," where more progressive rotations involving root breaks and artificial meadows failed to keep the fields clean.[14] The inability to prepare the soil, as much as lack of animal manure, both due to a small stock of draft animals and an underlying scarcity of fodder, seems to have been a major factor limiting cereal yields.

The importance of tillage on crop yields and the opportunities that improvements in this area afforded for growth in productivity can be guessed at from the Rothamsted experiments on unmanured land, which show that a rotation of wheat and fallow produced yields of seventeen bushels per acre, or nearly twice the yields reported for eighteenth and early nineteenth-century

---

[13] *Agriculture française, Aude*, pp. 157–58.

[14] "Are the seeds of wild oats, rye-grass, thistles, and corn-cockles—carried in part by manure and in part by the wind—destroyed by such cultivation? Not at all. One should not be surprised at this. Weeded crops that are *negligently cultivated with imperfect tools leave almost intact the weeds* springing up after the corn. The insufficiency of these methods is so strongly felt that it is necessary to resort to fallowing. How otherwise can one explain fallowing and plowing fields after crops whose role in the rotation is to loosen and clean the soil. Fallowing is thus a remedy *in extremis*." *Agriculture française, Tarn*, p. 153.

France.[15] The difference must surely have been due to better soil care on the experimental plots. The 1852 census returns from the canton of Givonne, a district in the Ardennes near the Belgian frontier, reported that where farmers neglected to plow the fallow crop, yields fell twenty to thirty percent.[16] A textbook on weed control states that the presence of wild mustard in cereal fields could cut yields by forty percent, and infestation by sow-thistle or quackgrass by as much as eighty percent.[17] From these scattered evidences of the ravages of weeds and nitrogen deficiency in unturned soil, it seems as though improved tillage and weeding was capable of increasing crop yields by twenty to fifty percent.

The improvement in field care was commonly reported as the main source of the increase in crop yields over the previous twenty-five years by the witnesses before the 1866 enquiry. Deeper plowing, more frequent harrowing and rolling, and row cultivation all seem to have increased the cleanliness of the fields, and supported the extension of new crops into land previously held in fallow.[18] This improvement was the result of parallel changes in the technology of animal-powered agriculture and methods of

[15] As reported by Witt Bowden, Michael Karpovich, and Abbott Payson Usher, *An Economic History of Europe since 1750* (New York, 1937), p. 59.

[16] Commission de statistique cantonnale: dictons concernant l'agriculture: comptes de frais de cultures par hectare de terres, Ardennes à Meuse (1852–1854), Ardennes, Archives Nationales, Paris, F20 561.

[17] Wilfred W. Robbins, Alden S. Crafts, and Richard N. Raynor, *Weed Control; A Textbook and Manual* (New York, 1942), p. 87.

[18] The relationship between draft animal power and rotations is especially well brought out by Daniel Faucher, "L'assolement triennal en France," *Études rurales* 1 (1961), 7–17. The effect of better plowing on weed control is noted in the report for 1866 from the Hautes-Pyrénées: "The progress accomplished . . . in the last thirty years comes down to very little. One must recognize nonetheless that the land is better cultivated and that plowing is deeper and more frequent. It is doubtless owing to these two circumstances that we have better cereal harvests and a diminution in the immense quantity of parasitical weeds that in times past invaded the corn and condemned the cultivators to carry out costly weeding. No doubt it is still necessary to weed the corn crops in rainy years; but this operation is becoming less expensive than it used to be because the weeds are less numerous." *1866 Enquête*, Vol. 18, Hautes-Pyrénées, 305.

The retrospective exhibition of agricultural technology for the International Folklore Conference in Paris in 1937 also emphasizes the improvement in plowing and the multiplication of superficial cultivation by harrows and row cultivators as the major source of growth in productivity. See Enquête sur l'ancienne agriculture, manuscripts deposited in the archives of the Musée des Arts et Traditions Populaires, Paris.

manual cultivation. Between 1840 and 1870 the introduction and diffusion of new plows, such as the Brabant and Dombasle, proceeded rapidly. It was associated with an improvement in the quality of the draft stock between 1840 and 1880, which resulted from an increase in the live weights of oxen of from 10 to 20 percent and an increase in the density of draft animals per hectare of cultivated land of from 75 percent in northeastern France to over 100 percent in the *Midi*.[19] The significance of these changes, which followed upon the increase in fodder supplies, can be seen from the draft requirements of agricultural implements of the period. At the end of the nineteenth century a simple iron plow required 400 to 600 pounds of draft, while the light Brabant plow of the 1840s weighed 145 pounds. Mowers and mechanical reapers generated resistances of 350 to 500 pounds. To meet these requirements a horse developing .80 horsepower could draw 250 pounds at a rate of one and a quarter miles per hour, while oxen and cows drew considerably less.[20] Improvement along these lines, however, was necessarily restricted to farms large enough to maintain draft animals and invest in the change of crop rotations.

The other way to raise crop yields was to use more manual labor. The extent and variety of the methods of working the soil by hand can be seen by examining the matrix in Table 8–4, which classifies the processes of soil preparation by their effect on the soil and by their means of power. Manual methods were usually more productive per hectare than mechanical ones, and provided an outlet for family labor. In addition, farmers could weed the standing crop by hand, for which there was no mechanical counterpart.

Manual preparation of the soil absorbed enormous quantities

[19] See Grantham, *Technical and Organizational Change*, pp. 65–66 and appendix II. Along with the increase in weight, the substitution of horses for oxen and oxen for cows was the main source of improvement.

[20] For the weights of agricultural implements, see L. Baily, ed., *Cyclopedia of American Agriculture*, Vol. 1, 204–207; and Anselm Payen, *Précis d'agriculture théorique et pratique à l'usage des écoles d'agriculture, des propriétaires et des fermiers* (Paris, 1851), p. 84. The horsepower and resistances are given in Baily, *Cyclopedia*, p. 218, W. J. Rankine, *Useful Rules and Tables*, 7th ed. (London, 1889), p. 251, and J. V. Poncelet, *Cours de mécanique appliquée aux machines* (Paris, 1877), pp. 268–70. The relative power that could be produced continuously by draft animals is as follows: Horse working against a capstan, 187; oxen working against a capstan, 96; horse working against a cart, 100; mule against a cart, 66; and ass against a cart, 28.

Table 8-4. Techniques of Tillage

Effect on the soil	Use in Agriculture	Tools	
		Manual	Draft Teams
turning the soil	deep plowing forming ridges and furrows	spade *pelleversoir*	mouldboard plow
breaking up the soil	shallow plowing, forming seedbed, covering seed.	hoe, *pioche*, *binot*	symmetric plow (*araire*) row cultivators
levelling or moving the soil	forming seedbed, encourage tillering	rake, hoe	harrow, horseshoe
packing the soil	firming up loose soils, breaking clots	mallets	roller

of labor. The census accounts of labor inputs for hand-worked crops such as hemp and flax or garden crops indicate that it took on the average twenty to thirty days to work a hectare of land with a sod fork, and that forty to sixty days were needed to prepare the seedbed.[21] In the heavier soils of western France these requirements might rise as high as sixty to eighty days.[22] In contrast, the preparation of the soil by plow and harrow took from seven to twenty-five days, depending on soil conditions and the type of draft animal employed.[23] There seems to have been some improvement in hand tools in the first half of the century as a result of the cheapening of metal and the replacement of the broadbladed wooden spade by the sod fork or *pelleversoir*. A man working heavy soil with a wooden spade dipped in water or rubbed with fat to facilitate its entry into the

[21] See Commissions de statistique cantonnale: comptes de frais de cultures par hectare de terres (1852–1854), Côtes-du-Nord, Archives Nationales, Paris, F20 560, and Ardennes à Meuse (1852–1854), F20 561. These data are evaluated and criticized in appendix III of Grantham, *Technological and Organizational Change.*

[22] See Charles Parain, "L'évolution de l'ancien outillage dans l'Aude et les départements voisins au cours de XIXe siècle (Culture des céréales)," *Folklore* (Carcassonne), Vol. 3 (July-December 1940), 48–61; Pierre Coutin, "L'évolution de la technique des labours dans le Nord de la Limagne depuis le début du XIXe siècle jusqu'au 1938," *Folklore Paysanne* (March-April, 1938), pp. 31–32; *1866 Enquête*, Vol. 22, Gard, 342; Vol. 15, Charente-Inférieure, 287; Vol. 7, Loire Inférieure, 683; Leclerc-Thouin, *L'Agriculture de l'Ouest*, pp. 181–82.

[23] See Grantham, *Technical and Organizational Change*, pp. 296–97.

ground could work about 150 square meters a day—a rate of approximately sixty days per hectare. With an iron blade his rate doubled, and with the *pelleversoir*, which penetrated the soil more easily and did not foul on roots or weeds, two or three men working together could plow a hectare in ten days.[24] These figures refer to deep spading, which had to be periodically carried out to clean the fields. The improvement in metallurgical technology, then, seems to have extended the possibilities of labor-intensive agriculture.

Subsequent operations on the soil do not seem to have experienced technological progress, and they continued to soak up great amounts of labor. Hoeing absorbed twenty to thirty man-days per hectare. The breaking up of earth clots, which rarely needed more than a day or two when performed by harrower or roller, could take up to twenty days when performed by hand, although ten seems to have been more usual.[25] References to the practice of manual clod beetling are most frequent in southwestern France and Languedoc, where it was thought to encourage tillering and thus promote higher yields.[26] Row cultivation by multishared cultivators was ten times faster than the same operation carried out with a single plow or *araire*.[27] In the post-tillage operations, hand weeding and sarcling, sickling, and hand threshing gave greater yields per hectare than their labor-saving counterparts.[28] In all these operations it was possible to use labor lavishly when its marginal cost was low.

The enquiry of 1866 supplies two explicit comparisons of the relative costs of labor-saving and labor-absorbing methods of

[24] Coutin, "L'évolution de la technique des labours," pp. 31–32; Parain, "L'évolution de l'ancien outillage," p. 49; *Agriculture française, Tarn*, pp. 72–73; Musée des Arts et Traditions Populaires, Enquête sur l'ancienne agriculture, departments of Puy-de-Dôme, Indre-et-Loire, Corrèze, Haute-Loire, Hérault, Basses-Alpes; Cros-Mayrevieille, "Les premiers résultats de l'enquête sur l'outillage agricole," *Folklore* (Carcassonne), Vol. 3, (July-December 1940), 39–41.

[25] Grantham, *Technical and Organizational Change*, pp. 311–12.

[26] *Agriculture française, Haute-Garonne*, pp. 66–67; *Tarn*, pp. 198–99.

[27] Roger Brunet, *Les Campagnes toulousaines; une étude géographique* (Toulouse, 1965), p. 340; *Agriculture française, Hautes-Pyrénées*, p. 116; *Tarn*, p. 302.

[28] The scythe shattered the grain on some varieties of wheat, and it was difficult to use on land plowed in a pattern of ridges and furrows. See *1866 Enquête*, Vol. 3, Ille-et-Vilaine, 158; Vol. 8, Loire-Inférieure, 632; Vol. 7, Vendée, 216, Deux-Sèvres, 434; Vol. 9, Yonne, 120; and Pierre Coutin, "La Moisson en Limagne," *Le Mois d'ethnographie française* 10 (1950), 22.

cultivation. In the Breton department of Loire-Inférieure, cereals produced on hand-spaded ground cost about 12 percent more per hectare than on soil plowed up with oxen. In the Jura costs per hectare of wheat were 237 francs when it was sickled, as compared with 218 francs when it was not.[29] Isolated references do not prove the case that the cost differentials between animal and manual methods of cultivation were often narrow, but there is one major piece of indirect evidence that links differences in the labor requirements of plowing and hand preparation with changes in the distribution of farm size. Table 8–5 presents the average plowing and spading times by region in the middle of the nineteenth century, as reconstructed from census returns and other contemporary sources. We see here that it was in precisely the areas where small farming seems to have expanded most rapidly—the departments of the west, center, and south of France—that the differences in labor requirements for plowing and hand spading were smallest. The rapid movement of horses on the loams of northeastern France conferred a far greater advantage than the slow-moving and expensive oxen on the heavy soils of the *Midi*. This advantage in turn could be expected to have some influence on the evolution of farm size.

[29] *1866 Enquête*, Vol. 7, Loire Inférieure, 683; Vol. 27, Jura, 369.

Table 8–5. Preparation of the Seed Bed (man-days per hectare)

	By Plow	By Hand
Northeast	5–7.5	45
Normandy	6–12	45
Champagne	4–7	40
East	12	50
Brittany	12	50
West	8–12	60
Loire Plains	10–15	45
Massif Central	15–25	50
Southwest	20	50
Southeast	8–12	50

Sources: Commissions de statistique cantonnale: comptes de frais de cultures par hectare de terres (1852–1854), Archives Nationales, Paris, F[20], pp. 560–561; Ministère de l'Agriculture, *Enquête sur la situation et les besoins de l'agriculture, 1866–1872* (Paris, 1867–1872). The derivation of these estimates is in George W. Grantham, *Technical and Organizational Change in French Agriculture between 1840 and 1888; An Economic Interpretation* (Ph.D. dissertation, Yale University, 1972), Appendix iv, pp. 287–317, and Appendix v, pp. 318–35.

Social Influences on the Agrarian Structure

The simultaneous advance of mechanical technology and the increase in the number of small peasant holding suggests that French agriculture was dividing into two sectors—a relatively modern and capital-using sector of large farms, and a large mass of peasants employing traditional labor-using techniques. Such developments are now seen to reflect differences in factor costs, especially labor, that faced peasant and nonpeasant farmers. The "costless" character of labor on peasant farms was a frequent theme in the accounts of French agriculture of the last century. The maintenance of clod-beetling over the harrow and roller in the Tarn was explained by the fact that "the breaking up of clods is, in [the peasant's] eyes, only a matter of more work, with no increase in expense whenever it can be accomplished by himself or his family. His own time and that of his family does not enter into account. Thus it is that in the final analysis, he will give little attention to the inconvenience of this practice as long as it does not cost him anything." [30] Family members are described as "workers" or "servants," and it was recognized that "the more children a *métayer* has to help him farm, the fewer hired hands he requires and consequently the lower his costs." [31] Faucher suggests that the destruction of rural cloth-making probably reinforced the farm family as an autonomous unit by freeing large numbers of women for work in the fields.[32] In any case, family workers conferred a real advantage over hired hands, who had to be supervised and could not be swiftly shifted from one task to another in response to changes in the weather or the existence of idle time.[33]

[30] *Agriculture française, Tarn*, p. 200. The cultivation of hemp by peasants in the Sancerre was also explained by the abundance of "free labor": "The inhabitants of the countryside . . . do not count this time as an expense. It is the women who are occupied once the field is sown. Since little or no cash outlay is required they believe they have struck a good bargain in doing this. This is true in the sense that all too often the women and children of our canton are not sufficiently employed. One could strictly regard this work as costing nothing, since it costs nothing but their labor and in its absence they would not have worked at all." Report of statistical committee of Henrichemont, Cher, Archives Nationales, Paris, F20 561.

[31] *Agriculture française, Côtes-du-Nord*, p. 96. For similar observations see *1866 Enquête*, Vol. 7, Loire-Inférieure; Vol. 24, Var, 382; Vol. 7, Vendée, 215; Vol. 18, Haute-Garonne, 266.

[32] Daniel Faucher, "Aspects sociologiques du travail agricole," *Etudes Rurales*, Vol. 13–14, 127.

[33] See the report of the committee of Charleville for the 1852 census, Archives Nationales, Paris, F20 561.

Direct statistical measurement of the differential cost of labor on and off family farms is nonexistent. Such fine reckonings of time spent did not come naturally to farmers, who measured their days by the tasks to be done, and who determined profits and losses on the basis of whether they had maintained their working capital through another crop year.[34] We must rely, therefore, on the casual observations that peasants worked longer hours and more intensively per hectare on their own farms than they did on those of others.[35] A more important question is whether one can isolate some of the reasons for the persistence of a privileged access to labor on peasant farms.

The factors favoring peasant family farming in nineteenth century France divide roughly into two categories: economic reasons, in which the calculation of anticipated benefits and costs determined the marginal movement of labor in and out of family farms; and moral or psychological reasons, so deeply embedded in the rural mind as scarcely to be susceptible of a marginal analysis.

The economic reasons are the more accessible to analysis and understanding. The most fruitful point of entry is through a consideration of the risks and earnings of the different occupations available to peasant farmers. Until late in the nineteenth century peasants were held to their tiny farms by several types of insecurity. Laboring jobs and incomes in agriculture and industry were insecure. There was little provision for aged and retired workers in rural areas, and for some time in towns.[36] Harvest failures created ripples of income effects through the rural and industrial economy, causing unemployment in the fields and provoking sharp declines in the demand for industrial goods as a result of the rise in food prices.[37] Lack of transport

[34] See the remarks by Leclerc-Thouin, *L'Agriculture de l'Ouest,* p. 105.

[35] See, for example *1866 Enquête,* Vol. 18, Gironde, 378; Vol. 7, Eure-et-Loir, 31, 349. For later observations see Direction de l'Agriculture, *La Petite propriété rurale.*

[36] The avoidance of penury and the possibility of pensions for work in towns was a great consideration in the eyes of rural people. Vaury reports that in the Sologne at the beginning of the twentieth century, young people were leaving agriculture for trades that would yield them a pension so that they would not be reduced to begging "or what amounts to the same thing, living with their children." L. Vaury, *Étude d'économie rurale sur la commune de Saint-Florent-le-Jeune* (Paris, 1921), p. 84.

[37] The statistical commission of Charleville noted in 1852 that "The time is long past when everyone was contented with bread, gruel and buckwheat. As industry has penetrated the countryside, so has the luxury of white bread

and commercial storage for grain redistributed income away from wage-earners towards farmers and all those who could support themselves directly from the land. The spread of manufacturing into rural areas and the consequent specialization of the labor force increased the vulnerability of rural people to fluctuations in market prices.[38] Workers holding land were better protected from harvest failure and disruption of food markets than the landless proletariat, and self-sufficient peasants were safer still. The great harvest failures of the mid-1840s, producing recrudescence of rural bread riots at the end of the July Monarchy, mark the end of the century-long expansion in the rural population. They must have deeply printed on the minds of the rural poor the notion that security lay in the soil.[39]

The impact of other less catastrophic forms of economic insecurity could also be softened by holding land. Of these the most important perhaps was seasonal unemployment.[40] This condition, implicit in cereal farming everywhere, produced not only seasonal migration, but a steady dissatisfaction with farm work. A steady industrial job, the chance that when he finished his days he would have a pension, and higher wages were the chief incentives attracting a hired worker away from farming. A landholder, by way of contrast, could keep himself fully occupied with the manifold tasks of farm life, and when he was too old to work, could arrange the transmission of his property to

---

and practically all the workers now buy from the baker. As a result, in periods of commercial crisis or of scarcity of cereals, no one has at home any reserve of grain or flour." Archives Nationales, Paris, F[20] 561, Ardennes.

[38] The work of Labrousse and his students on short-term economic fluctuations in eighteenth and nineteenth-century France has been concerned with this problem. On the crisis of 1846 see C. F. Labrousse, ed., *Aspects de la crise et de la dépression de l'économie française au milieu du XIXe siècle, 1846–1851*, Bibliothèque de la Revolution de 1848, Vol. 19 (La Roche-sur-Yon, 1956), especially the introduction. The research of Jean Meuvret, although bearing on an earlier period, also sheds light on early modern food and labor markets. See especially his "Circuits d'échanges et travail rural dans la France du xvii siècle," in *Studi in onore di Armando Sapori* (Milan, 1957), Vol. 2, 1129–42.

[39] Sharp fluctuations in grain prices continued through the 1850s and 1860s, doubling between 1851 and 1856, and rising more than sixty percent between 1865 and 1868.

[40] The relative stability of industrial employment is mentioned frequently as a cause of rural emigration. See *1866 Enquête*, Vol. 2, Mayenne, 506; Vol. 7, Vendée, 214; Vol. 17, Basses-Pyrénées, 218. It became even more important at the end of the century. See Ministère d'Agriculture, *La Petite Propriété rurale* and *Enquête sur les salaires agricoles*.

ensure his maintenance. Even in the absence of an heir, he could work out an annuity with the village notary. The uncertainties of market relations provided an important class of causes for peasants to hold and work land at returns below those paid in the labor market. By extension, such calculations may be supposed to have entered into the reckonings of the members of his family as well, although here moral and social motives immediately come into play. The expectation of inheriting land, and the appreciation of the farm as an intergenerational enterprise must have induced many sons to work alongside their fathers rather than seek wages elsewhere. Some of this labor was an investment in learning the peculiarities of the soil and the lay of the land that made each plot more productive under the hands of its owner than those of a stranger. In most cases economic motivation for staying on the family farm grew out of the lack of other opportunities for work in rural areas and the high cost of coming into a landed estate except through inheritance.[41]

After 1850 the economic motives for staying on the land must have diminished. Improved markets and an aggregate demand that was less dependent on the grain harvest reduced the frequency of short-term depression and unemployment, while rising wages gave greater compensation for the risks of taking employment off the family farm. Some of these changes were internal to agriculture. The suppression of the fallow led to a growing demand for hands at the same time as many landless laborers were emigrating to the towns. One reads, then, of a loosening of family ties and a decline in the number of large peasant farms staffed exclusively by members of the same family. The breakdown of family control was, of course, of long standing, and by the middle of the century there were only enough truly extended families to provide sociological documents for the curious.[42] But

[41] Delord estimates that in the 1870s and 1880s in the Limousin it would have required ten years for a young man to amass two thousand francs working as a hired hand. With these savings he would be able to enter a small *métairie* whose total capital requirements were eight thousand francs, the balance being supplied by the landlord. The high costs of establishing a new household must have greatly increased the value of entering into the existing family farm through inheritance or through its promise. See Jeanne-Marie Delord, *La Famille rurale dans l'économie du Limousin, 1769–1939* (Limoges, 1940), pp. 118–22.

[42] See Guy Thuillier, *Aspects de l'économie nivernaise au XIXe siècle* (Paris, 1966), pp. 42–43; Henriette Dussourd *Au même Pot et au même Feu . . .*

there is also much comment on the separation of younger sons from family operations, which in certain parts of France seems to have affected the viability of large-scale peasant farms. In the Vendée, it was "generally recognized that [the *métairies*] are less united; and that the great communities of cultivators are progressively disappearing." [43] In Brittany, the 1866 enquiry notes that families are still large, but they now tend to divide more easily "as a result of the weakening of paternal authority." [44] In southwest France "the difference is just barely noticeable, but families tend to break up from about the age of puberty of the children. Each one wants to work on his own account." [45] As it became easier to establish families at an early age, the younger members of the farm family began to leave the parental home.

The breakdown of the peasant family generated much nostalgic vaporing among the upper classes and the clergy, which for all its bluster gives an important insight into the ways peasants preserved control of their labor force. In the Landes the disappearance of *métairies*—a term that included not only sharecrop tenures, but any substantial peasant holding—was attributed to the abandonment of field work by the young, who left it "to their old parents who without the aid of their children cannot execute it." [46] A more indignant reporter from Perigord claimed that "It would be extremely shameful from every point of view to see the children who work alongside their father on the *métairie* scatter and seek work elsewhere as laborers. It would mean misery for their parents, who alone could not work their land." [47]

Helping the parents man their farm belonged in the category of moral actions that admitted of few trade-offs. Roger Thabault has related that in his Poitevine commune of Mazière-en-Gatine in the 1870s, a carpenter's son who had through his ability and elementary education carved out a position in the army con-

---

Étude sur les communautés familiales agricoles du centre de la France (Moulin, 1962).

[43] *1866 Enquête*, Vol. 7, Vendée, 215.

[44] *1866 Enquête*, Vol. 7, Loire-Inférieure, 627, 629. An almost identical statement came from Allier: "The union is smaller and each of the members tends much more easily to separate and retire from it" (Vol. 9, 246); in Haute-Vienne we read that families were becoming smaller "less by the fact of diminution in the number of births than by the division of families, which are less united than they used to be" (Vol. 15, 219).

[45] *1866 Enquête*, Vol. 18, Haute-Garonne, 278.

[46] *1866 Enquête*, Vol. 16, Landes, 413.

[47] *1866 Enquête*, Vol. 16, Dordogne, 289.

sciously sacrificed his career to rejoin his father in the shop.[48] Before the 1860s, even the possibility of leaving the homestead probably would not have been entertained. Henri Mendras reports that modern peasants conceive of themselves as being born to their profession, not as having chosen it. Sons were duty-bound to honor their fathers, and any *père* who failed to obtain the labor and respect of his spouse and offspring also lost his standing in the village community.[49]

Among the other psychological or moral qualities that maintained the peasant farm in the face of attractive employment outside was what Mendras calls *courage*—what we perhaps might once have called steadfastness. It meant self-discipline in work, self-control in society, and the acceptance of one's condition in the world.[50] To be *courageux* was to be respected in the small community of farmers. This puritannical conception of life and work found some support from the clergy, who emphasized the life-sustaining quality of agricultural work, and it was singularly well-suited to a technological regime in which success depended on continuously hard labor and on the slowly acquired specific knowledge of how plants and animals grew. Such moral justifications for effort, as they were held up as a community ideal, probably retarded the movement of laborers from family farms to commercial ones. Such ideas change slowly, and their persistence kept the implicit costs of family labor lagging behind the rise in the market wage.

The Evolution of Farm Organization

The technological and social factors sketched above explain the coexistence of commercial and peasant farms, but they do not explain the movement in the distribution of size of farms, and presumably of farm types, that occurred. For the causes of that evolution we must look to external factors acting on what seems to have been a relatively free and competitive set of markets for land and labor. The evolution of the size distribution of farms

[48] Roger Thabault, *Education and Change in a Rural Community*, pp. 101–102.

[49] *Ibid.*, pp. 100–101.

[50] Henri Mendras, *The Vanishing Peasant, Innovation and Change in French Agriculture*, translated by Jean Lerner, (Cambridge, Mass., 1970), pp. 163–65.

during the nineteenth century—a period in which the insignificant fraction of a few hundred properties was fettered by entail and primogeniture during the Restoration and July monarchies—seems to illustrate the natural selectivity of competition among peasants and nonpeasants for land and labor. A rise in the labor intensity of the crop mix coming from, say, an increased demand for fodder-intensive products, tended to favor the peasant sector with its relatively easier access to labor supplies; conversely, improved grain marketing and wider outlets for cereals encouraged the growth of large farms specializing in the production of bread cereals; and any advances in the productivity of animal-powered farm machinery tended to favor capitalist farms with their favorable connections with the capital market and access to technical knowledge. Rising opportunities outside agriculture tended to loosen family bonds, and increased the required rate of return to family farming, discouraging the expansion of that sector. Tighter labor markets favored the sector with the easiest access to labor. The movement of these functions, some deriving from changes in agricultural technology and others from differences in the psychology and perceived opportunities of peasant and nonpeasant producers, determined the relative advantage of the two types of farm organizations over time.

PRODUCT DEMAND.

It is commonly supposed that growing demands for fine fruits, table vegetables, poultry, and dairy products after 1850 created many new opportunities for the establishment of small farms.[51] According to this view any increase in peasant farming after 1850 can be attributed to rising urban incomes and falling transport costs, which increased demand for luxury garden crops and extended the area from which they could be supplied. Most of these new products demanded large amounts of labor—250 to 300 man-days per hectare in the case of garden vegetables—and demanded so much judgment and supervision that it was not feasible to use machines for men, or to employ gang labor in place of an occupying proprietor. As a result, the growing demand for such foods led to a multiplication of small family farms.

[51] See, for example, J. H. Clapham, *The Economic Development of France and Germany, 1815–1914*, 4th ed. (Cambridge, 1936), p. 162.

At first glance, this hypothesis seems to command assent. Gardens increased by 128,000 hectares between 1852 and 1882 in response to the new demands. But against this increase must be placed the decline in land planted to hemp and flax.[52] Between 1862 and 1882 the area in the two fiber crops dropped 98,000 hectares, and the amount of land in colza and other oil crops fell another 159,000. Since the area in other garden crops and vineyards remained constant, the net change in the area in highly labor-intensive crops was small and could not, therefore, have exerted much impact on the size distribution of farms. The evidence is summarized in Table 8–6.

Changes in the patterns of demand for livestock could also affect the size distribution of farms. Levy has demonstrated that in the late nineteenth century in England livestock husbandry was associated with much smaller farms than was grain farming.[53] This was also true in France. Table 8–7 compares the percentage of farms over forty hectares with the share of agricultural land in arable in France in 1882. The relation is clear. Cereal-producing regions—associated here with a high proportion of arable land—had larger farms than livestock regions.

When one considers the impact of changes in the number of livestock held on the distribution of farm sizes, the relation is less clear. In Table 8–8 the percentage change in the number of livestock other than draft animals, sheep, pigs, and goats is

[52] The labor requirements per hectare of flax and hemp were about the same as for gardens: 240 to 250 man-days per hectare. These figures are averages taken from the accounts of labor inputs per hectare in the 1852 census manuscripts, Archives Nationales, Paris, F[20] 560–561.

[53] Hermann Levy, *Large and Small Holdings: A Study of English Agricultural Economics,* translated by Ruth Kenyon, 1st ed (New York, 1966), pp. 104–106.

Table 8–6. Area in Labor-Intensive Crops, 1852, 1862, 1882 (hectares)

	1852	1862	1882
Gardens			
Market	35,936		90,093
Domestic (family)	265,417		339,608
Hemp and Flax	205,693	205,555	107,632
Oilseeds		295,266	136,846
Other Crops		30,685	30,897
Vineyards	2,190,909	2,320,809	2,196,799

Source: *Enquête décennale de 1882,* p. 97.

Table 8–7. Share of Agricultural Land under the Plow and Share of
           Farms over 40 Hectares

Share of Arable (percent)	No. Depts.	Average Share of Arable (percent)	Farms over 40 ha. (percent)
More than 70	9	74.5	6.7
60–70	18	64.5	5.7
50–60	15	54.5	3.6
40–50	13	44.7	2.8
30–40	8	36.4	2.4
Less than 30	15	22.9	4.9

Source: *Enquête décennale de 1882.*

compared with the changes in the size distribution of farms.
Although cattle-raising appears to have some effect in the twenty
to forty-hectare range of farm size, the changes are not large,
and the relationship between animals and changes in farm size in
the range under twenty hectares is not close. Over long periods
of time, farm sizes adjusted to the crop mix—this is reflected in
a cross-section comparison of land use and farm sizes. But in
the thirty-year period covered here, the effects of animal husbandry on average farm size had not yet worked themselves out.
Again we are permitted to conclude that demand patterns had
some effect on farm size, but they were not the main forces acting
upon the evolution of the agrarian structure.

Table 8–8. Change in Livestock other than Draft Animals, Pigs, Goats,
           and Sheep, 1852–1882 and Changes in Number of Farms
           1862–1882

Livestock (1852 = 100)	Farms (1862 = 100)				
	Average	5–10	10–20	20–30	40+
More than 200	338	151	125	123	121	105
150–200	170	123	131	120	102	101
125–150	137	120	113	103	114	108
100–125	109	136	123	114	104	95
75–100	90	150	125	116	109	92

Sources: Statistique Générale de la France, *Statistique de la France, Statistique agricole décennale de 1852,* 2 vols. (Paris, 1858, 1860); *Enquête décennale de 1862; Enquête décennale de 1882.*

LABOR MARKETS.

The most potent influence on the evolution of peasant farming and farm sizes was the tightening of the rural labor market after the middle of the century. Rising real wages—over a hundred percent in some areas between 1840 and 1870—had their exogenous cause in the rising demand for industrial labor and increased demand within agriculture as farmers adopted more labor-intensive courses of root breaks and fodder crops in their rotations. Falling birth rates were probably having some effect on labor supplies by the 1860s. The consequence of rising rural wages were two-fold. Large farmers saw their costs rise more rapidly than did those of small farmers, who were insulated from the labor market because of their use of family labor. The workers, for their part, benefited from an increased cash flow, which helped them to finance acquisitions of land for themselves. These simultaneous movements helped sustain the final surge of peasant proprietorship in the second half of the century.

The main difficulty facing large farmers in the 1860s and 1870s lay in the narrow range of machines and processes that could be substituted for labor in agricultural production. It was difficult to replace harvesters by reapers and haymakers by mowers, when mechanics were scarce and fields and meadows stony or uneven. Such machines as had appeared by the 1860s had been introduced "more with the idea of improving them than with the intention of drawing any real service." [54] The diffusion of mechanical harvesters was still in its early and exploratory stage. Moreover, by compressing the length of the harvest, the reaper greatly exacerbated the problem of labor supply by creating a huge short-term demand for gatherers and binders.[55]

[54] *1866 Enquête,* Vol. 6, Seine-et-Marne, 84. The reporter from Montargis stated that "It would be desirable . . . that the population be initiated to the operation of agricultural machinery . . . and that the level of instruction be raised so as to place the peasant in a position to understand mechanical concepts" (Vol. 11, Loiret, 122). See also Vol. 5, Nord, 165; Vol. 15, Charente-Inférieure, 369: Vol. 11, Nièvre, 423; Vol. 10, Indre, 8; Vol. 6, Seine-et-Oise, 179; Vol. 11, Yonne, 443; and Vol. 23; Vancluse, 16. The Enquête sur l'ancienne agriculture lists only five departments where mechanical reaping was common before 1880; Meurthe-et-Moselle, Meuse, Vôsges, Nièvre, and Bouches-du-Rhône.

[55] See *1866 Enquête,* Vol. 19, Aveyron, 212–13, and Vol. 18, Haute-Garonne, 302–303.

The main problem, however, was that rural life was not organized for the mechanization of the harvest. Large farms had
traditionally drawn on small holders, rural manufacturers, and
migrants for their seasonal labor needs. These needs were very
large and can be appreciated by noting that in addition to the
plowman needed for every ten to twenty hectares of arable land
and the permanent employees hired to keep the stock and clean
the stables, a large arable farm normally took on temporarily one
scyther and six helpers for every four hectares of meadow, six
sicklers or two scythers for every four hectares of winter wheat
or rye, and a *bineur* to perform stoop labor on every three or
four hectares of row crop. In southern France a common rule of
thumb was four harvest hands for every plowman.[56]

In the past the supply of *saisonniers* had been dipped from the
pool of landless and partly landed laborers who constituted the
rural poor, and from the class of rural artisans who entered the
fields for a summer's work in open air. By 1860 the old pattern
of labor supply had begun to break down. Throughout much of
northern and western France the traditional rural textile industry, depending on locally produced supplies, was being destroyed,
and with it the source of support for a numerous class of summer
workers.[57] It seems to have remained strong in the Vosges and
in the industrial districts west of Lyon, but on the whole rural
industry no longer seems to have supplied great numbers of
workers to the summer fields.[58] The second source of labor—that
of small farmers—was more enduring, but the prosperity of the
period and rising wages seem to have enabled them to withdraw
their services from the market.

The employment of smallholders as a seasonal labor force can
be traced to medieval times, and had its roots in the techno-

[56] Labor requirements for a typical northern farm are given in the textbook by Louis Gossin, *L'Agriculture française, principes d'agriculture ap-
pliqués aux diverses parties de la France* (Paris, 1858), pp. 360–61. Those from
southern France can be found in the series *Agriculture française, Isère*, pp.
63–68; *Aude*, pp. 81–86, 89, 101; *Haute-Garonne*, pp. 47–55; *Tarn*, pp. 75–80;
and Leclerc-Thouin, *L'Agriculture de l'Ouest*, pp. 95–96. More permanent
employees were required per hectare in southern and western France because
plowing was carried out with oxen and cows instead of horses, as in the
northeastern regions.

[57] See Claude Fohlen, *L'Industrie textile au temps du second empire*
(Paris, 1956), pp. 161–249.

[58] See *1866 Enquête*, Vol. 26, Vôsges, 33; Vol. 27, Rhône, 148; Vol. 17,
Loire, 78–79; Vol. 2, Orne, 425–26; and the *Enquête sur les salaires agricoles*.

logical requirements of large-scale cereal farming.[59] Traces of earlier institutions could still be seen in the exchange of carting and plowing services by larger farmers for the harvest and haying labor of small ones. The exchange in some areas was in fact almost as asymmetric as it had been in ancient days, the plowing and carting costing more in labor than a hired team, if one were available. By the 1860s the cooperative purchase and maintenance of draft teams by several small farmers had broken down these patterns, but they were still common throughout a great arc of northern France stretching from Brittany to the Vosges, and constituted a means by which large farmers secured their labor.[60] Another method was to give or lease out small plots to workers to induce them to stay, on condition that they render labor services on demand. In the 1866 enquiry many witnesses attested to the value of small holdings as a means of retaining labor. "The smallholder, not being able to live by cultivating his own land, is much disposed to supplement his resources by working for wages." "The worker who is also proprietor cannot live on his possession without hiring himself out to his neighbors." In many other regions the smallholder was extolled for his willingness to work and his reluctance to emigrate. A land of many small farms, therefore, was frequently one of *grande culture*. Large and small farms coexisted and complemented each other.[61]

In this slight sketch of the relations between large and small farmers we find economic elements of a village structure that

[59] See, for example, the regulations published in Warren O. Ault, "Open-field Husbandry and the Village Community: A Study of Agrarian By-laws in Medieval England," *Transactions of the American Philosophical Society,* n.s. Vol. 55, part 7 (1965).

[60] The 1866 enquiry for the Breton department of Ille-et-Vilaine noted that "The farmers who are not able to maintain a team of draft animals are obliged to reimburse the large farmers in day labor for their plowing and carting services. As a result, they often become the customary workers of these farmers and they lose more from their day labor off their farms than what it would cost them to hire a team for money" (*1866 Enquête*, Vol. 2, Ille-et-Vilaine, 113). See also Vol. 3, Morbihan, 235; Vol. 1, Manche, 12; Vol. 26, Vosges, 264, 266; Leclerc-Thouin, *L'Agriculture de l'Ouest*, pp. 109–110.

[61] See *1866 Enquête*, Vol. 17, Hautes-Pyrénées, 363; Vol. 24, Var, 530. See also Vol. 12, Ardennes, 277; Vol. 26, Meurthe-et-Moselle, 530; Vosges, p. 32. The practice of leasing land to laborers at artificially low rents in exchange for their rendering services on demand is described by Vaury, *Etudes d'économie rurale*, p. 71; and *Agriculture française, Côtes-du-Nord*, pp. 47–48; *Tarn*, p. 105; and *Nord*, p. 30.

could be reproduced throughout rural France in the nineteenth century. At the top of the agricultural ladder were the great nobles, and, more frequently, the village *notables,* squires, notaries, and doctors, holding tracts of land that gave them political importance, and whose rents gave them leisure to undertake local administration. Below them were the large peasants, who might hire workers to help them farm. Lower still were self-sufficient peasants and part-time workers. The bottom of the social scale was occupied by the landless poor.

This world, lovingly described in Roger Thabault's biography of his village, began to break down after 1850 with the improvements in transportation, the spread of education, and the growth in opportunities for work outside agriculture. Higher wages and the spread of education among the lower classes did much to reduce the social gap between the *notables* and the workers, who became more independent in their politics, and, in the words of one disgruntled farmer from Poitou, *américain* in their labor relations.[62] Wages increased nearly thirty percent between 1852 and 1862 and ten to fifteen percent over the next twenty years, the latter of which had falling grain prices. For France as a whole, the summer wage seems to have risen even more rapidly than winter wages—a sign of growing shortages at harvest time and haying. These changes hit large farmers more severely than small, as they were unable to cut rising costs by substituting machines for labor. Peasants, for reasons discussed above, were able to hold down the rise in their labor costs by drawing on family labor. It was in this period that the advantage of a family organization made itself felt on the structure of farm sizes. Family farms became relatively more profitable than capitalist ones.

There were regional variations in the size of this gap. It is likely that the relatively swift demise of large farming in southern France was due to the higher labor intensity of production in a land of weak plows and tough soils. Here, where the substitution of capital for labor was especially difficult because of the scarcity of fodder and the high cost of maintaining draft animals, the rise in the cost of labor must have greatly reduced the viability of large-scale farms. In the northeastern region of three-field

---

[62] *1866 Enquête,* Vol. 10, Vienne, 80. The same report notes the "diminution of the authority of the master over his servant" (p. 665).

farming, less labor had always been needed, and the effect of rising wages on costs was less severe.

The Response to Rising Wages

Workers responded to rising wages in a variety of ways. Men withdrew their wives and children from the fields as their incomes rose enough to support a family.[63] Work became less intense, "either through indolence or from the loss of time spent in an augmented number of meal breaks."[64] Some reports suggest that the working day had fallen by two hours by the mid-1860s.[65] Against this decline in the quantity of work supplied must be placed the improvement in the stamina and intelligence of workers in areas that had long been poor, notably in Brittany and the Massif Central.[66]

The most important response, however, worked itself out only over a longer period: rising wages and incomes permitted workers to save more. Already in the 1840s a careful observer of peasant life in Maine had remarked that hired hands were lending money to their employers, so great was their propensity to save.[67] By 1852 potential savings rates among single laborers were of the order of fifteen to thirty percent of income, if estimates of income and expenditure on consumption published in the census of that year can be believed (see Table 8–9). These savings provide the final link between land and the labor market, for they financed the redistribution of the land.

Savings were crucial to the evolution of peasant farming because there were no large alternative sources of finance available

---

[63] The presence of an income effect can be inferred from the responses to the question "how has the amount of labor supplied by workers changed in recent years?" prepared by the 1866 Enquête. In nearly all departments respondents noted a decline in the amount of labor supplied per worker, and also the withdrawal of women and children from the fields. "The men earn enough to be able alone to feed the whole family (Vol. 6, Seine-et-Marne, p. 587). See also Vol. 9, Aube, 156, Allier, p. 206; Vol. 7, Indre-et-Loire, 28; Vol. 17, Basses-Pyrénées, 135; Vol. 16, Gironde, 349, 445; Vol. 19, Aveyron, 213; Vol. 18, Tarn-et-Garonne, 100; and Vol. 24, Var, 405.

[64] *1866 Enquête*, Vol. 22, Gard, 360.

[65] *1866 Enquête*, Vol. 5, Nord, 165; Vol. 2, Orne, 32; Vol. 3, Côtes-du-Nord, 521.

[66] *1866 Enquête*, Vol. 14, Saône-et-Loire, 234; Vol. 27, Rhône, 150; Vol. 25, Isère, 263; Vol. 26, Vôsges, 262, Haute-Saône, p. 417; Vol. 7, Loire-Inférieure, 632, Indre-et-Loire, p. 28; Vol. 22, Gard, 302–303.

[67] Leclerc-Thouin, *L'Agriculture de l'Ouest*, p. 106.

Table 8–9. Potential Savings Rates for Single Workers, 1852

	Low Estimate	High Estimate
Northeast	.14	.28
Normandy	.25	.32
Champagne	.03	.07
East	.06	.14
Brittany	.12	.19
West	.28	.32
Loire Plains	.28	.34
Massif Central	.16	.25
Southwest[a]	.16	.25
Southeast[b]	.12	.19

[a] Excluding Basses-Pyrénées, Hautes-Pyrénées, Ariège.
[b] Excluding Pyrénées-Orientales.
Source: Savings estimated by subtracting estimated consumption from annual earnings. In column 1, annual earnings are calculated from daily wages and number of working days in the year. In column 2, income has been adjusted for summer wages, assuming fifty days of summer labor. Income from non-agricultural employment is not included. Basic data from *Statistique agricole, 1852*.

to the rural working class. Loans could be arranged, but interest rates ranged from ten to twenty percent per year, in contrast to the three to five percent rate of return earned on investments in land.[68] The lack of credit had always been a problem in rural France, owing to the high cost of handling small loans and the many legal and political difficulties of expropriating land when debtors defaulted. Well into the nineteenth century, agricultural credit was limited mainly to short-term and self-liquidating loans to finance cattle fattening and the movement of products to markets.[69] The demand for an organized credit system was also lacking in rural areas. Leclerc-Thouin noted that "in the vulgar opinion of the countryside, to borrow except it be to acquire land is almost synonymous with bankruptcy."[70] To borrow was to admit failure to produce enough in the year to maintain the

[68] The rates of return to land are calculated from rents and land prices published in mid-nineteenth-century agricultural censuses. On the cost of rural credit, see Bertrand Gille, *La Banque et le crédit en France de 1815 à 1848* (Paris, 1959), p. 136. His estimates are consistent with those mentioned in the 1866 *Enquête*.

[69] Gille, *Banque et crédit*, pp. 127–38, and Guy Thuillier, *Aspects de l'économie nivernaise*, pp. 13–14, 26, 117–18.

[70] Leclerc-Thouin, *L'Agriculture de l'Ouest*, p. 94.

family, and it forced the peasant once more to open his affairs to the descendants of families that had collected tithes, rents, and other feudal charges in the Old Regime.[71]

The high cost of external funds and the imperfection of the rural credit market helps explain why peasant investments in land should have been so sensitive to changes in the cash flow. Because creditors did not lend and peasants did not wish to borrow to finance their acquisitions of land, the price of land did not always reflect the peasant demand or the capitalized value of the peasant rent—the difference in costs between family and hired labor. When wages rose workers and smallholders were able to make effective their demand for more land. It is this new source of income that explains in large part why the growth in peasant farming accelerated after 1850.

The rounding out of worker's plots and small holdings had a secondary impact on the agricultural labor supply. It can be easily predicted from the economic theory of occupational choice that as workers increased the size of their holdings, it would become profitable to shift their labor from the market to their own farms. The 1866 enquiry contains many complaints such as one from Indre, where "many workers, having become proprietors, no longer supply their services to those who used to employ them." In the Charentes it was the same. "The great division of property . . . has extended the field of work for small cultivators, who no longer supply their hands to the large and medium-sized farms." "It is only after having exhausted their strength in their own work that they go to work for others," explains the report for Tarn-et-Garonne. "It has resulted from this that the hands are scarcer and the work of the day laborers is less than before, although better paid." [72] Between 1862 and 1882 the number of workers classified as landholders dropped by 400,000. Many of these, perhaps most, made up the 300,000 new full-time farmers enumerated in the census of 1882. The movement finds a voice in the complaints of landowners about the loss of their laborers to small farming. "The medium-sized farm is in its final throes and will soon expire—that is, will

[71] These points are discussed in connection with modern peasants by Mendras, *The Vanishing Peasant*, pp. 82, 122.

[72] *1866 Enquête,* Vol. 15, Charente-Inférieure, 821; Vol. 18. Tarn-et-Garonne, 110. Similar remarks can be found in the reports of nearly every other department.

inevitably pass into the regime of small farming as a result of subdivisions. For large farming requires large families, and in a few years they will have entirely disappeared. Day laborers, both men and women, are no longer to be found, and the number of hired hands is also considerably diminished." [73] In Gascony, the respondents to the enquiry noted that while "The agricultural work force has not diminished, since there is more land in cultivation and it is more vigorously cultivated than it used to be, . . . the number of available rural laborers has fallen, and workers are lacking to those who still demand as many as in times past." [74] The problem of labor shortages for large farms seems to have been common to every part of France, and it is remarkable that the descriptions from the southwestern plains should be almost perfectly reproduced in the reports from Picardy and Artois. "Fundamentally, only the large and medium farms have any reason for complaint. Agriculture in general has had nothing to blame. Her hands have not been removed, but have been transferred to small farms, which require more labor and are more productive. The only change is that this displacement has forced the large and medium farmers to offer higher wages." [75]

The shift in the labor force from large farms to small thus had a marked effect on the profitability of the capitalistic sector. Not only did land acquisition reduce the amount of labor supplied from the peasant sector to the commercial sector, it also made this supply less elastic. As agricultural laborers derived a greater proportion of their income from their own land, increases in the wage rate could be expected to induce a decline in the supply of work offered to large farms through the strong income effect on the choice between work and leisure. Under these conditions, the small farm with its reserve of family labor found its advantage growing in relation to the farms that drew their labor from the market. One finds many reports—some of them cited above—of the inability of large farms to maintain themselves in the face of the labor drain into self-sufficient farming. [76]

[73] *1866 Enquête*, Vol. 18, Tarn-et-Garonne, 97.

[74] *1866 Enquête*, Vol. 18, Gers, 473.

[75] *1866 Enquête*, Vol. 5, Pas-de-Calais, 93.

[76] The sequence of events reported here may be represented by a two-sector economic model, in which one of the sectors possesses a more labor-

A process of redistribution then worked itself out in the competition between the large and small-farm sectors for land and labor. As workers purchased land they transferred their labor from large farms to small, which caused the wage rate to rise to the point where it equalled the marginal revenue produced by labor on large farms after the reallocation of land and labor. At the same time, the decline in the labor-land ratio on large farms lowered the rate of return to land and thus provoked some landlords to sell their land to peasants in small lots. The tendency for land to be redistributed in favor of the small farmers was thus reinforced by the process of redistribution itself. The process continued until the rise in commercial wage was sufficient to shut off the movement from one sector to another.

Conclusions

Redistribution of the land and increase in the class of self-sufficient peasants in France grew naturally out of technological changes and economic expansion in the second half of the nineteenth century. Given the long-standing peasant demand for land, the increase in peasant farming after 1850 was a logical consequence of the improvement in wages and incomes. The preservation and growth of the peasantry was aided by the fact that mechanical technology in the late nineteenth century did not yet give large farms the competitive advantage that would have enabled them to draw land away from the peasant sector. The changes in agricultural technology and organization in France thus seem to reflect the normal response of a peasant society to the pressures and opportunities created by economic growth.

Technological change was induced by rising market demand for food and by rising wages. Peasants and larger farmers did

---

intensive production function than the other. Under these conditions, shifting land from the more land-intensive to the more labor-intensive sector will result in (or be associated with) a rise in the wage-rental ratio in both sectors, assuming that there are diminishing returns to land and labor and constant returns to scale in both sectors. This arises from the fact that the transfer of land and labor out of the land-intensive sector is likely to raise the land-labor ratio in both sectors, because the proportion of land to labor reallocated, although less than the existing land-labor ratio in the "capitalist" sector, would be greater than that in the "peasant" sector. The result of this shift was to make large farming less profitable than before.

not resist innovation, but accepted them as they became profitable following changes in relative factor prices. Had the recently
settled lands of North America and Russia been less suited to
wheat farming, the growing world demand might have induced
a greater degree of mechanization in France, since the growth in
the export sector would probably have favored large farms over
small. As it was, the rate of change in French agriculture was
consistent with her rate of industrial growth, and was fast enough
to satisfy the demands for food and labor that were created by
growth in other sectors.

The period from 1850 to 1880 was one of profound change
for the French rural order. The traditional links between crop
rotations, common farming, and the allocation of land and labor
were decisively broken by rapid movements in the relative prices
of grains and livestock and the rise in the wage rate. The 1880s
saw a new equilibrium emerging in the countryside, in which
advances in mechanical technology in the commercialized sector
of large farms were balanced by the ease with which family labor
could be substituted for land and machines on small peasant
farms. The distribution of the labor force and the land among
farms grew out of the balancing of the advantages of these two
forms of organization. It was, however, a transitory resting
place. Advances in mechanical and chemical technology in the
first half of the twentieth century were to wipe out the advantages
that intensive manual cultivation had held over cultivation by
plow and harrow, while the bonds of family that had encouraged
the use of such labor-intensive techniques on peasant farms
weakened under the strains of rising incomes and the pull of a
superior standard of living in the towns.

Afterword

ERIC L. JONES

I think biology furnishes the necessary background against which
social studies must be built. And we must take care that these
various fields of inquiry do not really develop as separate worlds,
with communication among them increasingly difficult. We need
to remember that all human knowledge is continuous, and that
no part can successfully be cultivated for long as a thing-in-itself.
This, at least, is my belief; and written out, I hope that it will
serve me as a naturalist, by way of a passport for travel into the
territories of the historians, the anthropologists and the economists.
Marston Bates, *Where Winter Never Comes*

The Concerns of Agrarian History

Scholars have perhaps two main purposes in studying the agrarian
past. One is to recover the record of the techniques and organization of farming and the evolution of the social and physical environment of rural life. The other is to explain the pattern and
pace of change in these things, and to examine the relation between them and change in the economy at large. To the extent
that the tasks may be pursued separately, an historian may be
tempted to concentrate on the former and an economist on the
latter. Both parts of the program are extremely intricate, particularly if the record is to be unearthed at the depth of detail
that many local studies now reach, and if explanations that can
bear the burden of that detail are to be put forward. The
thoroughness in research and the intellectual adroitness needed
to fit the two approaches together, indeed to prevent them flying
asunder, are obviously formidable requirements. Nevertheless,
progress has been made in recent years. Our knowledge of past
agrarian environments and farming methods is wider and more
exact than could readily have been anticipated twenty years ago.
The standards of factual delving into European agrarian history

are at their best very high.[1] Our understanding of the social and economic processes at work in those environments has likewise been enriched. And now the new breed of scholars represented by the authors of the essays in this volume is turning its attention to the subject: scholars trained as economic historians within North American departments of economics. While they often come to economic history with little formal training in archival work and little initial familiarity with the topography of Europe, their more rigorous training in the methods of economics may enable them to offer exciting solutions to old historical puzzles. In short, they can see the wood for the trees. While there may be some criticisms about their free American hand with the tracery of the branches, my own view, as someone brought up to admire the foliage and underbrush of English agricultural history, is that not only does their eye for essentials more than compensate, but that the contributors to this volume have in fact descried a great deal of detail.

Many of the interpretations by scholars of this type must nevertheless rely for orientation—and often substance—on published sources. There may be Europeans who will secretly feel that the Americans are "free riders" on European scholarship. Good relations have not been encouraged by the missionary tone of the first "new economic historians" to address European audiences. This will die down as Europeans become familiar with the methodology of cliometrics, as cliometrics itself is supplemented by largely American initiatives at reintroducing the systematic study of institutions into economic history, and as it becomes evident that young American economists can be scholarly as well as scientific in their approach to history.

An issue of more enduring substance, since published sources are going to be reworked by the Americans, is the representativeness of the existing secondary literature. In many respects it is still patchy. At this stage there is an evident demand for survey articles in English codifying material on topics in European agrarian history that possess only an antiquated, exiguous, or inaccessible literature. Writing good survey articles is hard work, like that of the bibliographer, "a horrible drudgery that no mere drudge could perform."[2] Yet only inspired searches of the more

---

[1] A single illustration should suffice: see the voluminous and detailed contributions to *A. A. G. Bijdragen* (Wageningen, continuing).

[2] Elliot Coues, quoted in Peter Matthiessen, *Wildlife in America* (New York, 1959), p. 289.

recondite literature can pull together the fragments of knowledge about significant but unfashionable aspects of the agrarian past, and so open up the possibility of spotting unsuspected relationships.

If these surveys do open up new lines of work, who will pursue them? One might expect that young scholars will move into new fields as they observe the onset of diminishing marginal returns in well-worked areas. But opening up new territory means high start-up costs, and exploration entails high risks. A fanning-out of research effort seems, moreover, to be slowed by the factory organization of scholarship. Quite obviously there exist Ph.D. programs in which dissertation topics are chosen, or assigned, in follow-the-leader fashion, and vested interests ensure that the work of a young man who attends to minor extensions of the literature—"normal science" in Thomas Kuhn's phrase—may well receive disproportionate notice. Ventures into unfashionable areas have to chance being dismissed as mere "fishing expeditions," less purposeful as well as less rewarding than the retesting of standard hypotheses about familiar topics. Such extreme intellectual risk-aversion makes for a dull world. The history of scientific research suggests that in scholarship as in prospecting, rich seams may be struck by those who are bold enough to cast about in zones to which they have been guided by intuition or chance.

Along with the pressures towards scholarly conformity that a network of journal editors, referees, thesis supervisors, and the awarders of grants can unconsciously generate, there clearly exists the danger today that the agrarian past will be presented anachronistically. By background, training, and even inclination, students of economic history have become less familiar than ever with rural life, the pace of farming routines, the old primitive techniques and empirical character of decision-making in agriculture, and its complex biological linkages and constraints. Few Anglo-American students nowadays can have much firsthand sense of the customs in a communal village, or feel for hand-tool technologies. The peasant past, its concern for daily detail, its perpetual hand-to-hand combat with a sly and brutal world of nature, is nearly impossible to recover in the western world, especially within close reach of the city dweller. Yet when reconstruction is carried out with the tools of economic analysis and a sensitivity to the constraints of the physical and biological world, the results are illuminating.[3] We should be heartened about the prospects for such a symbiosis, though watchful against both scholarly conformity and agricultural anachronism.

Anachronism may derive from treating the past as the ancestor of the present, as the child is father to the man. The temptation to do this is strong where the students are trained in the social sciences, with their present-mindedness and proclivity for abstracting with little respect for time, and with the focus of economists on generalizing the process of growth. The temptation should be resisted, for no former economic system was a miniaturized version of the modern economy; each was, in terms of the present, a misshapen dwarf. A past economy cannot be fully understood, for it is not being correctly described, by reference only to those embryonic limbs that have since grown large. Other features, long shrivelled, must be recognized and made the objects of study. What follows in this Afterword is a personal view of some current and future problems of the agrarian past that deserve attention, with a string of queries about them, and a sprinkling of introductory references. Three sections shadow some of the main concerns of the essays in this book, and three take up neglected biological aspects of the agricultural economy during historical periods.

Spatial divisions and differences

Does western Europe form a distinctive unit of study for the economic historian? The significant questions here are, did a region which can be identified as "western Europe" become agriculturally differentiated from the remainder of Europe, and if so at what period, and what relation did the causes bear to the forces that by early modern times effectively placed northwestern European economies ahead of the rest of the world? What were the connections between subsequent agricultural change there and economic advance, particularly industrialization? These matters ought to engage the development economist as well as the historian. Professor George Dalton has recently urged economic anthropologists who are concerned with modernization in

---

[3] An excellent example is Paul David, "The Landscape and the Machine: Technical Inter-relatedness, Land Tenure and the Mechanization of the Corn Harvest in Victorian Britain" in Donald N. McCloskey, *Essays on a Mature Economy: Britain after 1840* (London, 1971).

the "third world" to look for parallels in the extensive literature on early medieval Europe.[1] This intellectual catholicity, long discouraged, is in my view likely to prove fruitful and, in fact, irresistible.

There are formal climatic and biological answers as to what constitutes western Europe, but no clear definition of the region in terms of the agricultural systems of given periods. At least two views of the dating of the crucial agricultural advances in Europe north of the Alps have some currency. One is that expressed by Professor Lynn White: "The prime event in Europe's history during the Middle Ages was the development, between the sixth and the late eighth centuries, of a novel system of agriculture appropriate to the northern lands."[5] A second view, not necessarily incompatible with the first, though often presented in isolation, is that parts of northwestern Europe, notably the Low Countries, drew ahead of formerly more advanced areas such as Lombardy during the fourteenth or fifteenth century.[6] How much of the change at either period was in methods of cultivation and cropping, and how much was in the *organization* of farming? Put another way, to what extent did institutional changes encourage technical changes of a productivity-raising kind, and to what extent did institutional arrangements for farming the land or sharing the produce adapt to independent or semi-independent changes in technology? These questions haunt us throughout history. With the renewed emphasis by economists on the primacy of institutional change, reflected in this volume by the contributions on the open fields and enclosure, it is becoming almost necessary to insist on the parallel importance of examining technical change.

Neither national agricultures nor regional agricultures within nation states developed at all evenly. There is a flavour of new wine in old bottles about the achievement of the agricultural sector in the growing regions of Europe, and the discrepancies in the rate of development offer an obvious field for comparative

[1] See especially George Dalton, "Peasantries in Anthropology and History," *Current Anthropology* 13 (1972), 385–415.

[5] In *The Fontana Economic History of Europe: The Middle Ages*, edited by Carlo M. Cipolla (London, 1972), p. 146.

[6] On developments in Flanders, see A. Verhulst, "Sources and Problems of Flemish Agrarian History in the Later Middle Ages," in *Ceres en Clio, Zeven Variaties op het Thema Landbouwgeschiedenis*, Agronomisch-Historisch Bijdragen, Zesde Deel (Wageningen, 1964), pp. 205–35.

studies. One of the larger issues is the backwardness of farming
under the *Ancien Régime* in France contrasted with that of the
Low Countries or England. Why did productive investment
look so specially attractive to the English and so unappealing to
the French?[7] The French preferences for holding assets in a
liquid form and for conspicuous consumption were surely parts
of a widespread syndrome of "underdevelopment,"[8] and while
the French were probably extreme in western Europe in these
respects, it is the oddity of English landed investment that really
calls for explanation. English landowners were peculiarly closely
concerned with productive techniques; for example, they encouraged major developments in livestock breeding as a spinoff
from their interest in breeding sporting animals.[9] Yet other
European landed aristocracies were interested in breeding horses
and dogs—there are more ancient bloodlines in French packs
of hounds than in English packs[10]—without an equivalent
transfer of economically influential techniques to farm animals.
French landowners drained capital away for conspicuous consumption in Paris and at Versailles: France was absolutist while
England was parliamentary, and the social obligations for heavy
expenditure at the center of affairs, away from their estates, were
more oppressive on the French. But why did a desire for cash
not spur more French landowners to positive attempts at estate
improvements with the aim of increasing their rent rolls?[11] Why
did so many of them farm out their rights to bourgeois agents in
the "feudal reaction" of the second half of the eighteenth century, causing the meticulous collection of some old dues and the
ingenious revival of others; why did so very few French landowners try to raise their income by positive means—by adopting
the English farming measures advocated by the Physiocrats?

   At least two strands of explanation do come to mind and invite further inquiry. The first relates to the divergent political
history of France and England (and the Netherlands), in which
the more commercial economies saw political influence tip in-

[7] See Robert Forster, *The House of Saulx-Tavanes* (Baltimore, 1971).

[8] Cf. Nathan Rosenberg, "Capital Formation in Underdeveloped Countries,"
American Economic Review 50 (1960), 706–15.

[9] Peter Mathias, *The First Industrial Nation* (New York, 1969), pp. 79–80.

[10] Sacheverell Sitwell, *The Hunters and the Hunted* (New York, 1948),
p. 73.

[11] See Robert Forster, "Obstacles to Agricultural Growth in Eighteenth-
Century France," *American Historical Review* 75 (1970), 1613.

creasingly into the hands of forward-looking interests, leaving France relatively behind. It may therefore be necessary to consider the political matrix more explicitly than economic historians have latterly done when trying to account for differences in investment behavior and the diffusion of agricultural technologies. Second, perhaps the simple underlying fact is that the *market did not encourage productive investment in French agriculture*, or, since there was in fact a growth in output, not to nearly the same extent as in England. London and some industrial conglomerations grew rather rapidly, but Paris grew very slowly, and movements of foodstuffs in France were also impeded by internal customs barriers and barriers of custom that had dissolved in England. Hence, perhaps, the vigour of the search for substantial and energetic tenants on English landed estates, for men to pay good but fixed cash rents for their farms, and the lethargy in France, the acceptance of men to be penalized and pay dues.

In late medieval and early modern times, when overland transportation costs were very high, pockets of land around many European towns became intensively cultivated in response to the local concentration of demand.[12] In the Low Countries there were enough cloth-working towns closely spaced for whole provinces to become agriculturally developed, and knowledge about intensive methods of farming and about wetland reclamation was diffused from there to far-flung parts of Europe.[13] England imported techniques from the Low Countries in the sixteenth and seventeenth centuries,[14] and translated the specialist Flemish and Brabanter production of animal feed into the lynch-pin of mixed cereal and livestock rotations. The reverse flow of agricultural knowledge in the eighteenth and nineteenth centuries, when English practices were discussed and adopted in continental Europe,[15] deserves a more systematic inventory than

[12] See B. H. Slicher van Bath, "The Rise of Intensive Husbandry in the Low Countries," in J. S. Bromley and E. H. Kossman, eds., *Britain and the Netherlands* (London, 1960), pp. 130–53.

[13] For drainage schemes carried out across Europe by Dutchmen, see C. T. Smith, *An Historical Geography of Western Europe before 1800* (London, 1967), figure 9:7.

[14] G. E. Fussell, "Low Countries' Influence on English Farming," *English Historical Review* 74 (1959), 611–22.

[15] See, for example, A. J. Bourde, *The Influence on England on the French Agronomes, 1750–1789* (London, 1953); H. H. Müller, "Christopher Brown—an English Farmer in Brandenberg-Prussia in the Eighteenth-

it has had, together with an appraisal of the demand for productivity-raising improvements. Clearly, effective demand was unevenly distributed, and we are brought back to the need to explain those differences between regions that are noted in local studies. Existing generalizations about the nature and timing of agricultural change tend to rest on a handful of much-studied areas within each country. A considerable opportunity exists to advance our understanding of the processes of development by collating local studies, and by starting research on neglected regions to encourage a more balanced synthesis. The narrow base of our case studies at present may be inducing tunnel vision. In the British case, for instance, cropping changes that had come in slowly, experimentally, and piecemeal in southern England were later lifted bodily to less-developed parts of Scotland, and introduced as integrated systems within much shorter periods. It is difficult to conceptualize how this diversity of regional experience may be weighted in the framework of national or western European history, but the effort needs to be made and the time for making it is propitious.

Enclosures

Another central topic that is already starting to receive attention from historically-minded economists is enclosure. This has always received a large slice of all scholarly interest in English agrarian history, but mostly by historians who have been vastly more concerned with effects on equity than with effects on productivity.[16] It is probably fair to say that many of the studies have been purely descriptive and local, but that recent work runs the risk of over-generalizing, of being too insensitive to the variety of enclosures in such an intricate landscape. Without doubt, too much work deals exclusively with the last phase of the movement, enclosure by act of Parliament, which offers the convenience of good documentation, and somewhat spuriously makes enclosure march in time with the "Industrial Revolution."

Century," *Agricultural History Review* 17 (1967), 120–35; and the useful contemporary summary in *Encyclopaedia Britannica* 1, 3d ed. (Edinburgh, 1797), 248–49.

[16] J. G. Brewer, *Enclosures and the Open Fields: A Bibliography,* published by The British Agricultural History Society ([Reading], 1972), is the latest list, which should, however, be supplemented by other sources.

This bias ought not to go on distracting attention from earlier enclosure by agreement. Only if that is studied in detail can it be discovered why the legal vehicle was changed, and with what effect on the total rate of enclosure. Perhaps it would be instructive to look on the one hand at the special circumstances surrounding the handful of Parliamentary enclosures undertaken before 1760, and on the other at the circumstances that kept a tiny number of communal systems in being into the twentieth century. These categories may be regarded to some extent as limiting cases of enclosure.

Inhabitants of a parish who felt their livelihood threatened by an enclosure that a local notable or powerful lobby was promoting had two modes of recourse: "exit" or "voice," market or nonmarket responses.[17] They could abandon independent farming, possibly quitting agriculture altogether, or they could try to resist the enclosure by political means, perhaps by raising a common purse to finance a defense in the courts, perhaps by raising a riot that might, just might, bring the central authorities to their aid against the local gentry. Popular resistance to enclosure was not uncommon in the Tudor and early Stuart period, with hedges torn down and fences thrown open. Less dramatic combinations to offer resistance by legal means were apparently much less common—inarticulate rage was easier to whip up than articulate protest—but more cases may turn up in the records. As late as the period of parliamentary enclosure, legal opposition was sometimes offered and riots did still take place, but the distinct impression is that resistance of all kinds had faded away in comparison with Tudor times.[18]

What were the factors influencing the choice between market and nonmarket responses to enclosures, and which were responsible for the change in proportions over time? Higher legal expenses may have dissuaded villagers from putting their case to the courts. Rioting ceased to attract the sympathy of the authorities as threats of major famines became remote and as the central government came, after 1660 and especially after 1688, to reflect

[17] The terminology is that of A. O. Hirschman, *Exit, Voice and Loyalty: Responses to Decline in Firms, Organizations, and States* (Cambridge, Mass., 1970).

[18] See W. E. Tate, "Parliamentary Counter-Petitions during the Enclosures of the Eighteenth and Nineteenth Centuries," *English Historical Review* 59 (1944), 392–403, and "Opposition to Parliamentary Enclosure in Eighteenth-Century England," *Agricultural History* 19 (1945), 137–42.

landowner opinion more strongly. But the diminution of opposition to enclosure may also have been in part the result of a
shift in attitudes in favor of market solutions. By the late eighteenth century, when acts of parliament had become the normal
means of enclosing, economic expansion meant that more employment options were open to a displaced small farmer or a
commoner who had lost his rights. There was more chance of
earning cash wages in an increasingly commercialized agriculture
or in the widening range of nonfarming occupations. The economy was producing more manufactured goods that could only
be obtained for cash, and preferences for cash over leisure may
accordingly have increased.

If, in any event, political protest, or "voice," failed, some of
the opponents of enclosure would probably be obliged to "exit,"
to leave the business of farming, and others might follow should
their share of enclosure costs prove too onerous and the closes
allotted to them appear too small to support a family. Small-
holders might sell their land and leave, depriving the village
community of leadership. In the more developed market economy of the late eighteenth century, greater opportunities than
ever before presented themselves to the more articulate villagers
with some small capital. They could more freely choose "exit."
Thus the widening of economic opportunity may itself have
been important in easing the way for parliamentary enclosure,
and our sights should not be set so fixedly on the economic
changes that parliamentary enclosures themselves induced. There
was a more involved process of economic change in which growth
built growth.

The role of enclosure in agricultural change, and hence in
economic growth as a whole, is easy to exaggerate. For example,
its significance may be overplayed in assessing trends in the
formation of farm capital. Many farm buildings in England are
very old, and even modern farmsteads not infrequently en-
capsulate structures that are centuries older. Until we obtain
more architectural dating information, we hardly know what
periodicity of capital investment has to be explained.[19] With
parliamentary enclosure a lag of a few years tended to occur be-

[19] But see R. B. Wood-Jones, *Traditional Domestic Architecture of the
Banbury Region* (Manchester, 1963); Nigel Harvey, *A History of Farm
Buildings in England and Wales* (Newton Abbot, 1970); and J. E. C. Peters,
*The Development of Farm Buildings in Western Lowland Staffordshire up
to 1880* (Manchester, 1970).

tween the act and the award, drawing out as more complicated parishes were dealt with. Only after the award could land remodelling and new building properly begin. With nonparliamentary processes of enclosure it would be surprising if expenditures on land improvement followed as quickly. With parliamentary enclosure, the date of the award often seems to mark the start of investment in fences, accommodation, roads, and other items of farm layout, but there is no real evidence that new farm building followed within a standard interval. The awards were in this respect nothing but enabling legislation. Neither may we assume that the length of lag between enclosure, by any process, and investment in land improvement is a simple function of the degree of difficulty experienced in rearranging open-field strips into compact, ring-fenced parcels. What, for example, are we to make of the case of a Midlands parish which was legally enclosed in Elizabethan times but did not acquire most of its roads, fences, or hedges until the nineteenth century?[20] In that parish, right into the nineteenth century, visits to all but the nearest neighbours had to be put off from October to April because the weather made the ways impassable to the lightest vehicles. The rights-of-way that had been laid out at the time of the Elizabethan enclosure were not actually sealed into hard roads until the second half of the nineteenth century, and the subdivision into the 150 fields of Victorian times (rather than the 18 large enclosures and 16 small crofts of the Elizabethan surveyors) also came late. Perhaps, like so many in the Midlands, the original enclosure had been for sheep farming. The investment that converted virtual ranches into the mixed arable farms recognizable today was deferred for three centuries. If there were many cases like this it hardly seems that the chronology of capital investment in agriculture may be read off from the record of enclosure, and definitely not of parliamentary enclosure alone. The seductive appeal of numerical data from the last, parliamentary, phase of enclosure should not so captivate scholars that the inherent gradualness of economic change in England is slighted.

Rural Domestic Industry

Mixed occupations characterize imperfectly developed economies, such as those of western Europe until the nineteenth century.

[20] Albert Pell, "The Making of the Land in England: a Retrospect," *Journal of the Royal Agricultural Society of England,* 2d ser. 23 (1887), 362.

In such circumstances to distinguish an "agricultural sector," as though a section of the population and only that section operated exclusively within it, is a matter of the loosest convenience. The uses of agriculture's products also differed from those of later years. Farming supplied the raw materials for a number of industries that are not now supplied directly from the land, and for other trades which, though once important, have shrunk relatively and absolutely. The agriculturists of many districts engaged in by-employments, producing small manufactures as well as the products of their farms. These rural domestic industries formed a large part of the total "manufacturing sector," which was, hence, not distinct. Agriculture itself was supplied and served by crafts, and its products were processed by industries, which together accounted for another large fraction of all manufacturing activity. The rural domestic industries have recently attracted a good deal of scholarly interest that has rescued them from undeserved obscurity.[21] The servicing and processing industries have not yet attracted comparable attention, for all their evident size, complexity, and economic significance. They do not seem to have been passive companions of agriculture, but to have been instrumental in the early emergence of metal-working and the manufacture of machinery: grain millers were major customers for the makers of steam engines, farm implements and machines were almost a joint product with railroad equipment in nineteenth-century foundries, while Denmark virtually based her industrialization on the demand for cream separators and dairy-farm equipment.

The current interest in rural domestic industry promises to bring about a fruitful union of industrial and agricultural studies, with further hybrid vigor introduced by cross-mating with demography. The frequently rigid separation between studies of farming and industry can hardly outlast the recognition that so very much manufacturing, well into the "Industrial Revolution," was the resort of cottagers who were making use of odd hours and seasons when they could not profitably work on

---

[21] See Charles Tilly and Richard Tilly, "Emerging Problems in the Modern Economic History of Western Europe" (1971, mimeographed), summarized as "An Agenda for European Economic History in the 1970's," *Journal of Economic History* 31 (1971), 184–98, and Franklin F. Mendels, "Protoindustrialization: The First Phase of the Industrialization Process," *Journal of Economic History* 32 (1972), 241–61.

the land. The lingering notion of a late and abrupt "take-off" into sustained economic growth can hardly survive recognition of how widespread rural industry was and how long and gradually it grew. And the stature of some of the English heroes of cotton-spinning, iron-puddling, and pot-throwing in the late eighteenth century is bound to diminish as industrialization is recognized as a broad and prolonged, not a once-over, process.[22]

Can the rise or intensification of diverse rural domestic industries in a number of countries be accounted for in a general model? [23] The answer seems to be in the affirmative, bearing in mind, however, that the problem is more an interregional than an international one. Western Europe, as well as parts of central Europe and Scandinavia, appears to have been bifurcated into "good" arable plains and smaller regions of pastoralism, where peasants increasingly added rural domestic manufacturing for the market to their economic activities. The production possibilities of these two topographical categories were different. Within the pastoral zones some sections of the lowlands of several countries, infertile sandlands, and heavy clays stand out as places where the countryside thickened with cottage industry, and so, at the other topographical extreme, do many highland districts.[24]

The phenomenon was evident in lowlands from the infertile sands of the Veluwve in the Netherlands to the eastern fringe of the Jutland Heaths in Denmark, and on intractable clays in parts of the Midland plain of England. These lowland areas tended to be, or to become, pastoral, and in hindsight the suitability of the associated routines and skills of, say, dairying for meshing with home textile production seems providential. Perhaps the special advantages should, however, be alluded to lightly. The absolute advantage for rural manufacturing may still have resided in the fertile, arable plains, which nevertheless stressed grain-growing

[22] Closer study of these industries has already deemphasized the role of some hero figures. An interesting example is Lorna Weatherill, *The Pottery Trade and North Staffordshire 1660–1760* (Manchester, 1970).

[23] E. L. Jones, "Agricultural Origins of Industry," *Past and Present* 40 (1968), 58–71, and "Le origini agricole dell' industria," *Studi Storici* 9 (1968), 564–93.

[24] E. L. Jones, "Economic Options in Highland Europe," paper presented to Council of European Studies Conference, M.I.T., September 1971. The role of the highlands in European industrial development was discussed by Max Barkhausen, "Government Control and Free Enterprise in Western Germany and the Low Countries in the Eighteenth Century," in Peter Earle, ed., *Essays in European Economic History* (Oxford, 1974), p. 263.

because that was where their comparative advantage lay. The comparative advantage of infertile districts, highland as well as lowland, lay in rural domestic industry. As to why the population did not migrate to the better agricultural areas, the answer seems to be in general terms that the most desirable land had been early settled and remained most heavily manorialized, so that further entry became difficult. Indeed the movement of population was likely to be towards marginal farmland, where squatters could settle on the waste with little fear that manorial lords would eject them. Population did, certainly, move from all rural areas to the cities over the centuries, but before industrialization proper, cities were mostly trading and administrative centers that could not cushion whole societies against the pressure of population on resources. In any case, the farm occupier or cottager even on poor land would not easily quit his holding, because this represented not only his "farm business" but his homestead. The competitive pressures on him were more subtle, and he initially took up cottage industry to supplement rather than completely to replace his income from agriculture.

Highland districts had often experienced sharp outbreaks of socio-economic disorder during the rise of population in the late sixteenth and early seventeenth centuries. They were deeply scarred by banditry, peasant revolts, and witchcrazes; they sent out streams of mercenaries and temporary migrants, such as harvesters, domestic servants, and building workers, to make a living elsewhere; and still they suffered worse food shortages than the plains. Rural domestic industrialization proved one way of offsetting the fundamental problem that their populations pressed hard against local supplies of arable land or other resources.[25] In Germany, for example, medieval colonization in the Erzgebirge, the Thuringian forest, and the Frankenwald led to a depletion of mineral resources. Farmland was scarce and the population had to turn to the domestic manufacturing of woolens, toys, musical instruments, and nowadays precision instruments to make a living. The pattern does differ in part from the English emergence of industrial towns out of clustered manufacturing villages on the coalfields, with industry in Germany

[25] A recent study that stresses this point is Arnošt Klíma, "The Role of Rural Domestic Industry in Bohemia in the Eighteenth Century," *Economic History Review* 2d ser. 27 (1974), 48–56.

often arising quickly in the old medieval trading towns, which tended to be at route centers in the good arable areas that could support urban growth. Nevertheless, the Ruhrgebiet is a prime example of the transition from rural domestic to coalfield industrialization, and the uplands of Germany are more densely populated than agriculture alone could account for.[26] Cottage industry was usually rather easy to enter, and by encouraging earlier marriage than might have occurred in a farming community obliged to wait on the inheritance of land before marrying, may have revived the problem of population pressure that it affected to solve.

Readers of Michael Crichton's novel, *The Andromeda Strain*, will recall that the problem teasing the physician is the link between the two unlikely bedfellows who alone survived an unidentified disease—a Sterno drinker of sixty-nine with an ulcer, and a baby of two months. The problem of the causes of rural domestic industrialization is analogous: what had extreme lowland and highland areas in common? The answer is that they could not fully feed their populations from internal agricultural resources. If, however, they could buy enough food with the earnings from cottage industry, the implication must be that some other regions, not necessarily within the same country, had become sufficiently productive to export food. The existence of interregional-cum-international exchanges of foodstuffs against the wares of cottage industry is, however, more easily inferred than documented.[27] It would be useful to have more hard evidence on this reciprocal trade and to know how far this, rather than rural-urban exchange (which can hardly have been a powerful motor of growth over much of the interior of northern continental Europe before the nineteenth century) was responsible for improvements in communications and the expansion of commerce. In practice, the interdependence between types of region, arable plains and areas of rural domestic industry, lowland and highland, must have been considerable, and the benefits of trade

[26] R. J. Harrison Church, *et al.*, *An Advanced Geography of Northern and Western Europe* (London, 1967), pp. 167–70.

[27] There is one source that shows that the trade in foodstuffs was extensive as early as the 1580s in central Europe, and that the fertile plains even then were specializing in different crops: Josef Petran, "A Propos de la formation des régions de la production specialisée en Europe centrale," *Contributions*, Second International Conference of Economic History, Aix-en-Provence, 1962 (Paris, 1965), pp. 220–22.

were surely an important force in Europe's gradual economic advance. Some cottage manufacturing districts, perhaps part agricultural, became quite prosperous, though the more specialized and remote ones were taking the risk that the exchange value of their wares would not be high enough to override the occasional famine price of grain. Some suffered direly at times. Switzerland in the winter of 1816–1817 felt "the pressure of absolute famine," attributed to "an excessive population, for which sustenance cannot be found within its scanty territory." [28]

The transition from cottage industry to the factory system is another puzzle. The customary view is that total demand for manufactured goods was large and growing fast enough in late eighteenth-century England to elicit a technological breakthrough in textile production. The supply of rural spinners was exhausted, and putting-out merchants are thought to have drawn on the pool of mechanical talent in Lancashire and the surrounding area to devise and substitute water-powered spinning machines. Thereupon the inducement to mechanize was transferred to the weaving operation, where hand-loom operators could not process the new flow of cheap yarn. Rural textile production concentrated into factories that housed inanimately-powered machinery. Hand workers, their competitive edge eroded, were willing to shift their labor into the factories. In this best of all unbalanced growth sequences, rural domestic industrialization can be portrayed as an indispensable basis for the factory system.

The danger is of portraying it as a sufficient requirement. Understandably, it has hardly occurred to British (or European) scholars that there could have been too much industry, except in the sense that the welfare of a swollen body of hand-loom weavers was eventually undermined by competition from factories that could not absorb the domestic weavers fast enough for comfort. Yet many parts of the world had vast populations of cottage workers producing for the market (and extensive interregional trade) without spontaneously generating modern industry. Rural domestic industry seems to have been present in Britain and Europe within a range of capital-to-labor ratios suitable for growth. The relevant parameters and the peculiar nature of the organizational forms would repay analysis.

[28] *The Observer* (London), 27 April 1817.

This is not to imply that the shift from domestic industry to the factory was freely made in Britain or Europe. T. S. Ashton's study of the nailmaker, Peter Stubs, showed that it could be extremely difficult to induce skilled workers to leave their own homes to work together under one roof.[29] A framework knitter summed up the attractions of working on one's own frame, in one's own loft, at one's own speed, as, "then ye can take credit for a sound article and time for a nap." [30] On the continent of Europe the transition, when it came, may admittedly have been more a matter of necessity than inducement. Competition from British factory-made textiles and other goods was evident from the time of the Eden Treaty in 1786, and forced down the incomes of rural domestic workers in the nineteenth century, when many of them no longer had any foothold in farming. Industrialization became a "political imperative" if European governments were to avoid mass unemployment and disorder.[31]

In western Europe, with rural domestic manufacturing for the market widely distributed, a breakthrough to the factory in one industry in one region of one country—Britain was merely *primus inter pares*—could set up sufficient competition to force the introduction of the factory system in that industry in other countries. Emulation proved more attractive and successful than protective tariffs. The "follower" countries obviously shared powerful features—great responsiveness—or could offer efficient substitutes that the laggards or nonstarters lacked. Like England, western Germany and the Low Countries were coming close up against the limitations of hand-spinning and available water power during the eighteenth century, and were very ready to change over to machinery devised by the English.[32]

The limited distribution of sources of fuel and power prompted the shrinkage from sprawling cottage industry to factories. Mechanized production could grow only at water-power sites or near coal mines. Districts with rural domestic industries and a supply of both these resources tended to become centers of nineteenth-century industrialism. Districts with rural domestic

[29] T. S. Ashton, *An Eighteenth-Century Industrialist: Peter Stubs of Warrington 1756–1806* (Manchester, 1961).

[30] E. G. Nelson, "The English Framework-Knitting Industry," *Journal of Economic and Business History* 2 (1930), 494.

[31] David S. Landes, *The Unbound Prometheus* (Cambridge, 1969), p. 139.

[32] See Barkhausen, "Government Control and Free Enterprise," p. 266.

industry but neither source of power sank back into pastoral poverty, their cottage industries withered by outside competition. An area with fast hillside streams but no coal might negotiate the transition to factory industry based on water mills, only to succumb eventually to competition from steam-powered industry on a coalfield or at a railroad node.[33] Its excess labour would be obliged to migrate, seasonally, or temporarily, or forever. Next to nothing seems to be known about the effect of these regional retrogressions on the industrial economy of the nineteenth century, despite the fact that the outflows of people created sizeable minority groups in the cities. "When the labourers of Paris strike for higher wages, it is often the hunger for land in the Limousin Mountain that is the impelling motive."[34] Some men obviously worked in the city in the hope of accumulating capital enough to return and buy farmland, which had once again become the prime resource in the once-industrialized countryside from which they had come. But only a rare flash like this reveals that here may be hidden a source of light on the behavior of the industrial labour force.

Agricultural Pests and Diseases

In farming man alters natural ecosystems to divert the energy flows of plant production to his own ends. This interference with the tendency of plant communities towards biological climax causes various unpredictable disturbances. Echoes are set up throughout delicate and complicated ecosystems. Perhaps the fundamental tension may be explained in this way: agriculturists tend to put more and more of the land under more uniform and heavier crops, resulting at the extreme in monoculture, with the fields used as though they were roofless factories. But each step in this direction unintentionally offers a larger and better habitat to a few other species—microorganisms, weeds, insects, mammals,

[33] *Ibid.*, p. 263. Compare Church, *et al.*, *An Advanced Geography*, pp. 169–70, 231.

[34] M. I. Newbigin, *Man and his Conquest of Nature* (London, 1917), p. 143. Chapter 10, "Some Communities Outside the Coal Zone," lists options taken by the inhabitants of these districts. It is possible that the differing economic experience of rural areas was linked to the behavior of the two labouring groups distinguished by Peter N. Stearns, "Patterns of Industrial Strike Activity in France during the July Monarchy," *American Historical Review* 70 (1965), 371–94.

and birds—which flourish well enough to become significant pests. The increase in the numbers of these competing species may be considered a negative externality of man's effort to intensify production within interlocked biological systems. Controlling pests in the interests of the desired crop (or, indeed, species of farm stock) has a habit of raising a new succession of problems. The biological control agents that have been introduced, that is, the predators and parasites of existing pests, have sometimes themselves increased so as to become pests. And the modern solution of saturating the fields with chemical biocides has sometimes been dangerous to the men spraying, or to neighbouring crops and stock, or to consumers through chemical residues in foodstuffs.

In former centuries there were no chemical sledgehammers to use against pests. The outcome was the whole depressing history of blights and rusts, the tragedy of the potato famine in Ireland, the phylloxera in the French vineyards.[35] Pest control was a makeshift or extemporized affair, undertaken with little scientific understanding. Even the compensation of insurance was lacking until a late date. Damage that was not properly understood and could not be prevented was conceived of as an "act of God." In France, the first society to write insurance for losses of standing wheat in hailstorms was actually suppressed by the state in 1809 as a flagrant interference with divine providence. Permanent insurance against hailstorm losses dates only from 1823 in France, with an average premium of 1.05 percent and an average annual loss of 0.81 percent over the next fifty years.

In England, the first formal insurance against hailstorms was not written until 1842 (at a premium of 1.6 percent). The crown and the church had earlier encouraged a primitive form of risk-sharing, however, which performed some of the functions of insurance schemes without their precision or orderliness. The instrument was the Royal Brief, which was a licence to collect alms for the relief of those who had suffered some mishap such as storm or flood damage. The expectation was that should the givers themselves ever experience a similar misfortune, there would be a general collection for their relief. This was a halfway house between primitive economies where family or tribal responsibilities offered some protection, and modern economies

[35] See E. C. Large, *The Advance of the Fungi* (New York, 1940).

where formal insurance markets exist. Of course, this interpretation of the brief is of its latent function. There is no clear evidence that contemporaries saw the system as insurance pure and simple, and there are other explanations of postdisaster charity.[36]

The old system of licensing to collect alms represented by the briefs was renewed by Charles II after the Restoration, decayed in the second half of the eighteenth century when formal insurance markets had emerged, and was finally abolished in 1828. For the hundred years or so after the Restoration, and possibly earlier, the briefs offer a neglected source of quantitative data on the incidence and relief of certain types of agricultural mishap in England. As late as the 1890s in one Norfolk Breckland village, a brief would be sent round for the assistance of a small farmer who had lost a cow or a villager who had been struck by sudden misfortune.[37] By that date the brief was a private subscription list, but its survival indicates that full insurance cover had not spread so far down the income scale, although the national Friendly Societies pooled weekly pennies for relief in the case of a breadwinner's illness. Other countries had been quicker than England to offer at least hail insurance—besides France, Scotland by 1780 at the latest, and Germany by 1797 (the Mecklenburg Hail Insurance Association charged an average premium as high as 3.8 percent for fifty years, while a second company formed in 1812 charged from 2.5 percent to 5 percent). The first hail insurance in Austria was written in 1824, still eighteen years before England. It would be interesting to know whether charitable schemes comparable to the brief offered protection in these countries before the emergence of formal insurance markets, and whether or not the system of the brief actually delayed formal provision in the English case. The brief was originally a papal instrument, taken over in England by the crown; one may

---

[36] For examples of heavy losses in hailstorms and floods, the collections at Whitchurch, Oxfordshire, may be cited, according to the Brief Book for 1723–1769. John Slatter, *Some Notes of the History of the Parish of Whitchurch, Oxon.* (London, 1895), p. 111. On charitable responses to disasters, see C. M. Douty, "Disasters and Charity: Some Aspects of Co-operative Economic Behavior," *American Economic Review* 62 (1972), 580–90. On early formal crop insurance schemes, see P. T. Dondlinger, *The Book of Wheat: An Economic History and Practical Manual of the Wheat Industry* (New York, 1912), p. 186.

[37] Michael Home, *Winter Harvest: A Norfolk Boyhood* (London, 1969), p. 28.

wonder whether or not it was continued in this way in other Protestant countries, and if not, whether the ending of an informal system of insurance was one cause of the early rise of proper insurance cover.

This history of the actual reduction of losses from animal and plant diseases, predators, weeds, and weather warrants more systematic treatment than it has had. The gains probably account for a substantial fraction of Europe's economic advantage over the third world, where losses are estimated still to run at twenty to thirty percent of the crop yields which would otherwise be had at the rates of sowing. The patterns of reduction in losses to pests of standing crops and stored grain in Britain and Europe are recoverable.[38] The aggregate damage formerly done to standing crops by rabbits and reared game, to grain stores by rodents and insects, to pastureland by moles, and to livestock by wolves, was not negligible even in the gentle environment of western Europe, especially when many rural communities were close to subsistence. In the long process of reducing these sources of loss, England stood at a peculiar advantage. In lowland England wolves were exterminated during the high Middle Ages, and by the sixteenth century foreign observers remarked on the fact that sheep and cattle could be left to graze without watchers as peculiar to England.[39] Such a freedom from wolves (or rustlers) did not extend to the Welsh or Scottish borders, or most of the Continent. When Napoleon's administration wished to increase France's sheep stock, they felt compelled to establish a special wolf-hunting organization.[40] By that date, which was 1804, wolves had been exterminated throughout Great Britain. It might be possible to impute a value to the protection afforded by Britain's island site against losses of this kind, for unlike France and other mainland European countries, once the wolf was destroyed in Britain it could not be replaced from other populations farther east.

An island site was also a positive external factor for the British when it came to freedom from the worst ravages of the cattle plague.[41] Systems of government and political will were im-

---

[38] Compare E. L. Jones, "The Bird Pests of British Agriculture in Recent Centuries," *Agricultural History Review* 20 (1972), pp. 107–25.

[39] G. M. Trevelyan, *History of England* (London, 1942), p. 90, note 1.

[40] R. B. Holtman, *The Napoleonic Revolution* (Philadelphia, 1967), p. 109.

[41] C. F. Mullett, "Cattle Distemper in Mid-Eighteenth-Century England,"

portant too. Besides the natural protection of the Channel, Britain minimized the harm done by cattle plague by developing a scheme of compensation for farmers whose beasts were slaughtered to reduce the spread of infection. Obligatory slaughter was, of course, the important feature; financial compensation made it acceptable. It was a rare continental country that could insist on a policy of slaughtering and change the odds in favor of compliance by offering compensation, but Brandenburg, which lacked Britain's watery *cordon sanitaire,* did rather successfully prohibit the import of cattle from plague-ridden countries when in 1709–1716 the disease was brought to central and Baltic Europe by Swedish and Russian troops. The policy in Brandenburg was not, however, a matter of rational calculation, in that it was a means whereby the "paternalistic" ruler, William I, protected the privileges of the public executioners over fees for carcase disposal, rights to hides, and so forth, in the face of evasion and indifference by noble landowners. In the Netherlands, where the immediate slaughter of all beasts in contact with infected animals was required in a calculated attempt to contain the plague, the measure was ineffective. In the absence of a strong central government it could not be enforced. Eighteenth-century Britain hardly possessed an authoritarian central government, but it seems to have possessed rational public authorities, and it had the Channel as a first line of defense.

The history of plant diseases is another poorly explored subject. According to Blith in 1652, the "blasting" of wheat in the ear was "one of the Kingdom's curses." [42] Problems such as this, once so significant, have been reduced today to the concern of specialists or rare and bizarre occurrences that seldom strike a chord of awareness among economic historians. When something does arouse our awareness, we begin dimly to perceive the extent of our ignorance about the immediacy of natural calamity in earlier centuries. In 1951 an attack of psychotic disorders in a single French village was traced to a fungoid growth on damp

---

Agricultural History 20 (1946), 145–46; Reinhold A. Dorwart, "Cattle Disease (Rinderpest?)—Prevention and Cure in Brandenburg, 1665–1732," *Agricultural History* 33 (1959), 79–85; and J. A. Faber, "Cattle-Plague in the Netherlands during the Eighteenth Century," *Mededelingen van de Landbouwhogeschool te Wageningen* 62:11 (1962), 1–7.

[42] Quoted by Sir E. John Russell, *A History of Agricultural Science in Great Britain 1620–1964* (London, 1966), p. 40.

rye that had been baked for bread. It was a freakish twentieth-century outbreak of ergotism. But in medieval France and into the eighteenth century there were often such outbreaks, with eight thousand deaths in the Sologne district as late as 1777. Before 1951, however, the last instance had been in 1816.[43] The condition is caused by a chemical constituent of ergot, a fungus parasitic on rye. When rye became a popular field crop across Germany and into Poland in the sixteenth century, ergotism followed. The first Russian outbreak was in 1722. Subsequently, the adoption of the potato reduced the dependence on rye bread in Europe, and ergotism diminished. The incidence of ergotism has not, however, been tabulated, and until that has been done its rise, consequences, and decline cannot be investigated adequately. Obviously the sources on a subject like this are scattered and obscure. They are unlikely to come under the notice of any but the most inquisitive econometric historian, or the one most blessed by serendipity, yet cost-benefit analysis of programs of pest and disease control and other measures to tame the environment would be feasible subjects for quantitative research.

Plant and Animal Breeding

The study of agricultural losses through pests and diseases could well be supplemented by a fuller examination of plant and livestock improvement. Our view of this process is distorted by the undue attention paid to the work of the leading British livestock breeders in the period from 1750 to 1850. These men selected the cattle and sheep that stocked farms in Britain and colonized

[43] J. G. Fuller, *The Day of St. Anthony's Fire* (London, 1969); G. L. Carefoot and E. R. Sprott, *Famine on the Wind: Plant Diseases and Human History* (London, 1969), pp. 19–29. Again, England seems to have escaped what the Continent suffered, presumably because less rye bread was eaten. There was an outbreak in the eighteenth century in Suffolk, where rye was eaten mixed with barley or wheat. J. C. Drummond, Ann Wilbraham, and D. F. Hollingsworth, *The Englishman's Food* (London, 1964), p. 87. Other cases probably await discovery, but the large European outbreaks cannot be matched. Another example of Britain's natural advantage was her escape from the locust plagues that occasionally reached southern France. Stanley Baron, *The Desert Locust* (New York, 1972), pp. 4–6. Yet another was the failure of the Angoumis grain moth to establish itself because the climate was not warm and dry enough, whereas in France it caused great losses of grain. George Ordish, *The Living House* (Philadelphia, 1960), p. 160. Britain's foolishly derided climate actually imposed lower overhead costs on her agriculture.

vast temperate grasslands overseas. The plasticity of breed types and the speed with which they were molded to supply the growing markets for fat beef and mutton, wools of varying lengths of staple, and beasts to dung and tread in the foldyards of arable farms, were remarkable. Trade-offs between joint products from the same animals—mutton and wool, for example—were struck with consummate skill. The saga of the breeders of that period has accordingly become the great dramatic episode in the history of the livestock industry. It was very fully recorded while it took place, and since there was no comparable documented episode of plant breeding, has dominated the history of the improvement of the biological materials of agriculture.

We need more information on the less-publicized upgrading of livestock in earlier centuries. In addition, some attention ought to be given to possibly adverse effects of the work of the great breeders. The new breeds were of fixed conformation and color patterns. The registers of their pedigree were better kept and more jealously guarded than those of their owners. Agricultural shows inculcated the "prize marrow fallacy" by rewarding markings and fashionable conformation more than the economic attribute of efficient feed conversion. The resultant veneration of instantly recognizable breeds, each protected by a breed society, restricted genetic interchange. New productive purposes have since had to be met by breeds imported from abroad, pure or for crossing, against the entrenched resistance of the breed societies.[44] The introduction of the French Charollais to Britain is a case in point.

Cropping changes also ought to be given some attention. Written material on improvements in plant strains is harder to come by than for prize stock, but there is untapped information in the old botanical literature, while herbarium specimens may be treated as a primary source. Modern plants themselves bear evidence of their ancestry. This has mostly been looked into with reference to very long-term changes and the diffusion of crops between continents, and there is little in the secondary literature on the selective pressures that have consciously or unconsciously been brought to bear in recent centuries.[45] Plant breeders had to

[44] See Sir Joseph Hutchinson, *Farming and Food Supply: The Interdependence of Countryside and Town* (Cambridge, 1972).

[45] A useful introduction is Franz Schwanitz, *The Origin of Cultivated Plants* (Cambridge, Mass., 1966).

make tradeoffs of a slightly different kind from the livestock breeders, in that they had to balance the size and palatability of the edible parts against the retention of the plant's means of mechanical protection against pests. The small-grain crops have long, barbed protrusions from the glumes that enfold the kernels. These protrusions are called awns, and make the kernels difficult for birds to get at and eat. The small grains also have loose pannicles, which are difficult for birds to perch in. It has been suggested that under effective husbandry, implying breeding for edibility, selection against mutants lacking these protections will disappear.[16] This suggestion, however, ignores the problem of pests. The evidence indicates that in reality the trend towards monocultural crop-growing reached the stage in the nineteenth century at which there were very few crops grown in any one district, and those in uniform stands, favouring the increase of a few well-adapted species of pests. The problem that arose of bird pests feeding on the grain in the fields then necessitated a deliberate selection of discarded strains of wheat. These were "archaic" strains carrying their own protection in the form of long awns.[17]

Different and constantly changing farm technologies selected against different characters of crop plants. An example was the premium that mowing with the scythe instead of gentler reaping with the sickle placed on varieties of grain with less easily shattered ears. The unsuitability of a crop could limit the scope for technological innovation. Biological and technical changes were like two people repeatedly stepping to the same side while trying to pass one another. During the nineteenth century advances in mechanical technology probably did outstrip biological advances, as is usually stated, but the former are so much more noticeable that the gap in achievement may well be exaggerated. What seems especially desirable in tackling problems in this area is cooperation between economic historians and those ecologists who have evolved, this last decade, into "ecological historians." In that way the economic significance of subtle environmental changes may be identified and studied. The subject has been quite unduly neglected. As Edgar Anderson wrote twenty years ago, "lack of interest in the humble everyday mainsprings of one's

[16] G. E. Hutchinson, *The Enchanted Voyage and Other Studies* (New Haven, 1962), pp. 51, 53.

[17] Jones, "Bird Pests," p. 120.

own existence is mandarinism. . . . A bringing together of men in different disciplines for the study of cultivated plants and weeds, an active co-operation of historians, anthropologists, and enthnobotanists would have as its immediate aim the advancement of understanding in the particular problem. Its greater ultimate effect would be the catalytic transfer of techniques and attributes from one field to another." [48] Anderson's hopes have been abundantly realized by a coalition of prehistorians and agricultural botanists, and by the "ethnobotanists" who study remnant primitive societies. As a result we now possess a better understanding of ecology and its economic implications for prehistoric man, and for remote corners of the modern world, than we do for Europe in historic times. Let us hope for similar exchanges in future between biologists and economic historians.

Human Nutrition

Agrarian historians have largely concerned themselves with supply side-conditions and changes: with technology and organizational forms. Development economists and economic historians have widened the work to include links between agrarian change and economic growth, but the demand side has been left far behind. Rather little is known about the marketing of farm products, less still about their processing, and very, very little about the consumption of food and the food consumed. Nutritional history, in short, has been almost ignored by agrarian specialists and economic historians. In view of its enormous implications for health and well-being, the output of human energy and the numbers of people, this is unfortunate.

Man is a multivariate organism. The consequences of a given diet for a human population are little understood today, when there is some prospect of anatomizing the population and analyzing the composition of the food intake. What we are obliged to do for earlier periods is to speculate about the interactions between diets of uncertain volume and dubious constituents, and populations of virtually unknown biochemical needs. Nutritional history becomes a nightmare where, since the exact size of past populations is seldom known, let alone the age and sex

[48] Edgar Anderson, *Plants, Man and Life* (Boston, 1952), pp. 121–23. Note also his chapter on "Uneconomic Botany."

composition, we can scarcely reduce them to modern "reference man" and "reference woman" equivalents to calculate the adequacy of calorie intakes. (These reference standards live under nicely specified conditions and engage in clearly defined activities.) It is, consequently, *not an easy matter to identify in the past any diet-induced condition short of actual famine.*

Although the subject is too important to be passed over, one of the results of this miasma of uncertainty is that it is very hazardous to attribute any clear effects in terms of improved average diet, health, and energy output to the "agricultural revolutions" that scholars variously identify. Attempts have, of course, been made to do this. Professor McNeill argues that *cheap salt in the late medieval and early modern periods made it possible in the Baltic lands to preserve herring and cabbage,* which with rye bread permitted denser settlement in that part of Europe. Apparently the critical factors were vitamin C and protein for a winter diet in a region of poor soil and short growing season, conditions which meant that the beans and peas that provided the poor of western Europe with protein would not grow well.[49]

If starvation is almost the only nutritional state that we can unequivocally detect in the past, we may nevertheless be convinced by analogy that it was no more than the tip of an iceberg of nutritional deficiencies, each with specific health and mortality patterns and repercussions on the human agent and his economic performance. The potential significance for the long-run economic development of Europe of the progressive eradication of deficiency diseases is such that despite the historiographical gaps, it makes no sense to ignore it.[50]

[49] W. H. McNeill, *The Shape of European History* (New York, 1974), pp. 112–13 and note 5. See also Lynn White's provocative *Medieval Technology and Social Change* (Oxford, 1962).

[50] The chief literature is in French and deals largely with medieval nutrition. See, for example, various issues of *Annales: Economie, Société, Civilisation in the 1960s,* and for recent surveys, Hughes Neveux, "L'Alimentation du xiv⁰ au xviii⁰ siècle," *Revue d'Histoire Economique et Sociale,* 51 (1973), 336–79; and Maurice Aymard, "The History of Nutrition and Economic History," *Journal of European Economic History* 2 (1973), pp. 207–19. There have also been recent analyses of nineteenth-century diets by workers at Queen Elizabeth College, London. The only source known to me that tries to correlate changes in mean human stature with the incidence of famine over a long period is Steffensen's study of Iceland, discussed by D. R. Brothwell, "Dietary Variation and the Biology of Earlier Human Popula-

The suggestion has been made that cereal and pulse-based diets in the Middle Ages tended to produce a sluggish metabolism, due to a high consumption of carbohydrates with too little protein. There are technical arguments that such a diet may have been sufficient when it did in fact contain plenty of grain, even without additional protein, just as the Italian diets at the end of the sixteenth century, which Professor Cipolla regards as unsatisfactory, may have been adequate because, though scanty, they were balanced.[51] It remains true, however, that medieval and later diets may often have been simply too small for populations to maintain mechanical efficiency. A decrease in activity would have been quick to follow. If this happened in the seasons of the year when farm work was at a minimum, it is still possible to argue that damage to the economy may have been slight, yet resistance to disease was surely impaired, and some effects would carry over to the busy seasons. We cannot escape the implication that improvements in the volume, makeup, and regularity of diets must account for some part of Europe's economic advance.

In medieval Europe much of the population may have had mild scurvy, or at least have been in a subscorbutic condition, during late winter and early spring because of the shortage of fresh food. In agricultural terms, there was a hungry gap for men as well as beasts. For men this meant a vitamin C deficiency, with blackened gums, loss of teeth, haemorrhages ultimately into most body tissue, and progressively incapacitated victims. The incidence of scurvy among seamen separated from fresh food on long voyages was appalling,[52] and may have risen with the increase of transoceanic trade in the days of slow sailing ships. Before Lind's experiments in the mid-eighteenth century—the first to lead to cure and prevention—writings on scurvy show that it was already ceasing to be a winter epidemic among the town dwellers of northern Europe and was being reduced to an occupational disease of sailors.[53] Scurvy had been called the

---

tions," in P. J. Ucko and G. W. Dimbleby, eds., *The Domestication and Exploitation of Plants and Animals* (London, 1969).

[51] See P. V. Sukhatme, "India and the Protein Problem," *Ecology of Food and Nutrition* 1 (1972), 267–78; C. M. Cipolla, *Cristofano and the Plague* (London, 1973), pp. 137–38.

[52] Harriette Chick, "Early Investigations of Scurvy and the Antiscorbutic Vitamin," *Proceedings of the Nutrition Society* 12 (1953), 210–19.

[53] A. J. Lorenz, "Some Pre-Lind Writers on Scurvy," *Proceedings of the Nutrition Society* 12 (1953), 306–24.

"Disease of London" or the "Dutch Distemper" during the sixteenth and seventeenth centuries because it was prevalent among urban populations. It was also common in armies and among the rural poor, if they could not maintain a supply of the lowlier herbs, cresses, and scurvy grass in their diets. Besieged garrisons and townsfolk were very hard hit. Gibraltar was only saved in 1780 by the chance capture of a Dutch boat with a cargo of lemons, the juice of which was used to treat already hospitalized victims of scurvy, and—mixed with brandy to preserve it—used as a preventive. Even so, when the Great Siege was lifted in 1783, the garrison had lost only 333 men killed in action compared with almost 500 dead of scurvy.[54] Sometimes whole populations were affected in peacetime, as in Brabant in 1556 and Holland in 1562, while the disease was endemic in other parts of the Low Countries, Iceland, Greenland, Cronstadt, northern Russia and parts of Germany and Scandinavia. Scurvy occurred sporadically in the rest of Germany and the British Isles. It was a disease of poverty (and tended to keep its victims poor), and its eradication awaited improvements in farming and distribution that brought down the price of fresh food.

Most deficiency diseases were associated with poverty. This is a complication, because the improvident expenditure of otherwise adequate incomes can also give rise to deficiency diseases, and the so-called "malnutrition of affluence." Even what at first sight seems to be increased variety in the food supply may lead to deficiency diseases. An example is the introduction of the disease pellagra into Europe in the early eighteenth century following the spread of maize as a staple cereal in the Mediterranean countries. Overreliance on maize as a foodstuff means a diet deficient in nicotinic acid and tryptophan, which may lead to pellagra unless maize beer is drunk, too. Unhappily for them, maize eaters in Europe did not change their drinking habits.

The difficulty in relating nutritional disorders to the performance of agriculture within Europe itself is indicated by dental caries, the human disease of which there is the longest record. Carious lesions have been found in teeth buried for hundreds of thousands of years, since the bacteria causing the lesions cease to work after the death of the sufferer, while the hard dental tissues are resistant to other forms of decay. The extent of caries at the time of death is thus preserved. Caries

---

[54] John Masters, *The Rock* (London, 1971), pp. 263, 281.

is particularly associated with the so-called civilized diet—really the diet of agricultural rather than hunting populations—which reduces mastication and therefore the natural cleansing of the teeth. A cereal-based diet contains plenty of quickly fermentable carbohydrates that are broken down by the bacteria on the teeth to form acids that attack the dental tissues. By Saxon times in England there is evidence of regional variation in caries rates, though there is much still to be done in standardizing the methods of study.[55]

As regards caries, the real villain of the piece has been the growing consumption of sugar. From the twelfth century A.D., England began to import sugar from the eastern Mediterranean, and by the early fifteenth century 100,000 lb. per annum were coming in. Although this represented an average of only about one-half ounce of sugar per head for a population of three millions or thereabouts, consumption was probably far from evenly distributed among the population. Conceivably, the rich were identifiable by bad teeth as well as tall stature. By the late sixteenth century sugar-blackened teeth were thought to be characteristic of the English. Thereafter, West Indian sugar became available. Greater caries frequency was due mostly to an increase in occlusal cavities, which occur when food particles are trapped not between the teeth or around their base (where cervical cavities form), but in the fissure patterns on the occlusal surfaces. This suggests that another factor had entered: the generally "softer" diets of the English from the seventeenth century meant that the fissure patterns were not worn off, but remained to trap acidulous food particles on the occlusal surfaces and give rise to cavities there.[56] This is one of the rather few areas where bio-archeology has come together with economic history, for the evidence of these shifts comes from skull collections. From the period from the seventeenth to the early nineteenth centuries, these show up to twice the caries incidence of

[55] J. L. Hardwick, "The Incidence and Distribution of Caries throughout the Ages in Relation to the Englishman's Diet," *British Journal of Dentistry* 108 (1960), 9–17, and Brothwell, "Dietary Variation," p. 537.

[56] The earlier English pattern occurs today among many Asians, the cusps and fissure patterns of whose teeth are often worn to planed surfaces by a gritty diet, and who have fewer occlusal cavities than Europeans or North Americans. Information supplied by Mr. J. Greenwood, B.D.S., L.D.S., of Tadley, Hampshire, and Dr. David Stone of Newbury, Berkshire, and Northwestern University.

Anglo-Saxon times, when occlusal cavities were few because the fissure patterns on the occlusal surfaces were worn off by a coarse diet including fibrous matter not washed free of grit.[57]

Nutritional history must thus take account of agricultural production in the entire area from which a population draws its food, as well as considering a multiplicity of other factors such as income levels, health provision, and dietary habits. On nutritionally-important changes that seem to have had their origin in home agricultures and strictly European phenomena, we need to discover more about subfamine conditions and European food prejudices.[58] It would be interesting to examine the reward system that produced margarine, food-bottling and canning, and the spread of beet sugar production in Napoleonic Europe, as marking a break with an older resignation to nature's ways. Similarly it would be useful to see codified the scattered data on the changing availability of fish and feral animals that bulked so large among medieval sources of protein. The histories of river fisheries, fishponds, dovecots, duck decoys, orchards, market gardens, and the hunting of wild game for the pot, all have specialist, antiquarian literatures, which, pieced together, might be illuminating. Students of the transfer of property rights from communal to private hands have not dealt with rights in anything except cropland and pasture. They should be encouraged to take an interest in changes in title to these individually minor but together major sources of protein.

The Future of Agrarian History

In Alvin Toffler's book, *Future Shock,* there is a remark about "students so ignorant of the past that they see nothing unusual about the present." We are all in some way guilty here. One of the defects of the most accessible literature of economic history is that the problems studied and debated show more cerebral

[57] D. Brothwell, "Teeth in earlier human populations," *Proceedings of the Nutrition Society* 18 (1959), 59–65; Warren Harvey, "Some Dental and Social Conditions of 1696–1852 Connected with St. Bride's Church, Fleet Street, London," *Medical History* 12 (1968), 62–75. See also Calvin Wells, *Bones, Bodies and Disease: Evidence of Disease and Abnormality in Early Man* (New York, 1964), figure 19.

[58] See R. U. Sayce, "Need Years and Need Foods," *Montgomeryshire Collections* 53 (1953), no pagination; Frederick J. Simoons, *Eat Not This Flesh: Food Avoidances in the Old World* (Madison, Wisc., 1967).

ingenuity than true curiosity about the world. Many economic historians who were trained as economists seem so persuaded of the power and scope of existing theory that they do not on principle act as one anthropologist claims to do: "curiosity also impels me to study whatever seems significant, even though I do not see its *immediate* relation to the problem." [59] This is not the road to the quick kill, but it is the path of the poacher who finds new game.

One result of the modern methodology of economic history is that the industries about which most material is published are essentially modern. If this were not so, there would be almost as big a literature about ship-building, fishing, tanning, or lumbering as about cotton, iron, pottery, or coal. Agriculture is a fortunate half-exception. Despite its shrinking role in western economies, economic historians have not neglected it—though it would be fair to say that they have partly shunted it into the siding of agrarian history. But agriculture's extensive use of one factor of production, land, guarantees its visibility. So does the fact that agriculture attracted earlier scholars, say Tawney and Gonner and Slater and Gray in the first years of this century, and historians tend to poke in the bushes along the paths their teachers frequented. Yet the thought remains: we study the big conventional themes and accumulate knowledge round and about them, but do not venture far off the beaten track.

How may students be convinced that dusty technologies and obscure products were once of vital economic significance? How may they be sensitized to spot the importance of things now neglected? One way may be to humble ourselves and encourage observation of little things. No economic historian should think it beneath his dignity to visit the reconstructed buildings of the open-air museums that are growing in numbers and excellence in all the western countries. Even better may be the "living farms" that have been proposed in several countries, where antique methods of husbandry are to be reenacted. The obsolescent breeds of livestock being kept as "gene banks" in zoos and game parks would repay inspection—after all, some breeds that have lingered obscurely, as virtual curiosities, like Jacob's Sheep and Warwickshire Longhorns, have made unexpected comebacks.

[59] Hortense Powdermaker, *Stranger and Friend: The Way of an Anthropologist* (London, 1967), p. 269.

Surviving examples of the open fields should be visited if possible: the most famous in England is Laxton, Nottinghamshire.[60] Experience at archeological excavations will help students to sense the immediacy of the past. No chance of talking with farmers or agriculturists should be passed up. Best of all for scholars from northwest Europe, the United States, or Australasia, is to visit and probe into the problems of less specialized agricultures than their own. Without a "feel" for older ways of doing things there is a tendency to substitute the known for the unknown, and to overplay the importance in the past of what is important today.

Economic analysis has its own beauty. Its cunning is to appear independent of cultural setting. Its power comes from its generality and abstractness, but its durability in historical explanation can only come from the closeness of its fit with the evidence. The evidence promises a second kind of beauty: the beauty of restoration and reconstruction. The mark of the economist is a dexterity with logical tools, an ability to select the common elements from a number of situations. Selection is unavoidable, and it is a blessing that economics does offer the historian one efficient scheme for choosing what to study. The mark of the historian, on the other hand, is a desire to get behind generalizations to the textured reality on which they rest, to find sense in the individual truth. To some degree the historian may be right to object to economic models that discard everything they do not explain, as mere "noise" in the system. However, the economist's numeracy is now so formidable that few historians can really inhabit the same universe and offer unsolicited advice with much conviction. The increase in quantitative studies in departments of history in American universities fortunately shows that some historians are, however, willing to acquire numerical skills in addition to their traditional subtleties. Are economists coming to meet them halfway? Deep immersion in the broadest subject matter is incumbent on the economic historian of agriculture—something of the observational, diagnostic skill of the medical man or motor mechanic approaching complex systems imperfectly giving off signals of their working. This open-endedness, plus the fatigue of collecting data from miscellaneous sources,

[60] See J. D. Chambers, *The Last English Open Field Village. A Guide.* (London, 1964).

bears as an emotional strain on some formally-minded economists who approach agrarian history. But the contributions to this volume show that others can and do bear it. With their minds roaming free over Europe's ghostly fields, the prospects for agrarian history suddenly look bright.

Index

Library of Congress Cataloging in Publication Data

Main entry under title:

European peasants and their markets.

  Includes index.
    1. Agriculture—Economic aspects—Europe—His-
tory—Addresses, essays, lectures. 2. Peasantry—
Europe—Addresses, essays, lectures. 3. Land
tenure—Europe—-History—Addresses, essays, lectures.
I. Parker, William Nelson. II. Jones, Eric L.
HD1917.E86   338.1'094   75-15281